The Principles of Social Order

The Principles of Social Order

Selected essays of Lon L. Fuller, edited
with an introduction by Kenneth I. Winston.
Duke University Press, Durham, N.C. 1981

Library of Congress Cataloging in Publication Data

Fuller, Lon L.   1902–1978
   The principles of social order.
ISBN 0–8223–0477–5 (pbk)

   "Bibliography of the published writings of
Lon L. Fuller, compiled by Kenneth I. Winston and
Stanley L. Paulson":p.
   Includes bibliographical references and index.
   I. Natural law—Addresses, essays, lectures.
2. Legal positivism—Addresses, essays, lectures.
3. Law—Philosophy—Addresses, essays, lectures.
4. Fuller, Lon L., 1902–   —Bibliography. I. Winston,
Kenneth I. II. Title.
K474.F84A2 1981   340   80–68477
ISBN 0–8223–0448–1   AACR1
ISBN 0–8223–0477–5 (pbk)

for Marnie Fuller

Contents

Acknowledgments   9

Introduction   11

I. *Eunomics: The Theory of Good Order and Workable Social Arrangements*

Means and Ends   47

II. *The Principles and Forms of Social Order*

Two Principles of Human Association   67

The Forms and Limits of Adjudication   86

Mediation—Its Forms and Functions   125

The Implicit Laws of Lawmaking   158

The Role of Contract in the Ordering Processes of Society Generally   169

Irrigation and Tyranny   188

Human Interaction and the Law   211

III. *Legal Philosophy, Legal Education, and the Practice of Law*

The Needs of American Legal Philosophy   249

The Lawyer as an Architect of Social Structures   264

On Legal Education   271

Philosophy for the Practicing Lawyer   282

Appendix

Letter from Lon L. Fuller to Thomas Reed Powell   293

Bibliography of the Published Writings of Lon L. Fuller   305

Index   309

Acknowledgments

I wish to express my gratitude to the many individuals who encouraged and supported my interest in Lon Fuller. Martin Golding first introduced me to Fuller's work in a graduate seminar at Columbia University in 1965. He also supervised my doctoral dissertation, submitted to Columbia in 1970, which dealt (sceptically, I might note) with some alleged connections between justice and legal rules. In the early 1970s I had the privilege of joining a small group of lawyers and philosophers who met weekly at Harvard Law School to discuss matters of mutual interest. The principal members of this group—which we called, with playful ambiguity, the Austinian Society—were all, at one time or another, Fuller's students. It was from them that I began to appreciate the respect inspired by Fuller as a teacher and the seriousness of the commitment to a moral conception of the legal enterprise. Although there were no formal rules of membership in the Austinian Society and our weekly meetings were attended by a shifting cast of characters, the continuing members to whom I am most indebted are John Bruce Moore, Richard B. Parker, Stanley L. Paulson, David A. J. Richards, and Peter C. Williams. During the same period, I also had the good fortune of spending considerable time at the Center for the Study of Law and Society in Berkeley, California, including the academic year 1972–73 when I was an American Council of Learned Societies Fellow. These sojourns in Berkeley proved to be decisive for my attachment to Fuller's thought (as well as for my intellectual maturation generally) principally because of the influence of Philip Selznick, who has written the most sympathetic and perceptive comments on Fuller's work of which I am aware.

I first had occasion to meet Fuller in 1971 when we were both participants in the World Congress for Legal and Social Philosophy in Brussels, he as a principal speaker and I as an invited contributor. After that we got together in Cambridge several times a year for informal conversation. When Fuller died in April, 1978, his widow asked me to put his private papers in order for placement in the Harvard Law School archives. It was in carrying out that assignment that I discovered several of the items that are printed here for the first time. For her confidence in me and her cooperation in making possible this collection of essays, I am deeply grateful to Marnie Fuller; it is indeed a great pleasure to dedicate the volume to her. I also want to thank the various people at the Harvard Law School who aided my efforts in countless ways, especially Morris Cohen, Head Librarian, and Erika Chadbourn, Curator.

Permission to reproduce previously published essays was generously granted by the *Harvard Law Review* for "The Forms and Limits of Adjudication," the *Southern California Law Review* for "Mediation—Its Forms and Functions," the *Stanford Law Review* for "Irrigation and Tyranny," the *American Journal of Jurisprudence* for "Human Interaction and the Law," the *Record of the New York City Bar Association* for "Objectives of Legal Education," Praeger Publishers for the selection from *Anatomy of the Law*, and West Publishing Co. for chapter 2 of *Basic Contract Law*. I am also grateful to the American Society for Political and Legal Philosophy for forgoing its share of the reprinting fee charged by Lieber-Atherton, Inc., for "Two Principles of Human Association."

I should note that some of the principal ideas in my Introduction were first formulated in a working paper entitled "Toward the Development of Legal Naturalism" presented in 1973 to the Center for the Study of Democratic Institutions in Santa Barbara. Many people, too numerous to mention, offered helpful criticisms of that paper. For comments on the final draft of the Introduction I want to thank Richard B. Parker and Stanley L. Paulson. Indeed I owe a special debt of gratitude to Stan Paulson, who collaborated during the early stages of this project and provided useful assistance in putting together the bibliography of Fuller's writings. Finally, my greatest debt is to my wife, Mary Jo Bane, whose active involvement in government policymaking provides me with a standard for assessing the significance of my jurisprudential speculations. Her encouragement has meant more to me than I can hope to express.

K.I.W.

Boston, Mass.
August 1980

Introduction

Kenneth I. Winston

This volume is a collection of some published and some previously unpub-lished essays and addresses of Lon L. Fuller, late Carter Professor of General Jurisprudence at the Harvard Law School. At the time of his retirement from Harvard in 1972, Fuller was undoubtedly the most renowned American legal philosopher. He had first established his presence in American letters a few years after his graduation from Stanford Law School with the publication of three articles on legal fictions.[1] These studies displayed a mind not only thor-oughly at home in the law but deeply versed in philosophy and linguistics and intimately acquainted with European legal scholarship. Fuller was also an early critic of the excesses of legal realism; his 1934 essay on the subject won him the prestigious Phillips Award of the American Philosophical Society.[2] In addition, he was an innovative and influential theorist of contract law, both through his work on "the reliance interest" and by the widespread use of his casebook, *Basic Contract Law*.[3] And Fuller's hypothetical "Case of the Spelun-cean Explorers"[4] is a classic of the legal literature, indeed probably the single most frequently reprinted portrayal of judicial reasoning in the English lan-guage.

Yet because of his passionate defense, over a span of more than thirty years, of a modest "secular natural law" theory, Fuller has received a largely unsym-pathetic hearing from the scholarly community for his jurisprudential writ-ings. His most widely read book of recent years, *The Morality of Law*,[5] was severely attacked by many eminent lawyers and philosophers. None of the criticisms, however, attempted to place the arguments regarding the connec-tion between law and morality in the context of the general theory which

1. "Legal Fictions," *Illinois Law Review* 25, nos. 4, 5, 6 (1930–31): 363–99, 513–46, 877–910; reprinted as *Legal Fictions* (Stanford: Stanford University Press, 1967).

2. "American Legal Realism," *University of Pennsylvania Law Review* 82, no. 5 (1934): 429–62.

3. "The Reliance Interest in Contract Damages" (with William R. Perdue, Jr.), *Yale Law Jour-nal* 46, nos. 1, 3 (1936–37): 52–96, 373–420; *Basic Contract Law* (St. Paul, Minn.: West, 1947; 2d ed. with Robert Braucher, 1964; 3d ed. with Melvin Eisenberg, 1972).

4. *Harvard Law Review* 62, no. 4 (1949): 616–45.

5. (New Haven: Yale University Press, 1964; rev. ed., 1969).

informs the body of Fuller's work. Admittedly Fuller did not make such a task at all easy for his commentators, since he never published a full exposition of his views. The elements of the theory were scattered in diverse journals, chapters of books, and lectures. What tentative efforts he made to draw these elements together remained unfinished, as well as unpublished, at the time of his death in April, 1978.

This volume aims to correct that situation by bringing together for the first time the published and unpublished materials that compose the most comprehensive picture we have, in Fuller's own words, of his general conception of law and legal institutions. The organizing principle of this collection is the idea of *eunomics*, a term Fuller coined in a 1954 review of Edwin Patterson's *Jurisprudence: Men and Ideas of the Law*.[6] The context for the introduction of the new term is a distinction Fuller draws between two central concerns of traditional natural law theory. The first is the derivation of substantive moral principles from a knowledge of human nature. Fuller expresses his sympathy with this aspect of the tradition: "I cannot see what standard there can be for passing ethical judgments if it is not that which is in keeping with man's nature as it would be if it were able to resolve its disharmonies and to surmount its imperfections."[7] Yet he is not preoccupied by this problem and does not attempt to address it in detail anywhere in his writings. Rather, Fuller's principal concern is the second aspect of the tradition: the discovery of natural laws of social order, that is, the compulsions and opportunities necessarily contained in particular domains of objective social reality, in certain ways of organizing men's relations with one another.

Fuller was led to this study, I believe, by reflecting on his experience as a practicing lawyer. He practiced law in the early 1940s for the prominent Boston firm of Ropes, Gray, Best, Coolidge and Rugg, being primarily involved in the negotiation of labor contracts in the textile industry. He returned to full-time teaching at the end of the war, but for the next two decades he was often asked, both by labor and by management, to serve as an arbitrator in contract disputes. This experience, I think, stimulated Fuller's efforts at delineating the two quite distinct processes arbitrators engage in—adjudication and mediation—and subsequently the other legal processes discussed in this volume. In any case, what seems to have impressed Fuller most during his tenure at Ropes and Gray is the role of the lawyer as the chief architect and manager of the social mechanisms that structure human relationships. Thus he wrote in his review of Patterson's book:

6. Fuller, "American Legal Philosophy at Mid-Century," *Journal of Legal Education* 6, no. 4 (1954): 457–85. The inspiration for the neologism probably came from Jeremy Bentham.

7. Ibid., p. 473.

The lawyer drafts constitutions, treatises, charters, by-laws, statutes, contracts, wills, and deeds. All of these serve to impose forms on men's relations with one another. The lawyer is constantly studying these forms and discovering, by reflective analysis and practical experience, what results flow from particular forms of order. This is, indeed, the most creative side of his work.

One might expect that the major effort of legal philosophy would be directed toward this department of the lawyer's activities. Instead we find it almost entirely neglected.[8]

Fuller suggests that the reason for the neglect of what he liked to call *problems of institutional design* is the disrepute into which natural law theory has fallen. Natural law, he noted, is now considered an unpleasant, discredited, outmoded doctrine. The discrediting of natural law of course was largely the work, at least in Anglo-American legal thought, of the English jurist John Austin and his compatriot utilitarians, who advocated the doctrine that became known as legal positivism. They viewed laws as morally neutral phenomena and instrumental to external ends, such as utility. Laws are positive, according to the utilitarians, not only in the sense that they issue forth from individuals holding readily identified positions (such as that of sovereign or judge) but also in the sense that they are formally imposed by fiat on the individuals to whom they apply, brute facts compelling obedience regardless of their content or their connection to legitimate purposes. Fuller believed that this conception of law offered a distorted picture of the work of the practicing lawmaker, who finds that he must more often conform his own creative activity to an external order than impose an order on others to which they must conform. The external order is both moral and practical. There are moral principles at stake in the effort to channel human conduct into legal structures, as well as in choosing among the variety of possible structures. And there are practical constraints—the limits of available resources, the state of social invention, general features of communal life—which determine the effectiveness of different structures in managing social problems or in achieving agreed upon ends. Thus the work of the lawmaker is better viewed as a process of reasoned discovery, rather than sheer invention, of the legal forms appropriate to introducing coherent and authoritative decisionmaking into particular social situations. It is this necessity of being responsive to external realities, I think, that Fuller took to be the fundamental insight of traditional natural law theory.

Fuller's alternative to the positivist conception is nicely illustrated for the

8. Ibid., pp. 476–77.

office of judge in his "Reason and Fiat in Case Law,"[9] in which he imagines a group of shipwrecked men isolated on a desert island. Disputes arise among them, and recognizing the need for their settlement they designate one of the group to be an arbiter. From the beginning the arbiter realizes that his decisions cannot be mere expressions of his personal predilections; his task imposes definite constraints on him. He knows, for example, that his decisions will be seen as precedents, that a body of rules will emerge from his treatment of individual cases, and that the group will tend to adjust itself to those rules. These are what we might call institutional constraints on the arbiter. Then he realizes that his decisions must accord with the basic aims and commitments of the group, as they might be expressed in a charter or constitution, if such existed. The point, I think, is not only that standards of decisionmaking are derived from the community but that the arbiter sees himself as an agent, perhaps an oracle, of the group's purposes. These are communal constraints. And then the arbiter realizes that he must conform his decisions to "the natural principles underlying group life," utilizing his knowledge of social regularities for the benefit of all. This reference to what we might call sociological constraints (about which very little is said in this context) reveals at least that, in Fuller's view, the effort at governance must be informed by the cumulative learning of the social sciences.

The desert island scenario, of course, only hints very tentatively at what developed eventually into the idea of eunomics, which Fuller defines as "the science, theory, or study of good order and workable social arrangements." However, it is sufficiently suggestive, when taken in conjunction with the brief discussion in the review of Patterson's *Jurisprudence*, to make apparent the principal preoccupations of a eunomical approach to legal institutions. (Each of the following points, I should note, will be discussed in subsequent sections of the Introduction.) First, it views the emergence of legal institutions as conscious and reasoned responses to problematic situations common to all societies. This entails a concern with both the social origins and the social effects of legal order and so disposes the theorist toward a functional analysis of legal structures. Second, it sees the forms of legal ordering as constituted in part by basic moral principles which are independent of the ends sought by means of those forms. Legal structures embody moral aspirations and define moral relationships. Third, it focuses on the question of legal competence, that is, the distinctiveness of different legal institutions in purpose, structure, and capacity to resolve substantive problems. This entails a subsidiary concern with the limits of effectiveness of different institutions and the pathological forms they

9. *Harvard Law Review* 59, no. 3 (1946): 376–95.

are liable to generate. Indeed this third matter is the one Fuller wrestled with most in the years following his call for a new jurisprudence.

In the late 1950s and early 1960s, he planned a systematic "essay in eunomics" entitled "The Principles of Social Order" to carry out his suggested program, but only the introductory chapter, "Means and Ends," was actually written. (It is printed in this volume as part 1.) Yet, in the decade following, he devoted the bulk of his scholarly attention to the enumeration and description of a wide variety of legal processes and their diverse manifestations—including adjudication, mediation, legislation, contract, and managerial direction. The result is that much of the detail of the eunomics program was actually worked out, in something of the form one might have expected, but without any extended theoretical exposition to display the unity of the program or to clarify the conception of law underlying the particular analyses. In bringing together these "exercises in eunomics" in a single volume, I expect that the connectedness of their concerns will be apparent. However, I think it might be helpful to the reader if I attempt an exposition of the underlying conception of law. I should say immediately that I do not wish to treat here the question whether eunomics is correctly viewed as a natural law theory, however modest and however secular. Its importance does not depend on an answer to that question. I also do not wish to prejudge the question of the ultimate coherence of the program itself. The essays are rich and illuminating in themselves; their value does not depend on any particular way of tying them together. What I shall focus on, rather, in my introductory remarks is the issue that has produced the greatest controversy about Fuller's jurisprudential work, namely, the claim that there is a necessary connection between law and morality. I shall not by any means try to resolve the controversy once and for all but simply try to shed some light on Fuller's side of the debate, light generated through the broad perspective offered by the essays in this volume. This attempt will also of course involve some discussion of legal positivism.

Since a principal failing of Fuller's critics, it seems to me, is that they have not been sufficiently reflective about what is at stake in the choice among competing conceptions of law, I begin in section 1 by deriving three requirements of a conception of law. I do not presume that these requirements are neutral among all the competing conceptions that have currency in contemporary legal philosophy, but neither do they constrain us necessarily to the single choice I am elaborating. In section 2 I introduce what I construe to be Fuller's conception of law by expanding an argument—or, more properly, a sketch of an argument—drawn from the work of H. L. A. Hart, former Professor of Jurisprudence at Oxford University. There may be a certain irony in so proceeding, since Fuller regarded Hart as a principal spokesman for legal positivism, but I think there is a point to showing the similarity of some of their concerns. Once the outline of Fuller's conception of law is presented, I offer a few observations, in section 3, on how this conception clarifies what Fuller called the internal morality of law. Indeed, if I am successful, I will have displayed how internal moralities abound in the law. This result is certain to set some teeth on edge, so I close with brief remarks on some common objections to a moral conception of law.

1. Criteria of a Conception of Law

To grasp Fuller's general conception of law, we may pursue his frequent admission of sympathy with the position of Justice Foster in the famous "Case of the Speluncean Explorers." In this case, which remains Fuller's most engaging mythopoeic device, five men are accused of the murder of a companion with whom they had been trapped in a cave, without sufficient food to sustain them until a rescue could be effected. Justice Foster takes the view that the defendants' "barbaric" act of consuming one of their fellows in order to remain alive was not contrary to law; hence, the men ought to be acquitted. He offers two arguments to support this conclusion. First, the special circumstances of the case, he claims, place it entirely outside the reach of positive law. The familiar forms of legal regulation presuppose that certain basic features of human life obtain: for example, that the survival of some individuals does not depend on the killing of others. These features were not present in the cave, so the accused must be judged in terms of a legal framework befitting their situation, specifically in terms of the (social) contract made by the parties in their "state of nature"—an agreement to cast dice to determine which of the group would be sacrificed. Alternatively, if one rejects the first argument and insists on deciding the case in accordance with established law, it still does not follow that the men committed murder. Admittedly the law as presently written does not permit a defense to the charge of homicide covering the special circumstances that obtain here. However, a proper understanding of the purpose of the law of homicide, Foster claims, requires judicial recognition of certain exceptions or defenses, even if not previously formulated in relevant legislation. In the present case, it is irrational to suppose that convicting the accused would have any deterrent effect on individuals who might find themselves in such an extreme situation in the future. Therefore, it would not further the purpose of the law to convict the defendants. Again, they ought to be acquitted.

Three Requirements

Fuller was quite aware of the weaknesses in Foster's opinion, as the other justices in the case make clear, but Foster alone (among the five opinions) reflects the conception of law, I think, that Fuller found compelling. What I shall attempt to do is to articulate the underlying contentions in Foster's proposed resolution of the case and restate them as a set of requirements that we should expect any conception of law to meet. There are three of special importance.

First, Foster's state of nature argument suggests that forms of legal regulation each have their own ecological niche, their own sustaining environment, which partly accounts for their authority when conditions are suitable and for their limits when conditions are not. If the ecology is altered dramatically, as in the speluncean case, the familiar legal forms lose their import and must be replaced by others that, however alien to our ordinary sensibilities, provide the basis for assessing what is lawful in the new situation. The failure of the other justices to appreciate this observation is a failure to understand the dependency of legal ordering on material circumstances and thus reflects a parochial attachment to their own legal environment. In a similar way, traditional theorists of law have too often tied a definition of law to a specific institutional configuration—such as a sovereign or a court—and then been forced to identify practices that share many familiar features, but not the allegedly critical ones, as nonlegal. It may be that ulterior political motives account for much of this artificial narrowing of conceptions of law (perhaps a desire to lend support to a particular form of government), but there are theoretical exigencies which may also lead to such a result, for example the temptation to offer an overly systematic rendering of legal phenomena or the felt need (to which philosophers are especially liable) to enumerate necessary and sufficient conditions for applying the term *law*. Fuller consciously avoided definitional questions precisely because they pretend to settle matters that need to remain open. In his view, a conception of law should be generous, attuned to the diversity of historical and cultural manifestations of legal regulation. This, accordingly, is the first requirement of a conception of law.

Second, Foster's argument about the purpose of the law of homicide suggests that legal regulation, whatever form it takes, should be seen as consciously designed by intelligent beings for definite ends. This point may seem too obvious to dwell on, but it is too often neglected both by legal officials and by legal theorists—by officials, such as several justices in the speluncean case, when they mechanically apply a rule to a case without considering whether the purpose of the rule is being served, and by theorists who become wholly absorbed in the structural details of legal processes and forget the human context that gives them meaning. Fuller believed, only somewhat unfairly, that legal positivists characteristically focus on the structural features of legal systems, especially the types of rules and the hierarchical relations among them, in abstraction from the role they play in human interaction. In any case, he believed a proper corrective to such an emphasis would stress the nature of legal regulation as a purposive and problem-solving enterprise. Like John Dewey, he saw the principal virtue of legal order as bringing intelligence to bear on human affairs in an organized way. With this orientation the legal theorist becomes sensitive to conditions for the effective operation of legal institutions, a topic Fuller explored in many of his essays. Also, with the attempt to make plain the foundations of positive law in the realities of group life, the theorist becomes cognizant of manifestations of law in its less articulate forms, as it is implicit in or emergent out of existing patterns of conduct. Hence Fuller's special concern with customary law. John Austin came close to Fuller's conception when he described law, in its most general sense, as a rule provided by an intelligent being for the guidance of other intelligent beings.[10] In the end, however, Austin reduced law to an expression of will, a superior's wish backed by the threat of force in the event of noncompliance. For Fuller, legal regulation must be understood rather as a product of intellect, the rational element that inheres in social organization.

Third, underlying Foster's opinion as a whole is the suggestion that it is part of the aim of legal regulation to promote moral order among persons. This is most apparent in judicial decisionmaking to the extent that there is a felt need to do justice in each case, as far as possible. Foster makes this point by declaring that if the speluncean explorers are found to have committed a crime, then the law itself is convicted in the tribunal of common sense. Translating this observation into a criterion of a conception of law, we may say that a conception of law should clarify the function of legal institutions in granting public recognition to the principles that are binding on individuals, a function that renders them the most important social agencies through which conduct, decisions, and rules acquire legitimacy. Clearly this requirement can be met only by a normative conception of law, that is, only if the source of legitimation is conceived to be internal to legal regulation itself. Otherwise the pursuit of justice and other legal values would appear to be an entirely accidental feature of law and would have to be described in an ad hoc or nontheoretical way.

This criterion may seem to be the most controversial of the three I have proposed and the one most likely to separate Fuller from the tradition of legal positivism. It is important, therefore, to explain that positivists have consis-

---

10. John Austin, *Lectures on Jurisprudence*, 5th ed. by Robert Campbell (London: John Murray, 1885), vol. I, p. 86.

tently attempted to meet this requirement—and therefore, we may conclude, consider it a proper one—and that the disagreement with Fuller comes in assessing the sufficiency of their account.

The Problem of Normativity

To focus the issue most sharply, let us concentrate on the single positivist contention that it is in no sense a necessary truth that law conforms to the demands of morality. To support this contention positivists offer a morally neutral conception of law. At the same time, they allow that one of the principal features of law is that it makes certain forms of conduct nonoptional. In other words, laws impose obligations, and any adequate account of law must explain that fact. For a positivist, then, there must be a way of recognizing legal obligations independently of moral considerations, and indeed positivists can be distinguished from one another by their proposals on this matter. For present purposes, it will be helpful to consider the views of Austin and Hart, whom Fuller considered as the advocates of positivism most in need of rebuttal. Austin provides what I shall call a *political* account of legal obligation, Hart a *sociological* account.

Austin's view is manifest in his "refutation" of the famous apologist of English law, Sir William Blackstone. Austin allows that when Blackstone says that human laws are not valid if contrary to the laws of God, he *may* mean simply that all human laws ought to conform to the laws of God. If so, Austin has no quarrel. However, what Blackstone seems to mean is "that no human law which conflicts with the Divine law is obligatory or binding; in other words, that no human law which conflicts with the Divine law *is a law*, for a law without an obligation is a contradiction in terms."[11] Blackstone's claim is simply "stark nonsense," says Austin. All manner of pernicious enactments have been "enforced as laws" by judicial tribunals. If he, as a defendant in court, objects that the enactment in question is contrary to the law of God and hence not obligatory, "the Court of Justice will demonstrate the inconclusiveness of my reasoning by hanging me up, in pursuance of the law of which I have impugned the validity."[12]

One may well wonder whether Blackstone would have denied that a court could "hang a person up" in pursuance of an invalid law! Austin's argument seems curiously misdirected. Both he and Blackstone agree that a law without an obligation is a contradiction in terms, but the agreement is deceptive since

---

11. Ibid., p. 215.

12. Ibid. As Albert Camus said in a different context: "the guillotine becomes a logician whose function is refutation." *The Rebel*, trans. Anthony Bower (New York: Vintage, 1956), p. 126.

a shift has occurred in the meaning of *obligation*. In his effort to make jurisprudence a science, Austin thought it necessary to eliminate normative terms
from his vocabulary, or at least to give to such terms as appeared indispensable
a definite empirical meaning. So to say a person is under a legal obligation to
act in a certain way becomes, for Austin, the claim that the person is "obnox-
ious to" or liable to a sanction (pain) in the event of noncompliance with the
wish of the politically sovereign power. The obligatoriness of law, in other
words, is an alternative description of the readiness of the sovereign to make
its threat of a sanction effective. The sovereign, it is important to note, does
not invoke a principle of legitimation in an effort to *justify* its claim to obedience; to attempt justification would be to shift from the empirical fact of superior power to a (disputable) rationale for its existence. Austin's conception
is a stark form of legal voluntarism: the exercise of superior force alone accounts for the creation of legal duties.

As a refutation of Blackstone, Austin's shift in meaning is of course without
consequence, since it is perfectly consistent to say that one is under a duty to
obey (in the sense of being liable to a sanction) and that one is not under a
duty to obey (in the sense of being morally obligated). If Austin's view is more
persuasive, it is only for reasons that make an empirical conception of law
preferable.[13] However, Austin had an unduly narrow idea of what matters can
be treated empirically. He excluded from criteria of legal validity not only the
merit or demerit of laws but any feature that might give to law a normative
authority not based on the exercise of force. In this he showed an insensitivity
to the dynamic of the resort to force in human relationships, which evokes
demands for its justification and hence requires support from acceptable principles of legitimation.

Hart rejected Austin's narrow empiricism on the ground, among others,
that it did not take seriously the idea of a *rule* of law.[14] According to Hart, the

13. The only point Austin makes in this context bearing directly on this issue is that Blackstone's view amounts to preaching anarchy. The laws of God, according to Austin, are not always
certain. Even the principle of utility, which Austin considers an index to God's laws, does not yield
noncontroversial moral judgments. So if the laws of God are used to assess the validity of positive
laws, there will be innumerable opinions as to what a subject's legal duties are. Thus, "to proclaim
generally that all laws which are pernicious or contrary to the will of God are void and not to be
tolerated, is to preach anarchy. . . ." Austin, *Lectures*, p. 216. Contemporary legal theorists who
seek to identify forms of legal ordering only by nonevaluative criteria are the heirs of the Austinian
tradition, though they seldom invoke the fear of anarchy. Joseph Raz, for example, defends such
a view in *Practical Reason and Norms* (London: Hutchinson, 1975), pp. 164–65. However, assuming it is possible to produce nonevaluative criteria to identify legal order, it does not follow
that the choice of one set of nonevaluative criteria over another is itself nonevaluative. Also, if the
theorist's aim, as Raz suggests, is to clarify the special sort of social institution that a legal order
is, nonevaluative criteria may fail to do that job. That indeed is the essence of Fuller's critique of
legal positivism.

14. Hart's views are most fully elaborated in *The Concept of Law* (London: Oxford University
Press, 1961). On the particular point under discussion, Hart accuses Austin of conceptual confu-

key to what Austin called the science of jurisprudence is the combination of two types of rules: restraining rules and empowering rules. Restraining rules make certain types of conduct obligatory, such as refraining from violence and paying taxes. In the present context, this category also subsumes the set of facilitative rules by which private parties realize their wishes in the form of marriages, wills, and contracts—with the effect of creating new structures of rights and duties. Empowering rules, by contrast, are second-order rules in accordance with which public agencies introduce, apply, modify, and repeal restraining rules. Hart elaborates this distinction between types of rules by enumerating the defects of "primitive communities," by which he means communities governed by norms consisting only of restraining rules. Specifically, such communities lack procedures and criteria for (a) identifying the rules that are obligatory on them, (b) changing those rules once they are identified, and (c) determining when a violation of a rule has occurred. Only when empowering rules are introduced to remedy these defects has the step been taken "from the prelegal into the legal world." [15] Thus for Hart empowering rules constitute the distinctive mark of a legal system. They serve both to define the public agencies that are (thereby) authorized to recognize valid restraining rules and to state the criteria to be met by any particular restraining rule for attaining legal status. These elements Hart refers to collectively as the rules (or rule) of recognition.

Accordingly a citizen's having a legal obligation is explicated in two steps: first by showing that the obligation is entailed by a restraining rule and then by showing that the restraining rule meets the criteria of membership set by the rules of recognition (it is a valid rule of the legal system). The difficult point in this analysis is explaining the nature of the bond between a given citizen and the rules of recognition. Why is a particular rule of recognition binding on the citizen? Charting a middle course between a moral ground for obligations (such as a promise or contract) and a coercive ground (such as the threats of a political sovereign), Hart offers a sociological account of this relationship by positing the adoption of what he calls "an internal point of view" toward the rules. The internal point of view is a form of acceptance, somehow short of explicit consent yet stronger than mere acquiescence. The person who adopts an internal point of view toward the rules of recognition employs the rules as authoritative guides to the identification of binding restraining rules and as a basis for criticizing deviations from them. Hart seems at first to conceive of the internal point of view as a necessary condition of a legal system on the part of all, or at least the great majority of, citizens within

---

sion for failing to distinguish *obliging* and *obligating*. This criticism, I think, obscures Austin's voluntarism.

15. Ibid., p. 91.

that system. In this formulation, the binding character of legal rules appears to be, directly or indirectly, self-imposed. Subsequently, however, Hart allows that for a legal system to exist it is necessary only that the officials, especially the judiciary, adopt the internal point of view. It is sufficient for the majority that they simply obey the officials. Here the obligations of ordinary citizens appear to result from what Fuller refers to as a one-way projection of authority.[16]

How this understanding of the relation between official and citizen would be revised by Fuller is a matter I shall discuss in section 3. For the present I wish to focus on the role of the official alone. The core of Hart's account is that the criteria employed by judges to determine the validity of laws, and hence the obligations of citizens, have their status (as criteria) simply from being "accepted" by (the majority of) judges. That is, these criteria (whichever they are) happen to be the ones toward which the judges have taken an internal point of view. When stated this baldly, Hart's account bears a striking resemblance to the notorious assertion of some legal realists that the law is simply what the judges say it is. Perhaps the account should be modified by adding that the judges not only agree in accepting specific criteria—and thereby confer on them their status as criteria—but they consider their agreement as essential to their acceptance. The fact of their agreement would then constitute a *reason* for choosing among different possible criteria or sticking with criteria already agreed upon. If we take this step, however, we are then bound to ask whether the fact of agreement (among judges) is a good or bad reason for accepting or sticking with a specific criterion of validity—and what *other* reasons (good or bad) might there be? Once this issue is pressed, we can observe that judicial choice of criteria is not, and cannot be, whimsical or ad hoc; there are a variety of constraints on judicial choice, constraints deriving from many sources not the least of which, as Fuller would stress, is the nature of the enterprise in which the judges are engaged. (Recall the story of the arbiter on the desert island who discovers numerous institutional, communal, and sociological constraints on his decisionmaking.) The relevance of these constraints to the judicial task does not depend upon their being, in Hart's sense, accepted (especially by judges), yet they are decisive in establishing the authority of judicial decisions.

This reflects the fact that a judge's authority, and hence the bindingness of the judge's pronouncements, has two quite distinct sources, only the first of which is given a place in Hart's account. A judicial pronouncement may be authoritative in the sense of being institutionally conclusive: it is issued by the public agency specifically designated to make such pronouncements and the

16. Compare Hart's discussion in *The Concept of Law* at pp. 87–88 with that at pp. 111–13.

citizen has no further *official* appeal. One function of the criteria of validity is to ensure conclusiveness of this sort, to guarantee an orderly and consistent mode of social decisionmaking. A judicial pronouncement may also be authoritative, however, in the sense of being well founded, that is, based on sound reasons. And even though the question of well foundedness may be debated intelligently by officials and nonofficials alike, whether or not a judicial pronouncement is well founded is a *legal* question that is essential for determining a citizen's legal obligations.[17] Thus the weakness of Hart's analysis is that the account of judicial authority is incomplete. To base that authority solely on the judge's own adoption of an internal point of view toward certain rules (the criteria of validity) is to omit the conditions inherent in legal ordering that constrain the judicial choice of rules and that render some choices more legitimate than others—more legitimate, that is, in terms of the enterprise in which the judges are engaged. This weakness is a consequence, I think, of Hart's taking the task of understanding law to be an exercise in descriptive sociology.[18] For sociology tends to conflate or simply ignore the distinction between what is accepted as authoritative and what is actually authoritative. Yet the former notion is parasitic on the latter for its meaning, and the latter notion cannot be explicated by sociological analysis alone. It requires the introduction of moral principles of legitimation, which in turn entails an excursion into moral theory. Furthermore, such an excursion into theory would leave behind the actual functioning of legal institutions were it not made clear that the institutions themselves are caught up, necessarily, in the articulation and application of the relevant moral principles. What Fuller's conception of law promises is a clarification of this moral dimension of law— thereby offering a more adequate account than the positivists have been able to provide of the legitimating character of legal institutions.

At this point let us remind ourselves of the three requirements of a conception of law generated from Justice Foster's opinion: it should generously encompass the variety of forms of legal regulation; it should illuminate the purposive character of legal regulation; and it should explain the fact that legal institutions are the most important social agencies of legitimation. It now remains for me to sketch Fuller's conception of law and to show how it meets these requirements.

17. A similar point is made by Philip Selznick when he writes: "The availability of a specialized staff for the enforcement of norms may be highly correlated with the existence of a legal order and thus may serve as a reliable *indicator* of norms that have been selected for special treatment. However, it does not follow that this is what basically distinguishes legal from nonlegal norms and institutions." Selznick adds: "The special work of law is to identify claims and obligations that *merit* official validation and enforcement" (emphasis added). See "The Sociology of Law," *International Encyclopedia of the Social Sciences*, vol. 9 (1968), p. 51.

18. "Notwithstanding its concern with analysis the book may also be regarded as an essay in descriptive sociology. . . ." *The Concept of Law*, p. vii.

2. Fuller's Conception of Law

To introduce Fuller's conception of law, I shall employ the philosopher's device of arguing from something familiar to something unfamiliar. What is familiar, at least to students of jurisprudence, is H. L. A. Hart's redemption of a "core of good sense" in the doctrine of natural law.[19] Hart argues that any system of municipal law will find it necessary to enforce rules protecting persons against violence, securing their property, and imposing liability for breach of promises in order to ensure the voluntary conformity and cooperation upon which social order depends. The argument proceeds by noting a few salient features of human life which, given the minimal aim of survival, provide compelling reasons for the rules in question. The critical features include: the extreme vulnerability of human beings to bodily attack; the approximate equality of persons in their powers of domination; their limited altruism and consequent lack of confidence in the future conduct of others; the scarcity of natural resources and the special advantages of a division of labor; and, finally, limited knowledge, understanding, and strength of will. Given these "natural facts" or "truisms," as Hart calls them, there is a "natural necessity" for legal systems to contain rules restricting the use of violence, rules recognizing minimal forms of property, and rules enabling people to transfer, exchange, or sell goods and services. Indeed in the absence of such rules, says Hart, people would have no reason for voluntarily obeying *any* rules.

Now it is not so much the details of this argument as its general form that I wish to highlight. The form may be represented as follows:

A. Given certain purposes or conscious aims (such as survival); and
B. given certain natural facts about human life (vulnerability to attack, etc.); then
C. there are compelling reasons for any legal order to include certain rules (restricting violence, etc.).

I believe this form of argument is more powerful than Hart has imagined, for the logic of the argument does not require the very restricted elements that Hart has inserted at each step. I want to sketch briefly how each step may be expanded.

(A) The purposes people have in associating with one another are not limited to survival. Although Hobbes regarded the fear of death as the strongest passion that inclines people to obey a common power, he also gave a prominent place to the desire of such things as are necessary to commodious living

19. Ibid., pp. 189–95.

and the hope by industry to obtain them.[20] The resulting competition for scarce goods probably has a more profound impact upon the structure of social life than the common wish to survive. And no doubt other universal aims of human beings could be added. My purpose is not to construct a definitive list but only to suggest that the list is longer than Hart supposes. Furthermore, the conscious aims that could be inserted into this form of argument need not be ones that are universally shared. It is possible to confine the argument to aims that are special to a particular culture and then to derive rules necessary for that culture, given the natural facts of human life. For example, if a culture is deeply committed to democratic forms of governance, then natural facts about human motivation (subsumable under Hart's reference to limited altruism) may provide compelling reasons for rules that severely restrict private financial contributions to public officials. Of course any detailed argument of this sort will be complicated by the shifting relationships between means and ends, as Fuller would stress. Nonetheless the argument schema is clearly open to more precise and more restricted assertions.

(B) The natural facts taken into account in the second step of Hart's argument need not be "truisms" about human life. For the argument to remain compelling, it would be sufficient to insert factual statements about social regularities confirmed by scientific inquiry. Such statements also afford reasons why, given specified aims, rules of law should have a definite content. (I am not arguing of course that scientific findings made by detached observers will necessarily affect the fashioning of legal rules within a particular system. The import of discoveries must be appreciated by appropriate officials and considered as reasons for the adoption of one set of rules over another.) One must also allow that conclusions reached in the social sciences—in psychology or economics, say—may have very limited application. Specific patterns of behavior or of motivation may be more or less deeply entrenched at particular times and places, so we can imagine a good deal of variation in what features of social life provide compelling reasons for what rules. The possibility of this variation does not undermine the type of argument being offered as long as the statements at the second step have some empirical validity, though it does make the range of valid generalization more problematic.

(C) Finally, even if the previous two steps remain as Hart presents them, the conclusions compelled in the third step of the argument are not limited to *rules* embodying a certain *content*. In fact Hart's set of basic rules protecting persons, property, and promises suggests a kind of static, fixed structure of obligations and expectations of the sort one might anticipate finding in his prelegal primitive community. Rather, we should conclude that each society will estab-

---

20. Thomas Hobbes, *Leviathan*, ed. C. B. Macpherson (Baltimore: Penguin, 1968), p. 188.

lish a variety of procedural *mechanisms* for creating, modifying, applying, or (generally speaking) giving authoritative recognition to basic and nonbasic rules alike. These mechanisms will constitute public agencies, institutionally guaranteed forms of decisionmaking for facilitating social interaction. As Fuller has written: "In all significant areas of human action formal arrangements are required to make choice effective. . . . Our more important choices are meaningless if there is no way of carrying them over into the larger social order on which we are dependent for almost all our satisfactions. But to give social effect to individual choice, some formal arrangement, some form of social order, is necessary."[21] The particular forms that emerge in a given society, of course, need not be identical to those in other societies, especially if the variation in aims and in natural facts which I noted above has any effect.[22]

The Idea of Legal Processes

This final expansion of Hart's argument is the springboard for Fuller's most decisive departure from a positivistic analysis of law, so I shall devote some attention to its details.[23] It is important to stress, however, that the derivation of the mechanisms for public decisionmaking conforms to the pattern of the derivation of Hart's basic rules. The connection between the first two steps of the argument and the third is mediated, as Hart says, by reason. I take that here to mean that, since human beings have the capacity to think about what they are doing, they will begin the foundation of social order by constructing *models* of possible procedural mechanisms. These models will then serve to guide the emergence of specific practices and institutions that utilize or embody the mechanisms; the models will also provide standards for assessing the extent to which such practices or institutions are successful in their implementation. I should make it clear that I do not mean to overestimate the power of human rationality in inventing these models of ordering. The task for a historian who wished to trace their descent would not be to locate their point of origin, which could well be inexplicable (the accidental, spontaneous out-birth

21. Fuller, "Freedom—A Suggested Analysis," *Harvard Law Review* 68, no. 8 (1955): 1312.

22. This point is suggested by Lloyd Fallers when he argues that only the most parochial theorist would deny that it is possible to have a legal system without a legislature. Natural facts make a difference. A legislature is appropriate to a complex social order undergoing rapid change. But in a static and homogeneous culture one may find only a judge or arbiter, whose reasoning consists in the repeated unpacking of a single set of principles in response to stereotypical conflicts. See Lloyd A. Fallers, *Law Without Precedent* (Chicago: University of Chicago Press, 1969), p. 312.

23. In these paragraphs I am enlarging the account I offered in "Visions of the Law," *Working Papers for a New Society* 3, no. 2 (1975): 69–71.

of an excessively instable brain, in William James' image), but to identify the forces in the human environment which confirmed or sustained them once they appeared. It is also important to note that, when human purposes are embodied in the structure of an institution, they may, over time, come to operate independently of the wishes of its agents or of the population it serves. There appear to be limits to the human capacity to control institutions once they are entrenched. However, I am putting aside these complicating factors for the sake of a smooth exposition.

Adopting a designation from Fuller's vocabulary, I shall call these models of ordering *legal processes*, though Fuller sometimes preferred the generic term *social processes*. Over the course of the nearly three decades that Fuller worried about these matters, he made several attempts to distinguish diverse types of legal processes, with each succeeding enumeration turning out to be somewhat different from the one before.[24] However, since people are endlessly inventive, there is no reason we should expect to generate a definitive list of legal processes. In Fuller's writings, we can identify two essentially historical sources that contributed to the formation of a working list of processes (as well as a variety of hypotheses about how they relate to one another): namely, the common law institutions which are the inheritance of every Anglo-American lawyer and Fuller's extensive study of non-Western legal cultures. From these two sources, Fuller came to focus on five legal processes in particular—adjudication, mediation, contract, legislation, and managerial direction—each of which is represented by a selection in part 2 of this volume. Although Fuller sometimes describes customary law as a distinct form of ordering, it does not appear to involve any mechanism radically different from those already mentioned. Its special feature, rather, is that it operates without necessarily implicating any official agency.[25] Property is also frequently cited by Fuller as a distinct process, but in the end he seems to have regarded it as an adjunct of contract. As he once wrote, "The institution of private property is, in fact, only the static and relatively less important side of the institution of private contract."[26] Finally, Fuller often mentions two other processes, elections and the resort to chance (the lottery), both of which may be employed when substantive criteria of decisionmaking are absent or otherwise considered inappropriate.

24. The last and longest enumeration of types is presented in "The Role of Contract in the Ordering Processes of Society Generally." See this volume, p. 170.

25. More generally, Fuller thinks of customary law as consisting of spontaneous, self-regulating normative practices, in which rules (or understandings) are generated and enforced informally, resulting in a systematic regulation of conduct in the absence of centralized power.

26. Fuller, "The Philosophy of Administrative Law" (unpublished, undated manuscript [c. 1944] in the archives at the Harvard Law School).

More important than generating a definitive list of legal processes is clarifying the internal composition of those already identified. As a model of ordering, each legal process contains two central elements: the design of a mechanism and moral principles appropriate to that design. The first element is a determinate structure of decisionmaking (or rendering individual choices socially effective). It gives decisionmaking an organized form, with steps to be followed. The second element stipulates a set of moral requirements distinctive of the process. For example, contract is a method of creating binding obligations between private parties based on the practice of promising; it is regulated by principles of reciprocity or fair exchange. Adjudication is a form of third-person dispute settlement requiring impartiality between the contending parties and a resolution that invokes authoritative precepts. Legislation is the enterprise of governing in accordance with general rules, which is regulated by what is known in our tradition as principles of legality. Similarly for other legal processes.[27] These brief descriptions are drastically simplified. In the next section I shall offer detailed observations about one particular process, legislation, but for a more complete account of the other forms of ordering I must refer the reader to Fuller's essays themselves.

In addition to the design of a mechanism and associated moral principles, each legal process may be characterized in terms of the types of problems it is best suited to handle and the social conditions that make it, when it succeeds, an effective decisionmaking process. It is important to stress, however, that there is no strict correlation between a given problem, a given legal process, and a given institutional configuration. For example, a court (understood simply as a social entity) which has the task in our legal culture of determining criminal culpability will employ the process of adjudication. This is in part because we conceive of criminal conduct as a violation of principles of right. In other legal cultures, under different natural conditions, disputes engendered by comparable activities may be resolved through mediation. The occurrence of a crime would be treated as a sign of a deeper social disharmony, which could be dealt with directly in the mediational process. By the same token, the process of mediation is sometimes employed by our courts for other sorts of problems: for instance, in settling the division of property in complex probate cases. In general, the selection of a particular process will depend very much

27. Philosophers may be aided in getting an intuitive grasp of the conception being presented here by recalling recent discussions in the philosophical literature of the practice of promising. A correct description of the practice is understood to include both the steps by which promises are made (constituted by one or more enabling rules) and the regulative principle that "one ought to keep one's promises." See John Rawls, "Two Concepts of Rules," *Philosophical Review* 64 (1955): 3–32, and John Searle, "How to Derive 'Ought' from 'Is,'" *Philosophical Review* 73 (1964): 43–58. Cf. David Lyons, *Forms and Limits of Utilitarianism* (London: Oxford University Press, 1965), pp. 177–97.

on the kind of problem at issue, the institutional resources available, and the values to be realized in proceeding one way rather than another.[28]

For these reasons, it would be a mistake to confuse actual institutions (social entities) with the legal processes they may, more or less, embody. The identification of what is distinctively "legal" in a legal institution rests on the logically prior articulation of the models of ordering. It is these models that define what it means for a legal process to achieve institutional embodiment. Fuller is quite explicit on this point: "It is only with the aid of this nonexistent model [of adjudication] that we can pass intelligent judgment on the accomplishments of adjudication as it actually is. Indeed, it is only with the aid of that model that we can distinguish adjudication as an existent institution from other social institutions and procedures by which decisions may be reached."[29] Fuller adds that there is surely a good deal of tosh, as he calls it, in the adjudicative process as we observe it: superfluous rituals, rules of procedure without clear purpose, needless precautions preserved through habit. "Our task is to separate the tosh from the essential."[30] It follows, obviously, that positive law alone is not an adequate basis for carrying out this task.[31]

28. It should also be kept in mind that the process types I have enumerated are actually genera within which there may be several species; relevant moral principles would need to be adjusted accordingly.

29. Fuller, "The Forms and Limits of Adjudication," *Harvard Law Review* 92, no. 2 (1978): 357 [p. 90 in this volume].

30. Ibid., p. 356 [p. 89 in this volume].

31. To underscore the difference in orientation between Fuller and the positivists, Philip Selznick has suggested that "Fuller's approach might best be referred to as legal naturalism. In the debate with legal positivism, this terminology evens up the sides a bit, because naturalism has credentials that are in many quarters better respected than natural law." Book Review of *Anatomy of the Law, Harvard Law Review* 83, no. 6 (1970): 1475. If we regard Fuller as the principal theoretician of legal naturalism, we might distinguish positivist and naturalist studies as follows:

I. The sciences of positive law
    A. Analytical jurisprudence—(1) Analysis of concepts employed in existing legal systems, including specific concepts such as strict liability or general concepts such as rights and obligations. (2) Rational reconstruction of legal systems (as suggested by Hans Kelsen), including elaboration of the logical apparatus for such a task.
    B. Descriptive jurisprudence—(1) Factual accounts of legal systems or particular legal practices. (2) Explanatory or developmental accounts of legal institutions from an historical or sociological perspective.
    C. Prudential jurisprudence—(1) Identification of opportunities for legal innovation. (2) Prescription of legal means for predetermined ends.
II. Philosophy of Law
    A. Casuistical philosophy of law—(1) Application of the moral principles associated with legal processes to specific cases, for example employing the principle of reciprocity in finding consideration for a contract. (2) Justification of institutional innovation, such as reform of the adversary system.
    B. Legal theory proper (eunomics)—(1) Elaboration of the theory of good order and workable social arrangements, including detailed accounts of each model of legal ordering. (2) Establishing the theoretical and empirical validity of a moral conception of law.

Conformity to the Three Criteria

Although these remarks so far have been quite schematic, I think I have said enough to make it evident how Fuller's conception of law (as a set of models of ordering) meets the three criteria set out in the previous section. First is the matter of generosity. On this point one would have assumed "that as, in the course of history, the various forms of social ordering and dispute-settlement became separated in practice, they would [have] become the subject of an earnest discussion among scholars as to their distinctive functions and their most appropriate applications."[32] Instead, Fuller says, we find in the history of legal thought a succession of distortions and misrepresentations in which one or another process is claimed to be the paradigmatic form of legal order. Some theorists, for example, have reserved pride of place for legislation (or the commands of a sovereign) and regard other forms of legal ordering as subordinate or derivative.[33] Others have been inclined to the particularly American failing of regarding the adjudicative process as the true form of law and have relegated statutes, constitutional provisions, contractual agreements, and so on, to the status of "sources of law." Both groups have been puzzled by the encounter with some non-Western societies which, from their point of view, seem to have no forms of legal ordering at all, or only such "inferior" forms as mediation. At a more abstract level are those theorists who posit contractual relationships as the only basis of social order—either in the guise of an original compact from which all authoritative restraints on citizens are derived, or in the fantasy of an ideal community founded on the principle that persons have obligations only from agreements voluntarily entered into. A proper antidote to these distortions is a comprehensive vision of legal processes sensitive to the relative virtues and defects of each and therefore open to an empirical determination of which areas of human activity are most amenable to regulation by which processes. It is with this vision in mind that Fuller sometimes thought of himself as a legal pluralist.

(This scheme is modeled on a similar construction for political studies presented by Robert Paul Wolff in a lecture at Columbia University, February, 1965.) One difficulty with this scheme is that it suggests a false division of labor. For once the priority of eunomics is acknowledged, it transforms the character of empirical studies of existing legal institutions by setting them within its own normative framework. They become opportunities for assessing the possibility of achieving moral order in public agencies. See, for example, Philippe Nonet, *Administrative Justice: Advocacy and Change in Government Agencies* (New York: Russell Sage, 1969), and Philip Selznick, *Law, Society and Industrial Justice* (New York: Russell Sage, 1969).

32. Fuller, "Mediation—Its Forms and Functions," *Southern California Law Review* 44, no. 3 (1971): 339 [p. 156 in this volume].

33. Fuller himself suggests such a view in *The Morality of Law*, pp. 46ff., when he characterizes law as the enterprise of subjecting human conduct to the governance of rules. However, when seen in the context of his other writings, it is clear that such a characterization is meant to define not law in general but only the process of legislation.

Second is the problem-solving orientation of Fuller's conception of law. Law in all its forms is purposive, a product of conscious responses to pervasive features of human life. There is a temptation to regard this aspect of Fuller's conception as favoring a kind of functional analysis of legal institutions (indeed I have already mentioned his inclination toward a functional approach), but that suggestion can be misleading. At a minimum it must be dissociated from any commitment to the metasociological theory known as functionalism; legal processes are not to be explained simply in terms of their contribution to the maintenance of social harmony. That is one function they may perform, but it is neither the only nor necessarily the most distinctive function. An enumeration of functions would note at least that legal processes facilitate voluntary transactions and arrangements, help define social ideals, promote education and civic participation, confer legitimacy on persons and policies, as well as provide vehicles for maintaining public order and settling disputes.[34] More importantly, an enumeration of functions (however extensive) remains unsatisfactory as a way of identifying legal processes for two reasons. First, any defined set of functions will not be exclusive to law. Other social institutions (such as schools, churches, business corporations) make, or are capable of making, similar contributions to human interaction. Second, a functional analysis requires an instrumental conception of law, that is, the aims of law are seen as wholly external rather than intrinsic to legal forms of ordering. Obviously an instrumental conception precludes Fuller's view that the law itself embodies moral aspirations and defines moral relationships.[35]

If the talk about functions seems apt in trying to understand the problem-solving aspect of Fuller's conception of law, it is perhaps because in ordinary discourse the term is ambiguous between causal efficacy and purpose. For example, if I say, "The function of the Federal Reserve Board's current monetary policy is to increase unemployment," I could be making a statement about a consequence of monetary policy (whether the consequence was intended by anyone or not), or I could be making a statement about the conscious aim of some government officers (whatever the actual consequence of the policy). Similarly, identifying the functions of a legal institution could mean either describing the work it does as a social entity (a court, for example, is an official keeper of records as well as an instrument of social control) or articulating its

34. See Selznick, "The Sociology of Law," pp. 52–55. Cf. Joseph Raz, "On the Functions of Law," *Oxford Essays in Jurisprudence* (2nd series), ed. A. W. B. Simpson (London: Oxford University Press, 1973), pp. 278–304. Raz attempts a comprehensive classification of legal functions but does not argue for the necessity or exhaustiveness of his enumeration.

35. Most commentators have understood, even while they have criticized, Fuller on this point, so it is surprising to see Ronald Dworkin claim that Fuller holds a conception of "law as an instrument for moving society toward certain large goals," a conception which "ended by distorting jurisprudential issues . . . by eliminating just those issues of moral principle that form their core." *Taking Rights Seriously* (Cambridge: Harvard University Press, 1977), p. 4.

animating purpose (the impartial resolution of disputes on the basis of authoritative precepts). Between these two possibilities, the latter is, for Fuller, the preferred description. It employs the model of adjudication to render intelligible the institution's activities, including such effects as record keeping. One could of course describe the institution without reference to its animating purpose, just as one could describe a pencil without saying that it was for writing or drawing, but it would be an impoverished description, making the very existence of the artifact mysterious.

Finally, Fuller's conception satisfies the third requirement of normativity. Since moral principles have a central place in the models of ordering, legal processes constitute modalities through which particular outcomes—decisions, rules, acts—acquire legitimacy. Legitimation results from conforming to the moral conditions stipulated in a legal process. For example, a judicial ruling influenced by an ex parte communication between the judge and one of the parties is *to that extent* illegitimate and not binding on the other party, except in the Austinian sense of making the party liable to a sanction. Of course, the qualification "to that extent" is important because there may well be other principles at stake that counterbalance or outweigh the violation of impartiality. In general, the standards that compose part of the model of a legal process are not the only moral criteria relevant to the assessment of particular decisions, rules, or acts; there are also substantive criteria whose status is independent of legal processes. Fuller made this point once by distinguishing "a natural law of institutions and procedures" from "a natural law of substantive aims":

> Thus we may list [the following principles] as injunctions of what may be called broadly a procedural law of nature: laws should be clear in meaning and ought not to require anything beyond the powers of the subject; a retroactive criminal statute is an abuse of legislative power; no one should act as judge in his own case. Injunctions of a substantive natural law might include such diverse assertions as the following: . . . no tax can be just that takes from the citizen more than the equivalent of what government renders to him; any attempt to restrict the free sexual life of responsible adults is a violation of the principle of individual freedom.[36]

Fuller suggested that "essentially the same distinction" is familiar in American constitutional law as the distinction between procedural due process and substantive due process. In any case, while both sets of standards could be used to evaluate the legitimacy of particular legal outcomes, it is obviously only the

36. Fuller, "La Philosophie du Droit aux États-Unis," trans. into French by Mme Van Camelbeke, *Les Études Philosophiques* no. 4 (1964), p. 566. The English version is from the original manuscript in the archives of the Harvard Law School.

former standards that are constitutive elements of the models of ordering. That is sufficient to establish that the law, in Fuller's view, is not a set of instrumental devices which are neutral to the ends they may serve.

In sum, Fuller's idea of legal process meets the three requirements of a conception of law—generosity, purposiveness, and normativity—set out in the previous section. The details of (and variations in) each process I must leave to the reader to discover in Fuller's essays. However, I have ventured to present a skeletal outline of the processes in the form of a chart, which offers a cohesive summary of the essays, albeit at the risk of oversimplifying their content.

3. Application to Legislation

Now that I have indicated the sense in which, for Fuller, there is a necessary connection between law and morality, I shall attempt to utilize that conception to illuminate what has become the most widely known and most controversial of Fuller's contentions: namely, that the process of legislation contains an internal morality the violation of which by legislators logically precludes them from making any laws at all. Whatever the shortcomings of this contention— according to Fuller's critics there are many indeed[37]—there has been a notable failure to appreciate the contention, because it has not been placed in the context of Fuller's general conception of law.

The central vehicle of Fuller's argument is the hypothetical story of the hapless king, Rex, who nobly attempts to make laws for his subjects and fails.[38] The failure is instructive, since each of the eight ways in which Rex bungles the job involves a violation of "the morality that makes law [i.e., legislation] possible." The canons of this morality may be summarized as follows: (1) there must be (general) rules; (2) the rules must be promulgated; (3) the rules must typically be prospective, not retroactive; (4) the rules must be clear; (5) the rules must not require contradictory actions; (6) the rules must not require actions that are impossible to perform; (7) the rules must remain relatively constant over time; and (8) there must be a congruence between the rules as declared and the rules as administered. Only by adherence to these canons will

---

37. For some representative criticisms, see Ronald Dworkin, "Philosophy, Morality and Law—Observations Prompted by Professor Fuller's Novel Claim," *University of Pennsylvania Law Review* 113, no. 5 (1965): 668–90; H. L. A. Hart, Book Review of *The Morality of Law*, *Harvard Law Review* 78, no. 6 (1965): 1281–96; David Lyons, "The Internal Morality of Law," *Proceedings of the Aristotelian Society* 1970–71 (London: Methuen, 1971), pp. 105–19.

38. The story is presented in *The Morality of Law*, pp. 33–38.

Features of the Principal Legal Processes

Elements of the mechanism of each process are given in rows 1 and 2. The animating purpose of each process is reflected directly in 3 and indirectly in 5 and 6. The moral principles associated with each process are indicated in 4.

	Adjudication	*Mediation*	*Contract*	*Legislation*	*Managerial direction*
1. *Manner of participation*	Presentation of proofs and reasoned arguments	Negotiation and accommodation	Bargaining and consent	Acting in accordance with rules	Following orders of superior
2. *Role of process manager*	Assessment of arguments, declaration of principles	Fostering harmonious interaction of parties	—	Governing in accordance with rules	Issuing orders or commands
3. *Intended outcome*	Impartial decision based on relevant facts and defensible principles	Harmonious settlement, social peace	Reciprocal self-determination	Impersonal direction of citizen's conduct	Coordination of collective activity for a common end
4. *Internal morality*	Conditions of impartial adjudication (no person can be judge in his own case, etc.)	Conditions of impartial mediation	Conditions of equal bargaining (no coercion, no monopoly of resources, etc.)	Conditions of impersonal direction (generality of rules, clarity, consistency, etc.)	Conditions of hierarchical coordination
5. *Province (types of problems or activities)*	Questions of right or fault	Conflicts in dyadic relationships with heavy interdependence	Exchange of goods and services	Restraints or guidelines necessary for operation of other processes	Efficiency (e.g., in the military) or social justice (securing welfare rights)
6. *Limits*	Polycentric problems, coordinating collective activities	Triadic or more complex relationships, absence of interdependence	Where impersonal, limited, non-continuous obligations to others are inappropriate	Decisions aimed at individuals	Where individual autonomy is valued

a legislator be successful at his enterprise, subjecting human conduct to the governance of rules.

Fuller's critics have not quarreled, by and large, with the proposition that these canons, or some set closely resembling them, are necessary conditions of success in the legislative enterprise or even necessary conditions of the existence of a legal system. What they have contested is, first, the claim that these canons are *internal* to the law—or, as one might say, part of the nature of law—and, second, the claim that they constitute a *morality* in a sense sufficiently interesting to warrant the assertion of a necessary connection between law and morality. It is not my intention here to examine and respond to the critics' arguments in detail; I shall rather offer two extended observations regarding the status of the eight canons, in the light of the discussion above, and thereby indicate where I think the critics have gone wrong in understanding Fuller's argument. The first and longer set of remarks focuses on the reciprocity between a citizen's obligation to obey laws and a legislator's obligation to adhere to the eight canons. The second considers the eight canons as judicial criteria for invalidating legislation.

The Legislator's Obligations

One of Fuller's most perspicuous formulations of his argument runs as follows:

> Certainly there can be no rational grounds for asserting that a man can have a moral obligation to obey a legal rule that does not exist, or is kept secret from him, or that came into existence only after he had acted, or was unintelligible, or was contradicted by another rule of the same system, or commanded the impossible, or changed every minute. . . . There is a kind of reciprocity between government and the citizen with respect to the observance of rules.[39]

In this passage, Fuller is saying that certain formal features of laws and lawmaking have moral import. The point is that the moral obligation of citizens to obey laws depends crucially upon the legislators' not causing needless harm to citizens or treating them insultingly or unjustly by the manner in which they exercise their authority. There is, in other words, a correlativity of duties between the two parties in this relationship: the duty of the citizen to obey the legislator and the duty of the legislator to govern well. It does not follow from this argument, nor does Fuller claim, that the eight canons constitute a set of

---

39. Ibid., p. 39.

jointly sufficient conditions of a citizen's obligation to obey laws; there are other (especially substantive) considerations of at least equal weight. The canons resemble more closely a set of necessary conditions of obligation, but even that is not quite correct, since cases may arise in which a violation of one or more of the canons is innocuous or actually beneficial. It would be more helpful simply to regard the eight canons as stating conditions that *generally defeat* the claim of an obligation or that warrant saying no obligation has been established.

This formulation of Fuller's claim is not uninteresting, but it hardly seems contentious enough to have elicited so much criticism. In order to deepen the controversy we must see the claim as a characterization of the nature of law. Let us revise the argument, then, by beginning with the proposition that is in some ways the most disputed and in other ways the most neglected premise of Fuller's argument: namely, that the purpose of legislative regulation (or governance by laws) is to provide a special sort of guidance to citizens' conduct. What is most disputed in this premise is the reference to purpose. Even critics who concede that the eight canons are necessary conditions of the existence of legislation assert that a theorist may recognize the necessity of those conditions without knowing what the point of legislation is. To revert to my previous example: that is like claiming to know the conditions necessary for an object's being a pencil, without knowing that a pencil is used for writing or drawing.

However, rather than arguing in general terms for the relevance of purpose, I shall simply observe that legal positivists tend to assume its presence without, as it were, noticing its effect. Hans Kelsen provides an instructive example of this phenomenon. In *General Theory of Law and State*, Kelsen asserts that for a legislative act to count as a law it must constitute a norm, that is, it must be possible for citizens to regard it as indicating how they ought to act. But a legislative act that contains an internal contradiction, he notes, cannot perform this function, and therefore cannot be a law. Similarly, two distinct norms that are in direct conflict cannot both be legally valid, so the judge who confronts them must either give them a meaning, if possible, that will reconcile them or declare that one of them supercedes the other.[40] Fuller reports that he brought up this matter in a conversation with Kelsen.

> I pointed out that this [task assigned to the judge] is in no sense a compulsion of logic; a logician might set himself the task of so interpreting the provisions of [the law] as to produce the maximum internal contradiction. When we try to resolve apparent contradictions it is because we realize that

40. Hans Kelsen, *General Theory of Law and State* (Cambridge: Harvard University Press, 1945), esp. pp. 374–75. Kelsen says: "The principle of noncontradiction must be posited in the idea of law, since without it the notion of legality would be destroyed," p. 406.

[the law] is intended to provide a workable framework for human relations. But if this is so, why then not go a step further and ask more definitely what task this framework was intended to perform?[41]

Fuller apparently did not receive a satisfactory answer to this question.[42]

Another revealing statement is offered by Hart in the course of his attempt to distinguish the idea of making laws from the Austinian notion of ordering people to do things. The latter activity, he says, entails actually addressing the order to the persons to whom it applies; the former does not.

> It may indeed be desirable that laws should as soon as may be after they are made, be brought to the attention of those to whom they apply. *The legis-lator's purpose in making laws would be defeated unless this were generally done*, and legal systems often provide, by special rules concerning promulgation, that this shall be done. But laws may be complete as laws before this is done, and even if it is not done at all.[43]

What it means for laws to be "complete as laws" is a question I shall leave aside; it is the claim about purpose that I wish to stress. For it seems to me that Hart is talking not of the purpose of a specific piece of legislation but of the purpose of *legislating*, as opposed to governing in some other way. Perhaps I could clarify this point by drawing a general distinction between purposes that are internal to, that is, peculiar to and distinctive of, a legal process on the one hand and purposes that are external to a process on the other hand. The first sort of purpose is cited in response to the question: What is the point of using *this* process, namely legislation, as opposed to other processes such as contract or managerial direction? The second sort of purpose is cited in response to the question: What can be *achieved* by the use of this process: for example, helping low-income students obtain a college education by making available federally guaranteed loans? It is obvious that innumerable external purposes may be promoted by a single legal process. It is less obvious, I think, how wide the range of possible internal purposes is for a single process. And this leads me to the neglected part of Fuller's first premise.

What Fuller's critics have failed to notice is that the argument for an internal morality invokes the conception of legislation that is part of our received

---

41. Letter to Louis Del Duca, 15 April 1954. Kelsen was a Visiting Scholar at the Harvard Law School in the early 1940s. For further discussion of this issue, see Fuller, *The Morality of Law*, pp. 65–70.

42. It should be noted that in later writings Kelsen retracted his claims about the status of internal contradictions. See Kelsen, *Essays in Legal and Moral Philosophy*, ed. O. Weinberger, trans. P. Heath (Boston: Reidel, 1974), ch. 10. (I am indebted to Stanley L. Paulson for this reference.) From Fuller's point of view, I think we can say that when Kelsen retracted his earlier claims, it became less certain that he was still talking about the norms of legal systems.

43. Hart, *The Concept of Law*, p. 22 (emphasis added).

political tradition, a conception that stipulates what form legislation takes and what its point is. In adopting this conception, Fuller was simply following the strategy of traditional liberal thought, the main thrust of which is to render the exercise of legislative power impersonal by imposing formal requirements on laws themselves. For the traditional liberal, the utterances of a legislative body are not considered laws—and therefore represent an illicit use of power—unless they conform to at least one or both of two conditions: (1) they must be formulated in general language, referring only to classes of acts and persons, not specific acts and specific individuals (a requirement which was thought somehow to guarantee equal treatment) and (2) they must not posit specific ends to be pursued (which would reflect preferences of the legislators, or a majority, regarding what is good or valuable).[44] Fuller invokes both of these requirements in the course of his account of the internal morality, and he makes it clear why. Legislative enactments, simply put, are baselines for self-directed action by citizens, securing the minimal restraints necessary for continuing interaction. Legislation properly conceived permits citizens to arrange their own affairs—to pursue their own good in their own way, in John Stuart Mill's phrase—which they do principally through contractual relationships. This is the fundamental respect in which legislation differs from managerial direction, for the latter involves regulations (commands, orders) for accomplishing objectives set by a political superior. Legislation, to the contrary, entails the deference of governing officials to citizens' powers of self-determination and so can be said to promote their autonomy. Thus Rex's failure to make *laws* is a special affront to each citizen's dignity as a responsible agent.[45]

It is generally assumed today, though the matter is not much discussed, that these conditions (generality and the absence of specific ends) are either unsat-

44. The most systematic uses of this traditional liberal strategy are made by Jean-Jacques Rousseau, *The Social Contract*, ed. Charles Frankel (New York: Hafner, 1947), and Immanuel Kant, *The Metaphysical Elements of Justice*, trans. John Ladd (Indianapolis, Ind.: Bobbs-Merrill, 1965).

45. See Fuller, *The Morality of Law*, pp. 162, 207, 210, 229. Although it is not completely clear what laws would (or could) meet the two stipulated conditions, Fuller sometimes illustrated the kind of distinction he had in mind. For example, in "Freedom and Planning," a talk delivered in Chicago to The Associated Harvard Clubs (April 19, 1951), he distinguished laws prescribing maximum hours of work and laws providing for price controls.

> Here, certainly, are two forms of governmental intervention that are as unlike economically as they can be. A law prescribing maximum hours can be stated in general terms and be left unchanged for decades. People can adjust their affairs with reference to it just as they do with reference to the rule that a will requires two witnesses. The passage of such a law does not commit the state to any further action, nor does it necessarily set loose forces that will require still further state intervention. A price control is, of course, an entirely different thing. It is essentially a managerial intervention of the state, and like any managerial decision it is subject to change or reversal on very short notice. The imposition of a fixed price on one commodity is likely to bring about a diversion of productive capacity that will require still further controls, etc.

isfactory as a means of guaranteeing legislative neutrality or are impossible to meet. Some contemporary theorists have suggested that the requisite neutrality is maintained if legislators formulate laws under the constraint of a modest veil of ignorance. Specifically, they must be ignorant of the likely effect of laws on particular persons, whether themselves or others.[46] Fuller would undoubtedly have been sympathetic to this proposal but just as surely would have had difficulty imagining how it could be instituted, at least before the invention of an electronic device for producing selective amnesia (of particular but not general knowledge). Other theorists seem to despair altogether of a strictly legislative solution and instead assign a special role to courts to countermand inevitable legislative acts interfering with citizens' autonomy. The task of the courts is to uphold a set of basic rights attaching to individuals which override the forms of encroachment that legislative majorities can be expected to attempt.[47] The effect of this proposal is to shift the burden of neutrality from legislatures to courts, a shift that Fuller, I think, would not have regarded with equanimity. He would not have understood why the legislature should be relieved of its role as guardian of the people's liberties, and he would not have thought it likely that the courts could form an effective bulwark for individual autonomy if truly under seige by majoritarian pressures.

However that may be, recognition of the role of the traditional liberal conception of legislation allows us to reconstruct Fuller's argument in a form closer to what he seems to have intended:

(1) The purpose of legislative regulation (or governance by laws) is to provide baselines for self-directed action by citizens.

(2) Rules that do not fulfill this purpose are, to that degree, not laws.

(3) Rules that systematically violate the eight canons cannot function as baselines for self-directed action, therefore are not laws.

(4) Since laws promote autonomy, to govern by law is to treat citizens with respect.

(5) The conditions that constitute treating someone with respect comprise a morality.

(6) Therefore, the eight canons comprise a morality the systematic violation of which defeats the legislator's effort to make laws.

This is not the place to assess the soundness of this argument, but I wish to

46. See Friedrich A. Hayek. *The Constitution of Liberty* (Chicago: University of Chicago Press, 1960), ch. 10, and John Rawls, *A Theory of Justice* (Cambridge: Harvard University Press, 1971), sec. 31.

47. See Ronald Dworkin, *Taking Rights Seriously*, esp. ch. 7, and his "Liberalism," in *Public and Private Morality*, ed. Stuart Hampshire (Cambridge: Cambridge University Press, 1978), pp. 113–43; also David A. J. Richards, *The Moral Criticism of Law* (Encino, Calif.: Dickenson, 1977), ch. 3.

point out that a critical appraisal would need to confront directly the question of how our conception of legislation has evolved, to the extent that it has, from the traditional liberal view. I think Fuller believed that, as liberalism developed toward giving greater prominence to the welfare of citizens, the institutional entities we call legislatures came increasingly to take on the features of managerial direction—or they delegated their authority to administrative agencies which act, in many ways, in accordance with a managerial model. From Fuller's point of view, then, the question for contemporary liberals is whether legislation (as a distinct process) is still a valued form of governance.[48] Further, even if the characterization of legislation in Fuller's first premise is accepted, it is likely that objections would be raised to the definitional matter in the second premise. Here it is helpful to recall the quotation with which I began these remarks. What is at stake in the definition of law, for Fuller, is a matter of rightly understanding the moral relationship between legislator and citizen. The teaching of liberalism is that the quality of that relationship determines a citizen's legal obligation to obey.

The Judge's Obligations

I can now suggest a second point regarding the status of the eight canons which involves a slight change of perspective. In his detailed analysis of the canons, Fuller generally takes the viewpoint of conscientious legislators meeting their responsibilities to citizens. But when he gives examples of the identification and enforcement of the canons, he cites judicial pronouncements, such as the famous opinion of Sir Edward Coke in Dr. Bonham's case.[49] Part of Fuller's thesis is that the institution of judicial review of legislation has its strongest justification in the protection it provides for the internal morality of legislation: in this area, he says, judicial review is most needed and most effective. And the fact of the matter is that during at least four centuries of Anglo-American legal history the eight canons have been regularly invoked as grounds for the judicial invalidation of legislative acts.[50]

The question raised by Fuller is whether his conception of law provides a more plausible explanation than legal positivism of the status of the internal

48. Fuller's attachment to the traditional liberal conception of legislation may explain his opposition to viewing law as a form of social engineering, which seems to involve a central coercive agency enforcing specific ends. A minimalist conception of legislation is also consonant with his view of legal ordering as emergent out of individual choice and interaction. See "Human Interaction and the Law," pp. 230–237 in this volume.

49. 8 Rep. 118a (1610). See Fuller, *The Morality of Law*, pp. 99–101.

50. Note that in this context it is indifferent whether the judges have regarded the internal morality as a set of natural law principles that control legislation or simply as rules of statutory interpretation.

morality as a source of criteria of judicial review (or, in Hart's terms, as elements of the rule of recognition). I cannot give a full answer to that question here, but I shall offer a few observations that build upon the discussion of legal positivism in section 1. I shall assume that a positivist would attempt to account for the status of the eight canons as criteria of judicial review in terms of the doctrine of legal validity, which is a doctrine of official sources. That is, whether or not a particular rule of conduct qualifies as a proposition of law crucially depends upon locating officials who have the authority to find, declare, approve, or apply standards of conduct. (I have already pointed out that positivists differ among themselves in the methods they employ to explain this authority.) This is a doctrine of official sources because the status of propositions of law, as law, is determined strictly by the acts of special persons or groups—officials acting in their official capacities—and not by the requirements of morality.

Positivists do not of course assert that moral ideas can have no place in assessing the validity of a law; such a claim would obviously be suspect in the United States, since the Constitution places important moral restrictions on the legislative process (such as the requirement of equal protection of persons). Rather, the point is that any particular moral idea must itself always be traceable to an official source that has the power to effect formal recognition of that idea, and its status as a criterion of review comes solely from that recognition. Thus the provisions of the Constitution are traced to the constitutional assemblies in which "the people" adopted them. Similarly, in a nonconstitutional (or preconstitutional) setting, the eight canons may gain recognition simply by being adopted and applied by judges who take Hart's internal point of view toward those principles.

This positivist account is unsatisfactory, however, because it inverts the true relation between official sources and moral ideas, at least for judicial decision-making. To understand this point, recall the two senses in which a judicial ruling may be said to be authoritative. It may be institutionally conclusive, that is, issued by the public agency that has jurisdiction for that question, or it may be well founded, that is, based on the most persuasive argument that can be constructed with extant legal resources. Fuller's thesis is that the legality of a judicial pronouncement is only minimally established, at best, when it is traced to a formal source. Since any legal order, as we have noted, has a need for institutional conclusiveness, there may be substantial political reasons for wanting to confine the recognition of valid law to officials. We know that institutional life is liable to various pathologies, especially deviations from what morality requires. So the continuous need for order and harmonious interaction may make us think that nonofficials should (be made to) abdicate their determination of particular obligations. But a contrary argument would point out that institutional conclusiveness is the element of fiat in legal order-ing, which it is the business of legal regulation to minimize.[51] In this view, a judicial decision increases in legality as it becomes increasingly well founded. If the issue at stake in the decision is the enforcement of a legislative enact-ment, the question of whether the law was made in accordance with accepted rules of formation will not be a substitute for the question of whether it meets the requirements of certain general principles, such as the eight canons.

The fundamental difficulty with the positivist view is that it must regard the general principles employed by the courts in reviewing legislation as having received judicial recognition, where they have, simply as a matter of histori-cally contingent fact. It suggests that the judiciary could have, with equal ease, settled upon altogether different criteria of review. As though, as Fuller has said, the proposition that laws ought to be clearly expressed were simply a subjective preference of the judges. But respect for the integrity of legislation as a distinct process requires adherence to the eight canons, and that places objective constraints on judicial choice. So we could say against the positivist that the eight canons are not legal principles because they are accepted and applied by judges; they have legal status because they are principles that judges have a duty to accept and apply. In this respect, the canons are like the basic rules derived in Hart's natural law argument. They are standards to be ignored only at the peril of the entire enterprise.

4. Concluding Remarks

These considerations in support of "the internal morality of law" are not conclusive, just as the earlier elaboration of Fuller's conception of law was not exhaustive. My aim has been to bring into focus a line of inquiry that was more or less explicit in Fuller's writings since the late 1940s but has not been sufficiently appreciated by his commentators. I hope at least to have made plain that the theory of eunomics provides a different perspective on Fuller's work. The principal obstacle to assent is likely to be the moral conception of law that is central to the theory of eunomics, so I shall close this introduction with a few remarks on some familiar objections to a moral conception of law.

It is sometimes said that a consequence of a moral conception of law is that it is logically impossible to have moral criticism of the law. Since morality is a

---

51. See Fuller, "Reason and Fiat in Case Law," *passim*; and Philip Selznick, "Sociology and Natural Law," *Natural Law Forum*, 6 (1961): pp. 84–104.

condition of legality, there can be no independent moral basis for questioning the obligatoriness of legal decrees. However, when directed against Fuller's conception of law, this objection rests on a double confusion. First, it fails to distinguish the limited moral aims peculiar to each legal process from substantive aims that may be invoked to assess the outcomes of any process whatever. If a judicial decree, for example, must meet *some* moral criteria (stipulated by a structural model) to attain legal status, it may still be criticized in terms of *other* moral criteria (directed to its content). More important, the objection fails to take into account the distinction contained in Fuller's conception between a legal institution as a social reality and a legal process as a model by which the institutional activity is guided. Thus, from the fact that the legality of a judge's decree depends on the judge's conduct satisfying certain moral standards (such as impartiality), it does not follow that the standards cannot be employed to criticize the judge's conduct. The conduct is open to moral criticism precisely to the extent that it fails to meet the standards.

The worry that appears to underlie this objection is that a moral conception of law will preclude moral criticism of existing institutions and practices, that it will necessarily result in support of the present order of things. But such a consequence is certainly not entailed by Fuller's conception. By distinguishing the model of a legal process from the social institution which may more or less embody or give effect to it, Fuller's conception brings into focus the element of human striving in law, the earnest endeavor to fulfill the ideals that are definitive of legality—and hence the ways in which that endeavor can go wrong, can fail to realize its aims. Thus his conception provides a critical measure for assessing the performance of institutions, even though the aims sought through legal processes are internal to the processes themselves.

It may also be objected that a moral conception of law presupposes the truth of certain evaluative propositions which are at best controversial and at worst mere expressions of personal preference. Thus, according to the theory of eunomics, the legality of a rule or act or decision depends on its meeting, at least to a degree, the moral conditions stipulated by a particular legal process. Such claims of moral propriety, it will be said, are too precarious to provide a foundation for legal order. (Note that this scepticism is not easily voiced by theorists who press the first objection, wishing to make room for moral criticism of the law.) But I would like to suggest, to the contrary, that the contents of the internal moralities are much less controversial than this objection supposes, and the determination of what each model requires in specific cases presents no greater casuistical problem than is involved in ordinary legal reasoning. Differences of view are more likely to arise in judging whether particular activities are best regulated by one legal process rather than another, for example, whether the allocation of economic resources and opportunities is best left to the operation of a free market (contract) or placed in the hands of centralized planners (managerial direction). But most theorists who engage in such debates assume that these questions have answers and that sound arguments can be made in defense of one side or the other. However that may be, it is important to observe that, while the eunomic conception of law does make some demands on moral cognition, they are far more modest than those of other moral conceptions of law. Thus eunomics does not require a moral backdrop of the sort that characterizes traditional natural law theories, that is, a set of immutable rules of transcendent origin. Also the eunomic conception is not tied to any particular theory of a just (or otherwise ideal) society. For Fuller, the emergence of specific models of ordering is less systematic than practical: it happens as part of an uncertain historical development in which people discover, expound, test, and reformulate governing principles to facilitate their interaction.

Finally, it may be objected that a theorist who employs a moral conception of law cannot distinguish law and morality. Now there is an obvious sense in which this claim begs the question whether or not there *is* an important distinction between law and morality, and what its basis might be. Putting that aside, we may imagine that this claim arises because of those recurring occasions when it seems perfectly intelligible to say of an act that it is legally obligatory but morally wrong, or legally forbidden but morally permissible, and so on. These bifurcations reflect a pervasive view that legal—or, more generally, institutional—considerations are not alone dispositive of what a person ought to do. However, it does not follow from this view that a person's legal obligations can be determined without recourse to moral considerations, only that additional (extra-institutional) moral considerations may override initial (institutional) moral considerations. Clarity of perception and argument may require distinguishing the legal from the nonlegal, but it does not preclude the legal from being a species of the moral.

Whether or not these admittedly fragmentary remarks in defense of a moral conception of law are at all persuasive, it should be evident by now why Fuller rightly resisted the suggestion of many commentators that his views were basically consistent with or complementary to those of legal positivists. Instead he persisted in believing that the clash between legal positivism and a natural law perspective was the central jurisprudential controversy of his time. If his almost casual manner of argument left him especially vulnerable to attack, his critics nonetheless failed, in my view, to touch his fundamental insight of the central place of moral theory in developing an adequate conception of law. This insight remains to be restated in a more rigorous form.

1. *Eunomics: The Theory of Good Order and Workable Social Arrangements*

Means and Ends

Editor's Note

In the late 1940s, Lon Fuller assembled a set of readings for his course at Harvard Law School on jurisprudence, including a long essay he had written entitled "The Principles of Order." When the collection was published in 1949 as The Problems of Jurisprudence, *in a "temporary edition" by The Foundation Press, he announced in an editor's note that he already planned to revise his own essay, as well as to add a variety of readings to the collection. The revision was never completed, however, and no further edition of the collection appeared.*

Fuller's plan to revise his essay persisted for at least ten years. Among the supplementary readings distributed to his jurisprudence class in the academic year 1956–57, there was a five-page outline of "an unwritten final chapter for The Problems of Jurisprudence" *intended to take the place of the essay in the temporary edition. It was entitled "The Principles of Social Order: An Essay in Eunomics." The outline was distributed to his classes again in 1958–59 and 1959–60. Fuller's correspondence reveals that by 1960 the intended essay had grown, in thought, into a whole new volume.*

So far as I have been able to determine, only the introductory chapter, "Means and Ends," was actually written. Part of the original outline contained a section on adjudication, and it was during this same period that Fuller wrote "The Forms and Limits of Adjudication." However, the latter essay took on a life of its own and was never revised to fit the plan of the outline. We are left, then, with an introductory chapter to a nonexistent volume—serving here as an introduction to a collection which comes as close as possible, I believe, to the volume that might have been.

Fuller did not add any footnotes to the text of "Means and Ends," but he did indicate, by angle marks, where he thought footnotes were called for. I have provided them, as I have throughout this collection, wherever I could tell what was intended.

1. *Introduction*

Ambitious as the title of this book is, it would be still more ambitious if it were truly to represent what is here attempted. For, of course, we are not interested merely in order—the order, say, of a concentration camp—but in an order that is just, fair, workable, effective, and respectful of human dignity. Indeed, I once suggested a term for describing the kind of study undertaken in this book. That term was *eunomics*, which I defined as "the science, theory, or study of good order and workable social arrangements."[1]

This book is, then, a set of exercises in eunomics. Its purpose is to examine, not simply the principles of social order, but the principles of *good* social order. If this is so, why is that objective not made explicit in its title? The answer is that such a title would raise false hopes and would encourage a set of mind—on the part of some readers at least—that would inevitably lead to misunderstanding.

To avoid misapprehension we should be clear at the outset about what is here attempted and what assumptions—of method and of substance—underlie the analysis to be presented. The main purpose of the present chapter is to advance this clarification.

The first thing to be observed is that while a quest for the principles that underlie good social order animates everything said in this book, it nowhere attempts to answer questions like the following: What is the highest human good? What is the ultimate aim of human life?

Anyone who turns to the book for help in answering such questions will therefore be disappointed. Nor will it be likely to please those who consider that until the question of ultimate values is resolved no meaningful judgment can be passed on particular ways of ordering men's relations with one another. To them the book will probably seem to suffer from a fundamental flaw in logic: it attempts to chart its course by a compass that lacks a pole toward which it can point.

If the analysis here presented is such as to alienate those who demand absolutes, it is perhaps equally true that the book will have little persuasiveness for those who stand at the opposite pole of social thought. Its analysis is not likely to appeal to the cultural relativist who considers that all value judgments are impressed on the individual by his social environment. Nor will the appeal be any greater for the ethical skeptic who asserts that any judgment expressing a preference for one state of affairs over another must be emotionally grounded and hence not properly a judgment at all.

The book abounds in what may be called affirmations of the middle range. As the analysis proceeds I do not hesitate to take—and to support by what I consider to be rational argument—distinctions between sound and unsound social institutions. Indeed, in some cases I go further and stigmatize certain forms of social ordering as perverted and parasitic. I also present an analysis of the conditions under which particular forms of social order may be said to approach perfection.

---

1. [Lon L. Fuller, "American Legal Philosophy at Mid-Century: A Review of Edwin W. Patterson's *Jurisprudence: Men and Ideas of the Law*," *Journal of Legal Education* 6, no. 4 (1954): 477.]

These affirmations are, of course, open to the criticism that the middle range in which they fall is a logical monstrosity, even though it is in this area that most of us make our intellectual home and feel ourselves most comfortable. But the analysis here presented is open to another kind of objection which does not have to come from extremists of the left or right. It is an objection that must be faced candidly.

The objection to which I refer is that the analysis is upside down; it seems to begin with means and concludes with the ends they serve. It starts by inquiring, What are the ways open to human beings to arrange their mutual relations so as to achieve their individual and collective ends, whatever those ends may be? This question is pursued at some length, and a good many distinctions are taken, before any serious attention is devoted to the problem whether the ends sought are such as ought to be achieved. Ethical judgments are postponed until a framework has been constructed for them by an analysis that appears to be ethically neutral. In this sense the book seems to exemplify a sort of "technological natural law," to use an epithet that has been applied to previous tentatives in the same general direction.

It may be said against this procedure that every social arrangement or institutional practice is a means to some end. We cannot pass on its effectiveness, nor determine what form it should take, until we know precisely what that end is. It is all very well to eschew absolutes, but clarity about ends, even if they be only ends "of the middle range," is essential in any serious analysis of the forms of social order. And this clarity about the precise end sought must exist at the outset, for without it there exists no subject matter either for disinterested analysis or for moral judgment.

So that no portion of the force of this objection may be missed, let me refer to the discussion of it in the opening paragraphs of John Stuart Mill's *Utilitarianism*. Mill observes that in science and mathematics the paradoxical situation obtains that clarity about fundamental concepts generally comes at the end of an analysis, not at the beginning. In mathematics, for example, elaborate calculations were possible for a long time before men even raised such questions as the nature of number itself. Mill continues:

> But though in science the particular truths precede the general theory, the contrary might be expected to be the case with a practical art, such as morals or legislation. All action is for the sake of some end, and rules of action, it seems natural to suppose, must take their whole character and color from the end to which they are subservient. When we engage in a pursuit, a clear and precise conception of what we are pursuing would seem to be the first thing we need, instead of the last we are to look forward to.[2]

2. [John Stuart Mill, *Utilitarianism, Liberty, and Representative Government*, ed. A. D. Lindsay (New York: Dutton, 1951), p. 2.]

To the argument he thus states so persuasively, Mill really gives no explicit answer. In attempting an answer here I shall first invoke an analogy—that of architecture—which will serve to open up the subject. I shall then attempt a more general and abstract analysis of the means-ends relationship as it affects social arrangements.

2. *The Analogy of Architecture*

This whole book may be described as an essay in social architecture. It may therefore be useful to consider the means-ends relation as it arises in architecture in the more literal sense.

Let me paraphrase and extend Mill's argument as it might be applied to architecture. Architecture is not an abstract science but a practical art. It exists for the satisfaction of certain human ends, which may be described as utility and beauty. The means to those ends are materials such as cement, lumber, and steel to which must be added the technical skill necessary to assemble them. All of these means are subservient to the ends of utility and beauty. In any particular structure they take their character and color from the particular kinds of utility and beauty sought in designing that structure. It therefore follows that the study of architecture must begin with ends, with a definition of utility and beauty, for it is only when these ends have been clarified that it is possible to deal intelligently with means, or even to know what means are relevant to the objects of architecture.

It will be worthwhile to analyze the reasons why this argument is unconvincing. At the outset it may be observed that one particular response to it would scarcely be taken seriously. This is a response that would accept the primacy of architectural ends over means and proceed then to argue that, since utility and beauty cannot be defined, architecture itself does not exist. Paraphrased into terms of social architecture, the argument has seemed persuasive to many. As applied to physical architecture it scarcely rises to the level of a bad joke.

A more serious response to the suggested primacy of architectural ends over means would be to point out the futility of discussing ends in abstraction from available means. We must know what is possible before discussing what is desirable. A building suspended in mid-air might have a certain esthetic appeal, but since there is no means for constructing such a building we may dismiss it from consideration, or at best turn our minds to the problem of creating the most effective illusion of such a building by the means at hand.

It is an obvious economy of thought, therefore, to survey available means before addressing ourselves to ends. But the point goes deeper. Some limitation of means is essential to liberate the creative spirit. I know of no better way to make this point than to quote at some length from Igor Stravinsky's *Poetics of Music*:

> The creator's function is to sift the elements he receives from [imagination], for human activity must impose limits on itself. . . .
>
> As for myself, I experience a sort of terror when, at the moment of setting to work and finding myself before the infinitude of possibilities that present themselves, I have the feeling that everything is permissible to me. If everything is permissible to me, the best and the worst; if nothing offers me any resistance, then any effort is inconceivable, and I cannot use anything as a basis, and consequently every undertaking becomes futile. . . .
>
> What delivers me from the anguish into which an unrestricted freedom plunges me is the fact that I am always able to turn immediately to the concrete things that are here in question. I have no use for a theoretic freedom. Let me have something finite, definite—matter that can lend itself to my operation only insofar as it is commensurate with my possibilities. And such matter presents itself to me together with its limitations. I must in turn impose mine upon it. . . . [I]n art as in everything else, one can build only upon a resisting foundation; whatever constantly gives way to pressure, constantly renders movement impossible.[3]

What Stravinsky applies to the actual business of creation applies equally well to the abstract definition of ends. It is easier to define a perfect omelet than it is to describe the most delectable dish imaginable. To say that a lawyer arguing a case within the limits of forensic procedure achieved perfection in his art is to convey more meaning than to assert of an argument that it is the best conceivable in any context. In all areas, from the most trivial to the most exalted, the mind is compelled to sharpen its judgment by narrowing its range. Some limitation of means, imposed by circumstances or voluntarily accepted, is essential for an intelligent definition of the end sought.

These observations should be enough to remind us that the relation between ends and means is far from being simple. It is certainly not the one-way affair implied when Mill wrote that "rules of action [and we may suppose he meant to include also the social institutions that rest on such rules] must take their whole character and color from the end to which they are subservient."

But because it is a mistake to assign an unconditional primacy to ends over means in thinking about creative human effort, it does not follow that the

3. [Igor Stravinsky, *Poetics of Music*, trans. Arthur Knodel and Ingolf Dahl (Cambridge, Mass.: Harvard University Press, 1947), pp. 63–65.]

mistake can be corrected by a turn of a hundred and eighty degrees. Because our architectural paraphrase of Mill's argument is false as stated, it does not follow that it can be corrected by reversing every assertion in it. Some vague conception of architectural ends at the outset is essential to define the range of means worthy of consideration for architectural purposes. In the development of architecture it is safe to assume that an obstinate quest for new forms of beauty and utility has sometimes led to the discovery of means capable of realizing them, so that firmly held ends stubbornly pursued can sometimes create means that were previously nonexistent.

What is needed is obviously a more exact analysis of the role played in human thinking by the means-ends relation. We shall also need to explore carefully the peculiar function performed by this category of thought in the design of social institutions. Is it true, for example, that the means available for constructing social institutions are, like the means available to the architect, limited in range? If so, why is this? Stravinsky not only rejoices in the physical restrictions of his subject, but recommends that the artist voluntarily impose on himself what may be called liberating limitations. Is there anything like this in problems of social design? These are questions that if not broached directly may lurk disturbingly in the background. They are questions that cannot be answered without a somewhat tedious exercise in analysis.

3. *Means and Ends in Social Architecture*

I have already sufficiently indicated my own view that the need for greater clarity about the means-ends relation as it affects social philosophy is a most urgent one. Let me emphasize this point by juxtaposing two quotations, each taken from a writer by no means deficient in analytical powers.

The opening paragraphs of Aldous Huxley's *Ends and Means* read as follows:

> About the ideal goal of human effort there exists in our civilization and, for nearly thirty centuries, there has existed a very general agreement. From Isaiah to Karl Marx the prophets have spoken with one voice. In the Golden Age to which they look forward there will be liberty, peace, justice and brotherly love. "Nation shall no more lift sword against nation"; "the free development of each will lead to the free development of all"; "the world shall be full of knowledge of the Lord, as the waters cover the sea."
>
> With regard to the goal, I repeat, there is and for long has been a very

general agreement. Not so with regard to the roads which lead to that goal. Here unanimity and certainty give place to utter confusion, to the clash of contradictory opinions, dogmatically held and acted upon with the violence of fanaticism.[4]

Compare this passage with the opening words of an inaugural address by Isaiah Berlin:

> If men never disagreed about the ends of life, if our ancestors had re-mained undisturbed in the Garden of Eden, the studies to which the Chi-chele Chair of Social and Political Theory is dedicated could scarcely have been conceived. For these studies spring from, and thrive on, discord. Some-one may question this on the ground that even in a society of saintly an-archists, where no conflicts about ultimate purpose can take place, political problems, for example constitutional or legislative issues, might still rise. But this objection rests on a mistake. Where ends are agreed, the only ques-tions left are those of means, and these are not political but technical, that is to say, capable of being settled by experts or machines like arguments between engineers or doctors.[5]

With all allowance for a difference in context and for the license that enti-tles a writer, and especially a speaker, to overstate a point for the purpose of driving it home, there remains in these quotations a significant residue of genu-ine disagreement. Even if we make the improbable assumption that the two speakers were basically in accord, the very fact that they could express their agreement in language so directly opposed in ordinary meaning is evidence enough of the need for greater clarity. What are the important problems of social theory—those of means, or of ends, or of both, and if of both, how are the two to be related in the process of analyzing social problems? If the proper concern of social philosophy is with ends, while means are for the mere tech-nician, how does one assure oneself of his qualifications?

It will be convenient to begin a discussion of these questions by examining critically certain assumptions that seem to be commonly made about ends and means as they affect social arrangements—assumptions which I believe to be plainly untenable. The primary object of this examination will be to reveal the difficulties that are implicit in commonly accepted modes of thought. It will only be after the nature of these difficulties has been revealed that I shall try to trace them to their source and suggest an analysis that will avoid them. The first and negative part of this exposition will not present an easy flow of

---

4. [Aldous Huxley, *Ends and Means: An Inquiry into the Nature of Ideals and into the Meth-ods Employed for Their Realization* (New York: Harper & Bros., 1937), p. 1.]

5. [Isaiah Berlin, *Two Concepts of Liberty* (London: Clarendon Press, 1958), p. 3.]

thought, for the assumptions I shall examine are interrelated in various complex ways, some indeed being perhaps merely alternative formulations of a single basic premise. To trace all of the relevant interrelations, distinguishing carefully logical entailment from a mere congeniality of ideas, would be wearisome and would not, I think, contribute greatly to the objective sought.

In what follows I shall speak primarily of institutions, in which I mean to include legal, political, and economic institutions, as well as those which do not fall readily under any of these rubrics. Most of what I shall have to say will apply, with some modification, to social arrangements which would not ordinarily be described as institutions, such as relatively transient orderings of human relations.

The first common mode of thought I want to examine is one which supposes that the ends served by social institutions are severable, that they stand as distinct entities, each capable of a separate appraisal. If we say that an institution takes its whole character and color from the end to which it is subservient, we assume its end to be something that can be severed from those of other institutions, so that a clear conception of its end is a necessary and sufficient condition for an understanding of any institution. Even if we recognize (as we certainly should) that most institutions serve more than one end, we may still assume (as I think we should not) that the several ends served remain essentially discrete, having been assembled merely for reasons of economy—something like railway cars united for a haul across the country and then shunted off toward so many final destinations.

Against this way of thinking we must set the plain fact that human aims and impulses do not arrange themselves in a neat row of desired "end states." Instead they move in circles of interaction. We eat to live and we live to eat. We love that we may be loved, and we want to be loved that we may love freely. The pattern of our private desires reflects itself in the pattern of our social institutions. We keep up with public affairs so that we may vote intelligently, and we believe in democracy partly because it gives us an incentive to keep informed. We take legal measures to insure the impartiality of jurors, and we defend the jury system because it tends to inculcate a habit and taste for impartiality.

We should not conceive of an institution as a kind of conduit directing human energies toward some single destination. Nor can the figure be rescued by imagining a multipurpose pipeline discharging its diverse contents through different outlets. Instead we have to see an institution as an active thing, projecting itself into a field of interacting forces, reshaping those forces in diverse ways and in varying degrees. A social institution makes of human life itself something that it would not otherwise have been. We cannot therefore ask of it simply, Is its end good and does it serve that end well? Instead we have to ask a question at once more vague and more complicated—something like this: Does this institution, in a context of other institutions, create a pattern of living that is satisfying and worthy of man's capacities?

A second mode of thinking that seems to me both common and mistaken is that which assumes that the first task of social philosophy is to arrange human ends in a hierarchical order. This conception follows rather naturally from the fallacy just discussed. If particular social means are subservient to distinct and diverse social ends, so that in each instance the end sought must first be precisely defined before it is possible to select an apt means for achieving it, then it follows that the first task of institutional design is to draw up a schedule of ends in the order of their urgency. This hierarchical schedule then becomes a master plan into which the details of social architecture can be fitted.

Though such a table of priorities is often supposed to be indispensable, it is in fact never really drawn up, though verbal facsimiles are sometimes offered. There are reasons why this default does and must occur. Let us suppose a consensus that *End A* is generally "more important" than *End B*. Can we on the basis of this agreement place *End A* ahead of *End B* on our schedule of urgency? Before we can do this we must know at least what such a listing would imply. Would it mean, for example, that if the two ends come into conflict any satisfaction of A, however small, is to be preferred to any satisfaction of B, however complete? Can we really know how much we want A and B respectively until we know how much each will cost in terms of a sacrifice of other ends? If we try to solve this problem we shall have to abandon our project of defining priorities and explore the problem of available means. In this exploration we shall discover two things: First, no abstractly conceived end ever remains the same after it has been given flesh and blood through some specific form of social implementation. Reversing Mill, we may truthfully say that a social end takes its "character and color" from the means by which it is realized. Second, we must appraise not only means-cost (How much will *End B* be sacrificed to *End A* if we realize the latter through *Means X*?) but also what may be called means-surplus. Can we discover a means of realizing *End A* that will yield, as a kind of by-product, some satisfaction of *End B*? When these complexities are taken into account it becomes plain that the so-often recommended hierarchical ordering of ends is not the proper place to start in dealing with problems of social architecture.

There is one superficially persuasive defense of such an ordering that requires at least passing mention. It can be said that without human life, no other human end can be meaningful. It therefore follows that the preservation of human life must have the highest priority in the design of any social edifice.

If the resulting table is one that has only two places—preserving life comes first, everything else in second place—it is nevertheless a table of priorities on which every other decision must be based.

An easy answer is to point out that such a table cannot solve the problem presented where life is inexorably pitted against life, as in the ancient example of the two shipwrecked sailors holding to a single plank capable of supporting only one of them.[6] The true objection, however, runs deeper. We do in fact undertake enterprises, not necessarily those of war, knowing full well their cost in human life. Actuarial science could predict with considerable accuracy, for example, the lives likely to be lost in constructing a transcontinental highway. If this cost seems not disproportionate, we do not hesitate to go ahead and build the highway. In all our affairs we gauge the value of keeping human beings alive by measures other than mere existence itself. The Hanseatic city of Bremen had as its motto, "To go to sea is necessary, to live is not." St. Thomas observed that if the highest duty of a captain were really to preserve his ship, he would keep it in port forever.[7] Hence, even the preservation of human life fails to secure a fixed schedule of ends.

The next common assumption I believe to be mistaken is a belief in what may be called the infinite pliability of social arrangements. Some such belief must in fact lie back of the assumption I have just been discussing, the assumption, namely, that the first task of social philosophy is to establish a hierarchy of social ends. If in planning a trip, I feel free to chart my itinerary point by point without consulting maps or timetables, it must be because I am assuming there will always be some mode of conveyance that will take me to any destination I may set for myself. The assumption that social institutions can always be shaped to any desired end reveals itself in the common notion that implementation is a mere matter of "technique." Curiously, though the technicians capable of devising the apt means for social ends are never identified, it seems to be assumed that their competence is unlimited. There are signs by which we know a good carpenter, one of them being his knowledge of the limitations of the materials with which he works. But the technician in social implementation seems to remain at once anonymous and omnicompetent.

I shall have occasion later to discuss the limitations intrinsic to the process of designing institutions and procedures to implement social ends. One such limitation may be mentioned in passing, and that is the requirement of simplicity. Human ingenuity has produced a considerable number of ways of holding elections, some of them quite complicated. But there is obviously an upper limit to complexity if in fact an election is to afford the voter a mean-

---

6. [See Jerome Hall, *General Principles of Criminal Law*, 2d ed. (Indianapolis, Ind.: Bobbs-Merrill, 1960), p. 418.]

7. [St. Thomas Aquinas, *Summa Theologica*, Pt. I–II, Q. 2, Art. 5.]

ingful participation in the decision of the issue up for vote. The voter must have at least some inkling as to what is going on if his participation is to be real. Furthermore, there are certain kinds of decisions that do not seem amenable to any kind of voting procedure. Even the ingenuity of Charles Dodgson (Lewis Carroll), fired by resentment toward Alice's father, the Dean, was unable to find a voting procedure that could resolve a dispute about the design of the new bell tower for Christ Church College.[8] It takes something more than a rub of the technician's lamp to bring into existence a social procedure apt for the solution of any given problem. And we must not overlook the possibility that a particular social task may turn out to be, in Michael Polanyi's words, unmanageable.[9]

The fourth common notion that I should like to challenge is one which assumes that elements of formal structure are to be found only in social means, not in ends. Means we design, ends we merely choose. Drawing up a hierarchy of ends is therefore not an exercise in social architecture, but a ranking of preferences. The element of formal design is supplied by our anonymous friend, the expert in means, the social technician—the specialist in implementation.

This mode of thought finds expression in, and at the same time is encouraged by, the now common usage which assigns to the word *value* the sense of a moral objective—a usage that appears to be chiefly owing to the influence of Nietzsche.[10] What used to be ethics is now often called value theory. Where we once judged a man by the cast of his character, we now inquire about his "value preferences." There is nothing about the word *value* that suggests any element of formal structure. Being a concept that is most congenial to economics, it suggests a formless end-utility, like the pleasure of eating or the comfort of keeping warm. Indeed, one "value-oriented" social philosophy explicitly defines a value as "a preferred event." It is characteristic that this philosophy begins with a table of eight "values" and never devotes explicit attention to the problem of social implementation.[11]

All of this line of thought is, I believe, profoundly mistaken. Any social goal, to be meaningful, must be conceived in structural terms, not simply as something that happens to people when their social ordering is rightly directed. In individual morality, I think it safe to say that the life worthy of

8. [See Duncan Black, *The Theory of Committees and Elections* (Cambridge, U.K.: Cambridge University Press, 1958), chap. 20.]

9. [Michael Polanyi, *The Logic of Liberty: Reflections and Rejoinders* (Chicago: University of Chicago Press, 1951), pp. 154ff.]

10. [Samuel Hart, *Treatise on Values* (New York: Philosophical Library, 1949), p. 13.]

11. [Myres S. McDougal, "The Comparative Study of Law for Policy Purposes: Value Clarification as an Instrument of Democratic World Order," *Yale Law Journal* 61, no. 6 (1952): 915–46. Bibliographical references to previous writings by Professors McDougal and Lasswell will be found in the notes to this article.]

emulation is one that forms a coherent pattern, not one that is manipulated to bring about a series of desirable states of mind and body. So I believe it is with society. There is, of course, danger in this analogy. It carries a disturbing suggestion of the organic theory of the state. But in this case surely we can manage to save the baby without having to keep yesterday's bath water. We can agree that it is definitely undesirable that the whole of human life should receive its pattern from social institutions. This does not preclude an equal agreement that our social institutions should be so designed as to give coherent meaning and direction to that portion of the life of man that is their proper province.

A fifth and final mode of thought that is here rejected has already been suggested in passing. This is the notion that social means—institutions, procedures, rules—are necessary evils and that the world would be better off if their costs could be avoided, that is, if social ends were attainable directly, without introducing any intervening rigidities of social structure. Enough has been said already to indicate the general line of argument that might be advanced against this view. It will be sufficient to suggest, as a counterbalance to the notion of means-cost, the notion of means-surplus or means-bonus.

We may say, for example, that the institutional role of the professional advocate (the lawyer pleading a case before a court, for example) is to insure that the deciding tribunal will have a full and sympathetic understanding of his client's situation. So that this function may be fulfilled, the advocate is permitted a certain license of partisanship; he may present both the facts and the law of his client's case in their most favorable light, leaving it to his adversary to present the case in its opposing aspect. It comes as a surprise to many laymen to discover that the practice of his profession often—though certainly not always—seems to confer on the advocate a special ability to judge issues objectively. A necessity of his professional role, that of understanding fully his opponent's position and of anticipating his arguments, develops an attitude of mind that carries over to questions arising outside the advocate's practice. An institutional license of partisanship becomes, then, the source of a habit of mind that can rise above partisanship. Our best institutions are, I believe, pregnant with these beneficial side-effects. It is chiefly for this reason that I have so vigorously objected to the view that institutions are mere inert conduits directing human energies, with much frictional waste en route, toward certain desirable end-states. Our institutions are a part of the pattern of our lives. The task of perfecting them furnishes an outlet for the most vigorous of moral impulses.

This completes our survey of certain common modes of thought which are being rejected here and of the reasons for that rejection.[12]

.   .   .   .

12. [What follows is condensed somewhat from the original manuscript.]

Despite a steady expansion of the functions of government, large and small, formal and informal, during the last hundred years, freedom as an objective of social policy is still conceived largely in Mill's terms, as a mere absence of constraint. Its relations with other social goals, and in particular with that of security, are scarcely mentioned. In a tacitly assumed hierarchy of ends, freedom is accorded a high position—perhaps the highest position—this ranking being assigned to it, not because of any assumed structural relation with other ends, but because of an attributed intrinsic value. Discussions of freedom are in fact permeated with the hierarchic conception. We are told, for example, that we not only can, but should, make up our minds whether we prefer freedom or order. Freedom as a form of social ordering, and order as something essential to freedom, are aspects of the problem generally passed over in silence.[13]

Society is, of course, impossible without some limits on individual freedom, that is, without some form of constraint. If freedom means the absence of constraint, the problem then becomes that of avoiding constraint at particular points and for particular reasons—or, reversing the emphasis, of assigning sound reasons for imposing constraint at particular points. The respective functions of freedom and constraint are, therefore, two aspects of the same question. The pattern of freedom is the reversed image of the pattern of constraint. The two form the structure of society as a whole.

All of this is well expressed by James Fitzjames Stephen in his famous but little-read reply to Mill. Stephen is invoking his favorite analogy by which the rules of social living are thought of as bringing together and directing the flow of human energies, as pipes direct water to places where it can be most effective.

> The phenomenon which requires and will repay study is the direction and nature of the various forces, individual and collective, which in their combination or collision with each other and with the outer world make up human life. If we want to know what ought to be the size and position of a hole in a water pipe, we must consider the nature of water, the nature of pipes, and the objects for which the water is wanted; but we shall learn very little by studying the nature of holes. Their shape is simply the shape of whatever bounds them. Their nature is merely to let the water pass, and it seems to me that enthusiasm about them is altogether thrown away.[14]

We might reply to Stephen by pointing out that for a variety of reasons

---

13. [See Lon L. Fuller, "Freedom—A Suggested Analysis," *Harvard Law Review* 68, no. 8 (1955): 1305–25.]

14. [James Fitzjames Stephen, *Liberty, Equality, Fraternity* (Cambridge, U.K.: Cambridge University Press, 1967), p. 174. This is a reprint of the 2d edition, 1874.]

there are a good many people who have a strong penchant for pipes without holes—a distrust of human nature, ambitions toward vast projects of human engineering, or merely an innate tidiness. To offset their influence some enthusiasm for holes may not be misplaced. But the essential truth of Stephen's analysis remains, I believe, unimpaired.

Stephen is by no means alone in perceiving the fallacies that underlie so much of the literature of freedom. Michael Oakeshott, in particular, has emphasized the extent to which freedom, conceived as an object of social policy, is dependent upon formal arrangements for its realization. This aspect of the problem he expresses well—perhaps I should say he overstates effectively—when he writes: "The freedom which we enjoy is nothing more than arrangements, procedures of a certain kind: the freedom of an Englishman is not something exemplified in the procedure of Habeas Corpus, it *is*, at that point, the availability of that procedure." [15]

Other writers on freedom have made important contributions toward clarity of analysis. [16] In view of this it may seem unfair to pass so adverse a judgment on the literature generally. After all, it may be said, a writer must be judged in the light of his intentions. Most of the literature of freedom is in essence exhortatory and quite innocent of any intention toward analytical profundity. Should this literature not be simply accepted for what it is? Is not the only serious question whether it moves men's minds and hearts in the right direction?

I would respond to such questions by asking whether the very posing of them does not imply acceptance of one of the assumptions that has been rejected in this chapter. I refer, of course, to the assumption that the first and chief task of moral philosophy is to draw up a hierarchy of social ends, or in modern terms a schedule of personal value preferences. If such a schedule must precede and set the terms of any discussion of problems of social ordering, then it is quite difficult to see why one is not entitled to "sell" his personal value preferences by whatever rhetoric he commands. And if it be further assumed that social means are infinitely pliable, there is of course no reason why an exercise in persuasion should be encumbered by an irrelevant discussion of the problems of social implementation.

One of the strongest objections to the assumptions that have been rejected in this chapter lies in the fact that they encourage and appear to legitimate what may be called the salesmanship of value preferences. The general acceptance of these assumptions creates an atmosphere in which it becomes difficult

---

15. [Michael Oakeshott, "Political Education," in *Philosophy, Politics and Society*, ed. Peter Laslett (Oxford: Blackwell, 1956), p. 10.]

16. [See the collection edited by Ruth Nanda Anshen, *Freedom: Its Meaning* (New York: Harcourt, Brace, 1940).]

to make any distinction between serious efforts of analysis and what are essentially exercises in propaganda.

I want now to turn from the problem of freedom to that of equality.

4. *The Problem of Equality*

In the development of his utilitarian philosophy Jeremy Bentham made some tentatives in the direction of a hierarchical ordering of social ends, in which perforce pleasure had to occupy the highest place. In particular he discussed the proper ranking of security and equality as subsidiary objectives.[17] In his analysis of this problem the law of diminishing returns played a prominent role. Though he never articulated a general theory of marginal utility, he was thoroughly familiar with the notion that the value of a unit of money (say, a pound sterling), in terms of the happiness or "utility" it brings to its possessor, diminishes as the quantity owned increases. Indeed, it was on this principle that he founded his "disapprobation" of gambling for high stakes. To a man possessing a thousand pounds an apparently even bet of five hundred is not in fact even at all, since a loss of five hundred would visit on the gambler a deprivation much greater than the benefit he would derive if he won an equal amount.[18] In effect, then, when two men make an even bet for high stakes each enters, to the disadvantage of both (except under special conditions), a contingent trade of dear pounds for cheap ones.

From this law of the diminishing utility of money it would seem to follow that Bentham's highest good, namely, happiness, would be promoted by legislative measures deliberately directed toward equality of income. What the rich would lose by such a measure would be more than offset by what the poor would gain, measuring losses and gains not in pounds but in units of human happiness. But Bentham rejected the notion that total happiness would be increased by equality on the ground that in order to achieve and maintain equality repeated interventions by the state would be necessary, and such interventions would be destructive of security, itself an ingredient of happiness.[19]

This conclusion of Bentham's is severely criticized by the Danish legal philosopher Alf Ross. It is important to realize that in the passage about to be quoted Ross is himself neither advocating nor rejecting the principle of equal-

17. [Jeremy Bentham, *The Theory of Legislation*, ed. C. K. Ogden (New York: Kegan Paul, Trench, Trubner, 1931), pp. 96 and 119.]
18. [Ibid., p. 106n.]
19. [Ibid., pp. 119–20.]

ity. He is a thorough-going relativist whose object is merely to reveal what he regards as a naive dogmatism in Bentham. Ross in comment on Bentham's argument writes:

> The remarkable thing about this chain of reasoning is that Bentham does not mean by "insecurity" the disturbance and disappointment produced by a revolution in the rules which govern the distribution of ownership, a disturbance which takes place once and for all. Rather he plainly has in mind that equalization can be effected only through a series of repeated interventions in the rights of property, whereby something that is mine is transferred to you. Accordingly he assumes that an equalization in the distribution of wealth requires permanently recurring redivisions and continuing insecurity—in other words, a condition without order or stability. Apparently it never even occurred to Bentham that when a new mode of distribution was once introduced that which under the former order would have become mine would no longer become mine, and that the new mode of division could obviously be maintained with the same security as the old.[20]

Do we not have exemplified in Ross's criticism what I have called the fallacious assumption of the infinite pliability of social arrangements? In judging that question it is important to realize that neither Bentham nor Ross are addressing themselves to the old saw (perhaps not wholly without teeth) that after an equal division of wealth the shrewd and industrious will always find some way (including a change in the rules) of coming out on top. What Bentham and Ross are discussing is the possibility of a legal and economic order by which newly produced wealth would, as it came into being, be channeled so as to achieve and maintain an equal distribution. Bentham, whose mind was always intent on problems of implementation, apparently could not conceive how this could be done, or rather he could conceive of no way of doing it that would not require repeated redistributions. Ross, on the other hand, though he does not suggest any particular set of institutions that could achieve the desired objective, apparently assumes that any social goal can be given suitable implementation. Along with this assumption, there goes its corollary, that it is possible to define a social objective in abstraction from the means of realizing it.

It is difficult to conceive a social objective of which these assumptions are less true than they are of equality. Until we find some means by which equal treatment can be defined and administered, we do not know the meaning of equality itself.

20. [Alf Ross, *Kritik der sogenannten praktischen Erkenntnis* (Copenhagen: Levin and Munksgaard, 1933), p. 138. This passage was translated, I believe, by Fuller.]

Now of course Ross and Bentham were not talking about equality generally, but *economic* equality. This seems to transfer the question to a quite different plane. We all know, or we think we know, that to give two men each a hundred dollars a week is to give them equal treatment "from an economic point of view." The difficulties are those which lie concealed in the expression "from an economic point of view."

Living in a society where the economic market is taken for granted, we assume—and within limits we are entitled to assume—that one dollar is equal to another in terms of the command it confers over all kinds of goods. But there are serious qualifications on this apparent truism. The Negro who has the same monetary income as a white man does not generally gain by his dollars the same command over housing for his family and education for his children. Furthermore, there are numerous imperfections in the market which prevent it from bringing into a completely neutral calculation the comparison of one good with another. Among these imperfections are those resulting from a thousand and one government subsidies and penalties, introduced by the tax laws and otherwise, which run up the cost of some goods and reduce that of others. For example, measured by its drain on productive resources a quart of whiskey costs many times too much, this "overpricing" resulting from heavy taxes and, in some states, by a monopolistic position accorded the seller by "fair trade" laws.

With the qualifications suggested we are by and large justified in saying that a dollar is a dollar, and that if a loaf of bread carries the same price tag as a pound of asparagus it is because they are "worth the same" in terms of their drain on resources and their capacity to satisfy human desires. All of this goes by the board, however, so soon as we talk about a radical transformation in our legal and economic system such as was involved in the dispute between Ross and Bentham. We have no justification whatever for assuming, as Ross apparently does, that if the market were abolished some other institutional arrangement would be able to take over its function of establishing value ratios for goods of disparate kinds.

The notion that from an array of social objectives men can choose some particular end for highest priority, that this choice can be meaningful though reached without any consideration of means, that some means can always be found for any social end—this whole bundle of ideas has a curious vitality. These ideas also turn up, singly or in combination, in some curious places.

A divorce of the problems of ends from that of means is commonly encountered in treatises on economics, political science, and sociology. Such works are often prefaced by an explicit disclaimer of concern with, or at least of any special competence to deal with, the setting of social goals—sometimes called the problem of ultimate values. Thus in the second edition of a widely used textbook on economics the author declares, under the heading "Boundaries and Limits to Economics":

> When we come to the . . . question of the desirable distribution of wealth and income between individuals, we leave the field of science altogether. *De gustibus non est disputandum*: there is no disputing (scientifically!) tastes; and the same goes for ethics. We must leave the definition of social *ends* to the philosopher, the theologian, the statesman, and to public opinion.[21]

It may be assumed that the author of this passage took it for granted that those setting social ends would consult the economist to learn the "economic cost" of what they proposed. Thus, the setting of ends would at least require collaboration between the end-setter and the means-specialist. There are, however, two difficulties with this proposed division of labor. In the first place it is difficult to see how the philosopher or theologian, untrained in economics, could understand an explanation of all the economic problems involved in realizing, let us say, the objective of equality. The second difficulty is more fundamental. The concepts of "economic cost" and "economic efficiency" are themselves predicated upon the acceptance of certain means-ends relations. Thus I would argue that economics takes as its province a certain kind of social ordering which may be called broadly a regime of reciprocity.[22] An "economic cost" is, then, a set-back in the achievement of this particular form of social order. The economist means-expert, who warns of certain "economic costs," is therefore necessarily himself engaged in the business of end-setting.

In the passage last quoted it will be recalled that the author was not merely setting the limits of economics (it is concerned with means, not ends) but was also tracing the boundary between science and ethics, the former being concerned with means, the latter with ends. Now if the means-end relation is as simple as it is generally thought to be, then the distinction between science and ethics is equally simple. On the other hand, if the distinction between means and ends is, as I believe, urgently in need of reexamination, then this is equally true of the distinction between science and ethics.

---

21. [Paul Samuelson, *Economics: An Introductory Analysis*, 2d ed. (New York: McGraw-Hill, 1951), p. 15.]

22. [See Lon L. Fuller, *The Morality of Law*, rev. ed. (New Haven: Yale University Press, 1969), pp. 15–30.]

II. *The Principles and Forms of Social Order*

Two Principles of Human Association

Editor's Note

In his outline for "The Principles of Social Order," Fuller remarked that people come together in numberless ways to their injury. His interest was rather in the forms of coming together which are a benefit to the participants, and he suggested that such forms can be grouped under two principles: association by reciprocity and association to achieve common aims.

Association by reciprocity is formalized most notably in a regime of contract, in which social order is the cumulative product of innumerable individual agreements effecting voluntary exchanges of goods and services. The paradigm of such a regime, on a large scale, is a market economy combined with the private ownership of property. Association to achieve common aims is more commonly found in small or intimate settings, such as families, neighborhood groups, or nonprofit organizations. Fuller sometimes suggested that common aims are a source of spontaneous ordering, typically requiring few explicit rules and little formal structure. In a large society, however, members' interests are too disparate to sustain communal enterprises, and a vertical line of command is required, even if it is answerable ultimately to democratic majorities. Thus Fuller was sceptical of legislative control based on a notion of the public interest or the common good. The only common good, he once observed, is permitting citizens to realize the benefits of association by reciprocity. Accordingly he favored a conception of legislation which views laws as baselines for the self-directed pursuits of citizens, securing only the minimal restraints on conduct necessary for continuing interaction. The result is an impersonal scheme of duties and entitlements, without the imposition of specific ends by legislators.

While distinguishing these two principles of association—as Fuller did, in different ways, in a number of his writings—he was careful to stress that particular associations always manifest some mixture of the two. Thus he sometimes emphasized the element of reciprocity in family relationships and of shared objectives in the nation or the state. In the present essay, he was also concerned with observing how an association in which the principle of common aims was dominant could become transformed, and perhaps even undermined, by an increased formalization of relationships. He refers to this phenomenon as "creeping legalism," which shows itself in three ways: (1) a greater reliance on rules to define members' duties and entitlements, (2) a concordant shift in accountability based on tangible harms or benefits which flow from specific acts rather than on more judgmental assessments of character and motive, and (3) the articulation of strict procedural requirements for distributing benefits and burdens. When the bonds holding an association together consist of such formal structural elements, members are given greater leeway to pursue divergent aims. Fuller analyzes some of the conditions that promote divergence or convergence of aims and raises the question of the circumstances under which one or the other is desirable.

"Two Principles of Human Association" was initially presented to the American

Society for Political and Legal Philosophy, an organization of which Fuller was a founder. The Society's annual conference in 1966 was devoted to the topic "Private Associations." When the papers were published in the society's yearbook (Nomos XI, 1969), they appeared under the title Voluntary Associations, *edited by J. Roland Pennock and John W. Chapman.*

I

When I was in the fourth grade of grammar school a group of some five or six of us formed a modest "voluntary association" of our own. We met at recess in the corner of the school lot farthest from the school building. We sat about on the ground and talked. We were by way of being a literary society. We shared in common a very special interest in *The Idylls of the King* and *Treasure Island.* Toward those works we had some of the passion of the Baker Street Irregulars toward the writings of A. Conan Doyle. Like the Irregulars, we played a kind of game of one-upmanship with one another to see who could remember the most recondite passages in our favorites.

Shortly after we started holding our meetings we became aware of a figure hovering in the background. It turned out to be a somewhat unprepossessing classmate of ours named Wilber. We told him to go away; we were having a meeting. He retreated to a greater distance, but day after day continued to haunt our little camp. Finally we called him before us and asked him what he was up to. It turned out he was desperately lonesome and wanted to join our company. We told him we would see what could be done.

We finally administered an impromptu test of his literary competence. We decided he had just barely passed. He was, with some misgivings, admitted to formal membership.

Though Wilber became at once a faithful attendant at our meetings, it soon became apparent that we had made a serious mistake. Though he tried valiantly to take part in our discussions, it was clear that his interests and, in our opinion, his capacities did not move with ours.

We decided to expel Wilber. The deed had to be accomplished in a manner befitting the literary dedication of our society. It was decided he should be given the Black Spot. We carefully cut out a disk of white cardboard and painted one side with black shoe polish. There was some discussion as to whether we should amplify the message of the Black Spot with some words on the reverse side, there being authority in the scriptures for such a procedure. We decided, however, that this was unnecessary; with all his limitations as a student of literature, Wilber could not fail to understand what we meant. We then solemnly drew straws to select the messenger.

The next day at recess we stayed behind while our appointed agent carried the sinister symbol to our regular meeting place. We watched from a distance, confidently expecting to see Wilber take one look at the disk and then walk solemnly away with downcast head. Instead, to our surprise, he held the Black Spot out in one hand and gesticulated while our messenger engaged in some kind of explanation. Finally Wilber broke into tears.

Our messenger returned slowly.

What happened?

"Wilber didn't know what it meant. He said, 'What is this thing anyway?' I had to tell him."

Later we all had a talk with Wilber and found that he felt very bitter about the whole affair.

"What did I do wrong? Why didn't you tell me? Why didn't I have a chance to explain? And why did you give me that crazy piece of black paper instead of just plain saying you wanted me to get out?"

In short, Wilber felt that he had not been given due process of law. And indeed we had violated every principle of proper legal procedure. No rule had ever been announced that Wilber could be said to have broken. He was given no hearing; no specification of the charge against him was ever made; he had no chance to defend himself, no opportunity to consult counsel. We had even added insult to injury by adopting a grotesque and ambiguous way of conveying our decision to him.

I recall being very deeply disturbed by what we had done. On the one hand, it seemed plain that we had not played fair with Wilber. And yet, on the other hand, the more I thought about it the clearer it was to me that nothing Wilber could possibly have done—no violation of rules, no misconduct—could have demonstrated more clearly his unfitness to be of our number than the simple fact that he had never heard of the Black Spot. For this failing there could be no possible extenuation.

Many years later I became acquainted with a much discussed legal decision[1] concerned with the judicial review of expulsions from private associations. In October 1927, at the beginning of her fourth year as a major in home economics, Miss Beatrice Anthony was summarily dismissed from Syracuse University. She asked for a specification of the charges against her and a formal hearing. On the refusal of the university to meet her demand, she brought suit in the New York courts for reinstatement. The lower court ordered her reinstatement; on appeal this decision was reversed and the action of the university was upheld.

---

1. *Anthony v. Syracuse University*, 223 N.Y. Supp. 796 (1927); 224 App. Div. 487 (1928).

The only ground asserted by the university in justification of its action was that Miss Anthony was rumored to have caused trouble of an unspecified nature in the past and that they had concluded she "was not a typical Syracuse girl."

The decision upholding the university has been uniformly criticized by the commentators. While they have ridiculed the notion that Miss Anthony could properly be asked to leave because she "was not a typical Syracuse girl," the burden of their complaint relates to the failure of the university to give her a formal hearing. Yet if the charge remained the same—"not a typical Syracuse girl"—would not the holding of a hearing have compounded the university's offense? A formal hearing devoted to the issue Is she or is she not the type? would call to mind the horrors of Kafka's *The Trial* and the caricature of the judicial office presented by the Red Queen when she sat in judgment of Alice.

When I first became acquainted with *Anthony* v. *Syracuse University* it revived at once the painful memory of *The Petition of Wilber* v. *Five Young Literary Snobs*. This revival was not difficult; a guilty conscience had kept that earlier case on the threshold of recollection through all the intervening decades. Though it seemed to me that the action of Syracuse University was outrageous, I persisted in the belief that our own little group had acted properly in the premises. When I sought some satisfactory intellectual justification for distinguishing the two cases, however, I found myself in trouble. Nor could I take refuge in the belief that we were just children and that nothing of real importance was at stake. For aught I know, Wilber may to this day bear the psychic scars of the treatment he received at our hands. The wound we inflicted may still impair his effectiveness as a citizen, husband, and father.

II

Against this somewhat personal background I should like now to project a distinction between two principles of human association.[2] I ask you to note that I am speaking of *principles* of association, not *forms* of association. I am

2. The scope of my [essay] is, of course, affected by the circumstance that it is part of a general discussion of *voluntary* associations. I have made no attempt here to deal directly with relations of the sort commonly called those of domination or power. I would venture the opinion, however, that those relations, when they become stable, are not so divergent in principle from those herein discussed as is commonly supposed. In support of this view I would cite Talcott Parsons, "On the Concept of Political Power," *Proceedings of the American Philosophical Society* 107 (1963): 240; and *The Sociology of Georg Simmel*, trans. K. Wolff (New York: Free Press, 1950), pp. 181–303. As both authors remind us, we must not forget the interaction and reciprocal influence that exist in relationships that seem on the surface to present a unilateral projection of power.

concerned with the glue that holds together what one writer has called the furniture of society and not the structure of the furniture itself—though of course the efficacy of the glue limits the kinds of furniture that can be put together.

The first of my two principles of association is that of *shared commitment*. The opposing principle I shall call the *legal principle*; it refers to the situation where an association is held together and enabled to function by formal rules of duty and entitlement.

Obviously our little band in the school lot was held together by a shared commitment, by our dedication to the task of developing together the implications of certain common interests. We had, and for the time being at least needed, no rules or officers. At the other extreme, and exemplifying the legal principle of association, stands a government, a state, a polity.

I must confess to some qualms about the word *commitment* as a way of designating my first principle of association. The most obvious alternative would be to speak of an association for the achievement of shared *ends* or *purposes*. The trouble with this solution is that by taking a sharp distinction between means and ends it does violence to the nature of human motivation. Our little discussion group sought no clearly defined end-state; we wanted merely to be together in order to converse about certain shared interests. We had no conception of any ultimate development that might emerge from our conversations. Even in the case of a society explicitly formed to achieve some stated purpose, it may turn out that the objective sought is unattainable, so that some other end, not merely smaller in compass but actually different in nature, must be substituted. Or, again, an end originally selected, though attainable, turns out to require some unwelcome reordering of the internal relations of the group seeking to achieve it. This is frequently the case when an effective pursuit of the end originally sought is seen to require a formalization of the group's internal structure that is regarded as too high a price to pay for mere efficiency. Finally, and most important, in an association formally dedicated to the achievement of some stated end, the strongest element of commitment may not lie in the end itself (which may be trite and wholly acceptable to any normal person) but in a belief in the efficacy of the means pursued. It is usually on this point that the faint-of-heart fall by the wayside.

At one time I considered speaking of *aspiration* rather than *commitment* as the mark of my first principle of association. But, besides being a rather fancy word, *aspiration* would tend to rule out the case of men who are united by a shared hatred. Any attempt at dispassionate analysis must recognize that men may come together to express and cultivate a vast range of interests and desires, which may include the unworthy as well as the most commendable.

When I speak of commitment I do not have in mind anything like a formal or ritualistic pledge, any *rites de passage*. The members of our little club were not required to take an oath to maintain, midst all the vicissitudes of life, that Tennyson and Stevenson were the greatest writers that ever lived. We took that for granted.

Today the prevailing climate of opinion inclines us to assume that many lines of human activity, and many fields of human thought, involve no element of commitment whatever. The most obvious of these is supposed to be the pursuit of scientific truth. Yet as Michael Polanyi[3] and Thomas Kuhn[4] have shown, there is always in any given science, except during periods of radical reorientation, a tacit commitment to certain lines of inquiry as offering the only legitimate outlet for the scientific spirit. Accordingly, in terms of the analysis here presented, a scientific research group illustrates the principle of association by shared commitment. The commitment in this case extends not to the abstract goal of scientific truth, but to a body of doctrine and a set of procedures regarded as the indispensable means for arriving at that end.

III

In real life human associations normally present a blend, or perhaps I should say an uneasy mixture, of the two principles I have here distinguished.

Association by the principle of shared commitment is perhaps illustrated in its purest form in an association between a composer and a librettist, the collaboration of Richard Strauss and von Hofmannsthal being the most famous example. An equally relevant example would be the collaboration in scientific research of a theorist with an experimentalist.

It is not easy to find a corresponding "pure type" representing an association based on what I have called the legal principle, that is, an association wholly dependent upon formal rules of duty and entitlement. Perhaps the nearest thing to this model might be found in what anthropologists call silent barter. One party brings his offering—say, a tiger skin—to a clearing in the woods, leaves the skin on a tree stump, and then retires to a safe distance. The other party comes forward to inspect the offering and either declines it or puts his own offering alongside it, after which he in turn retires to a safe distance. In this way an exchange may ultimately be consummated without any words being spoken and without hostilities being risked by the parties' being brought

3. Michael Polanyi, *The Logic of Liberty: Reflections and Rejoinders* (Chicago: University of Chicago Press, 1951); *Personal Knowledge: Towards a Post-Critical Philosophy* (Chicago: University of Chicago Press, 1958 [rev. ed., 1962]).

4. Thomas Kuhn, *The Structure of Scientific Revolutions* (Chicago: University of Chicago Press, 1962; 2d ed., 1970).

in too close proximity with one another. All the parties need share for the possible success of such a transaction is a desire for disparate objects and a willingness to accept the few and simple restraints imposed by the rules of the game.

This illustration makes it clear that when I refer to a legal principle of association I do not mean to import into that description all the limitations that now surround the use of the word *law*. If anyone says that there cannot be law until there is a sovereign political lawgiver, then I will make my peace with him by stipulating that within the concept of law as I am using it I mean to include formalized rules of morality. And, of course, I have in mind formalized rules that govern the relations within an association, just as the rules of silent barter may be said to constitute a kind of internal law of that peculiar and singularly impoverished form of human association.

In most human associations the two principles stand in a relation of polarity—they fight and reinforce each other at the same time. As a shift occurs in the balance between them, this shift may both cause and reflect a corresponding shift in the quality of the human relationships encompassed by the two principles.

When all goes well with an association, it is usually difficult to say how much its success depends on a sense of shared commitment and how much derives from a well-designed internal legal structure. When trouble develops and a schism occurs, however, the latent tension between the two principles may come plainly into view.

This notably occurs when a quarrel within a church is taken to the ordinary courts for decision.[5] For quite obvious reasons the courts have generally steered clear of any involvement in the expulsion of church members, the discharge or discipline of the clergy, and other like matters. The matter stands quite otherwise when the issue is access to the church edifice itself. Here property rights are at stake, and the courts are compelled to take jurisdiction; the community simply cannot permit two contending groups to fight it out on the church steps to see who will be allowed to enter and hold his sort of service.

There are in the law reports literally hundreds of cases involving these intrachurch quarrels. It is estimated that each year in this area there go down in the books about twenty-five new appellate decisions.

It may be said that the courts have developed two standards for deciding these disputes. The first views the church as an association founded on a

5. In the comments that follow in the text I have drawn heavily on Note, "Judicial Intervention in Disputes over the Use of Church Property," *Harvard Law Review* 75, no. 6 (1962): 1142–86. Also useful have been Note, "Private Government on the Campus—Judicial Review of University Expulsions," *Yale Law Journal* 72, no. 7 (1963): 1362–1410; and "Developments in the Law—Judicial Control of Actions of Private Associations," *Harvard Law Review* 76, no. 5 (1963): 983–1100. Another source on which I have drawn has been the researches of two of my students, Leslie Ann Carothers and Peter C. Williams.

shared commitment, the commitment in this case running to a body of ecclesiastical doctrine. According to this view, the sheriff under court order holds the door of the church open to that faction which accepts most faithfully the creed to which the church edifice was dedicated. The opposing rule looks on the church as an association held together by formal rules. Access to the church building is then awarded in accordance with the internal law of the church itself.

Any judge faced for the first time with deciding one of these church fights would probably find choice between the two legal rules, just as we have stated them, quite uninviting. The choice becomes even less appealing when we examine how these two standards operate in the decision of actual cases.

Suppose the judge decides to steer clear of the internal law of the church by awarding the edifice to that faction whose commitment of faith most nearly corresponds to that of the church as a whole. At once the element of time enters the picture. The present church building may have been built with money raised some fifty years ago; those who contributed this money presumably anticipated that it would be used to propagate the faith as they then knew it. There are decisions that speak of a kind of implied trust in this situation, and by this principle the more conservative faction will normally win the argument. But is there any sound reason for supposing that those who contributed the money really laid great stake by purity of doctrine? And if they were alive today who can say what dogma they would embrace?

The opposite route—that of deciding the case according to the internal law of the church—is no smoother. "The lines of authority . . . are apt to be blurred, and the relevant church law chaotic, voluminous and unintelligible to a court, even with the aid of expert witnesses. Further, questions of authority are likely to depend upon matters of dogma. . . ."[6] On the surface the simplest form of church government is found in the congregational principle, by which the local congregation runs its own affairs. But matters affecting the congregation are not ordinarily put to a formal vote, and it may be difficult to know who actually counts as a member of the congregation. If the court undertakes—as has been done in one or two cases—to hold and supervise a vote it will inevitably be involved in questions of faith when it decides who can vote. And suppose that a vote has been taken by the congregation to sell the church or to convert it into a public facility for holding lectures on every kind of subject. Are there not tacit limits on the legal powers of the congregation that hold it at least within something like the broadest limits of the church's commitment to religious faith? And so it is that the attempt to follow out the implications of church law lands us back again in the uncomfortable position of determining the issues in part by religious doctrine.

6. Note, "Judicial Intervention," p. 1160.

These cases involving intrachurch disputes are interesting in the present connection because they reveal how the two principles of association become intertwined in complex patterns in any association that has functioned over a period of time. These cases are also interesting in that they reveal the repercussions on the internal ordering of an association that may result when the state intervenes to settle disputes within the association. This second aspect I shall return to later.

For the time being it should be pointed out that along the broad spectrum that includes, at one end, associations dominated by the principle of shared commitment, and at the other those dominated by the legal principle, the church occupies a peculiarly ambiguous middle ground. But along the whole stretch of this spectrum it is probably safe to say that, apart from a few atypical cases that I have suggested, all forms of human association involve in some degree both principles.

Our little gradeschool literary circle seemed, on the face of things, wholly animated by the principle of shared commitment. Yet if an expert in small-group research had been able to monitor our meetings and had kept a record of our interactions, he might well have detected the germs of a formal, rule-bound organization of which we ourselves were quite ignorant.

It is when we move to the other end of the spectrum and consider the political state—where the legal principle of organization dominates—that the problem of identifying the part played by the opposing principle of shared commitment becomes truly difficult and indeed, in some aspects, embarrassing. There is today in our prevailing legal and political philosophy a strong tendency to insist on the moral neutrality of law. We need only reinforce this disposition of mind by adding to it something like Hans Kelsen's theory of the identity of law and the state to arrive at the conclusion that the state, and the multitude of activities necessary to sustain it, are morally neutral except as the human actions involved may be judged by moral standards applicable to all forms of human behavior, governmental and nongovernmental alike. What is ruled out by this view is the concept of institutional role—the role of the citizen, the judge, the lawgiver, the cop on the corner. The result of this exclusion is to erect a strong taboo against any recognition that each of these roles requires for its proper discharge a distinctive kind of personal commitment.[7]

---

7. In my book *The Morality of Law* (New Haven: Yale University Press, 1964 [rev. ed., 1969]) I advanced the view that there is something that may be called, after the analogy of "political morality," *legal morality*—a morality that should constrain the lawgiver from enacting, for example, retrospective or incomprehensible laws, or laws that demand acts beyond the powers of the subject. This view was received with astonishment by a school of juristic thought that has recently been characterized as that of the New Analytical Jurists, of whom the principal figure is H. L. A. Hart of Oxford. Hart's review of my book will be found in *Harvard Law Review* 78, no. 6 (1965): 1281–96. Robert Summers, "The New Analytical Jurists," *New York University Law Review* 41 (1966): 861–96, lists other reviews of my book, all of which emphatically reject any

As a matter of sociological observation we may therefore assert that as an association becomes increasingly dominated by the legal principle, the element of shared commitment—though tacitly operative—tends to sink out of sight; any attempt to secure recognition for its role is likely to stir anxieties and meet with strong resistance. This reaction will extend, not simply to what may be called the element of shared substantive commitment, but to that minimum commitment essential to make the legal system itself function properly.

IV

I propose now to suggest some eight "laws" governing the interrelations of the two principles of human association. These laws will be particularly concerned with the manner in which the interactions between the two principles characteristically develop through time. I apologize for using so pretentious a term as *laws*; I adopt it simply as a device facilitating a kind of staccato presentation. Some of these laws are, I suspect, of dubious validity; some I know to be trite; and a few I have already more than hinted at.

First Law. In almost all human associations both principles are in some degree present.

Second Law. In a given case either principle may be tacitly operative or may emerge as an object of explicit and conscious concern.

Third Law. When an association is first brought into being the principle of shared commitment will tend to be explicit and dominant, even though the association from the outset adopts, or has imposed on it, an internal structure of formal rules.

Fourth Law. To the extent that an association is seen by its members as being held together by the principle of shared commitment, it will be hostile toward internal groups dominated by the same principle. This is obvious when the internal group—in the eloquent parlance of labor relations, "the splinter group"—is based on a commitment incompatible with that sustaining the larger association. But in a less uncompromising way, the same tendency holds

---

notion that an element of moral commitment to the job is essential to keep a legal system in effective operation.

toward internal groups supported by commitments that are consistent with, or even purport to [reinforce], the commitment sustaining the larger association. The sometimes uneasy relations between the Vatican and the various Catholic orders provide a familiar case in point. Even the incest taboo has been explained by some anthropologists as being grounded in a fear that the self-perpetuating and inward-turning family would constitute a threat to the solidarity of the larger group.[8]

A commitment seeks a voluntary summoning of energies that no formal legal duty can command or even purports to command. Most legal duties are "negative" and scarcely involve the principle of marginal utility as applied to the allocation of human energies. When the law says, "Thou shalt not kill," we assume that almost any alternative application of a man's talents would offer a better outlet than killing his fellows. But when we are told to render both to Caesar *and* to God, we are likely to ask, How much can a man be expected to give? All associations supported by the principle of a shared commitment are to some extent in competition for command over a limited stock of human energy.

In this connection it is well to remember that in the early days of our Republic—when the element of commitment was strong—there was a considerable suspicion of private associations, lodges, and societies. Madison in *The Federalist* (No. X) wrote of the "dangerous vice" of "faction." Our Constitution contains no explicit guaranty of the right to form associations, but speaks instead in the First Amendment of "the right of the people peaceably to assemble, and to petition the Government for a redress of grievances." The Founding Fathers seem to have contemplated that as soon as "the people" had respectfully filed their petition, they would quietly and submissively retire to their homes. Some of the attitudes that we now confidently ascribe to totalitarianism and its intolerance of dissent were not absent in the early, anxious days of our own country.

Fifth Law. As an association moves increasingly toward a situation in which it is dominated by the legal principle, it reaches a stage in which it not only can safely tolerate, but increasingly needs, internal groupings that are themselves sustained by the principle of shared commitment. Legal rules are not an effective device for directing human energies to those places where they can be most creatively and effectively applied. In *Democracy in America* Tocqueville observed that "a government can only dictate strict rules."[9] To see why

8. Frank W. Young, "Incest Taboos and Social Solidarity," *American Journal of Sociology* 72 (1967): 589–600.

9. [Alexis de Tocqueville, *Democracy in America*, trans. Henry Reeve (New York: Colonial Press, 1899), vol. 2, 2d Part, 2d Book, chap. 5, p. 117. The chapter is entitled, "Of the use which the Americans make of public associations in civil life."]

Tocqueville valued so highly the contribution of what he called public associations, but what we often call private associations, we need only ask ourselves,
viewing the contemporary scene, Where would educational television be today
if it had been left to market forces and the regulatory powers of government?
The usual analysis of private associations is that they enable their members to
pursue "special interests" of their own, not shared by the population generally.
Yet as the case of educational television demonstrates, the real contribution of
the private association may be to hold before the public possibilities it did not
know existed, and thus help it see what its "interests" really are.

Sixth Law. In the normal course of its development an association tends to
move toward dominance by the legal principle. At the end of this development,
the principle of shared commitment commonly sinks into a state of quiescence
until some crisis, such as an external threat to the association, brings it back
to life, commonly in an awkward kind of rebirth and often in a new form. The
tendency of the element of commitment to sink out of sight applies not only
to what may be called the substantive commitments of the association, but
also, as I have tried to show, to the prosaic kind of commitment that is an
indispensable support of the legal principle itself.

Seventh Law. Once under way the development toward dominance by the
legal principle feeds on itself and becomes accelerative. The aging association
commonly displays the symptoms of what may be called creeping legalism.

Eighth Law. The conditions of modern institutional life tend strongly to
break down the distinction between the law of the political state and the internal law of associations. The result is an expansion of the jurisdiction of the
regular courts of law to pass in review decisions of associations. The consequence of this external control through judicial review is to accelerate the
tendency I have described as creeping legalism and to convert it into something
more like galloping legalism.

V

My seventh and eighth laws have been presented in very brief form, for I
intend to enlarge on them in the remainder of this discussion. What I shall
attempt is an analysis of the social processes (internal and external to the as-

sociation) through which the principle of shared commitment tends to be supplanted by a juristic order. My first comments will relate to my seventh law.

Let us suppose an association newly formed and strongly animated by a sense of shared commitment. Within such an association it is probable that for some time nothing like a disciplinary problem may arise; the faint of heart will drop by the wayside of their own accord, and it may occur—though less dependably, as Wilber demonstrated—that those strong in spirit, but weak in the flesh, will also see fit to remove themselves. But as time goes on, the demands of membership will become less obvious to the member himself. It may become necessary to bring the backsliding brother back into line by an admonition. The procedure of admonition may itself become formalized and may contemplate the possibility of a request for resignation.

As the association prospers, affiliation with it will increasingly tend to carry tangible advantages, such as an interest in the common property or, in the case of a labor union, access to a job. Admission to membership may require some material contribution by the initiate. Under these circumstances, a demand will arise that any termination of membership be accomplished by some procedure that may be called due process. Yet plainly the mills of due process are an unsuited instrument for testing conditions of mind or degrees of inner resolution. They must be directed toward overt actions that can be clearly located in time and space. A change in procedure will, thus, inevitably bring with it a change in the substance of the issue inquired into. And with this change we shall discover that we are increasingly in an environment controlled by legal rules of duty and entitlement.

What I have here described as the phenomenon of creeping legalism may seem to suffer at least a partial refutation in the history of primitive societies. Notoriously the law of such societies tends to be rigid and technical; it is only as civilization develops that an early letter-bound law is supplanted by more supple legal notions. This development seems to oppose a kind of countercurrent to the tendency I have here described as typical. In answer to this possible embarrassment for my thesis, I would offer two observations. First, a change in what may be called the inner spirit of a legal system is something quite different from a basic shift away from a nonlegal ordering to one based on juristic principles. Second, and much more fundamentally, the law of primitive societies that is described as being strict and technical is not a law governing the relations of the individual with the community; it is concerned with the offenses committed between individuals or between families. In practice this law amounts to an institutionalization of the practice of private revenge. In modern terms it belongs, not to the law of crimes, but to the law of torts. When the question is the relation of the individual to the community as a whole, the situation of primitive society is quite different. Here the relevant measures are likely to be ostracism, outlawry, imposed exile, and the like. While the imposition of these measures is naturally an occasion of some solemnity, and there will be rules as to who is entitled to participate in the decision, the decision itself will not ordinarily be controlled by preexisting rules. In primitive society the senate of elders or the tribal council sits in judgment, not of specific acts, but of the man as a whole and of his fitness to remain of their number.

If the history of primitive societies requires at least some word of explanation in defense of the thesis here advanced, no similar qualms can arise concerning its application to religious associations. Here a whole vocabulary—from which I have already freely drawn—attests to the perennial conflict between two principles of association; some tension between the spirit and the letter pervades all religious faiths. I shall content myself with one quotation; it is drawn from a Catholic theologian who deplores "the innate tendency of legal categories to substitute their rigid framework for the order of charity which is a constant source of new life. The ideal state of the Church is not to be found in a plethora of canonical prescriptions, but in a minimum of these. To quote the witty remark of a well-known theologian: 'When the Spirit of God has burnt itself out, or lost its vigor, Canon Law proliferates.'"[10]

In religion the avowed champion of the spirit is likely to be regarded as liberal and progressive, even though he seeks to recapture a state of affairs thought to characterize the ancient church; adherence to the letter is in theology commonly stigmatized as reactionary. In secular matters this appraisal is apt to undergo a partial reversal. In some contexts at least it is those regarded as liberal and progressive who are most apt to take refuge in the letter; it is they who insist that formal judgments of the individual be attended by due process, and that the procedure of due process in turn be directed, not toward a man's spirit—not toward what he thinks, believes, and endeavors to be—but toward his outward acts measured against the letter of the law.

The urge to solve associational problems by a resort to formal procedures of due process can assert itself in contexts where it becomes incongruous. This point—which I have already more than intimated a number of times—can be illustrated by one of the incidents that occurred during the period of student unrest at the University of California in Berkeley. At the height of the tensions between the rebellious students and the administration a number of students went about the campus shouting obscenities. The proper handling of this "foul word" incident was, understandably, a subject of some discussion among the

10. Mgr. A. Pailler, "Considerations on the Authority of the Church," in J. M. Todd, ed., *Problems of Authority* (Baltimore: Helicon Press, 1962), p. 23. (After consulting the French original of this symposium, I have made a slight change in the translation of the quotation from "a well-known theologian.")

faculty. One member of the faculty asserted that if he had been chancellor he would have determined who were involved and then expelled them immediately without further ado. A colleague remarked that "unfortunately too many persons seriously respond in this way when a crisis is upon them."[11] This colleague was demanding due process for those who went about the campus shouting four-letter words. But once it was determined who actually engaged in this picturesque form of defiance, what was there to try? It is certainly doubtful that the principle of the Fifth Amendment should apply to such an offense. The man who is bold enough to adopt this symbolic form of rebellion ought to be willing to stand up and be counted when the question is asked, Who did it? The "foul word" incident may well call for charity toward the indiscretions of overwrought and, by some accounts, overtried, young men; it hardly provides grist for the mills of due process. If this kind of conduct is to be tried by formal rules, then we must have a paragraph we can point to, and we shall find ourselves arguing whether the words shouted met the legal test of being obscene, and other like issues. In such a discussion it would be quite immaterial that the shouting of the foul words was a kind of nose-thumbing at the whole educational enterprise as then conducted, yet that was the real meaning of the incident for everyone concerned.

There are many instances in which a man's acts are significant, not in themselves, but for what they reveal of the man himself and his beliefs and attitudes. In ethical philosophy a distinction is sometimes taken between the ethics of the act and the ethics of the person,[12] though the implications of this distinction remain largely undeveloped and its hidden complexities unexplored.[13] This distinction, while not identical with that here taken between two principles of association, is closely related to it, and certain it is that the legal principle must deal, not with the qualities of the person, but with his acts and their conformity to rule.

In general it may be said that as the intimacy of an association increases, the emphasis shifts from the act to the person. When I learn that a close friend of mine has done something censurable, I am not likely to measure his conduct against formal rules or to ask myself how far his act departed from duty. Instead, my reaction is apt to take some such form as: "Why, that's not like him; I wish I knew more about how this happened," or, "Yes, I can understand how

11. Ira M. Heyman, "Some Thoughts on University Disciplinary Proceedings," *California Law Review* 54, no. 1 (1966): 73–87.

12. John Laird, "Act Ethics and Agent Ethics," *Mind* 55, no. 218 (1946): 113–32. A notable contribution to an understanding of this relationship between the man and his deed appeared after my text was submitted to the editors; see John R. Silber, "Being and Doing: A Study of Status Responsibility and Voluntary Responsibility," *University of Chicago Law Review* 35, no. 1 (1967): 47–91.

13. An exception to this general neglect will be found in a perceptive work by Stuart Hampshire, *Thought and Action* (London: Chatto and Windus, 1959).

he might do a thing like that; his nature has always had that side to it." In an informal and intimate context this kind of attitude is, indeed, regarded as humane and perceptive. At the other extreme, when in the administration of criminal justice I am asked, as juror, to sit in judgment of another, then I am expected to make a conscious effort to direct my attention away from the person and toward the act; any failure in this effort may brand me as a poor citizen unable to respond to the demands of due process.

None of this means, of course, that we should expect to encounter pure forms at either end of the spectrum. Even within the family juristic notions will not be entirely excluded as a source of internal order, father perhaps being more inclined than mother toward this solution. The law of the state must, of course, act "impersonally," and in court proceedings a conscious and systematic effort is made to concentrate attention on the act and away from the actor. This effort is never entirely successful, and if we examine closely the legal system as a whole we shall detect latent tensions and hidden antinomies between the two principles of judgment.

This is true even of the basic philosophy underlying the criminal law. The familiar penal or retributive theory looks to the act and seeks to make the miscreant pay for his misdeed; the rehabilitative theory, on the other hand, sees the purpose of the law as recreating the person, as improving the criminal himself so that any impulses toward misconduct will be eliminated or brought under an internal control. Despite the humane appeal of the rehabilitative theory, the actual processes of criminal trial remain under the domination of the view that we must try the act, and not the man; any departure from this conception, it is feared, would sacrifice justice to a policy of paternalistic intervention in the life of the individual.

On the other hand, certain branches of the criminal law comport badly with the notion that our basic concern should be with acts and not with dispositions of the person. This is notably true of the law of criminal attempts. *A* shoots at *B* but misses by a wide margin. Common sense says that the occasion for an intervention by the public authorities in such a case arises, not because of any act of *A*'s that has caused harm, but because *A*'s act reveals that he is the kind of person who ought to be locked up. But this view runs counter to basic assumptions underlying the processes of criminal trial. The result is that the law of attempts is a battleground for theorists and, according to the point of view, either one of the most challenging or most distressing branches of the law of crimes.

As I have indicated, the procedures of a criminal trial are deliberately directed toward the act and away from the person of the accused. But we should remember that only a small proportion of criminal charges are actually brought to trial. The great majority are disposed of through various procedures of dismissal and by pleas of guilty. Plainly the prosecutor's notion of the dangerous propensities of the accused will play a central role in this process of extracurial settlement; here the act serves largely as an occasion for an appraisal of the person. A similar appraisal dominates decisions as to sentencing and probation. It is no accident that complaint is perennially raised that these vital processes of pretrial and posttrial decision occur informally, without effective public scrutiny and with few, if any, of the usual guarantees of due process.

There are instances where even in court procedures attention must be directed, in a frank and open manner, to the person and his propensities. This is true, for obvious reasons, in the judicial approval of adoptions (Are the proposed adoptive parents suitable persons?) and in contests between parents for the custody of children (Who is the most suitable person to have custody?). Again, it is no accident that these procedures depart radically from ordinary conceptions of due process, with the judge commonly pursuing inquiries on his own initiative, holding confidential meetings with one or both of the affected parties, and generally proceeding by inquisitorial and mediational methods rather than by those of trial in open court. Finally, there is that crossroads of legal confusion presented by the modern institution of divorce. Historically the law of divorce concentrates on the act; the "innocent" spouse can secure a divorce only by demonstrating on the part of the other some "matrimonial offense," such as adultery or desertion. This conception has long since been largely abandoned. It has been abandoned formally and openly by statutory reforms adding, as grounds for divorce, insanity and long-continued voluntary separation. In practice the reform has been, of course, much more substantial and approaches a total abandonment of the requirement of a wrongful act—a reform that has not been unaccompanied by gross hypocrisy and a knowing acceptance of perjured testimony. Confusions, however, remain, not only in the law but in the public mind. Thus, we can read in the newspapers of a prominent television star who, in bringing a bill for divorce, "charged [her husband] with incompatibility of character." [14]

To bring these last remarks into closer relation with our subject, I may observe that if the law of the state finds itself compelled to relax requirements of due process when it deals with the formation and dissolution of intimate associations then we must view with some caution any gross extension of legal forms throughout our whole associational life. The bonds that bind the member to a labor union, a school, a church, or a club may not be as intimate as those that unite husband and wife, but it does not follow that they are ready to be bent uncompromisingly to the demands of due process.

14. *Boston Herald*, 17 April 1967, p. 2.

VI

I come now finally to some brief comments on my eighth law. The first of these simply expands somewhat the bleak outlines of the law itself.

Let us assume the case of a typical university which has secured the official approval of a whole set of other associations called accrediting agencies. Such a university will enjoy tax exemptions and will receive many kinds of subsidies from government. Its students may enjoy draft deferment. Those holding its degrees will be given preference in securing jobs, both within and without the government. Some governmental and military jobs will formally require a degree from "an accredited school," such as this one. Students expelled from our hypothetical university will find it difficult, if not impossible, to secure admission to other universities, at least to those of equal standing. Small wonder, then, that it was reported from Berkeley that the students involved in the demonstrations there were not at all worried about going to jail for a couple of weeks—that would have been good fun—but were terrified by the prospect of being expelled. Thus stands—in the minds of those affected—the significance of the law of the state as compared with the internal law of the university.

All these considerations add up to the conclusion that we simply cannot deny to students the protection afforded by a judicial review of the disciplinary actions of universities, at least where discipline takes the form of expulsion. What are the implications of this review? It inevitably means a projection of "legalism" into the internal administration of the university. The university, to be sure its decisions will stand up on review by the courts, must itself adopt the modes of thought and action characteristic of courts of law. It must formalize its standards of decision, it must emphasize the outward act and its conformity or nonconformity to rule, instead of looking to the essential meaning of the act and the compatibility of that meaning with educational objectives. All this means inevitably some loss in the sense of commitment to educational aims, some diversion of energy toward secondary objectives. In the case of the universities this seems not too high a price to pay.

In the case of other associations the balance of pros and cons may become more delicate. We should recall that the term *association* covers a wide range of disparate institutional forms, demanding quite different things of their members and capable of imposing, through measures of discipline, hardships varying widely in kind and intensity. We should also recall that what appears as a simple demand for the reinstatement of an expelled member may in fact represent a strategem in an internal struggle for power between rival factions. The problems arising out of civil war—whether within nations or private associations—furnish refractory material for judicial determination. As the American Civil War demonstrated, it is usually futile to ask which side is right "legally." Under conditions of civil war, guarantees of due process for the individual are apt to be forgotten by both contending parties; believing right and talking right become as important as acting right.

In judging the wisdom of providing for the judicial review of associational decisions we are apt to have before us a picture of the helpless individual pitted against an intolerant majority or a corrupt "establishment." Procedures shaped by this vision become inept where a condition of civil war obtains within the association. When a court intervenes in such a case it is not vindicating legal integrity within the association, but deciding what the internal law of the association shall be and who shall control its processes; it is, in effect, defining the association itself.

VII

So far we have been attempting to view associational life through the eyes of an outside observer. Let us, in closing our account, attempt to look briefly at the problems we have been exploring from the standpoint of an individual member of an association.

May there not be in human nature a deep hunger to form a bond of union with one's fellows which runs deeper than that of legally defined duty and counterduty? May a man not feel an urge to enter such a bond even though he knows that it may later be ruptured, against his will, by those who consider him unsuited to it? And may not the possibility of this rupture lend a special value to the association by attesting its importance to both sides?

Corresponding to the nightmare world of Orwell's *1984*, where Big Brother watches over you to see that you believe right and think right, may there not be a counternightmare in which no one cares what you think or believe, but asks only: Did he file his papers on time? Has he passed Test 7-QW? Has he applied for reclassification under Section 63? What is his attendance record?

Has the frigid legal atmosphere of our basic associations driven some of us, in search of a richer bond of union with our fellows, into becoming Mods or Rockers, Hell's Angels, and shouters of filthy words?

These are difficult questions to which there can be no single big answer. What I am disturbed about is that we are every day, in a multitude of different contexts, giving little answers to them. No doubt most of these little answers are right. Yet in their cumulative effect they may push us along a path we do not like and would not have entered so blithely had we known where it was taking us.

The Forms and Limits of Adjudication

Editor's Note

The initial version of "The Forms and Limits of Adjudication" was circulated to the members of the Legal Philosophy Discussion Group at Harvard Law School in 1957. A revised and expanded version was prepared in 1959 for use in Fuller's course in jurisprudence and for discussion at the Round Table on Jurisprudence at the 1959 meeting of the Association of American Law Schools. Further refinements resulted in a third version for classroom use in 1961; that version was published posthumously in 1978 in the Harvard Law Review *and is abridged here.*

Fuller was apparently never convinced that the essay was sufficiently polished for publication, though it was widely circulated in manuscript form and frequently cited in scholarly discussions of adjudication. He did, however, incorporate parts of the essay into two articles—"Adjudication and the Rule of Law," American Society of International Law Proceedings (1960), and "Collective Bargaining and the Arbitrator," Wisconsin Law Review (1963)—and borrowed from it freely in other writings.

The central thesis of the essay is that adjudication is properly, or most usefully, distinguished from other forms of social ordering by the manner in which the affected parties participate in the process, namely, by presenting proofs and reasoned arguments. This formulation places great stress on the rationality of the decision making that occurs in adjudication. It should not be concluded, however, that Fuller meant to slight the rational character of other legal processes. For him law in all its forms is a conscious attempt to bring reason to bear on human affairs, though the way that striving manifests itself will vary from one process to the next.

In support of this view, Fuller was fond of quoting a passage from a little book by William Rawle entitled A Discourse on the Nature and Study of Law *(1832):*

> Law, *in all its divisions, is the strong action of* Reason *upon wants, necessities, and imperfections. No matter whether its ministration is by a legislative or through a judicial faculty, or by the consentaneous acts of individuals under no manifest compulsion; it is still the act of those on whom it has pleased divine Providence to bestow the attribute of reason, as distinguished from those who are guided only by instinct, and can make no rules for themselves.*

Fuller described this passage as "redolent with the flavor of a naive and vastly creative age"—an age, one might add, for which he had no little admiration.

1. *The Problems Toward Which This Essay Is Addressed*

The subject matter of this chapter is adjudication in the very broadest sense. As the term is used here it includes a father attempting to assume the role of judge in a dispute between his children over possession of a toy. At the other extreme it embraces the most formal and even awesome exercises of adjudicative power: a senate trying the impeachment of a president, a supreme court sitting in judgment on the powers of the government of which it is a part, an international tribunal deciding a dispute between nations, a faculty of law— in former centuries—undertaking to judge the rival claims of kings and popes, the Congregation of Rites of the Roman Catholic Church hearing the arguments pro and con in a procedure for canonization.

As the term *adjudication* is used here its application is not restricted to tribunals functioning as part of an established government. It includes adjudicative bodies which owe their powers to the consent of the litigants expressed in an agreement of submission, as in labor relations and in international law. It also includes tribunals that assume adjudicative powers without the sanction either of consent or of superior governmental power, the most notable example being the court that sat in the Nuremberg Trials.

The problems of concern here are those suggested by the two terms of the title, the *forms* and *limits* of adjudication. By speaking of the *limits* of adjudication I mean to raise such questions as the following: What kinds of social tasks can properly be assigned to courts and other adjudicative agencies? What are the lines of division that separate such tasks from those that require an exercise of executive power or that must be entrusted to planning boards or public corporations? What tacit assumptions underlie the conviction that certain problems are inherently unsuited for adjudicative disposition and should be left to the legislature? More generally, to borrow the title of a famous article by Roscoe Pound, what are the limits of effective legal action?[1]—bearing in mind that legislative determinations often can only become effective if they are of such a nature that they are suited for judicial interpretation and enforcement.

By the *forms* of adjudication I refer to the ways in which adjudication may be organized and conducted. For example, in labor relations and in international law we encounter a hybrid form called tripartite arbitration in which a public or impartial arbitrator sits flanked by arbitrators appointed by the interested parties. Such a deviation from the ordinary organization of adjudica-

---

1. [Roscoe Pound, "The Limits of Effective Legal Action," *American Bar Association Journal* 3, no. 1 (1917): 55–70.]

tion presents such questions as: What, if any, are its proper uses? What are its peculiar limits and dangers? Other deviational forms present less subtle questions, such as Judge Bridlegoose's decisions by a throw of the dice.[2] In general the questions posed for consideration are: What are the permissible variations in the forms of adjudication? When has its nature been so altered that we are compelled to speak of an abuse or a perversion of the adjudicative process?

Questions of the permissible forms and the proper limits of adjudication have probably been under discussion ever since something equivalent to a judicial power first emerged in primitive society. In our own history the Supreme Court at an early date excluded from its jurisdiction certain issues designated as political. This exclusion could hardly be said to rest on any principle made explicit in the Constitution; it was grounded rather in a conviction that certain problems by their intrinsic nature fall beyond the proper limits of adjudication, though how these problems are to be defined remains even today a subject for debate. In international law one of the most significant issues lies in the concept of "justiciability." Similar problems recur in labor relations, where the proper role of the arbitrator has always been a matter in active dispute.

It is in the field of administrative law that the issues dealt with in this chapter become most acute. An official charged with allocating television channels wants to know of one applicant "what kind of fellow he really is" and accepts an invitation to a leisurely chat over the luncheon table. The fact of this meeting is disclosed by a crusading legislator. The official is accused of an abuse of judicial office. Charges and countercharges fill the air and before the debate is over it appears that nearly everyone concerned with the agency's functioning has in some measure violated the proprieties that attach to a discharge of judicial functions. In the midst of this murky argument few are curious enough to ask whether the tasks assigned to such agencies as the Federal Communications Commission (FCC) and the Civil Aeronautics Board (CAB) are really suited for adjudicative determination, whether, in other words, they fall within the proper limits of adjudication. No one seems inclined to take up the line of thought suggested by a remark of James M. Landis to the effect that the CAB is charged with what is essentially a managerial job, unsuited to adjudicative determination or to judicial review.[3]

The purpose of this chapter is to offer an analysis that may be helpful in answering questions like those posed in the preceding paragraphs. Now it is apparent that any analysis of this sort, transcending as it does so many con-

2. [François Rabelais, *The Histories of Gargantua and Pantagruel*, trans. J. M. Cohen (Baltimore: Penguin Books, 1955), chap. 39.]

3. [See J. M. Landis, *Report on Regulatory Agencies to the President-Elect* (New York: Ad Press, 1960), pp. 41–45.]

ventional boundaries, will be meaningless if it does not rest on some concept equivalent to "true adjudication." For if there is no such thing as "true adjudication," then it becomes impossible to distinguish the uses and abuses of adjudication. Yet it is unfortunately also true that any suggestion of a notion like "true adjudication" goes heavily against the grain of modern thought. Today it is a mark of intellectual liberation to realize that there is and can be no such thing as "true science," "true religion," "true education," or "true adjudication." "It is all a matter of definition." The modern professional university philosopher is particularly allergic to anything suggesting the doctrine of essence and takes it as a sure sign of philosophic illiteracy when a writer speaks of the essence of art or the essence of democracy.

Yet we must examine critically the implications of this rejection. Does it imply, for example, that international lawyers are talking nonsense when they discuss the question of what kinds of disputes between nations are suited to decision by a tribunal? Are students of labor relations engaged in mere verbal shadowboxing when they ask how an arbitration should be conducted and what sorts of questions arbitrators are fitted to decide? Do those engaged in discussions of this sort deceive themselves in believing that they are engaged in a rational inquiry? Surely if adjudication is subject to a reasoned analysis in a particular context, there is no a priori reason for supposing that the context cannot be expanded so that adjudication becomes the object of a more general analysis.

A. D. Lindsay once observed that it is scarcely possible to talk intelligently about social institutions without recognizing that they exist *because* and *insofar as* men pursue certain goals or ideals.[4] The ideals that keep a social institution alive and functioning are never perceived with complete clarity, so that even if there is no failure of good intentions, the existent institution will never be quite what it might have been had it been supported by a clearer insight into its guiding principles. As Lindsay remarks, quoting Charley Lomax in Shaw's *Major Barbara*, there is a certain amount of tosh about the Salvation Army. Surely there is a good deal of tosh—that is, superfluous rituals, rules of procedure without clear purpose, needless precautions preserved through habit—in the adjudicative process as we observe it in this country. Our task is to separate the tosh from the essential. If in undertaking that task we go counter to a deeply held modern belief that there is nothing about society or about man's relations to his fellows that is essential and that all is in effect tosh, this is a price we shall have to pay to accomplish our objective.

4. [A. D. Lindsay, *The Modern Democratic State* vol. 1 (London: Oxford University Press, 1943), p. 42.]

Certainly there is nothing commendable in a procedure that avoids having to pay that price by keeping the discussion on a speciously ad hoc plane, where its broader implications raise no questions because they are not perceived.

Accordingly I shall have to begin our inquiry with an attempt to define "true adjudication," or adjudication as it might be if the ideals that support it were fully realized. In doing so I shall of necessity be describing something that never fully exists. Yet it is only with the aid of this nonexistent model that we can pass intelligent judgment on the accomplishments of adjudication as it actually is. Indeed, it is only with the aid of that model that we can distinguish adjudication as an existent institution from other social institutions and procedures by which decisions may be reached.

II. *The Two Basic Principles of Social Ordering*

It is customary to think of adjudication as a means of settling disputes or controversies. This is, of course, its most obvious aspect. The normal occasion for a resort to adjudication is when parties are at odds with one another, often to such a degree that a breach of social order is threatened.

More fundamentally, however, adjudication should be viewed as a form of social ordering, as a way in which the relations of men to one another are governed and regulated. Even in the absence of any formalized doctrine of stare decisis or res judicata, an adjudicative determination will normally enter in some degree into the litigants' future relations and into the future relations of other parties who see themselves as possible litigants before the same tribunal. Even if there is no statement by the tribunal of the reasons for its decision, some reason will be perceived or guessed at, and the parties will tend to govern their conduct accordingly. . . .

.   .   .   .

III. *Adjudication as a Form of Social Ordering*

In discussing reciprocity and organization by common aims, I pointed out that these two [principles] of social ordering present themselves along a scale of varying formal explicitness. To some extent the same thing is true of adjudication. We talk, for example, of "taking our case to the forum of public opinion." Or two men may argue in the presence of a third with a kind of tacit hope that he will decide which is right, but without any explicit submission of their dispute to his arbitrament.

On the very informal level, however, forms of social ordering are too mixed and ambiguous to make comparisons fruitful. It is only when a particular form of ordering explicitly controls a relationship that it can be set off clearly against alternative forms of ordering. For this reason, therefore, I am here employing contract to represent reciprocity in its formal and explicit expression. I shall take elections as the most familiar formalization of organization by common aims.

Adjudication, contract, and elections are three ways of reaching decisions, of settling disputes, of defining men's relations to one another. Now I submit that the characteristic feature of each of these forms of social ordering lies in the manner in which the affected party participates in the decision reached. This may be presented graphically as follows:

Form of social ordering	*Mode of participation by the affected party*
Contract	Negotiation
Elections	Voting
Adjudication	Presentation of proofs and reasoned arguments

It is characteristic of these three ways of ordering men's relations that though they are subject to variation—they present themselves in different forms—each contains certain intrinsic demands that must be met if it is to function properly. We may distinguish roughly between optimum conditions, which would lift a particular form of order to its highest expression, and essential conditions, without which the form of order ceases to function in any significant sense at all.

With respect to the principle of contract an analysis of optimum and essential conditions would be exceedingly complex and would require an analysis of the requirements of a market economy, of the peculiar qualities of bargaining in situations of oligopoly, etc. We can observe, however, that a regime of contract presupposes the absence of certain kinds of coercion; a contract signed at the point of a gun is hardly in any significant sense a contract at all. However, it will be simpler if we confine our attention here to a comparison of elections with adjudication.

Elections present themselves in many forms, varying from the town meeting to the "ja-nein" plebiscite. Voting can be organized in many ways: simple majority vote, PR [proportional representation], STV [single transferable voting], and various complicated mixed forms.[5] At the same time all of these expressions of political democracy have in common that they afford the person affected by the decision which emerges a peculiar form of participation in that decision, namely, some form of voting. The optimum conditions that would give fullest meaning to this participation include an intelligent and fully informed electorate, an active interest by the electorate in the issues, candor in discussing those issues by those participating in public debate—conditions, it is needless to say, that are scarcely ever realized in practice. On the other hand, there are certain essential conditions without which the participation of the voter loses its meaning altogether. These would include that the votes be honestly counted, that the ballot boxes not be "stuffed," that certain types of intimidation be absent, etc.

Now much of this chapter will be concerned in carrying through with a similar analysis of the optimum and essential conditions for the functioning of adjudication. This whole analysis will derive from one simple proposition, namely, that the distinguishing characteristic of adjudication lies in the fact that it confers on the affected party a peculiar form of participation in the decision, that of presenting proofs and reasoned arguments for a decision in his favor. Whatever heightens the significance of this participation lifts adjudication toward its optimum expression. Whatever destroys the meaning of that participation destroys the integrity of adjudication itself. Thus, participation through reasoned argument loses its meaning if the arbiter of the dispute is inaccessible to reason because he is insane, has been bribed, or is hopelessly prejudiced. The purpose of this chapter is to trace out the somewhat less obvious implications of the proposition that the distinguishing feature of adjudication lies in the mode of participation which it accords to the party affected by the decision.

But first it will be necessary to deal with certain objections that may be raised against my starting point, namely, against the proposition that the "essence" of adjudication lies in the mode of participation it accords to the affected party.

IV. *Adjudication and Rationality*

It may be said that the essence of adjudication lies not in the manner in which the affected party participates in the decision but in the office of judge.

5. [See W. J. M. Mackenzie, *Free Elections: An Elementary Textbook* (London: George Allen and Unwin, 1958).]

If there is a judge and a chance to appear before him, it is a matter of indifference whether the litigant chooses to present proofs or reasoned arguments. He may, if he sees fit, offer no argument at all, or pitch his appeal entirely on an emotional level, or even indicate his willingness that the judge decide the case by a throw of the dice. It might seem, then, that our analysis should take as its point of departure the office of judge. From this office certain requirements might be deduced, for example, that of impartiality, since a judge to be "truly" such must be impartial. Then, as the next step, if he is to be impartial he must be willing to hear both sides, etc.

The trouble with this is that there are people who are called judges holding official positions and expected to be impartial who nevertheless do not participate in an adjudication in any sense directly relevant to the subject of this chapter. Judges at an agricultural fair or an art exhibition may serve as examples. Again, a baseball umpire, though he is not called a judge, is expected to make impartial rulings. What distinguishes these functionaries is not that they do not hold governmental office, for the duties of a judge at a livestock fair would scarcely be changed if he were an official of the Department of Agriculture. What distinguishes them from courts, administrative tribunals, and boards of arbitration is that their decisions are not reached within an institutional framework that is intended to assure to the disputants an opportunity for the presentation of proofs and reasoned arguments. The judge of livestock may or may not permit such a presentation; it is not an integral part of his office to permit and to attend to it.

If, on the other hand, we start with the notion of a process of decision in which the affected party's participation consists of an opportunity to present proofs and reasoned arguments, the office of judge or arbitrator and the requirement of impartiality follow as necessary implications. The logician Frege once took the expression "I accuse" as exemplifying the complex implications contained in the most ordinary language. We may say that the verb *to accuse* presupposes five elements: (1) an accuser, (2) a person accused, (3) a person before whom the accusation is presented, (4) an act charged against the accused, and (5) a principle by which the act may be condemned.[6] The similarity to the analysis here presented is apparent; the fifth element, it should be noted, corresponds to the notion of a *reasoned* argument. Of course, Frege was concerned merely to spell out the implications contained in a phrase, not, as we are here, with the problem of creating and maintaining a social institution that will give effect to those implications.

6. [This analysis is taken from an anonymous review of *Translations from the Philosophical Writings of Gottlob Frege*, ed. Peter Geach and Max Black (Oxford: Blackwell, 1952), in *Times Literary Supplement*, p. 553, col. 1 (1952). The reviewer offers the analysis to illustrate the notion of "functional expression." The fifth element has been added by Fuller.]

It may be objected at this point that reasoned argument is, after all, not a monopoly of forensic proceedings. A political speech may take the form of a reasoned appeal to the electorate; to be sure, it often takes other forms, but the same thing may be said of speeches in court. This objection fails to take account of a conception that underlies the whole analysis being presented here, the conception, namely, of a form of participating in a decision that is institutionally defined and assured.

When I am entering a contract with another person I may present proofs and arguments to him, but there is generally no formal assurance that I will be given this opportunity or that he will listen to my arguments if I make them. (Perhaps the only exception to this generalization lies in the somewhat anomalous legal obligation "to bargain in good faith" in labor relations.) During an election I may actively campaign for one side and may present what I consider to be reasoned arguments to the electorate. If I am an effective campaigner this participation in the decision ultimately reached may greatly outweigh in importance the casting of my own single vote. At the same time, it is only the latter form of participation that is the subject of an affirmative institutional guarantee. The protection accorded my right to present arguments to the electorate is almost entirely indirect and negative. The way will be held clear for me, but I shall have to pave it myself. Even if I am given an affirmative right (for example, under the "equal time" rule of the FCC) I am given no formal assurance that anyone will listen to my appeal. The voter who goes to sleep before his television set is surely not subject to the same condemnation as the judge who sleeps through the arguments of counsel.

Adjudication is, then, a device which gives formal and institutional expression to the influence of reasoned argument in human affairs. As such it assumes a burden of rationality not borne by any other form of social ordering. A decision which is the product of reasoned argument must be prepared itself to meet the test of reason. We demand of an adjudicative decision a kind of rationality we do not expect of the results of contract or of voting. This higher responsibility toward rationality is at once the strength *and the weakness* of adjudication as a form of social ordering.

In entering contracts, men are of course in some measure guided by rational considerations. The subsistence farmer who has a surfeit of potatoes and only a handful of onions acts reasonably when he trades potatoes for onions. But there is no test of rationality that can be applied to the result of the trade considered in abstraction from the interests of the parties. Indeed, the trade of potatoes for onions, which is a rational act by one trader, might be considered irrational if indulged in by his opposite number, who has a storehouse full of onions and only a bushel of potatoes. If we asked one party to the contract, "Can you defend that contract?" he might answer, "Why, yes. It was good for me and it was good for him." If we then said, "But that is not what we meant.

We meant, can you defend it on general grounds?" he might well reply that he did not know what we were talking about. Yet this is precisely the kind of question we normally direct toward the decision of a judge or arbitrator. The results that emerge from adjudication are subject, then, to a standard of rationality that is different from that imposed on the results of an exchange.

I believe that the same observation holds true when adjudication is compared with elections. The key to the difference lies again in the mode in which the affected party participates in a decision. If, as in adjudication, the only mode of participation consists of the opportunity to present proofs and arguments, the purpose of this participation is frustrated, and the whole proceeding becomes a farce, should the decision that emerges make no pretense whatever to rationality. The same cannot be said of the mode of participation called voting. We may assume that the preferences of voters are ultimately emotional, inarticulate, and not subject to rational defense. At the same time there is a need for social order, and it may be assumed that this need is best met when order rests on the broadest possible base of popular support. On this ground, a negative defense of democracy is possible; the will of the majority controls, not because it is right, but—well, because it *is* the will of the majority. This is surely an impoverished conception of democracy, but it expresses at least one ingredient of any philosophy of democracy, and it suggests a reason why we demand of adjudication a kind of rationality that we do not expect of elections.

This problem can be approached somewhat obliquely from a different direction by asking what is implied by "a right" or by "a claim of right." If I say to someone, "Give me that!" I do not necessarily assert a right. I may be begging for an act of charity, or I may be threatening to take by force something to which I admittedly have no right. On the other hand, if I say, "Give that to me, I have a right to it," I necessarily assert the existence of some principle or standard by which my "right" can be tested.

To be sure, this principle or standard may not have antedated my claim. If one boy says to another, "Give me that catcher's mitt," and answers the question Why? by saying, "Because I am the best catcher on the team," he asserts a principle by which the equipment of the team ought to be apportioned in accordance with the ability to use it. He necessarily implies that, were the respective abilities of the two boys reversed, the mitt should remain where it is. But he does not, by necessary implication, assert that the principle by which he supports his claim is an established one. Indeed, up to the time this claim is made, the right to be catcher might depend not on ability but on ownership of the catcher's mitt. In that event the claim based upon the new principle of ability might, in effect, propose a revolution in the organization of the team. At the same time, this claim does necessarily imply *a* principle which can give meaning to the demand that like cases be given like treatment.

Now if we ask ourselves what kinds of questions are commonly decided by judges and arbitrators, the answer may well be, "Claims of right." Indeed, in the older literature (including, notably, John Chipman Gray's *The Nature and Sources of the Law*), courts were often distinguished from administrative or executive agencies on the ground that it is the function of courts to "declare rights."[7] If, then, we seek to define the limits of adjudication, a tempting answer would be that the proper province of courts is limited to cases where rights are asserted. On reflection we might enlarge this to include cases where fault or guilt is charged (broadly, "the trial of accusations"), since in many cases it is artificial to treat the accuser (who may be the district attorney) as claiming a right. Though it is not particularly artificial to view the lawbreaker as violating "a right" of the state, to say that when the state indicts the lawbreaker it is claiming a remedial "right" against him does seem to reflect a misguided impulse toward forcing a symmetry between civil and criminal remedies. To avoid any such manipulations of natural modes of thought, let us then amend the suggested criterion to read as follows: The proper province of adjudication is to make an authoritative determination of questions raised by claims of right and accusations of guilt.

Is this a significant way of describing the limits of adjudication? I do not think so. In fact, what purports here to be a distinct assertion is merely an implication of the fact that adjudication is a form of decision that defines the affected party's participation as that of offering proofs and reasoned arguments. It is not so much that adjudicators decide only issues presented by claims of right or accusations. The point is rather that *whatever* they decide, or *whatever* is submitted to them for decision, tends to be converted into a claim of right or an accusation of fault or guilt. This conversion is effected by the institutional framework within which both the litigant and the adjudicator function.

Let me spell out rather painstakingly the steps of an argument that will show why this should be so. (1) Adjudication is a process of decision that grants to the affected party a form of participation that consists of the opportunity to present proofs and reasoned arguments. (2) The litigant must therefore, if his participation is to be meaningful, assert some principle or principles by which his arguments are sound and his proofs relevant. (3) A naked demand is distinguished from a claim of right by the fact that the latter is a demand supported by a principle; likewise, a mere expression of displeasure or resentment is distinguished from an accusation by the fact that the latter rests upon some principle. Hence, (4) issues tried before an adjudicator tend to become claims of right or accusations of fault.

7. [John Chipman Gray, *The Nature and Sources of the Law*, 2d ed. (New York: Macmillan, 1921), p. 115.]

We may see this process of conversion in the case of an employee who desires an increase in pay. If he asks his boss for a raise, he may, of course, claim "a right" to the raise. He may argue the fairness of the principle of equal treatment and call attention to the fact that Joe, who is no better than he, recently got a raise. But he does not have to rest his plea on any ground of this sort. He may merely beg for generosity, urging the needs of his family. Or he may propose an exchange, offering to take on extra duties if he gets the raise. If, however, he takes his case to an arbitrator he cannot, explicitly at least, support his case by an appeal to charity or by proposing a bargain. He will have to support his demand by a principle of some kind, and a demand supported by principle is the same thing as a claim of right. So, when he asks his boss for a raise, he may or may not make a claim of right; when he presents his demand to an arbitrator he *must* make a claim of right. (I do not overlook the possibility of the arbitrator's proposing to the parties a "deal" by which the employee would get the raise but take on extra duties. But it is obvious that in such a case the arbitrator steps out of the role of adjudicator and assumes that of mediator. This kind of case presents the problem of mixed forms of ordering, which will be discussed later at some length. It may be observed that the American Arbitration Association strives to keep its arbitrators from assuming the role of mediators. Whatever the wisdom of this policy, it is apparent that it rests on some conception of the proper limits of adjudication and presents the sort of question toward which this paper is addressed.)

If the analysis presented here is correct, three aspects of adjudication that seem to present distinct qualities are in fact all expressions of a single quality: (1) the peculiar mode by which the affected party participates in the decision; (2) the peculiarly urgent demand of rationality that the adjudicative process must be prepared to meet; and (3) the fact that adjudication finds its normal and "natural" province in judging claims of right and accusations of fault. So, when we say that a party entering a contract, or voting in an election, has no right to any particular outcome, we are describing the same fundamental fact that we allude to when we say that adjudication has to meet a test of rationality or of principle that is not applied to contracts and elections.

In this connection it is interesting to recall that Langdell once argued that, although there are rights at law, there is no such thing as "a right in equity."[8] This is because, he contended, courts of law are bound by rules, while courts of equity proceed by discretion. A similar issue is presented by the question whether the regulations of administrative agencies create rights and by the common debate as to whether some dispensation resting within an agency's

---

8. [Christopher Columbus Langdell, "Classifications of Rights and Wrongs" (part II), *Harvard Law Review* 13, no. 8 (1900): 659, 670–71, reprinted in Langdell, *A Brief Survey of Equity Jurisdiction* (Cambridge, Mass.: Harvard Law Review Association, 1905), pp. 239, 251–52.]

power is a matter of right or of privilege. When it is said, for example, that entry into the legal profession is a matter of privilege and not of right, it is important to see that all that is really asserted is that a decision denying admission to the bar need not be supported by any general principle.

I have suggested that it is not a significant description of the limits of adjudication to say that its proper province lies where rights are asserted or accusations of fault are made, for such a statement involves a circle of reasoning. If, however, we regard a formal definition of rights and wrongs as a nearly inevitable product of the adjudicative process, we can arrive at what is perhaps the most significant of all limitations on the proper province of adjudication. Adjudication is not a proper form of social ordering in those areas where the effectiveness of human association would be destroyed if it were organized about formally defined rights and wrongs. Courts have, for example, rather regularly refused to enforce agreements between husband and wife affecting the internal organization of family life. There are other and wider areas where the intrusion of "the machinery of the law" is equally inappropriate. An adjudicative board might well undertake to allocate one thousand tons of coal among three claimants; it could hardly conduct even the simplest coal-mining enterprise by the forms of adjudication. Wherever successful human association depends upon spontaneous and informal collaboration, shifting its forms with the task at hand, there adjudication is out of place except as it may declare certain ground rules applicable to a wide variety of activities.

These are vague and perhaps trite observations. I shall attempt to bring them into sharper focus in a discussion of the relative incapacity of adjudication to solve "polycentric" problems. Meanwhile, the point I should like to stress is that the incapacity of a given area of human activity to endure a pervasive delimitation of rights and wrongs is also a measure of its incapacity to respond to a too exigent rationality, a rationality that demands an immediate and explicit reason for every step taken. Back of both of these incapacities lies the fundamental truth that certain kinds of human relations are not appropriate raw material for a process of decision that is institutionally committed to acting on the basis of reasoned argument. . . .

.   .   .   .

v. *Adjudication and the Rule of Law*

So far a point of crucial importance and difficulty has not been reached in this discussion. It has been repeatedly asserted that adjudication is institutionally committed to a reasoned decision, to a decision based on principle. But what is the source of the principle on the basis of which the case is to be argued and decided? Where do the parties and the adjudicator get their respective reasons?

Recent discussions of "the rule of law" reveal—or I should perhaps say, largely conceal—a very fundamental difference of opinion on this question of the source of principle. There is at present a very active movement aimed at extending the rule of law to international relations and at assisting peoples who have never known stable and constitutional government to achieve internally a condition known as the rule of law. Much of the discussion engendered is on an inspirational and rhetorical level that does not permit underlying difficulties to come to the surface. When, however, those difficulties are candidly faced a serious issue emerges that may be somewhat too simply stated as: Which comes first, courts or rules?

All are agreed that courts are essential to the rule of law. The object of the rule of law is to substitute for violence peaceful ways of settling disputes. Obviously peace cannot be assured simply by treaties, agreements, and legislative enactment. There must be some agency capable of determining the rights of parties in concrete situations of controversy. Beyond this point, however, disagreement begins.

On the one side the advocates of the view "first courts, then rules" see adjudication as the primary source of peaceful order. The essence of the rule of law consists of being assured of your day in court. Courts can be counted on to make a reasoned disposition of controversies, either by the application of statutes or treaties, or in the absence of these sources, by the development of rules appropriate to the cases before them and derived from general principles of fairness and equity.

Critics of this view assert that it does a disservice to a great and valid ideal. It dodges the whole issue of "justiciability" and assumes there can be no problem or controversy that lies beyond the limits of adjudication. It substitutes for critical judgment a naive trust in good intentions. It forgets that you cannot be fair in a moral and legal vacuum. It ignores the fact that adjudication cannot function without some standard of decision, either imposed by superior authority or willingly accepted by the disputants. Without some standard of decision the requirement that the judge be impartial becomes meaningless. Similarly, without such a standard the litigants' participation through reasoned argument loses its meaning. Communication and persuasion presuppose some shared context of principle.

Furthermore, say these critics, it is futile to assume that the void can be filled by contracts and treaties. Where the words of an agreement have a plain and obvious meaning, public opinion will ordinarily supply a sufficient sanction to ensure its performance. The necessity of a resort to adjudication will arise precisely in those cases where the proper meaning of the contract is in dispute. International treaties are often filled with purposeful ambiguities; some issues are simply too touchy to be resolved by agreement. When a dispute later develops around such issues, the agreement offers no guidance. To demand of a court that it simply resolve such issues fairly is to ask the court to decide something about which the parties themselves could not agree and for the determination of which no standard exists. Furthermore, the most troublesome issues arising out of treaties often involve cases where the original situation, on the basis of which the parties contracted, has been overtaken by events, so that the factual underpinnings of the agreement have been removed. In such a case, the court either has to declare the agreement no longer in force, thus leaving itself and the parties without any standard of decision, or it has to engage in a drastic revision of the contract, again without the guidance of any clear standard.

To all this argument the opposing party enters a rejoinder along these lines: The views just expressed are founded on a gross ignorance of history. The two great systems of law that dominate the world today—the common law and the civil law—took their origins in a case-by-case evolution of doctrine. Even today when developments occur in the common law it is usually only at the end of a series of cases that the governing principle becomes clear. In the civil law countries the codes from which courts purport to derive their principles often provide little beyond a vocabulary for stating legal results. They are filled with clauses referring to "good faith," "equity," "fair practice," and the like—standards that any court could apply without the aid of a code. One of the best of modern codes, the Swiss Code of Obligations, lays down very few rules and contents itself largely with charting the range of judicial discretion and with setting forth what might be called checklists for the judge to consult to make certain that he has overlooked no factor properly bearing on the exercise of his discretion.

To this argument the final reply would probably run somewhat as follows: The views just expressed themselves betray a deep ignorance of history. The developments related have occurred in situations where there was already outside the law a strong sense of community, where there were generally shared conceptions of right and wrong that could gradually be crystallized into legal doctrine. In a community of traders, apparently vague phrases like "fair practice" have a definiteness of meaning that they cannot have in international relations or among people just emerging from primitive feudalism. Where legal rules have evolved out of the process of adjudication, law has in effect been built on community. Uncritical proponents of extending the rule of law propose to build community on law. It cannot be done.

A less compromising reply would be given by Friedrich A. Hayek, a true stalwart of the "law first, then courts" school of thought. In his lectures *The Political Ideal of the Rule of Law*, he declares his conviction that the case-by-case methods of the common law are inconsistent with the ideal of the rule of law.[9] The startling conclusion seems to follow that precisely those nations that have most often been held up as ideals of a peaceful and just internal order themselves violate the rule of law by their systems of adjudication. Hayek further connects the decline of the liberal state in Europe and the rise of totalitarian philosophies with the increasing use of vague provisions in codes, such as those requiring "good faith" and "fair practice" without further specification of the kind of behavior intended.[10]

Now it seems to me clear that, if we exclude such extreme views as that of Hayek, there is much to be said for both sides. We need, I believe, to keep two important truths before us: (1) It is sometimes possible to initiate adjudication effectively without definite rules; in this situation a case-by-case evolution of legal principle does often take place. (2) This evolution does not always occur, and we need to analyze more clearly than we generally have what conditions foster or hinder it. . . .

.   .   .   .

I suggest more generally that where adjudication appears to operate meaningfully without the support of rules formally declared or accepted in advance, it does so because it draws its intellectual sustenance from the two basic [principles] of social ordering I have already described. It has done this historically with most notable success in the field where the accepted objective is to develop a regime of reciprocity or exchange. Students of comparative law are often struck by the fact that in the area of commercial transactions courts operating in entirely different environments of legal doctrine will often reach identical or similar results in the decision of actual cases.

But the possibility of a case-by-case development of principle is by no means confined to the field of commercial transactions. For example, the demands of a viable system of federalism are by no means immediately obvious. In gradually discovering and articulating the principles that will make federalism work, the courts may exemplify the process Mansfield had in mind when he spoke of the law "working itself pure."[11] Indeed, just such a development was envisaged by Hamilton in No. 82 of the *Federalist Papers*, where he wrote:

9. [Friedrich A. Hayek, *The Political Ideal of the Rule of Law* (Cairo: National Bank of Egypt, 1955), p. 19.]

10. [Ibid., pp. 35, 39–42.]

11. [See W. Holdsworth, *A History of English Law*, vol. 12 (London: Methuen, 1938), p. 551.]

The erection of a new government, whatever care or wisdom may distinguish the work, cannot fail to originate questions of intricacy and nicety; and these may, in a particular manner, be expected to flow from the establishment of a constitution founded upon the total or partial incorporation of a number of distinct sovereignties. 'Tis time only that can mature and perfect so compounded a system, can liquidate the meaning of all the parts, and can adjust them to each other in a harmonious and consistent *whole.*[12]

Obviously this kind of development—this gradual tracing out of the full implications of a system already established—can take place only in an atmosphere dominated by the shared desire to make federalism work.

It should be made clear that the view expressed here is radically different from one which it superficially resembles that threatens to become commonplace in sociology. I refer to the conception that in a sufficiently homogeneous society certain values will develop automatically and without anyone intending or directing their development. In such a society it is assumed that the legal rules developed and enforced by courts will reflect these prevailing values. In our own discussion, however, we are not talking about disembodied values but about human purposes actively, if often tacitly, held and given intelligent direction at critical junctures. In working out the implications of federalism or of a regime of exchange, a court is not an inert mirror reflecting current mores but an active participant in the enterprise of articulating the implications of shared purposes.

If the conception here advanced is sound, it follows that in extending the rule of law to international relations, law and community of purpose must develop together. It is also apparent that a community of purpose which consists simply of a shared desire to avoid reciprocal destruction is too impoverished to furnish a proper basis for meaningful adjudication. Where the only shared objective is the negative one of preventing a holocaust, there is nothing that can make meaningful a process of decision that depends upon proofs and reasoned argument. It is of course conceivable that, moved by a desire to prevent such a holocaust, two nations (say, Russia and the United States) might submit a dispute to arbitration, but they would do so in much the same spirit that they might resort to a throw of the dice—unless there were perceived by both some body of principle, however vague, that might control and give rationality to the decision. Such a body of emergent principle would have to derive from one of the two basic principles of order. In practice this would mean that it would have to derive from relationships of reciprocity. Hence a desideratum of overriding importance in the relations of Russia and the United

12. [Alexander Hamilton, *The Federalist*, No. 82 (New York: Random House, 1937), pp. 534–38.]

States is the development of every possible bond of reciprocity, every kind of useful exchange, between the two countries. This is essential not merely to promote "understanding" and an atmosphere of good will but to create a community of interest from which adjudication can draw intellectual sustenance.

VI. *The Forms of Adjudication*

Introduction

The remainder of this chapter will be divided into three main sections: The Forms of Adjudication, The Limits of Adjudication, and Mixed, Parasitic, and Perverted Forms of Adjudication. Of course, all of these topics stand in close relation to one another and some degree of anticipation will be unavoidable.

For example, the limits of adjudication are affected by its forms. Reference has already been made to so-called tripartite arbitration. This special and deviant form of adjudication sometimes makes it possible to undertake through an adjudicative process tasks that could not otherwise be handled satisfactorily through adjudication at all. At the same time, this form may impair the effectiveness of adjudication in its more usual employments.

The joining of "mixed, parasitic, and perverted" forms of adjudication in one title should not mislead the reader into thinking that all departures of adjudication from a state of pristine purity are condemned here. Certain mixed forms are valuable and almost indispensable, though their use is often attended by certain dangers.

In determining whether a deviant or mixed form impairs the integrity of adjudication the test throughout will be that already stressed repeatedly: Does it affect adversely the meaning of the affected party's participation in the decision by proofs and reasoned arguments? . . .

. . . .

May the Arbiter Act on His Own Motion in Initiating the Case?

In his *The Nature and Sources of the Law*, John Chipman Gray wrote:

A judge of an organized body is a man appointed by that body to determine duties and the corresponding rights *upon the application of persons claiming those rights.* It is the fact that such application must be made to him, which distinguishes a judge from an administrative officer. The essence of a judge's office is that he shall be impartial, that he is to sit apart, is not to interfere voluntarily in affairs . . . but is to determine cases which are presented to him. To use the phrase of the English Ecclesiastical courts, the office of the judge must be promoted by some one.[13]

A German socialist critic of "bourgeois law" [Anton Menger] once caricatured this view by saying that courts are like defective clocks; they have to be shaken to set them going. He, of course, added the point that shaking costs money.

Certainly it is true that in most of the practical manifestations of adjudication the arbiter's function has to be "promoted" by the litigant and is not initiated by itself. But is this coy quality of waiting to be asked an essential part of adjudication?

It would seem that it is not. Suppose, for example, the collision of two ships under circumstances that suggest that one or both masters were at fault. Suppose a board is given authority to initiate hearings in such a case and to make a determination of fault. Such a board might conduct its hearings after the pattern of court proceedings. Both masters might be accorded counsel and a full opportunity for cross-examination. There would be no impairment of the affected parties' full participation by proofs and reasoned argument; the integrity of adjudication seems to be preserved.

Yet I think that most of us would consider such a case exceptional and would not be deterred by it from persisting in the belief that the adjudicative process should normally not be initiated by the tribunal itself. There are, I believe, sound reasons for adhering to that belief.

Certainly it is clear that the integrity of adjudication is impaired if the arbiter not only initiates the proceedings but also, in advance of the public hearing, forms theories about what happened and conducts his own factual inquiries. In such a case the arbiter cannot bring to the public hearing an uncommitted mind; the effectiveness of participation through proofs and reasoned arguments is accordingly reduced. Now it is probably true that under most circumstances the mere initiation of proceedings carries with it a certain commitment and often a theory of what occurred. The case of the collision at sea is exceptional because there the facts themselves speak eloquently for the need of some kind of inquiry, so that the initiation of the proceedings implies nothing more than a recognition of this need. In most situations the initiation of proceedings could not have the same neutral quality, as, for example, where the occasion consists simply in the fact that a corporation had gone two years without declaring a dividend.

13. [Gray, *Nature and Sources*, pp. 114–15.]

There is another reason which justifies the common conception that it is not normal for the adjudicative process to be initiated by the deciding tribunal. If we view adjudication in its widest extension, as including not only the work of courts but also that of arbitrators in labor, commerce, and international relations, it is apparent that the overwhelming majority of cases submitted to adjudication involve the assertion of claims founded directly or indirectly on *contract* or *agreement.* It seems clear that a regime of contract (more broadly, a regime of reciprocity) implies that the determination whether to assert a claim must be left to the interested party.

A contrary suggestion is advanced by Karl Llewellyn in *The Cheyenne Way.* In answer to the question, Why do we leave it to the affected party whether to assert his claim for breach of contract? he gives the startling explanation that this is because as a matter of actual experience the motive of self-interest has proved sufficient to maintain a regime of contract.[14] He suggests that if in the future this motive were to suffer a serious decline, then the state might find itself compelled to intervene to strengthen the regime of contract. This curious conception is symptomatic of a general tendency of our times to obscure the role of reciprocity as an organizing principle and to convert everything into "social policy," which is another way of saying that all organization is by common aims (or by the aims that in the mind of the "policymaker" ought to be common).

Any individual contract serves society only insofar as society is interested in the individual enrichment made possible by a regime of reciprocity. (Naturally, "individual" here has to be given an extended meaning to include groups and formal entities like the corporation.) If two men discover that by an agreement each can profit by giving up something he values less than the thing he receives in exchange for it, the individuals are enriched by virtue of their own evaluations of the objects of the exchange. If ten days after the agreement is entered there is a change in those evaluations, so that neither party has any further interest in the performance of the agreement, this is as much their affair as was the original agreement. To enforce a contract for a party who is willing to leave it unenforced is just as absurd as making the contract for him in the first place. (I realize, of course, that there are contracts required by law, but this is obviously a derivative phenomenon which would lose all meaning if every human relation were imposed by the state and were called a contract.)

The belief that it is not normal for the arbiter himself to initiate the adjudicative process has, then, a twofold basis. *First,* it is generally impossible to keep even the bare initiation of proceedings untainted by preconceptions

14. [Karl N. Llewellyn and E. Adamson Hoebel, *The Cheyenne Way* (Norman: University of Oklahoma Press, 1941), p. 48.]

about what happened and what its consequences should be. In this sense, initiation of the proceedings by the arbiter impairs the integrity of adjudication by reducing the effectiveness of the litigant's participation through proofs and arguments. *Second*, the great bulk of claims submitted to adjudication are founded directly or indirectly on relationships of reciprocity. In this case, unless the affected party is deceived or ignorant of his rights, the very foundations of the claim asserted dictate that the processes of adjudication must be invoked by the claimant.

Must the Decision Be Accompanied by a Statement of the Reasons for It?

We tend to think of the judge or arbitrator as one who decides and who gives reasons for his decision. Does the integrity of adjudication require that reasons be given for the decision rendered? I think the answer is, not necessarily. In some fields of labor arbitration (chiefly, I believe, where arbitration is a facility made available without charge by the state) it is the practice to render "blind" awards. The reasons for this practice probably include a belief that reasoned awards are often misinterpreted and "stir up trouble," as well as the circumstance that the arbitrator is so busy he has no time to write opinions. Under the procedures of the American Arbitration Association, awards in commercial cases are rendered usually without opinion. (Written opinions are, however, usual in *labor* cases.) Perhaps the special practice in commercial cases has arisen because arbitrators in such cases normally serve without fee, and writing opinions is hard work. Perhaps also there is a fear that explanations ineptly phrased by lay arbitrators might open too wide a door to judicial review.

By and large it seems clear that the fairness and effectiveness of adjudication are promoted by reasoned opinions. Without such opinions the parties have to take it on faith that their participation in the decision has been real, that the arbiter has in fact understood and taken into account their proofs and arguments. A less obvious point is that, where a decision enters into some continuing relationship, if no reasons are given the parties will almost inevitably guess at reasons and act accordingly. Here the effectiveness of adjudication is impaired, not only because the results achieved may not be those intended by the arbiter, but also because his freedom of decision in future cases may be curtailed by the growth of practices based on a misinterpretation of decisions previously rendered.

May the Arbiter Rest His Decision on Grounds Not Argued by the Parties?

Obviously the bond of participation by the litigant is most secure when the arbiter rests his decision wholly on the proofs and argument actually presented to him by the parties. In practice, however, it is not always possible to realize this ideal. Even where all of the considerations on which the decision rests were touched on by the parties' arguments, the emphasis may be very different. An issue dealt with only in passing by one of the parties, or perhaps by both, may become the headstone of the arbiter's decision. This may mean not only that, had they foreseen this outcome, the parties would have presented different arguments, but that they might also have introduced evidence on very different factual issues.

If the ideal of a perfect congruence between the arbiter's view of the issues and that of the parties is unattainable, this is no excuse for a failure to work toward an achievement of the closest approximation of it. We need to remind ourselves that if this congruence is utterly absent—if the grounds for the decision fall completely outside the framework of the argument, making all that was discussed or proved at the hearing irrelevant—then the adjudicative process has become a sham, for the parties' participation in the decision has lost all meaning. We need to analyze what factors influence the desired congruence and what measures may be taken to promote it.

One circumstance of capital importance is the extent to which a particular process of adjudication takes place in a context of established rules. In branches of the law where the rules have become fairly settled and certain, it may be possible for lawyers to reach agreement easily in defining the crucial issues presented by a particular case. In such an area the risk is slight that the decision will fall outside the frame of reference set by the proofs and arguments. On the other hand, in areas of uncertainty, this risk is greatly increased. There are, to be sure, dangers in a premature crystallization of standards. On the other hand, one of the less obvious dangers of a too long delayed formulation of doctrine lies in the inevitable impairment of the integrity of adjudication that is entailed, for the reality of the parties' participation is reduced when it is impossible to foretell what issues will become relevant in the ultimate disposition of the case.

These are considerations often overlooked in criticisms of the conduct of administrative agencies and labor arbitrators. Ex parte posthearing conferences with the parties are often motivated by a well-intentioned desire to preserve the reality of the parties' participation in the decision. Where the standards of decision are vague and fluctuating, when the time comes for final disposition of the case it may be apparent that most of what was argued and proved at the public hearing has become irrelevant. A desire to give a litigant a meaningful "day in court" may, paradoxically, lead to giving him a lunch-hour out of court. In many cases this conduct should be characterized as inept, rather than wicked.

Those inexperienced in legal procedures often do not know of devices which have been developed by courts that will eliminate much of the need for such practices. In particular, requests for a reargument and the device of the tentative decree, with something like an order to show cause why it should not be made final, could often be used with advantage by labor arbitrators and administrative tribunals. This is not to say that these expedients will solve all problems. An arbitrator paid on a per diem basis by the parties may hesitate to run up his bill by requesting a second argument. In some situations a tentative decree may arouse expectations of such an intensity that a later modification becomes very difficult. The fundamental point made here, however, is that before we demand of lay arbiters that they act like judges, we must place them in a context, and arm them with procedures, that will make it possible for them to do their job properly and still act throughout like judges. It is distressing to see Congress assign to administrative agencies tasks that plainly lie beyond the limits of adjudication and yet demand of those agencies that they act as if their tasks fell within those limits. Even more distressing is it when they are compelled to announce standards and policies which they consider they cannot conscientiously follow in the discharge of their duties.

In this rather messy situation the influence of the individual practicing lawyer can be a most wholesome one. If he is an expert in a particular field of administrative law, he can often judge accurately in a particular case what issues will ultimately become crucial. This means that he will be able to present at the public hearing all that will be needed for a proper decision; thus the temptation of posthearing conferences may be removed. Generally the professional advocate can play an important role in preserving the integrity of adjudication. It is painful for a lawyer to attend the hearings of a board where most of the representation is by laymen; say, a board of appeals hearing applications for variances from zoning laws. The hearing is customarily devoted to irrelevancies, and the issues really pertinent to decision may be scarcely touched on in the arguments presented. This would be the situation in all fields of adjudication were we to remove from the scene the professional advocate. His presence is usually essential for adjudication to be in fact what it pretends to be.

I have mentioned two devices that can help to prevent a lack of fit between the case as argued and the case as decided—the request for a reargument and the tentative decree. Oral argument is also of the greatest importance in this connection, for a written submission is often truly a shot in the dark. In appellate cases it is also important that the judges have studied the record before oral argument, for without this preparation the virtue of the oral argument in defining the crucial issues may be lost.

So far I have been discussing precautionary measures that will reduce the risk that the arbiter will have to rest his decision on considerations not argued before him. I have assumed that the area of adjudication in question is such that these precautionary measures can have some measure of success. The matter stands quite differently when cases are assigned to a process called "adjudication" under circumstances such that the best informed advocate could not possibly present to the tribunal the grounds that must be taken into account in the decision. For example, G. D. H. Cole in his *Socialist Economics* proposes that under socialism wages should be set by "arbitrators" who would be "guided by common sense." [15] Presumably there would be public hearings and the affected employees would be permitted to present arguments in favor of an increase of their remuneration. However, Professor Cole recognizes that his "arbitrators" cannot be guided solely by what is argued before them. In fact, he recommends that they meet together from time to time to see to it that the combined effect of their awards will produce a proper flow of labor. Here, plainly, the bond of the affected party's participation has largely been destroyed. He is given the appearance of a hearing, presumably because this will make him happier, but the grounds of decision are largely unrelated to what occurred at the hearing. Professor Cole's "arbitrators" are in fact business managers who from time to time put on a show by going through the motions of adjudication. This is the kind of case I have in mind in speaking of problems that fall beyond the limits of adjudication.

Must the Decision Be Retrospective?

In practice both the decisions of courts and the awards of arbitrators are retrospective, both as to their effect on the litigants' rights and their effect as precedents for the decisions of other cases. A paradox is sometimes squeezed from this traditional way of acting, to the effect that courts, in order to avoid the appearance of legislating, cast their legislative enactments in the harshest possible form, making them ex post facto.

The philosophy underlying the retrospective effect of the judicial decision can be stated somewhat as follows: It is not the function of courts to create new aims for society or to impose on society new basic directives. The courts

15. [G. D. H. Cole, *Socialist Economics* (London: Victor Gollancz, 1950), p. 96.]

for various reasons analyzed previously are unsuited for this sort of task. Perhaps the most compelling objection to an assumption of any such function lies in the limited participation in the decision by the litigants who (1) represent generally only themselves and (2) participate in the decision only by proofs and arguments addressed to the arbiter. On the other hand, with respect to the generally shared aims and the authoritative directives of a society, the courts do have an important function to perform, that of developing (or even "discovering") case by case what these aims or directives demand for their realization in particular situations of fact. In the discharge of this function, at times the result is so obvious that no one thinks of a retroactive effect. Theoretically, a court might distinguish between such decisions and those which announce a rule or standard that seems new, even though it may represent a reasoned conclusion from familiar premises. But if an attempt were made to apply such a distinction pervasively, so that some decisions would be retrospective, some prospective only, the resulting confusion might be much less bearable than the situation that now obtains.

Generally the same considerations apply also to arbitration awards. It is not a matter of "concealing" the legislative nature of the arbitrator's award which makes him give it a retrospective effect. It is rather a conservative philosophy about the proper functions of adjudication, a philosophy which seeks to keep meaningful the adversary presentation, the participation of litigants only through appeals to reason, etc. . . .

．　　．　　．　　．　　．　　．　　．　　．　　．　　．

How Is Adjudication Affected by the Source of the Arbiter's Power?

The power to adjudicate may represent a delegated power of government, as in the case of a judge, or it may derive from the consent of the litigants, as in most forms of arbitration. Are these two basically different "forms" of adjudication? Obviously it has been a tacit assumption of this chapter that they are not.

On the other hand, this does not mean that the discharge of the arbiter's function is wholly unaffected by the source of his power. In a summary way we may say that the possible advantages of adjudication supported by governmental authority are: (1) The judge is under less temptation to "compromise" than is the contractually appointed arbitrator. (2) The acceptability of the judge's decision may be enhanced by the fact that he seems to play a subservient role, as one who merely applies rules which he himself did not make.

Among the possible advantages of adjudication which derives its power from a contract of the parties are the following: (1) Being unbacked by state power (or insufficiently backed by it in the case of an ineffective legal sanction), the arbitrator must concern himself directly with the acceptability of his award. He may be at greater pains than a judge to get his facts straight, to state accurately the arguments of the parties, and generally to display in his award a full understanding of the case. (2) Being relatively free from technical rules of procedure, the wise and conscientious arbitrator can shape his procedures upon what he perceives to be the intrinsic demands of effective adjudication. Thus, the "due process" which animates his conduct of the hearing may appear to the parties as something real and not something that has to be taken on faith, as allegedly inhering in technical rules that seem quite arbitrary to the layman.

As a special quality of contractually authorized arbitration, which cannot unequivocally be called either an advantage or disadvantage, we may note that the contract to arbitrate may contain explicit or implicit limits upon the adjudicative process itself. The arbitrator often comes to the hearing with a feeling that he must conduct himself in a way that conforms generally to the expectations of the parties and that this restriction is implicit in the contract of submission. Thus, if both parties desire and expect a more "literal" interpretation than the arbitrator himself would prefer, he may feel obligated to adopt an attitude of interpretation that he finds intellectually uncongenial.

VII. *The Limits of Adjudication*

Introduction

Attention is now directed to the question, What kinds of tasks are inherently unsuited to adjudication? The test here will be that used throughout. If a given task is assigned to adjudicative treatment, will it be possible to preserve the meaning of the affected party's participation through proofs and arguments?

Polycentric Tasks and Adjudication

This section introduces a concept—that of the "polycentric" task—which has been derived from Michael Polanyi's book *The Logic of Liberty*.[16] In approaching that concept it will be well to begin with a few examples.

16. [Michael Polanyi, *The Logic of Liberty: Reflections and Rejoinders* (Chicago: University of Chicago Press, 1951), p. 171.]

Some months ago a wealthy lady by the name of Timken died in New York leaving a valuable, but somewhat miscellaneous, collection of paintings to the Metropolitan Museum and the National Gallery "in equal shares," her will indicating no particular apportionment.[17] When the will was probated the judge remarked something to the effect that the parties seemed to be confronted with a real problem. The attorney for one of the museums spoke up and said, "We are good friends. We will work it out somehow or other." What makes this problem of effecting an equal division of the paintings a polycentric task? It lies in the fact that the disposition of any single painting has implications for the proper disposition of every other painting. If it gets the Renoir, the Gallery may be less eager for the Cezanne but all the more eager for the Bellows, etc. If the proper apportionment were set for argument, there would be no clear issue to which either side could direct its proofs and contentions. Any judge assigned to hear such an argument would be tempted to assume the role of mediator or to adopt the classical solution: Let the older brother (here the Metropolitan) divide the estate into what he regards as equal shares, let the younger brother (the National Gallery) take his pick.

As a second illustration suppose in a socialist regime it were decided to have all wages and prices set by courts which would proceed after the usual forms of adjudication. It is, I assume, obvious that here is a task that could not successfully be undertaken by the adjudicative method. The point that comes first to mind is that courts move too slowly to keep up with a rapidly changing economic scene. The more fundamental point is that the forms of adjudication cannot encompass and take into account the complex repercussions that may result from any change in prices or wages. A rise in the price of aluminum may affect in varying degrees the demand for, and therefore the proper price of, thirty kinds of steel, twenty kinds of plastics, an infinitude of woods, other metals, etc. Each of these separate effects may have its own complex repercussions in the economy. In such a case it is simply impossible to afford each affected party a meaningful participation through proofs and arguments. It is a matter of capital importance to note that it is not merely a question of the huge number of possibly affected parties, significant as that aspect of the thing may be. A more fundamental point is that each of the various forms that award might take (say, a three-cent increase per pound, a four-cent increase, a five-cent increase,) would have a different set of repercussions and might require in each instance a redefinition of the "parties affected."

We may visualize this kind of situation by thinking of a spider web. A pull on one strand will distribute tensions after a complicated pattern throughout the web as a whole. Doubling the original pull will, in all likelihood, not sim-

---

17. [See *New York Times*, 15 May 1960, p. 77, col. 1.]

ply double each of the resulting tensions but will rather create a different complicated pattern of tensions. This would certainly occur, for example, if the doubled pull caused one or more of the weaker strands to snap. This is a polycentric situation because it is many centered—each crossing of strands is a distinct center for distributing tensions.

Suppose, again, it were decided to assign players on a football team to their positions by a process of adjudication. I assume that we would agree that this is also an unwise application of adjudication. It is not merely a matter of eleven different men being possibly affected; each shift of any one player might have a different set of repercussions on the remaining players: putting Jones in as quarterback would have one set of carryover effects, putting him in as left end, another. Here, again, we are dealing with a situation of interacting points of influence and therefore with a polycentric problem beyond the proper limits of adjudication.

Let me now mention a polycentric problem that would be difficult to handle by adjudication as usually conducted, where the form of adjudication is sometimes modified to accommodate it to the nature of the problem. A textile mill is in agreement with a labor union that its internal wage scale is out of balance; over the years the payments made for certain kinds of jobs have "got out of line" and are now too high or too low in comparison with what is paid for other jobs. The company and the union agree that a fund equal to five cents an hour for the whole payroll shall be employed to create a proper balance. If the parties are unable to agree on the adjustments that should be made, the question shall go to arbitration.

Here we have a problem with strong polycentric features. If the weavers are raised, say, more than three cents an hour, it will be necessary to raise the spinners; the spinners' wages are, however, locked in a traditional relationship with those of the spinning doffers, etc. If there are thirty different classifications involved, it is obvious how many different forms the arbitration award might take; each pattern of the award could produce its own peculiar pattern of repercussions. If such a problem is presented to a single arbitrator, he will be under strong temptation to try out various forms of award in private conversations with the parties. Irregular and improper as such conversations may appear when judged by the usual standards of adjudication, it should be noted that the motive for them may be the arbitrator's desire to preserve the reality of the parties' participation in the decision—to preserve, in other words, the very core of adjudication.

Now it is in cases like this that the tripartite arbitration board finds its most useful application. The "impartial chairman" is flanked by two fellow arbitrators, one selected by the company, the other by the union. After the hearings the three consult together, the impartial chairman at some point proposing to the other members of the board various wage scales. He will in the process learn such things as that an increase for a particular occupation that seemed to him both proper and feasible will have repercussions in the bleachery of which he was unaware.

This is what I have called a mixed form of adjudication. In fact the device as I have stated it amounts to a mixture of adjudication and negotiation. All mixed forms have their dangers, and tripartite arbitration is no exception. The danger lies in the difficult role to be played by the flanking arbitrators. They can be neither wholly advocates nor wholly judges. They cannot perform their role adequately if they are completely impartial; it is their task during the deliberations to represent an interest, a point of view. It may be that they will wish to communicate with the parties they represent to inform themselves of the implications of some step proposed—though whether they should feel free to indulge in such consultations, and if so, to what extent, is one of the ambiguities that plague this form of arbitration. If, on the one hand, each of the flanking arbitrators must represent the party who appointed him, he must at the same time observe some of the restraints that go with a judicial position. If he runs back and forth between those he represents and the meetings of the arbitration board, reporting freely everything that happens during those meetings, the adjudicative process breaks down and there is substituted for it an awkward form of bargaining—in a situation, be it remembered, where negotiation has already failed to produce a solution.

As a prophylaxis against the arbitration's deteriorating into a mere continuation of bargaining—in an inept form—a variation on the tripartite pattern is now written into a good many labor contracts. It is provided that a unanimous decision of the three arbitrators shall control, but if such a decision cannot be obtained, the chairman shall determine the rights of the parties. Where there is from the beginning no real hope of a unanimous decision, this arrangement comes close to being little more than a contractual legitimation of the practice of holding posthearing conferences, though it has the advantage of officially designating the representatives who may take part in these conferences. On the other hand, where there is some genuine prospect of a unanimous agreement, the arrangement preserves for the flanking arbitrators a role that retains some of the functions, and with them some of the restraints, that go with judicial office.

The description just given is of tripartite arbitration when it is employed intelligently and with some appreciation of its advantages and dangers. In practice it is often used uncritically and tends to deteriorate, on the one hand, into a kind of continuation of bargaining behind closed doors, or, on the other, into an empty form, whereby it is understood from the beginning that the chairman is the "real" arbitrator.

It should be carefully noted that a multiplicity of affected persons is not an invariable characteristic of polycentric problems. This is sufficiently illustrated in the case of Mrs. Timken's will. That case also illustrated the fact that rapid changes with time are not an invariable characteristic of such problems. On the other hand, in practice polycentric problems of possible concern to adjudication will normally involve many affected parties and a somewhat fluid state of affairs. Indeed, the last characteristic follows from the simple fact that the more interacting centers there are, the more the likelihood that one of them will be affected by a change in circumstances, and, if the situation is polycentric, this change will communicate itself after a complex pattern to other centers. This insistence on a clear conception of polycentricity may seem to be laboring a point, but clarity of analysis is essential if confusion is to be avoided. For example, if a reward of $1000 is offered for the capture of a criminal and six claimants assert a right to the award, hearing the six-sided controversy may be an awkward affair. The problem does not, however, present any significant polycentric element as that term is here used.

Now, if it is important to see clearly what a polycentric problem is, it is equally important to realize that the distinction involved is often a matter of degree. There are polycentric elements in almost all problems submitted to adjudication. A decision may act as a precedent, often an awkward one, in some situation not foreseen by the arbiter. Again, suppose a court in a suit between one litigant and a railway holds that it is an act of negligence for the railway not to construct an underpass at a particular crossing. There may be nothing to distinguish this crossing from other crossings on the line. As a matter of statistical probability it may be clear that constructing underpasses along the whole line would cost more lives (through accidents in blasting, for example) than would be lost if the only safety measure were the familiar Stop, Look & Listen sign. If so, then what seems to be a decision simply declaring the rights and duties of two parties is in fact an inept solution for a polycentric problem, some elements of which cannot be brought before the court in a simple suit by one injured party against a defendant railway. In lesser measure, concealed polycentric elements are probably present in almost all problems resolved by adjudication. It is not, then, a question of distinguishing black from white. It is a question of knowing when the polycentric elements have become so significant and predominant that the proper limits of adjudication have been reached.

In speaking of the covert polycentric elements almost always present in even the most simple-appearing cases, it should be noted that the efficacy of adjudication as a whole is strongly affected by the manner in which the doctrine of stare decisis is applied. If judicial precedents are liberally interpreted and are subject to reformulation and clarification as problems not originally foreseen arise, the judicial process as a whole is enabled to absorb these covert polycentric elements. By considering the process of decision as a collaborative one projected through time, an accommodation of legal doctrine to the complex aspects of a problem can be made as these aspects reveal themselves in successive cases. On the other hand, if a strict or "literal" interpretation is made of precedents, the limits of adjudication must perforce be more strictly drawn, for its power of accommodation has been reduced.

If problems sufficiently polycentric are unsuited to solution by adjudication, how may they in fact be solved? So far as I can see, there are only two suitable methods: *managerial direction* and *contract* (or reciprocity).

The manner in which managerial direction solves polycentric problems is exemplified by the baseball manager who assigns his players to their positions, decides when to take a pitcher out, when and whom to pinch-hit, when and how far to shift the infield and outfield for a particular batter, etc. The relationships potentially affected by these decisions are in formal mathematical terms of great complexity—and in the practical solution of them a good deal of intuition is indispensable.

Many problems of economic management are of a similar nature. Substitution of plastic for aluminum in a component part may produce a paper saving of twenty cents on each unit produced but involve the disruption of a longstanding relation with a supplier, the possibility of a strike over the necessary changes in piece rates, though the strike might turn out in the long run to be a good thing, etc., etc. In the solution of some economic polycentric problems, recently developed mathematical methods, like those of Leontief, may reduce the necessity to rely on intuition, though they can never eliminate the element of human judgment.[18]

The other method by which polycentric problems are solved is that of contract or a reciprocal adjustment of each center of interest with those with which it interacts. Thus, an economic market can solve the extremely complex problems of allocating resources, "costing" production, and pricing goods. Whenever the literature of socialism actually deals seriously with those problems the only solution found is the establishment of something akin to a market among the various state enterprises.[19] It is interesting that the best solution even for problems of engineering calculation is often found by deriving an answer from a series of approximations, first from one center of stress, and then from another.[20]

18. [See Wassily Leontief, "Input-Output Economics," *Scientific American*, October 1951, pp. 15–21.]

19. See Oskar Lange and Fred M. Taylor, *On the Economic Theory of Socialism*, ed. Benjamin Lippincott (Minneapolis: University of Minnesota Press, 1938).

20. [Polanyi, *Logic of Liberty*, pp. 173–74.]

Recently a branch of mathematics known as game theory has been proposed as a method of adjusting adjudication to the solution of what are here called polycentric problems.[21] In essence these proposals convert adjudication into a kind of contractual game, in principle much like the classical solution already mentioned for dividing an estate equally between two sons. Each party draws up a priority list indicating his order of preference for the various possible solutions of the controversy; mathematical methods are then used to produce the "optimum" solution. The fault of this procedure is that it solves a polycentric problem only by grossly simplifying and distorting it. The priority list, for example, indicates one party's preferences as *A, D, E, B*; it does not indicate that if he gets one tenth of *A* he might be willing to move *E* ahead of *D*, etc.

It is important to note that the majority principle is quite incapable of solving polycentric problems. A baseball manager surveying in his mind all the possible ways of deploying the talent at his disposal may come up with the optimum solution; it would only be by accident that such a solution could result from a vote of the players or fans. Indeed, where voting is by the majority principle, the choice must be limited to two alternatives, say, solution *X* or *Y*, and most of the problems would have to be solved before a vote could be taken. But even when voting methods are modified, polycentric problems remain beyond the reach of anything like an election. Even if the choices are limited to three and voters are asked to list solutions *X, Y,* and *Z* in the order of their preference, the vote may result in a circle of priorities and thus yield no solution at all, either good or bad.

On the other hand, polycentric problems can often be solved, at least after a measure, by parliamentary methods which include an element of contract in the form of the political "deal." The parties in interest—or, more realistically, the parties most obviously concerned—are called together at a legislative hearing or in a conference with legislative leaders and "an accommodation of interests" is worked out. I suggest that we need a philosophy of the "political deal" that will discern its proper uses from its abuses. I believe the concept of the polycentric problem could help in drawing the line.

If we survey the whole field of adjudication and ask ourselves where the solution of polycentric problems by adjudication has most often been attempted, the answer is in the field of administrative law. The instinct for giving the affected citizen his "day in court" pulls powerfully toward casting exercises of governmental power in the mold of adjudication, however inappropriate that mold may turn out to be. It is interesting to observe, however, that during World War II the agencies charged with allocative tasks did not attempt

21. See Richard B. Braithwaite, *Theory of Games as a Tool for the Moral Philosopher* (Cambridge, U.K.: Cambridge University Press, 1955), pp. 53–54.

to follow the forms of adjudication. The War Labor Board proceeded after the pattern of tripartite arbitration, but it was theoretically barred from raising wages to influence the flow of labor, the allocative function in this case being assigned to the War Manpower Commission, which was not an adjudicative body. The Office of Price Administration and the War Production Board, vast as their powers were, did not pretend to act adjudicatively, except in trying alleged violations.

Generally speaking, it may be said that problems in the allocation of economic resources present too strong a polycentric aspect to be suitable for adjudication. Thus, a proposal made in England after World War II that scarce newspaper print be allocated by jury verdict could hardly have been the product of serious reflection. In a somewhat different category is the proposal by James B. Conant that a "quasi-judicial" procedure be used in allocating government funds among competing projects of scientific research. Obviously Dr. Conant has given serious thought to this question, and he seeks some procedure which will avoid the compromises that so often result in no project's getting enough money to make it effective. His desire to preserve the integrity of adjudication is shown by the fact that he suggests, "If there is no [competing project], some technical expert should be appointed to speak on behalf of the taxpayer *against* the proposed research. . . ." [22] Yet when one considers the nature of the problem of allocation, one wonders whether the "adjudication" here proposed could be that in anything but name. In allocating $100 million for scientific research it is never a case of Project A v. Project B, but rather of Project A v. Project B v. Project C v. Project D . . . bearing in mind that Project Q may be an alternative to Project B, while Project M supplements it, and that Project R may seek the same objective as Project C by a cheaper method, though one less certain to succeed, etc.

The final question to be addressed is this: When an attempt is made to deal by adjudicative forms with a problem that is essentially polycentric, what happens? As I see it, three things can happen, sometimes all at once. First, the adjudicative solution may fail. Unexpected repercussions make the decision unworkable; it is ignored, withdrawn, or modified, sometimes repeatedly. Second, the purported arbiter ignores judicial proprieties—he "tries out" various solutions in posthearing conferences, consults parties not represented at the hearings, guesses at facts not proved and not properly matters for anything like judicial notice. Third, instead of accommodating his procedures to the nature of the problem he confronts, he may reformulate the problem so as to make it amenable to solution through adjudicative procedures.

22. James B. Conant, *Science and Common Sense* (New Haven: Yale University Press, 1951), p. 337. [The sentence in the text is a slight misquotation; the original reads: "If there are no contrary arguments, some technical expert. . . ."]

Only the last of these needs illustration. Suppose it is agreed that an employer's control over promotions shall be subject to review through arbitration. Now obviously an arbitrator cannot decide whether when Jones was made a Machinist Class A there was someone else more deserving in the plant, or whether, in view of Jones's age, it would have been better to put him in another job with comparable pay. This is the kind of allocative problem for which adjudication is utterly unsuited. There are, however, two ways of obtaining a workable control over promotions through arbitration. One of these is through the posting of jobs; when a job is vacant, interested parties may apply for promotion into it. At the hearing, only those who have made application are entitled to be considered, and of course only the posted job is in issue. Here the problem is simplified in advance to the point where it can be arbitrated, though not without difficulty, particularly in the form of endless arguments as to whether there was in fact a vacancy that ought to have been posted, and whether a claimant filed his application on time and in the proper form, etc. The other way of accommodating the problem to arbitration is for the arbitrator to determine not who should be promoted but who *has* been promoted. That is, the contract contains certain "job descriptions" with the appropriate rate for each; the claimant asserts that he is in fact doing the work of a Machinist A, though he is still assigned the pay and title of a Machinist B. The controversy has two parties—the company and the claimant as represented by the union—and a single factual issue, Is the claimant in fact doing the work of a Machinist A?

In practice the procedure of applying for appointment to posted jobs will normally be prescribed in the contract itself, so that the terms of the agreement keep the arbitrator's function with respect to promotions within manageable limits. The other method of making feasible a control of promotions through arbitration will normally result from the arbitrator's own perception of the limitations of his role. The contract may simply contain a schedule of job rates and job classifications and a general clause stating that "discharges, promotions, and layoffs shall be subject to the grievance procedure." If the arbitrator were to construe such a contract to give him a general supervision over promotions, he would embark himself upon managerial tasks wholly unsuited to solution by any arbitrative procedure. An instinct toward preserving the integrity of his role will move him, therefore, to construe the contract in the manner already indicated, so that he avoids any responsibility with respect to the assignment of duties and merely decides whether the duties actually assigned make appropriate the classification assigned by the company to the complaining employee.

Let me take another example, where my interpretation of what has occurred may or may not be correct. The FCC early established the policy that generally applicants for radio or television channels must propose a well-rounded, general program. In rural areas, where only one or two channels are available for local receivers, this policy can be justified on grounds having nothing to do with the inappropriateness of using adjudication for allocative purposes. But in many areas there are available five to ten television channels and many more radio channels. What one would expect here would be the development of specialized markets: one station catering to the sports fan, another to the opera lover, etc. In England the BBC has three kinds of programs, ranging from lowbrow, to middlebrow, to highbrow. In this country some development of specialization has occurred—despite the FCC—in a general distinction in the appeal of AM and FM radio. Yet contests for television channels today are still competitions among applicants each of whom promises the most inclusive, "well-rounded" program, each undertaking to satisfy more incompatible tastes than his rivals. Is not this phenomenon to be explained by the fact that it is sensed by all, the FCC and the applicants alike, that the whole adjudicative procedure would break down if one applicant promised to satisfy one market, another a different market? In such a case, the meaning of the applicant's participation through proofs and arguments would be destroyed because (1) there would be no real joinder of issues and (2) the FCC would have to consider whether parties not present at the hearings were not already satisfying one or more of the markets proposed to be opened. To preserve some substance for the form of adjudication you have to judge pumpkins against pumpkins, not pumpkins against cucumbers, especially when there are some relevant cucumbers not entered in the show.

In closing this discussion of polycentricity, it will be well to caution against two possible misunderstandings. The suggestion that polycentric problems are often solved by a kind of "managerial intuition" should not be taken to imply that it is an invariable characteristic of polycentric problems that they resist rational solution. There are rational principles for building bridges of structural steel. But there is no rational principle which states, for example, that the angle between girder A and girder B must always be 45 degrees. This depends on the bridge as a whole. One cannot construct a bridge by conducting successive separate arguments concerning the proper angle for every pair of intersecting girders. One must deal with the whole structure.

Finally, the fact that an adjudicative decision affects and enters into a polycentric relationship does not of itself mean that the adjudicative tribunal is moving out of its proper sphere. On the contrary, there is no better illustration of a polycentric relationship than an economic market, and yet the laying down of rules that will make a market function properly is one for which adjudication is generally well suited. The working out of our common law of contracts case by case has proceeded through adjudication, yet the basic principle underlying the rules thus developed is that they should promote the free exchange of goods in a polycentric market. The court gets into difficulty, not when it lays down rules about contracting, but when it attempts to write contracts.

VIII. *Mixed, Parasitic, and Perverted Forms of Social Order Involving Adjudication*

Introduction

This concluding section will be sketchy and suggestive, without any pretense at dealing exhaustively with the problems it raises.

It may be well to warn against the assumption that every mixed or "impure" form of adjudication is here condemned. In the previous discussion of tripartite arbitration, I tried to show how useful this form might be, at the same time calling attention to the dangers contained in it and to the possibilities of its abuse.

When I speak of a form of order as being parasitic, I mean merely that, although it seems to possess an original strength of its own, it in fact draws its moral sustenance from another form of order. In labeling it parasitic, I intend no more condemnation than when a botanist calls a certain fungus parasitic. Just as, from the standpoint of human interest, there are good and bad fungi, so parasitic forms of order may be good or bad.

Mixed Forms of Social Ordering Involving Adjudication and Contract

Adjudication and Mediation. During World War II the War Labor Board undertook to revise the internal structure of wages in a number of industries. This polycentric task could not have been accomplished by adjudication in its usual forms. Instead, following the hearing, a member of the board met alternately with representatives first of industry, then of the union, and sounded them out on various changes in the wage scale. The result was a mediated contract negotiated under the threat of an exercise of adjudicative functions. For rather obvious reasons, this is a dangerous procedure, requiring the skill of a George Taylor and the capacity to make a rather uninhibited use of public power that characterizes a war economy.[23] In peacetime functions of this sort are usually exercised by a kind of industrial "czar." The fact that persons occupying this sort of role normally start as arbitrators has produced a very dangerous confusion. It has misled many uninformed persons into believing that "good arbitration" involves the formless exercise of a kind of wisdom-directed personal power. The fact is that these "czars" gradually drift into a kind of charismatic leadership, the peculiar magic of which is valid only within a limited context. Even within that context the business of "playing god" can be very dangerous, as experience has often demonstrated.

Obligations to Negotiate Under the Threat of an Exercise of Adjudicative Powers. A complex long-term supply contract provides for a renegotiation of the price from time to time and, failing agreement, for a determination of the price through arbitration. Here adjudication and contract reciprocally support one another. Parties desirous of entering a contract would hardly stipulate that on their failure to agree the whole contract should be written by an arbitrator. The function assigned to the arbitrator has to take place within the framework of an agreement, most of the terms of which are fixed. On the other hand, without the threat of arbitration it might be difficult for the parties to reach agreement on the terms left for periodic renegotiation.

In practice the arbitration clause in such a contract is included in the fervent hope that it will not have to be used; it is intended as a spur toward a negotiated agreement. On the other hand, the substance of the negotiations can scarcely escape being influenced by the parties' conceptions of what a resort to arbitration would probably produce. Expectations as to the way in which an arbitrator would view the case affect the relative bargaining power of the parties, and hence the outcome of the negotiations. This influence may detract from a full realization of the gains of reciprocity. On the other hand, if the arbitrator's powers are invoked he may try to decide the case by asking how the negotiations would have come out had the parties been more reasonable toward each other. Thus, each side of the arrangement—that is, the arbitrator on one side, the parties on the other—is likely to borrow its standards from the other, something generally undesirable and working against a fully effective use of either form of order, contract or adjudication.

This defect in the arrangement may become more serious when the parties have left for negotiated settlement something more complex than price, say, a seniority or vacation clause. Here the parties will realize that if the arbitrator's powers are invoked he will in all likelihood base his decision on standard or typical practice, simply because there is no other way of giving it a semblance

23. [See George W. Taylor, "Effectuating the Labor Contract Through Arbitration," an address to the National Academy of Arbitrators (January 14, 1949).]

of rationality. This anticipation of the results of arbitration strengthens the hand of that party who has the most to gain from an adoption of standard procedure, even though the needs of both parties might be better met by some deviation from that procedure.

Parasitic and Perverted Forms of Adjudication

Adjudication Parasitic on Contract. Since the participation of litigants in adjudication is limited to making an appeal to the arbiter's reason, it is of the essence that adjudication be based on "rational" standards in the senses previously discussed. Arbitrations to set wages and prices can under some circumstances derive their "rationality" from a market, as in the following cases: (1) In times of emergency, where the task of the arbitrator is to preserve normal relationships that threaten to be disturbed by the temporary crisis. Here the arbitrator's task becomes increasingly "irrational" as the normal pattern recedes in time and becomes increasingly inappropriate. (2) For a segment of industry, where the arbitrator's task is to preserve the "normal" relationship of this segment to industry as a whole. (3) For a single nation which is strongly dependent upon the world market.

The relative success of such adjudicative ventures has led to much confusion. We are told to follow the "middle way of Sweden," or to outlaw the strike by making all wages subject to arbitration, or to carry into peacetime the controls that were so successful in time of war, etc. These well-intentioned proposals can only arise because those who make them do not see that the adjudicative process they praise is parasitic upon a regime of contract.

Contract Parasitic on Adjudication. The leaders of a union privately agree with an employer on a five-cent-an-hour increase for the members of the union. Though the union leaders know the company's financial condition will not permit it to absorb a greater increase, they are doubtful of their ability to "sell" the five-cent settlement to their membership. Accordingly, an "arbitration" is arranged. The arbitrator is told that he is to render an award of five cents. Extended hearings are held during which the unsuspecting union members have the satisfaction of hearing their representatives argue vigorously that they are entitled to at least twenty cents an hour. The arbitrator "deliberates" for a month and renders an award of five cents an hour. The members of the union reluctantly acquiesce in the advice of their leaders that this is the most they could get with the aid of the best legal talent in town.

Here one form of order, contract, has not the strength to stand on its own feet; it has to be given an infusion from a phony arbitration. It seems to me that the term *parasitic* is here wholly apt, and I would not hesitate to add the designation *perverted*. Plainly, if *all* awards were "fixed," casting a contract in the form of an adjudication would accomplish nothing. Those who take advantage of the phony arbitration are able to do so only because their example is not generally followed. One is reminded of Schopenhauer's remark that the prostitute owes her bargaining power to the restraint of virtuous women.

It should be noted that the case I am speaking of (and such cases do in fact occur) involves an arbitrator who derives his power from an agreement of the litigants. The moot or "fixed" case before a court presents a different set of problems. Historically court procedure has often been employed to assure the legal effect of an agreement. "Fines" and "recoveries," two modes for conveying land in England, were based upon an innocently "collusive" suit. Developments of this sort seem in retrospect quite unobjectionable and even wholesome. The procedure now available in Reno and other places for converting an agreement into a legally effective divorce has not yet acquired the same shielding patina of history. In an interesting little book by a Soviet judge, the author tells of discovering that there were an extraordinary number of suits brought before him by consignees against railways claiming shortages.[24] In all of these cases the judgment was for the railway, on the ground that the alleged shortage was simply the shrinkage that would naturally occur in certain products in course of shipment. When the judge asked the plaintiffs why they persisted in bringing such suits, the answer was, "Well, in case any questions were raised about the amount we put into inventory, we thought we ought to have the protection of a court decree." I find in this little incident an eloquent though indirect tribute to commercial adjudication in Russia. If the commercial courts were not by and large "on the level," this mild abuse of judicial procedure would not have served any purpose.

Happily, the "fixed" labor award in the crass form I related is a rarity. In fairness, we must recognize further that the admixture of contractual elements in an adjudicative process is a matter of degree. Even in the most formal and adversary presentation an arbiter can often discern some indication of what the parties would regard as an acceptable settlement simply from the relative emphasis placed on the various issues and arguments. This discreet reading between the lines, far from being a perversion of adjudication, serves to enhance its efficacy. But the fact that all human relations are tinctured with a slight element of dissimulation is no reason to elevate dissimulation to the level of principle.

---

24. Georgii Ivanov, *Notes of a People's Judge* (Moscow: Foreign Languages Publishing House, 1950), pp. 55–56.

Mediation—Its Forms and Functions

Editor's Note

When student enrollment declined at the Harvard Law School during the Second World War, Fuller, like many of his colleagues, sought other employment. After attempting unsuccessfully to find a position with the federal government in Washington, he joined the prestigious Boston law firm of Ropes, Gray, Best, Coolidge and Rugg as an industry advocate in labor disputes. At the close of the war, he returned to full-time teaching but, from about 1947 to 1959, was often asked to serve as a labor arbitrator. Out of this experience, I believe, developed Fuller's long-standing interest in adjudication and mediation as authoritative processes of dispute settlement and his wrestling with the question of how they were properly to be distinguished. This experience also helps to explain the extended references to collective bargaining which appear in his analyses of both forms of social ordering.

It is not surprising in our legal culture, where courts are the only social institutions that take justice as a regulative ideal, that adjudication has been the object of considerable scrutiny by social theorists. Fuller stood almost alone among Anglo-American legal scholars in devoting similar attention to mediation. In part, his interest was sustained by extensive reading in legal history and anthropology, but he did not consider mediation as peculiar to alien cultures or periods.

Thus, in a letter to a colleague at Harvard Law School at the time of his retirement in 1972, Fuller wrote: "Anthropologists often state that it is a characteristic of primitive or tribal law that it puts a high value on consensus, hence uses mediation where we would employ adjudication. I am contending that when we encounter social contexts similar to those of a primitive society, we too resort to mediative rather than adjudicative methods of problem solving. (I would prefer 'problem solving' to the fashionable 'dispute resolution.') The contexts that make mediation preferable are in general those of a heavy and complex interdependence. Among such contexts in our society one might list: (1) marriage, (2) closely held corporations, (3) tenants packed together in public housing, (4) coauthors of a book. In all these cases some 'straightening out' may be essential, rather than an adjudicative determination of rights and duties."

The aptness of mediation, one might say, tends to be underestimated in a society which encourages litigation to settle personal and public conflicts. Of course to regard mediation as an alternative to adjudication does not mean that the one can always be substituted for the other. The efficacy of each process, as Fuller claims, depends on different social conditions, and each is most conducive to the resolution of different kinds of problems. At a practical level, we may expect to learn more about both the possibilities and the limits of mediation from the operation of such experimental institutions as "neighborhood justice centers." Meanwhile, Fuller's account provides a theoretical framework to guide further study and research.

"Mediation—Its Forms and Functions" was part of a festschrift *in honor of Fuller's colleague and close friend, Henry M. Hart, Jr. It appeared in the* Southern California Law Review *(volume 44, 1971) and is reprinted with permission.*

It is characteristic of the experienced mediator that he often proceeds most effectively to his goal, especially during the early stages of his efforts, by circumlocution and indirection. Perhaps I may be forgiven, therefore, if my approach to the subject of mediation itself displays something of those qualities. I have, in any event, thought it expedient to preface my analysis by putting mediation in the wider context of some assumptions of methodology that appear to shape our efforts to comprehend social phenomena generally.

I

In every branch of human study that has achieved or aspires to the name of science a fundamental difference seems to repeat itself in the assumptions men make as to the nature of the thing they are examining. This schism in basic orientations extends over a wide range of subjects. Something of its pervasiveness becomes apparent when we recall the slogan-like terms conventionally employed in describing this opposition of viewpoints: structure versus process, substance versus procedure, statics versus dynamics and—on a more elevated plane—Being and Becoming. As these terms indicate, this recurring difference is not so much thought of as a quarrel about the most profitable posture of the mind as it is about the essential nature of the thing being studied.

There are, of course, thinkers who with some difficulty—and often with some attendant obscurity—attempt to straddle the choice. Certain paradoxes also often emerge when we compare closely related subjects. For example, social anthropology, which has traditionally dealt with the more "static" primitive societies, tends, I believe, to be more "process-oriented" than its sister science of sociology, practitioners of the latter subject being inclined to stick with social structure without displaying much curiosity about how it got there.

Legal scholarship has, on the surface at least, been spared the anguish of choice visited on the practitioners of related disciplines. For one thing, law does not pretend to be a science and hence can permit itself a certain obscurity about its basic premises, attributing this condition simply to the nature of its subject. Legal reasoning is, in general, quite happy to proceed eclectically, fitting its methods and starting assumptions to the problem at hand. Then, too, American law teachers may assert that the case method combines in a happy mixture an analysis of both structure and process; it studies not only the established rules, but also, to the frequent discomfort of the beginning student, examines painstakingly and at great length the dialectical processes that bring them into being. Finally, a defense of legal scholarship against the charge of being one-sided can be derived from a glance at the law school catalogue where will be found listed, not only courses in substantive law, but also courses in procedure.

With respect to this last point it should be pointed out that law school courses dealing explicitly with procedure are concerned with the highly structured procedure observed in the trial of cases in court. It tells the student, for example, something about the problems of proving a contract in court; it tells him little about the extracurial procedures by which contracts come into being. In the case of the highly formal written contract, this omission may be quite innocent. But what of the contract "implied-in-fact"? Here any attempt to articulate clearly the modes by which contractual obligations arise tacitly out of human interactions would present structure and process in an uncomfortably intimate embrace, for in this case the thing that emerges from the process—"the contract"—is, as it were, simply an aspect of the process itself.

As for the case method as practiced in American law schools it can indeed be said of it that it combines in a felicitous mixture a study of both process and structure. The structure of the law of contracts as it goes into Restatements and textbooks is viewed as being in large measure a product of the judicial process. That process is in turn viewed as being shaped by the existing structure of rules and by the tensions that may arise between that structure and the court's conception of the proper disposition of the controversies (often of "novel impression") that are brought before it for decision. Thus, structure and process are viewed as interacting, each serving to shape the other.

The trouble with the case method, for all its explicit and perceptive orientation toward process, is that there is not enough of it in the law school curriculum. It is largely confined in practice to a particular kind of law-making, a species of legal ordering that for historical reasons has come to be known as the common law, though a more apt designation would have been adjudicative law. The adjudicative process is, however, only one way of bringing human relations into a workable and productive order. Other processes include statutory enactment, administrative direction, contractual ordering effected by the parties themselves, and the tacit accommodations that ripen into something equivalent to customary law. These various forms of social ordering are interrelated in complex ways; formal adjudication may of course serve as an adjunct to any of them for purposes of interpretation and enforcement.

The standard law school curriculum deals with the *results* of all these forms of social ordering; we do indeed teach students a little bit about customary law and a great deal about statutory law, administrative law, and contracts. We do not, however, spend much time exploring the social processes by which these various forms of "law" come into being. Because these processes are neglected we inevitably lack a perspective from which to appraise the relative aptness, for solving a given problem, of the various competing forms of social ordering.

No one has contributed more to a correction of this defect, and to an enlargement of this perspective than the late Henry M. Hart. His mind had a strong bent toward process and procedure. The famous course he created, which is now taught (still from multilithed materials) in some two dozen law schools, was and is called *The Legal Process*. The course consists in a series of diagnostic and prescriptive exercises. Instead of asking, What is the rule? or even, What is the best rule? it asks, What is the nature of the basic problem and how shall we choose among the various procedures of social ordering that might be applied to it?

II

I like to think there is a special appropriateness in dedicating a discussion of mediation to the memory of Henry Hart. For of mediation one is tempted to say that it is all process and no structure.

Casual treatments of the subject in the literature of sociology tend to assume that the object of mediation is to make the parties aware of the "social norms" applicable to their relationship and to persuade them to accommodate themselves to the "structure" imposed by these norms. From this point of view the difference between a judge and a mediator is simply that the judge orders the parties to conform themselves to the rules, while the mediator persuades them to do so. But mediation is commonly directed, not toward achieving conformity to norms, but toward the creation of the relevant norms themselves. This is true, for example, in the very common case where the mediator assists the parties in working out the terms of a contract defining their rights and duties toward one another. In such a case there is no preexisting structure that can guide mediation; it is the mediational process that produces the structure.

It may be suggested that mediation is always, in any event, directed toward bringing about a more harmonious relationship between the parties, whether this be achieved through explicit agreement, through a reciprocal acceptance of the "social norms" relevant to their relationship, or simply because the parties have been helped to a new and more perceptive understanding of one another's problems. The fact that in ordinary usage the terms *mediation* and *conciliation* are largely interchangeable tends to reinforce this view of the matter.

But at this point we encounter the inconvenient fact that mediation can be directed, not toward cementing a relationship, but toward terminating it. In a form of mediation that is coming to be called marriage therapy mediative efforts between husband and wife may be undertaken by a psychoanalyst, a psychiatrist, a social worker, a marriage counsellor, or even a friendly neighbor. In this situation it will not infrequently turn out that the most effective use of mediation will be in assisting the parties to accept the inevitability of divorce. In a radically different context one of the most dramatically successful uses of mediation I ever witnessed involved a case in which an astute mediator helped the parties rescind a business contract. Two corporations were entrapped by a long-term supply contract that had become burdensome and disadvantageous to both. Cancelling it, however, was a complicated matter, requiring a period of "phasing out" and various financial adjustments back and forth. For some time the parties had been chiefly engaged in reciprocal threats of a law suit. On the advice of an attorney for one of the parties, a mediator (whose previous experience had been almost entirely in the field of labor relations) was brought in. Within no time at all a severance of relations was accomplished and the two firms parted company happily.

Thus we find that mediation may be directed toward and result in discrepant and even diametrically opposed results. This circumstance argues against our being able to derive any general structure of the mediational process from some identifiable goal shared by all mediational efforts. We may, of course, indulge in observations to the effect that the mere presence of a third person tends to put the parties on their good behavior, that the mediator can direct their verbal exchanges away from recrimination and toward the issues that need to be faced, that by receiving separate and confidential communications from the parties he can gradually bring into the open issues so deep-cutting that the parties themselves had shared a tacit taboo against any discussion of them, and that, finally, he can by his management of the interchange demonstrate to the parties that it is possible to discuss divisive issues without either rancor or evasion.

But can we go beyond generalities of this sort? I believe we can, but to accomplish this we shall have to begin by examining in detail the functions mediation can perform in a specific illustrative situation. If this illustrative case is aptly chosen we may then, with appropriate adjustments, extend our conclusions to other situations that vary in specific ways from the model adopted for detailed analysis. The model I propose here is that presented by mediational efforts serving to facilitate the negotiation of a collective bargaining agreement between an employer and a labor union. Aside from the fact that this use of mediation happens to be one in which I have had some personal participation, I believe it to be especially suited to our present purpose because it combines in a single illustrative instance a number of the quite diverse functions a mediator can perform.

I begin, then, by supposing that an employer—say, a corporation engaged in manufacturing—and a labor union representing its production force are about to enter into negotiations concerning the terms of a collective bargaining agreement. I assume that these negotiations will range over a wide variety of issues, either because a collective bargaining agreement is being entered by the parties for the first time, or because an existing agreement has come open for renegotiation and the issues raised by the parties extend over a wide range of subjects, such as rates of pay, seniority provisions, grievance procedures, and the timing and length of annual paid vacations.

Now among the characteristics of this relationship that are relevant to our purposes, the *first* lies in the obvious fact that the parties mediated are two in number, they constitute a dyad, not a triad or more numerous group. To be sure, during the mediational effort some differences of opinion within the union and, less commonly, within the company, may come to the surface, but basically the mediator's efforts are directed toward an ordering of the relations between the company and the union and he will generally be at pains to stay out of quarrels arising within either of the participating groups.

The *second* characteristic of concern here lies in the circumstance that normally neither of the parties, the employer or the union, has any real choice but to reach an agreement with the other. The two parties are locked in a relationship that is virtually one of "bilateral monopoly"; each is dependent for its very existence on some collaboration with the other. The employer is not only under economic pressure to reach a contract with the union but in the United States is normally subject to a legal compulsion "to bargain in good faith" with the elected representative of his employees. The union, on the other hand, being organized for the purpose of collective bargaining, must, if it is to fulfill its reason for being, reach an agreement with the employer.

This "tied-in" relation, it should be noted, extends not only to the union as a collective entity, but in some measure to the individual union member as well. If, dissatisfied with what his union has achieved for him, he considers taking a job with another employer he is likely to be reminded that in his new position he will find himself at the bottom of the seniority ladder and vulnerable to lay-off at the first slackening of production. Furthermore, moving into a new employment may forfeit for him any nontransferable fringe benefits his union has obtained for him through collective bargaining, these benefits relating to such things as retirement pay, health benefits, paid vacations proportioned to length of service, and the like. We commonly find, then, between the unionized employer, on the one side, and the labor union and its members, on the other, a relationship that may be called one of heavy interdependence: they simply must find some way of getting along with one another.

The *third* characteristic of the relationship that is relevant here lies in the obvious fact that the negotiation of the collective bargaining agreement has elements of an economic trade. This is plainly true, of course, where rates of pay are being negotiated. But it is also true where non-monetary provisions of the contract come under discussion. For example, a manufacturer might be willing to accept a revision of the grievance procedure proposed by the union, in return for some expansion of the clause removing certain management decisions from arbitrational review. The question, Will this help or hurt *us?* is one the parties constantly put to themselves as they negotiate the contract— sometimes even when the issue is simply where a comma ought to be inserted. Into every aspect of the negotiations, then, there is likely to enter some calculation of relative "payoff."

The *fourth* characteristic of our illustrative situation stands in some contrast to that just described. The enterprise in which the parties are engaged is not simply one in which each seeks to attain the contractual language that will most favor his immediate interests. The parties are also caught up in the task of drafting a constitution, of putting on paper words by which they can in the future live together successfully. A perception of this aspect of their joint endeavor must temper and often redirect their efforts toward the achievement of their separate goals. A clause with hidden ambiguities that invite endless disputes will carry a heavy price tag for both parties, even though the party securing its adoption may at the time have congratulated himself on having served well his own advantage.

The fact that the actual negotiation of the collective bargaining agreement is conducted, not by principals, but by agents or representatives constitutes a *fifth* characteristic of the situation we are discussing. The employer is an abstract entity called a corporation; those who represent that entity act in a representative capacity and they are by no means commonly the chief executives of the corporation itself. Likewise, of course, the entire membership of the union does not and cannot participate directly in the negotiations; these are commonly conducted on their behalf by an out-of-town expert from the national union headquarters, assisted by a local committee.

The *sixth* and final characteristic of the relationship we are examining lies in the fact that one of the parties, the company, occupies toward the membership of the union a dual role. In the negotiation of the collective bargaining agreement the parties meet each other as equals, with neither having any recognized authority over the other; in the day-to-day management of the plant, however, the company is boss. Its foremen and superintendents, not the labor union, direct the manufacturing process. Indeed, experienced labor leaders exercise a canny reserve about invading this prerogative, for the responsibilities that go with it could be quite inconvenient for them and any sharing of those responsibilities would tend seriously to compromise their role as representatives of the union membership.

These, then, are six characteristics of the collective bargaining situation that have suggested to me it might be useful as a model in analyzing the functions of mediation generally. By way of a recapitulation: the parties concerned (1) being two in number, find themselves (2) in a relationship of heavy interdependence exerting a strong pressure to reach an agreement, an agreement that will (3) combine elements of an economic trade with (4) elements of a written charter or constitution for the governance of their future relations; this agreement is (5) negotiated by agents, not principals, and (6) the employer occupies throughout a dual role, being, on the one hand, director of the enterprise and, on the other, a coequal with the union in the negotiation and administration of the collective bargaining agreement.

In what immediately follows I shall attempt an analysis of the ways in which these six characteristics affect the need for and the functions performed by a mediator. Following that analysis I shall attempt to draw some analogies between the situation I have taken as my illustrative model and the uses of mediation in quite different social contexts. One context I shall discuss is that presented generally by "primitive" societies, where (in various guises) mediative processes play a prominent role in preserving (and sometimes in creating) a functioning social order. (By way of anticipation, I suggest that if the reader will glance through the summary presented in the last paragraph, he will discern that some of the six characteristics I have attributed to the collective bargaining situation bear a striking resemblance to those present in primitive societies; others, to be sure, are less obviously present, if they are at all.)

III

The first question is, then, how the need for a mediator, and the role performed by him, are affected by the fact that the parties whose relations constitute the subject of mediation are two in number. Here Simmel's famous discussion of the dyad and the triad becomes relevant.[1]

Simmel observes that among groups ranked in terms of the number of their members, the group of two, the dyad, is peculiarly handicapped in resolving problems of internal order. Even the triad confronting internal difficulties can be governed openly or tacitly by the majority principle; this is an expedient from which, of course, the dyad is excluded. Then, too, one member of a triad can often undertake to mediate between the other two, having perhaps preserved a posture of detachment precisely in order to assume this role; *A* seeing trouble brewing between *B* and *C* may initially have been inclined to favor *B* but decided to remain neutral in order to qualify for the role of mediator. This is obviously another resource denied to the dyad.

The dyadic relationship is, then, one eminently suited to mediation and often dependent on it as the only measure capable of solving its internal problems. Indeed, one may ask whether mediation in the strict sense is really possible in ordering the internal affairs of any group larger than two. If *A*, *B*, and *C* are all at odds with one another, it is extremely difficult for an outsider, say, *X* to undertake a mediative role without becoming a participant in the internal maneuvers of the quarreling members. If *X* asks *A*'s acquiescence in a proposed solution, *A* may reply that he will give his assent if *X* will undertake to persuade *B* to withdraw a concession *B* made in favor of *C*. *X* may thus end by becoming the manipulated tool of those he sought to guide. In this predicament he may face the alternative of retaining the empty title of mediator or becoming, in effect, a fourth member of the group and a participant in its internal games. If he chooses the latter alternative, his accession to membership may not increase but rather tend to diminish the chance for achieving a functioning order, since it introduces for the first time the possibility of a deadlock of two against two, in other words, it impairs an advantage the triad enjoys over the dyad, the capacity to resolve internal difficulties by something like a majority vote.

There is perhaps one situation in which an outsider may, with skill and good luck, serve usefully as a mediator among three. This would be where three different measures are proposed as the solution for some problem faced by the triad. *A* favors solution *X*, *B* favors solution *Y*, while *C* favors solution *Z*. Here the mediator might discuss with each of the parties the grounds upon which, and the degree of conviction with which, he supports his preference for one solution as against the other two. There are thus opened up, in somewhat embarrassing abundance, six separate entries for the mediator's intervention. Exploring these conscientiously he might discover that *A*'s preference for *X*

1. *The Sociology of Georg Simmel*, ed. Kurt Wolff (New York: Free Press, 1950), pp. 118–69.

over Y was based on a mistake of fact; with this mistake corrected A might then be ready to join with B in supporting Y. Or, the mediator might discover that B's preference for Y over Z was very slight and that he was almost indifferent between the two. The mediator might then persuade B to join with C in supporting Z, thus restoring the triad as a functioning entity. These happy outcomes are certainly possible, but it is obvious that the relationships involved are so complex, and the opportunities for misunderstanding so great, that the mediator may find it extremely difficult to maintain the integrity of his role as he makes the rounds among A, B, and C. Certainly if the mediational process can be said to have a home ground, it is to be found in the dyad.[2]

In my analysis of the characteristics of the collective bargaining situation I noted that it involved not only a dyad, but a dyad the members of which stood toward one another in a relation of heavy interdependence. Perhaps this observation served only to emphasize a characteristic that must be present before a resolution of the internal problems of the dyad becomes a matter of sufficient concern to justify mediative efforts. It is fairly obvious that mediation has scarcely any role to play in human relationships fluidly organized on what may be broadly described as the market principle. If X finds A, B, and C all competing to supply his needs through rival contractual arrangements, he may need the services of an expert adviser, but he will scarcely have occasion to call on those of a mediator. Likewise, in a society where transient and freely terminable sexual alliances took the place of marriage it is hardly likely that there would develop any institutional practice comparable to marriage therapy. Mediation by its very nature presupposes relationships normally affected by some strong internal pull toward cohesion; this is true whether the mediative efforts in question be directed toward the formation, modification, or dissolution of such relationships.

Those whose minds are intent on the structure of authority rather than on an analysis of social processes, are apt to ask of the mediator not What does he do? but Whence comes his capacity or authority to arrange the affairs of others? In this mood the inquiry is likely to be whether his power rests on a tacit contract with the affected parties, or derives from some charismatic qualities possessed by the mediator himself, or should be attributed to some role or

---

2. This does not mean, it should be observed, that a single mediator might not have occasion to cope with internal difficulties arising within a collectivity forming one member of a dyad. For example, in the course of mediating the negotiation of a contract between an employer and a union it might turn out that one of the chief obstacles to agreement lay in a clash between two factions within the union. An experienced (and courageous!) mediator might in some measure mediate the dispute between the union and the employer. This would involve, however, dealing successively with two dyads and not with any attempt to put in order a three-cornered pattern of opposed interests.

office assigned to him by tradition or higher authority. Now an inquiry along these lines is certainly not meaningless, but taking it too seriously may lead us to ignore the fact that the mediator's "power" may largely derive from the simple fact that he is there and that his help is badly needed. Thomas Schelling has some vivid and perceptive things to say about this aspect of the mediator's job:

> When there is no apparent focal point for agreement . . . [the mediator] can create one by his power to make a dramatic suggestion. The bystander who jumps into an intersection and begins to direct traffic at an impromptu traffic jam is conceded the power to discriminate among cars by being able to offer a sufficient increase in efficiency to benefit even the cars most discriminated against; his directions have only the power of suggestion, but coordination requires the common acceptance of some source of suggestion. Similarly, the participants of a square dance may all be thoroughly dissatisfied with the particular dances being called, but as long as the caller has the microphone, nobody can dance anything else. The white line down the center of the road is a mediator, and very likely it can err substantially toward one side or the other before the disadvantaged side finds advantage in denying its authority.[3]

A serious study of mediation can serve, I suggest, to offset the tendency of modern thought to assume that all social order must be imposed by some kind of "authority." When we perceive how a mediator, claiming no "authority," can help the parties give order and coherence to their relationship, we may in the process come to realize that there are circumstances in which the parties can dispense with this aid, and that social order can often arise directly out of the interactions it seems to govern and direct.

The third characteristic I found present in the collective bargaining situation lies in the fact that in reaching agreement each party is constantly calculating the relative advantage or disadvantage to him of any particular proposal. There is, in other words, a pervasive evaluation of "payoffs"; this evaluation extends even to provisions of the contract that seem unrelated in any direct way to monetary costs. In terms of the mediator's function, this means that the mediator participates in a bargaining situation where each party seeks to get as much for himself as he can at as small a cost as possible, the "cost" involved being, of course, that entailed in some concession to the opposing party.

In approaching this aspect of the situation I should like to begin with a quotation from a great student of the sociology of organization. It should be

3. Thomas C. Schelling, *The Strategy of Conflict* (Cambridge, Mass.: Harvard University Press, 1960), p. 144.

noted that in this passage the author makes it clear that his chief interest is not in something like a trade of economic goods, but in the calculations of utility that enter into any bargaining situation—sometimes even, as I have suggested, when the issue is where a comma ought to be inserted.

> . . . the rule must be that you give, so far as possible, what is less valuable to you but more valuable to the receiver; and you receive what is more valuable to you and less valuable to the giver. This is common sense, good business sense, good social sense, good technology, and is the enduring basis of amicable and constructive relations of any kind. This does *not* mean that you give as little as you can from the *receiver's* point of view. In terms of money, you give a man dollars for his services which are worth more to you than the dollars. No sane man would admit anything else. If you give services for dollars it must be that the dollars are worth more to you than the services. Unfortunately for simplicity, neither side of the transaction can be confined to or measured completely in dollars, even in commercial enterprises; and in non-commercial enterprises the exchange is extremely intangible.
>
> What conceals this simple fact of experience so often is that subsequent evaluations may change, though this is then beside the point. I may pay a man $10 today with pleasure, and find tomorrow that I need $10 very badly, but cannot use the services I paid for. I am then perhaps disposed to think I made a bad exchange. I read the past into the present. This leads to the false view that what exchanges *should* be is as little as possible of what the *receiver* wants, regardless of its value to me. This philosophy of giving as little as possible and getting as much as possible in the *other man's values* is the root of bad customer relations, bad labor relations, bad credit relations, bad supply relations, bad technology. The possible margins of cooperative success are too limited to survive the destruction of incentives which this philosophy implies.[4]

The closing sentences of the passage just quoted plainly suggest one function the mediator can perform in the collective bargaining situation, that of reminding the parties that their negotiations constitute a cooperative enterprise and that one does not necessarily make a gain for himself simply because he denies to the other fellow something he wants. In conveying this message the mediator only supplies the insight that the parties ought to have brought to the bargaining table without his aid. He simply makes them see, in Barnard's words, that "the rule must be that you give, so far as possible, what is less valuable to you but more valuable to the receiver; and you receive what is

---

4. Chester Barnard, *The Functions of the Executive* (Cambridge, Mass.: Harvard University Press, 1942), pp. 254–55.

more valuable to you and less valuable to the giver." Plainly it is this divergence between the cost of giving and the gain realized by receiving that makes possible the reciprocal advantages that can result from a properly negotiated exchange.

But if it is relatively easy to see that an apt exchange can yield advantages to both parties, it is much more difficult to discern the actual processes of discussion and negotiation that will maximize these gains of reciprocity. Suppose, for example, that one party reveals, intentionally or inadvertently, that he is desperately eager to secure some particular concession from his opposing number. It happens that granting this concession would visit very little disadvantage on the party from whom it is demanded. Does he at once reveal this fact, or does he hold back his concession as a resource on which to draw when he wants something badly that the other party is reluctant to give? Which course of action will, in fact, serve ultimately to maximize the gains of reciprocity for both parties?[5] In judging this last question it should be recalled that gratuitous concessions falling outside the frame of normal bargaining are apt to arouse suspicions as to their motivation and may be interpreted as requiring the benefited party to volunteer some counterconcessions, which may itself be unguided by any accurate understanding of its value to the other party—the "exchange" of Christmas presents is notoriously a poor example of maximizing utilities.

An obvious, but mistaken expedient would be to have both parties at once disclose to each other their internal evaluations of all the items under discussion. But there are many difficulties with this. As Barnard remarks, the values may be extremely intangible; there is no yardstick that can convert them into numbers. Furthermore, the items on a negotiating agenda may be interrelated in various complex ways. For example, suppose that one party, A, asks for concessions X, Y, and Z. Now it might be that if Y and Z were granted, X would become wholly unnecessary. On the other hand, if the other party were willing to concede both X and Y this concession might yield a return much higher than the value of X alone, say, roughly its double, although Y taken by itself would produce only a small fraction of the value that a grant of X by itself would yield, etc., etc.

Where the bargaining process proceeds without the aid of a mediator the usual course pursued by experienced negotiators is something like this: the parties begin by simply talking about the various proposals, explaining in gen-

---

5. I am aware that it is generally accepted in game theory that there is no objective way of defining an optimum settlement between two persons standing in a relationship of bilateral monopoly. Hence, when I speak of "maximizing the gains of reciprocity" I have in mind a settlement that would appeal to a reasonable man, familiar with the general posture of the utilities on both sides, as a close approximation to something that could be called an optimum settlement.

eral terms why they want this and why they are opposed to that. During this exploratory or "sounding out" process, which proceeds without any clear-cut offers of settlement, each party conveys—sometimes explicitly, sometimes tacitly, sometimes intentionally, sometimes inadvertently—something about his relative evaluations of the various items under discussion. After these discussions have proceeded for some time, one party is likely to offer a "package deal," proposing in general terms a contract that will settle all the issues under discussion. This offer may be accepted by the other party or he may accept it subject to certain stipulated changes.[6]

Now it is obvious that the process just described can often be greatly facilitated through the services of a skillful mediator. His assistance can speed the negotiations, reduce the likelihood of miscalculation, and generally help the parties to reach a sounder agreement, an adjustment of their divergent valuations that will produce something like an optimum yield of the gains of reciprocity. These things the mediator can accomplish by holding separate confidential meetings with the parties, where each party gives the mediator a relatively full and candid account of the internal posture of his own interests. Armed with this information, but without making a premature disclosure of its details, the mediator can then help to shape the negotiations in such a way that they will proceed most directly to their goal, with a minimum of waste and friction.

The fourth characteristic of the collective bargaining situation to be examined here lies in what I have called its constitution-drafting aspect. It should be kept in mind that the collective bargaining agreement serves, in effect, as the charter of a miniature government; it assigns functions, establishes procedures for the presentation of claims, and, in its provisions relating to arbitration, institutes what amounts to a private judiciary. Drafting such a document is a demanding exercise, not only in the accurate and unambiguous use of language, but in the apt design of institutional arrangements.

When I first mentioned this aspect of the collective bargaining situation I remarked that it stood in some contrast to that we have just examined at length. When the parties have reached the point where they are ready to express their future relationship in written words, their efforts will generally be

---

6. Probably the cautious and indirect approach just described is characteristic of all complex negotiations. This is certainly suggested in Walder's brilliant fictional account of the negotiation of the Peace of St. Germain. The following passage reports advice given to one of the negotiators: "You must mask your intentions, uncover them only a little at a time, tentatively, to find out where they agree. You must be able, behind your reserve, to change projects, purposes, allow your opinion the necessary fluidity, if there is to be the best possible outcome of your labors! Above all, do not commit yourselves, do not bind yourselves prematurely! Nothing is said, nothing is done until the very last moment." Francis Walder, *The Negotiators*, trans. Denise Folliot (New York: Heinemann, 1960), pp. 91–92.

directed toward an achievement of shared objectives, rather than toward a workable compromise of divergent aims. However, it is obvious that some elements of trade-off are likely to reappear when the parties undertake to reduce to numbered paragraphs an oral agreement previously reached in principle.

For one thing, there is often an inescapable compromise between what might be abstractly desirable and what can be clearly defined in words and effectively realized through formally instituted procedures. In exploring the reasons why this should be so, a hypothetical illustration drawn from a quite different field may be useful here. Let us suppose that for a century, two peoples, divergent in language and religion, have been united under one emperor. The empire is being dissolved and the two peoples will henceforth constitute separate nations. Under the empire, people *A* in general inhabited the area to the west of a large winding river, while the area to the east of the river was largely populated by people *B*. This simple line of division was, however, marred by some anomalies; at certain points on the river there were populations, as it were, on the wrong side. Now plainly there would be long-run advantages if the plainly visible, permanent boundary provided by the river could be established as the line dividing the new nations. On the other hand, the presence of these pockets of people on "the wrong side" of the new boundary might itself become a source of renewed friction and discord. An appraisal of relative advantages and disadvantages might be made differently by the two peoples; a skillful mediator might work out some acceptable compromise, which could, of course, include some relocation of populations.

Now the forms of language, like rivers, have a certain inertia of their own; they cannot always be readily bent to accommodate every nuance of thought, and a clause overloaded with qualifications may forfeit its meaning as a clear guidepost for human interaction. In the drafting of any complex agreement there is often an inescapable compromise between what can be simply expressed and what might be abstractly desirable. The mediational process plainly has a place in dealing with such problems.

There is another service that a mediator can render when the parties' efforts toward a formal agreement have reached the drafting stage. The mediator can bring to problems of drafting a third-party perspective; in George Herbert Mead's famous phrase he can serve as "the generalized other." This is important because the generalized other may in fact shortly appear on the scene in the person of Mr. X; six months after the contract is signed Mr. X may become personnel manager of the company in succession to the man who actually negotiated the contract on behalf of the employer and who was familiar with all the considerations that entered into its phrasing. The negotiators must keep in mind, not only what the words mean to them, but what they may mean to one who was not a participant in their deliberations and tacit adjustments. The mediator can help to supply that perspective.

We reach now the fifth aspect of the collective bargaining situation having some significance for the role of the mediator and the contribution he can make to a successful contract. This aspect lies in the circumstance that the contract is negotiated, not by principals, but by representatives or agents.

My first observation here relates to limitations, real or pretended, on the agent's authority. Let us suppose that the representative of one of the parties opens the first bargaining session by stating that he has been instructed by his principal that he may not, under any circumstances, make certain specified concessions. The excluded concessions will naturally relate to matters that might reasonably be expected to fall within the scope of the negotiations; the agent is hardly likely to warn the opposite party that his principal will sign no contract requiring him to commit a capital offense. In the collective bargaining situation the limitation on the agent's authority might, in the case of the employer, exclude a provision granting any version of the closed shop, or, in the case of the union, anything like a "management prerogative" clause.

Obviously the mediator will usually serve the cause of effective bargaining by freeing the negotiations from shackles imposed before any discussion of issues has begun and in abstraction from what the negotiations may later reveal about the actual posture of the two parties' interests. If the limitations on the agent's authority are feigned, the mediator can more readily and gracefully penetrate the pretense than can the opposing party. If the limitations have in fact been imposed by the principal, the mediator may induce the agent to ask for their removal and assist him in bringing about that result. None of this means, of course, that in the contract finally signed the principal will inevitably concede things he hoped to prevent from becoming subjects of bargaining; it simply means that the issues sought to be excluded will, in fact, enter into the discussions and be considered as possible ingredients in the final settlement, where, if included, they may of course undergo some modification.

The exploitation of feigned incapacities for the purpose of securing a bargaining advantage has been analysed at some length in "game theory." [7] Long before the device was subjected to any such sophisticated treatment it was familiar to lawyers and businessmen as the technique of "the wicked partner." *A* and *B* are discussing the terms of a contract. *B* demands some concession of *A*. *A* replies, "I wish very much I could let you have this. But my partner, who is in Europe and unfortunately cannot be reached, is dead set against it." In analysing the implications of this bargaining stratagem, it is important to realize that it becomes a serious problem only in situations I have described as

---

7. See Schelling, *Strategy of Conflict*, index entry, "commitment."

those of heavy interdependence, where the needs of the parties and the intertwining of their interests creates a strong pressure toward some sort of accommodation between them. It should also be noted that even in such situations it is a device that may miscarry and disserve the interest of the party who attempted to exploit it. When *A* refuses in advance even to consider making a particular concession he will realize that he might receive something in return for this concession, but he thinks he has grounds for believing that this counterconcession could not possibly compensate him for what he gave to secure it. This judgment may be misinformed for it has been reached before the internal structure of the other party's interests has been exposed through an open-ended exploration of the different ways in which the parties' diverse interests can be fitted together. But even if the party exploiting the wicked-partner technique is correct in his assumption that he will gain by forestalling in advance any granting of the concession, the bargaining process itself is distorted and it becomes impossible to secure the general and uninhibited exploration of diverse interests essential to a realization of the maximum gains of reciprocity. The scars left by this distortion may affect adversely the future relations between the parties.

All of this means that where the agent pleads in advance a lack of power to grant certain concessions and where the granting of these concessions would normally form an appropriate subject for bargaining between the parties, the mediator, by securing the removal of such restrictions, may make a substantial contribution, not only to the interests of the immediate parties, but to the integrity of the bargaining process considered as an essential in a functioning society.

So much for limitations, real or pretended, on the agent's power. There is a second and quite different implication for the mediator's role deriving from the fact that the parties to the negotiations are represented by agents. This lies in the observation that if there is no mediator the parties' agents may be forced, in effect, to join together in assuming the mediational role.

The negotiation of a collective bargaining agreement is commonly opened by a general session attended by delegations of persons representing both sides. On behalf of the union there may appear an attorney, a field representative from national headquarters, and a committee of the local. Management may be represented by an attorney, the personnel manager, the treasurer, and perhaps several other officers concerned with labor relations. Plainly this wide and miscellaneous audience constitutes a very poor human milieu in which to conduct the delicate sounding-out procedures by which the two parties' interests are revealed and gradually fitted together into some workable pattern. Spokesmen for both sides may be deterred, for example, from making anything like definite proposals by the fear of audible or visible dissents coming from their associates in the audience. The result is that the general opening session normally serves only a ceremonial and ritualistic purpose.

What is the next step? If a mediator is available, this is not difficult. Each of the two groups will, in turn, meet alternately with the mediator out of the presence of the other. At these repeated meetings each side will make, perhaps with some initial hesitancy but by degrees more openly, a relatively candid disclosure of the posture of its interests and preferences. Any differences within the ranks that may come to the surface during these meetings need not be damaging; on the contrary, some insight into these differences may furnish the mediator useful guidance as he works his way toward an accommodation of the parties' interests that will furnish a workable charter for their future relations.

What happens in the absence of a mediator? As I have previously expressed it, what not uncommonly occurs is that the two opposing agents join to take over the mediational function. This means that they meet together privately, explore possible ways of bringing to some workable accommodation the diverse interests of their principals, interrupt their discussions to secure advice from their colleagues, return to their joint sessions, and finally agree on the outlines of a settlement which they will propose for acceptance by their respective principals.

Obviously this procedure requires a degree of trust and mutual respect between the two negotiating agents. A good agent does not antagonize his opposite number, but is at pains to keep on good terms with him. When a lawyer representing industry has occasion over time to deal repeatedly and in different contexts with the same labor representative, a certain camaraderie will normally and quite usefully develop between them. This intimacy may, however, easily drift into a tacit reciprocity in the granting of favors that may in time become detached from the interests of the particular clients being represented. Thus, if a lawyer representing industry was forced by the intransigence of his client to deal rather harshly with his opposite number in Centerville, the question may arise, should he make up for this when the two representatives next meet in Zenith, where the employer is quite generous toward labor and ready to grant any reasonable concession recommended by his lawyer? I once heard an employer express himself in terms that left no doubt as to how he thought the lawyer would answer that question. He said, "You lawyers that represent industry and the labor people are like professional wrestlers. You travel around together and when you're in one town you agree on who'll take the fall in the next."

This was a harsh judgment, but it points to a real problem, a problem that the services of a mediator may do much to alleviate. The mediator can, by his explicit assumption of the mediational role, help those purporting to act as representatives remain what they offer themselves as being.

It should be noted that the problem here suggested is not a new one; it is by no means a sordid by-product of our complex modern industrial age. It was some one hundred and eighty years ago that Edmund Burke wrote the following: "The world is governed by go-betweens. These go-betweens influence the persons with whom they carry on the intercourse, by stating their own sense to each of them as the sense of the other; and thus they reciprocally master both sides."[8]

Burke's remarks contain important implications for the ethos of the mediator's office as well as for that of the agent; indeed, Burke seems to have in mind primarily the man who openly assumes the role of go-between. Is it in fact a common practice of mediators, in communicating the positions of the parties back and forth, to state "their own sense to each of them as the sense of the other?" Certainly when he receives from one party a statement of his position, the mediator, before conveying it to the other party, will normally strip it of vituperation and recrimination; his duty is to convey the substance of what was said, not its tone or the facial expression that accompanied it. But it is not always easy to effect this separation, especially since the depth with which a party feels about an issue is something that enters into the valuations that shape the final adjustment of diverse interests. At the same time an agreement obtained through an outright misrepresentation of the parties' own reasons for their proposals will certainly furnish an insecure basis for future relations, if indeed it does not lead to an immediate collapse of the agreement as soon as the false ground on which it was accepted becomes evident.

Like everyone else concerned with the mediational process, the mediator needs to reflect on his proper role and on the sources of his power. Mediators often pride themselves, and receive much newspaper publicity, for solving "tough" cases. But sometimes what makes the cases "tough" lies in the high stakes involved and the strong compulsion both parties are under to reach agreement. When he "solves" such a case, the mediator needs to reflect that his powers may derive as much from the urgency of the situation as from any special gifts of his. He may usefully recall Schelling's amateur who volunteers to call the dances at a square dance; the couples may follow his calls, not because the calls are especially apt, but because if they are not followed the dance cannot go on.

The sixth and final aspect of the collective bargaining situation requires

8. *The Writings and Speeches of Edmund Burke*, vol. 4 (Boston: Little, Brown, 1901), pp. 189–90. The quotation is from "An Appeal from the New to the Old Whigs" (1791).

only brief mention. This aspect lies in the fact that the employer occupies toward the union a dual role, being, on the one hand, director of an economic enterprise employing the union membership and, on the other, confronting the union as a coequal in negotiating and administering the collective bargaining agreement. In the present climate of labor relations in the United States this duality of role cannot be said to present any special problem for the discharge of the mediator's function. A few peripheral issues may arise; an example would be in working out the rules relating to lay-off in the case of reduced operations. The union is likely to seek formalized rules based on seniority, while management may want to retain some discretion in order to preserve a workable balance of specialized skills within the reduced force. The role of the mediator in helping to solve this sort of conflict is not different from that we have already analyzed at length with respect to other problems.

There are other contexts, however, in which this duality of role may create serious problems for the mediator. An example would be presented by a conflict between a municipality and some of its employees, as where teachers, firemen, or police threaten to go on strike—a strike that may be illegal. In solving such problems successfully the mediator will have to enlarge considerably the range of his concerns and in the process have to content himself with something short of perfection in the achievement of his more familiar objectives. So one may also suppose that in societies organized on a hierarchic principle, where personal status plays an important and diffuse role, the mediational process might have to be diverted to subsidiary issues (such as saving face) that are only indirectly related to the task of establishing a workable framework for future relations.

IV

Elaborate as the analysis just concluded has been, it has dealt only inferentially and indirectly with what may be said to be the central quality of mediation, namely, its capacity to reorient the parties toward each other, not by imposing rules on them, but by helping them to achieve a new and shared perception of their relationship, a perception that will redirect their attitudes and dispositions toward one another.

This quality of mediation becomes most visible when the proper function of the mediator turns out to be, not that of inducing the parties to accept formal rules for the governance of their future relations, but that of helping them to free themselves from the encumbrance of rules and of accepting, instead, a relationship of mutual respect, trust, and understanding that will enable them to meet shared contingencies without the aid of formal prescriptions laid down in advance. Such a mediational effort might well come into play in any of the various forms of mediation between husband and wife associated with family counseling and marriage therapy. In the task of reestablishing the marriage as a going concern the mediator might find it essential to break up formalized conceptions of duty and to substitute a more fluid sense of mutual trust and shared responsibility. In effect, instead of working toward achieving a rule-oriented relationship he might direct his efforts, to some degree at least, in exactly the opposite direction.

Because it does not bring this aspect of mediation into relief the illustrative model to which I have just devoted so many pages may seem inaptly chosen. The negotiation of an elaborate written contract, such as that embodied in a collective bargaining agreement between an employer and a labor union, does indeed present a special set of problems for the mediator. But in defense of the choice of this model it may be observed that complexity and formality of the processes involved may enable us to discern distinctive aspects of the mediator's task, which, though present in more informal contexts, would there have been blurred and resistant to separate analysis.

Furthermore, it should be remembered that the primary function of the mediator in the collective bargaining situation is not to propose rules to the parties and to secure their acceptance of them but to induce the mutual trust and understanding that will enable the parties to work out their own rules. The creation of rules is a process that cannot itself be rule-bound; it must be guided by a sense of shared responsibility and a realization that the adversary aspects of the operation are part of a larger collaborative undertaking. The primary task of the arbitrator is to induce this attitude of mind and spirit, though to be sure, he does this primarily by helping the parties to perceive the concrete ways in which this shared attitude can redound to their mutual benefit.

It should also be noted that the benefits of a collective bargaining agreement do not lie simply in the aptness of the numbered paragraphs that appear over the parties' signatures but derive also from the mutual understanding produced by the process of negotiation itself. I once heard an experienced and perceptive lawyer observe, speaking of complex business agreements, "If you negotiate the contract thoroughly, explore carefully the problems that can arise in the course of its administration, work out the proper language to cover the various contingencies that may develop, you can then put the contract in a drawer and forget it." What he meant was that in the exchange that accompanied the negotiation and drafting of the contract the parties would come to understand each other's problems sufficiently so that when difficulties arose they would, as fair and reasonable men, be able to make the appropriate adjustments without referring to the contract itself.

Certainly this beneficial by-product of carefully conducted negotiations is present in some measure in the case of the collective bargaining agreement. At the same time, it should be noted that the contractual relations between a labor union and an employer are not like a business deal where the relationship is scheduled for liquidation so soon as the reciprocal performances have been rendered. I have suggested that in one aspect the collective bargaining agreement is like a constitution; it must serve as a charter of government, if not for "generations as yet unborn," at least for a period that will in all likelihood extend beyond changes in the personnel administering the agreement. Since those who may have to administer the contract will not have had a chance to participate in the unverbalized understandings and expectations that went into its construction, I suggested that the mediator might usefully bring the perspective of "the generalized other" to the task of drafting the instrument. In this connection it should be observed that it may, paradoxically, sometimes be fortunate if disputes arise promptly under the new contract so that they may be resolved by those who participated in the negotiation of it and shared the perceptions that went into, and at the same time came out of, that process.

V

It is time now to bring mediation into some closer relation with the order-producing and order-restoring processes of society as a whole and in particular with those of state-made law. Some paragraphs back I spoke of the central quality of mediation, namely, its capacity to reorient the parties toward each other, not by imposing rules on them, but by helping them to achieve a new and shared perception of their relationship, a perception that will redirect their attitudes and dispositions toward one another. This suggests a certain antithesis between mediational processes, on the one hand, and the standard procedures of law, on the other, for surely central to the very notion of law is the concept of *rules*.

Insofar as our concern is with the problem of bringing laws into existence, this antithesis presents no difficulty at all. It is a commonplace of democratic government that statutes quite generally express some measure of compromise between opposing points of view. Individual legislators often find themselves, at times with some reluctance, cast in the essential mediative role that will effect this compromise. The crucial problem arises when we ask, not what role mediation should play in creating law, but how far and in what respects it should enter into the administration of laws. A general answer to this question is easy: once a law has been duly enacted its interpretation and enforcement is for the courts; courts have been instituted, not to mediate disputes, but to decide them.

It is not difficult to see why, under a system of state-made law, the standard instrument of dispute settlement should be adjudication and not mediation. If the question is whether *A* drove through a red light, or has paid his grocery bill, or has properly reported his earnings to Internal Revenue, even the most ardent advocate of conciliative procedures would hardly recommend mediation as the standard way of dealing with such problems. A pervasive use of mediation could here obliterate the essential guideposts and boundary markers men need in orienting their actions toward one another and could end by producing a situation in which no one could know precisely where he stood or how he might get where he wanted to be. As between black and white, gray may sometimes seem an acceptable compromise, but there are circumstances in which it is essential to work hard toward keeping things black and white. Maintaining a legal system in functioning order is one of those occasions.

It is, then, not in the making of legal rules, but in their enforcement and administration that a certain incompatibility may be perceived between mediative procedures and the rule of law. We may express something of the nature of this incompatibility by saying that, whereas mediation is directed toward *persons*, judgments of law are directed toward *acts*; it is acts, not people, that are declared proper or improper under the relevant provisions of law. This distinction is not quite so simple as it seems on the surface, for there are routine occasions within the operations of a legal system when judgment must be passed on persons. This necessity arises, for example, when a court must decide whether a convicted criminal should be admitted to probation or when a judge must determine which of two contesting parents should be given custody of a child. But in its core operations, in deciding, for example, whether a man has committed a crime or broken a contract, the standards of legal judgment are derived from rules defining the consequences of specific acts or failures to act; these rules do not attempt or invite any general appraisal of the qualities or dispositions of the person, exception being made, of course, for cases where the problem of legal accountability is raised, as when the defense of insanity is pleaded.[9]

9. I have attempted some analysis of the person-act distinction in "Two Principles of Human Association," *Voluntary Associations*, ed. J. Roland Pennock and John Chapman (New York: Atherton Press, 1969), pp. 17–19 [pp. 81–83 in this volume]; and in "Human Interaction and the Law," *American Journal of Jurisprudence* 14 (1969): 34–36 [pp. 244–46 in this volume].

The distinction just taken has been blurred in modern sociology by the indiscriminate use of the term *social norm*. This expression seems to be so used as to embrace indifferently, on the one hand, rules attributing legal or social consequences to overt and specifically defined acts, and, on the other, precepts eliciting dispositions of the person, including a willingness to respond to somewhat shifting and indefinite "role expectations." The word *norm* seems, indeed, to owe its popularity precisely to the circumstance that it lifts from the user the responsibility for making any such distinction. Complex and difficult as taking this distinction may in some contexts become, it is vitally important to keep it in mind in any inquiry directed toward discerning the limits of the effectiveness of "law," or toward defining the proper place and function of the various forms of social ordering, including mediation.

With reference to the uncertainties of our conventional vocabulary, I should also remark that there is a considerable ambiguity in the word *rule* itself. The Golden Rule is a magnificent expression of principle, but the "rule" that one should do unto others as one would be done by could hardly serve as a statutory injunction to be applied by courts. When in the remainder of this chapter I speak of rules I shall have in mind rules requiring, prohibiting, or attaching specific consequences to acts. Such rules are characteristic of enacted law; they are even more characteristic of what may be called contractual law, that is, of the legal regulation of the parties' relationship achieved through a contract. Though we do not speak of the "rules" contained in a contract, it is clear that contracts typically prescribe acts or performances, not resolutions of the will or dispositions of the spirit. Both the laws of the state and the requirements of a contract characteristically represent rules that may be called act-oriented.

In seeking now to delineate, within the processes of society as a whole, the proper domain of mediation, I suggest that we may usefully apply two tests; the first of these tells us when mediation *should not* be used, the second tells us when it *cannot* be used. The two tests are as follows: First, is the underlying relationship such that it is best organized by impersonal act-oriented rules? If so, then mediation will generally be out of place except as it is employed to create or modify rules. Second, is the problem presented amenable to solution through mediational processes? Mediation is itself subject to intrinsic limitations; I have discerned two of these: (1) it cannot generally be employed when more than two parties are involved; (2) it presupposes an intermeshing of interests of an intensity sufficient to make the parties willing to collaborate in the mediational effort.

In attempting an appraisal of the role of mediation in the total processes of society the most appropriate starting place is, I believe, offered by the institution of marriage. As I have already suggested, mediation has always played, and seems now increasingly to be playing, a role in the ironing out of marital difficulties. There is no mystery in this, for by the tests proposed here marital problems qualify on all counts for mediational solution. Marriage is, with us, a dyadic relation—one hesitates to think what it would be like to mediate the tangled affairs of a harem! The deterrents to separation or divorce, with the material and emotional costs either would entail, are generally sufficient to make the parties willing to collaborate in the mediational effort. Finally, the internal affairs of the marriage have generally been thought to be inappropriate material for regulation by a regime of formal act-oriented rules, whether imposed by law or by contract. There are, for example, no laws in the books prescribing which spouse is responsible for helping the children with their school work or allocating between husband and wife the right to invite their respective relatives to make weekend visits. In the few cases that have come to court where the spouses have attempted some contractual apportionment of rights and duties within the marriage relationship the courts have generally refused to lend their powers of enforcement to such agreements.[10]

The inappropriateness of formal, act-oriented rules as a means of organizing the internal affairs of a marriage can be rested on two grounds: first, that a "legalistic" conception of the relationship would be destructive of the spirit of mutual trust and confidence essential for the success of a marriage; second, that the shifting contingencies of married life—illness, pregnancy, loss of a job, the necessity for housing an indigent relative, etc.—would require reading so many tacit exceptions into the rules that they would, in any event, forfeit their efficacy as an organizing principle of the relationship. In refusing to enforce contracts between husband and wife regulating the details of their internal relationship, the courts have understandably had some difficulty in explaining just why such contracts should not be legally enforceable. The best one court could do was to say that "judicial inquiry into matters of that character, between husband and wife, would be fraught with irreparable mischief, and [is] forbidden by sound considerations of public policy."[11]

Recently there seems to have developed among students of marriage a greater inclination to approve an explicitly contractual organization of the relationship.[12] One physician has, indeed, recently proposed a kind of model contract to be entered before the marital vows are taken.[13] It includes a pro-

10. *Miller* v. *Miller*, 78 Iowa 177, 42 N.W. 641 (1889); *Graham* v. *Graham*, 33 F. Supp. 936, 938 (E. D. Mich., 1940); Caleb Foote, Robert J. Levy, and Frank E. A. Sander, *Cases and Materials on Family Law* (Boston: Little, Brown, 1966), pp. 297–366; Note, "Litigation Between Husband and Wife," *Harvard Law Review* 79, no. 8 (1966): 1650–65.

11. *Miller* v. *Miller*, 78 Iowa 177, 182, 42 N.W. 641, 642 (1889).

12. Banks McDowell, "Contracts in the Family," *Boston University Law Review* 45, no. 1 (1965): 43–62.

13. Carl T. Javert, "Guidelines for a Marriage Contract," *Trial* (1967–1968): 46–47. For a more extreme proposal, see Alix Schulman, "A Marriage Agreement," *Up From Under* 1 (1970): 5–8. The recommended contract contains a detailed apportionment of household duties between

vision for three bank accounts: "a joint checking account for the payment of household bills and expenses, and a savings account for the husband and one for the wife." (One is tempted to ask, if the husband drinks and the wife does not, is a supply of liquor and a cocktail shaker a "household expense"?) There are other provisions about the religion in which the children are to be reared, custody of children in the event of separation, etc. The contract makes no explicit provision for mediation except to state that when difficulties develop the parties will seek "counseling." On the other hand, the agreement expressly provides that when "a dispute arises that defies mutual solution, both parties agree to subject it to competent arbitration and to abide by the decision of the arbitrators." The references to "arbitrators" in the plural suggests an arbitrational board, truly a formidable (and expensive!) way of bringing the relationship of husband and wife within the rule of law. Whether a general adoption of this conception would for the first time elevate the marital relationship to a level worthy of human dignity or would, in the language of the Iowa Supreme Court, "be fraught with irreparable mischief," is something that perhaps only experience can answer.

A recent general reform in the law of divorce deserves brief mention here. It reveals with unusual clarity the tensions that can develop between the act-oriented perspective characteristic of legal processes and the person-orientation implicit in mediation. Though, as we have just observed, the marital relationship itself has generally been regarded as unsuited to regulation by act-oriented rules, the dissolution of marriage by divorce was, until recently, entirely dominated by the conventional legal approach; to secure a divorce the petitioning party had to prove the commission of a "marital offense" by the other spouse. The most obvious of such offenses was, of course, the act of adultery. Then, following an irregular pattern, different jurisdictions gradually began expanding the list of marital offenses in directions that tended to compromise its original act-orientation. The not easily defined act of mental cruelty might be added. Again, separation for a specified period of time, say, five years, was in some jurisdictions made of itself, and without regard to fault, a ground for divorce.

It is not necessary to describe here the hypocrisies and abuses that have developed out of this system; even when the only ground for divorce has been the act of adultery, the required act, when both parties wanted a divorce, might be feigned and proved in court by perjured testimony. As a cure for this and

---

husband and wife; the following extract illustrates the general tenor of the document: "8. Cooking: Wife does all dinners except Sunday nights; husband does all weekend breakfasts (including shopping for them and dishes), Sunday dinner, and any other dinners on his nights of responsibility if wife isn't home. Breakfasts are divided week by week. Whoever invites the guests does shopping, cooking, and dishes; if both invite them, split work."

numerous other evils, the reform in question has introduced the concept of "a complete and permanent breakdown of the marriage." In some jurisdictions this has been added to the conventional "marital offenses" as a ground for divorce; in others it has been made the sole basis for granting a divorce. This reform does not mean, in theory at least, that the parties can get a divorce simply by mutual consent; even if both declare that they wish a divorce they must convince the court that their marriage has in fact suffered "a complete and permanent breakdown." One asks at once, how does a judge go about deciding a question like that? What evidentiary proof will suffice to demonstrate that a given marriage has in fact broken down irretrievably?

Fortunately we now have a perceptive sociological study of the actual functioning of the new system as it operates in Poland.[14] It appears that if both parties want a divorce it is extremely difficult for the judge to penetrate behind their own self-serving declarations that their marriage has broken down. It would seem that the most logical way of going about deciding this issue would be to attempt reconciliation; if the parties do not succumb to skillful mediational efforts then it may be accepted that the marriage has indeed broken down. In a machine shop if the question arose whether a particular machine had broken down so completely that it ought to be consigned to the junkyard, one would certainly answer that question by asking a competent mechanic whether he could put it back in running condition; there would indeed be no other way of testing the matter. It appears that under Polish law the test of the breakdown of the marriage is not explicitly made its unamenability to conciliation. In fact, however, the courts commonly make repeated efforts during the divorce proceedings to accomplish a reconciliation, and it seems inevitable that they should take a failure in these efforts as the primary proof of the irremediable character of the breakdown.

What purports to be a finding of objective fact, that the marriage has broken down beyond repair, involves in fact a judgment of persons. Insofar as inquiry is directed toward finding out whether the two spouses are personally compatible, this is wholly in keeping with the spirit of the new law. But there is a third person involved, the judge himself. Górecki's study found that there was a very considerable difference in mediational skill among the judges of the divorce courts; a "factual" finding that the marriage is beyond repair may in reality reflect incapacities in the judicial mechanic attempting the repairs.

Experience in Poland has demonstrated that the new conception of divorce has by no means abolished the hypocrisies and abuses surrounding the old conception of "the marital offense." It appears that where both spouses want a divorce they may plead and attempt to prove a breakdown of their marriage

---

14. Jan Górecki, *Divorce in Poland* (The Hague: Mouton, 1970).

for a great variety of reasons. In the reported experiences of attorneys their clients "had claimed and obtained divorce in order to get a better flat, to escape the liability for the other spouse's debts, to retain a professional position endangered by an offense committed by the other spouse."[15] In one case the parties to a very happy marriage obtained a divorce so that the husband could get a visa to a foreign country where the wife planned later to join him.[16]

What has just been reported in no way represents any attempt to suggest that the reform in question was a mistake, or that the absurdities and abuses of the new system are any worse than those of the old. I have simply tried to suggest that in solving problems in the design of social institutions, as in those of engineering, compromises sometimes have to be made and that every advantage is likely to carry some cost. Unlike engineering, however, legal sociology, with its heavy orientation toward law as a simple exercise of "authority," has devoted little attention to the problems of institutional design or to a comparison of the pros and cons of rival processes of social ordering.

Resuming our more general inquiry into the proper place and function of mediation in the processes of society as a whole I should like to turn now to a subject that may seem remote from any we have so far considered. I refer to the problem of allocating scarce irrigation waters among competing uses.[17]

We are dealing, let us say, with a system of canals supplying perhaps a hundred different farmers with the water essential for growing their crops. The situation is one typical of areas where irrigation is necessary, that is, the available supply of water will fluctuate from year to year and even from week to week. During acute shortages an even distribution of water might result in a total failure of everyone's crop. In such an emergency, and in others less drastic, some decision has to be made as to how a vital resource shall be allocated among competing needs that exceed the available supply. The responsibility for making this allocation is generally placed in the hands of an official known as the watermaster. Can his decisions be brought within "the rule of law"? Is it possible to lay down in advance impersonal, act-prescribing rules that will determine just how much water each farmer shall receive? The answer is plain; no such system is possible.

In discussing the internal ordering of the family I spoke of the shifting contingencies of married life as precluding any regime wholly founded on fixed rules of duty and entitlement. The unpredictable dislocations to which the management of the household is subject are fully matched or exceeded by those affecting an agricultural system based on irrigation. The ability of the

15. Ibid., p. 56.
16. Ibid., p. 55.
17. In what follows I am drawing on sources cited in my article, "Irrigation and Tyranny," *Stanford Law Review* 17 (1965): 1021–42 [reprinted in this volume].

farmer to produce a satisfactory crop is not only dependent on the availability of canal water at the right time and in the right amount, but also on local conditions of rainfall, heat, light, wind, and atmospheric humidity, and on the balance of these factors as between night and day. Then there are the possible destructive effects of insect invasions and plant diseases. All of these factors may enter into the watermaster's decision. It would be foolish, for example, to give scarce water to a farmer whose crop will be destroyed by insects that have already begun their invasion; it would be equally foolish to save a crop if the same crop has in nearby areas come on in such abundance that there is no market for it and it lies unharvested in the fields. Typically the consideration of factors like these will be complicated by uncertainties that require a weighing of probabilities. The watermaster may also confront difficult and embarrassing questions of judging the person. One farmer can manage emergencies better than his neighbor; is that a reason for favoring the neighbor because he is handicapped or should his lack of expertise be a ground for denying him water? Again, another farmer notoriously tends to get drunk when a drought threatens his crop; during his conversation with the watermaster he seems already a bit tipsy. Should he be denied water because if he becomes drunk (as it now seems very likely he will) his condition will prevent him from operating effectively the system of ditches that serve to distribute the water over his land?

The problems involved in allocating irrigation waters are, then, not even remotely suited to solution through a regime of impersonal, act-oriented rules. Can these problems be solved by mediation? Plainly not. An irrigation system serving only two farmers would be a thing virtually unheard of; the number competing for the scarce supply may run into hundreds. Even if we were to assume that the users of the system formed a dyad, any mediational efforts between them would be unassisted by any felt sense of interdependence; far from standing in a relation of bilateral monopoly, they would be caught in a locked-in relationship of diametrically opposed interests. Where there are two farmers and only enough water for one of them, a solution in the mood of "game theory" might suggest itself—let them toss for it to see who gets the water; let the resulting crop be divided between them. Even this sort of solution, which is hardly "mediative" in any usual sense, could scarcely be extended beyond a quite small number.

Despite what has just been said one encounters in the literature references to the use of "mediation" in dealing with problems of irrigation, though generally without any indication of the kind of problems involved or the mode of their solution. Why is it that "mediative" procedures should thus have been associated with problems of irrigation? I think this association becomes understandable when we consider how a conscientious watermaster would view the nature of his responsibilities. The discharge of his duties requires not simply an inspection of the farmer's fields; it requires active consultation with the farmer himself as to his needs, plans, and wishes. The watermaster cannot just look at a crop and decide for himself how long it can go without water; the ability to withstand drought depends on the nature of the crop and the peculiarities of its location; these are matters likely to be better known to the farmer than to the watermaster. Furthermore, it may be desirable to give the farmer options and let him choose the one he considers most suited to his situation. The watermaster might ask the farmer, for example, whether he would rather be given today a certain amount of water or wait a week when there is a two-to-one chance he can be alloted twice as much.

In his relations with the persons affected by his decisions the watermaster occupies a role quite different from that, say, of the sanitary inspector, who has rules to enforce and can generally see for himself whether they are being observed. The "mediational" aspect of the watermaster's task lies in the fact that, though he issues administrative orders, those orders are informed and directed by consultation with the man whose interests are at stake. The official whose task it is to divide the waters seeks to accomplish this division, insofar as the relevant limitations permit, in a way that will suit the needs of the individual farmer as those needs are perceived by the farmer himself.

I suggest that in our modern society, where individual interests are becoming every day more interwoven and interdependent, we are witnessing a drastic increase in problems that resemble closely those of administering an irrigation system. Consider, for example, the numerous similarities between that undertaking and the administrative task of dispensing scarce public welfare funds to those most in need of them. Or consider the problem of the crowded public hospital which has to allocate, not utilities, but disutilities, when it has to ask a certain number of its patients, not yet entirely well, but on the mend, to give up their beds and go home to make room for patients more seriously ill. The discharge of responsibilities that cut as deeply into human lives as these certainly needs to be at least "mediative" (that is, as open-mindedly consultative) as those of the man who apportions scarce waters.

The standard American solution for problems of the sort just suggested is to move toward "judicializing" or "legalizing"[18] the administrative tasks they involve.[19] The obvious cost of this expedient is that it reduces inevitably the consultative and mediative elements in the operation. To say that "the law is

18. "le-gal-ize . . . 2. to interpret or apply in a legalistic spirit (you persist to legalize the gospel—J. W. Fletcher)." *Webster's Third New International Dictionary* (1966).

19. A perceptive sociological study of the gradual "legalization" of the functions of the California Industrial Accident Commission will be found in Philippe Nonet, *Administrative Justice* (New York: Russell Sage Foundation, 1969).

no respecter of persons" can, not unreasonably, be construed to mean that those exercising powers conferred by law need not bother to consult the preferences of persons and, indeed, that there would be some impropriety in doing so. This construction is likely to be especially appealing to the overburdened bureaucrat, who will find his task easier if he can confute those who press their special needs on him simply by saying, "Sorry, I have to follow the rules."

VI

At an early point in this chapter I spoke of the possible implications of the analysis it presents for primitive systems of law. I believe that the three models of mediation offered here—the mediation of a collective bargaining agreement, marriage therapy, and the consultative aspects of the watermaster's task—all have analogues in societies that would be called primitive.

Perhaps the aspect of mediation discussed here which seems most remote from early forms of social ordering is that I have described as an adjustment of interests designed to obtain optimum "pay-offs" for the participants. Yet Malinowski discerned in the principle of reciprocity a fundamental aspect of the ordering systems of "savage societies." [20] If he had in mind an explicit trade in which one party withholds his contribution until an opposite number has promised some reciprocal benefit, he would seem to be contradicted by his own report of relationships among the Trobriand Islanders. But we must remember that the silent slowdown is a more ancient phenomenon than the openly declared strike and that tacit contracting and trading were known and practiced centuries before the explicit verbal contract was perceived as an available expedient for arranging human affairs.

If we were to distinguish broadly among the various processes that contribute to social ordering we might discern six: legislation, adjudication, administrative direction, mediation, contractual agreement, and customary "law"—it being recalled of the last of these that it is often the intended product of a relegation of emergent issues to the tacit accommodations foreseen as developing out of future interactions. Even in modern societies these forms are interrelated in various complex ways and at times tend to shade into one another. In primitive society, I would suggest, they appear in still more mixed and muted forms; generally any scruple about blending or mixing them seems

20. Bronislaw Malinowski, *Crime and Custom in Savage Society* (London: Routledge and Kegan Paul, 1926).

to be absent, perhaps because they are simply not perceived as separate processes.

Something of the ambiguity of the social processes by which primitive societies are ordered is suggested in Barton's famous study of the Ifugao *monkalun* or "go-between." Barton refers to the parties who invoke the *monkalun's* office as "litigants"; the services rendered by the *monkalun* himself are described as follows:

> The office of the *monkalun* is the most important one to be found in Ifugao society. The *monkalun* is a whole court, completely equipped, in embryo. He is judge, prosecuting and defending counsel, and the court record. His duty and his interest are for a peaceful settlement. . . . To the end of peaceful settlement he exhausts every art of Ifugao diplomacy. He wheedles, coaxes, flatters, threatens, drives, scolds, insinuates. . . . The *monkalun* has no authority. All he can do is to act as a peace-making go-between. His only power is in his art of persuasion, his tact and his skillful playing on human emotions and motives.[21]

What appear to us as hopelessly confusing ambiguities of role were probably not perceived as such either by the occupant of the role or by those subject to his ministrations. In analyzing the social processes of primitive societies this often makes it an exercise in futility, as Gluckman has cogently observed, to try to sort out those processes that deserve to be called law.[22]

One might have been inclined to assume that as, in the course of history, the various forms of social ordering and dispute-settlement became separated in practice, they would become the subject of an earnest discussion among scholars as to their distinctive functions and their most appropriate applications. Instead of this, however, we find the substitution of one simplifying obfuscation for another. Now the tendency is to convert every form of social ordering into an exercise of the authority of the state, or, among sociologists, into a projection of "norms" by an abstract entity called society. Legislation, adjudication, and administrative direction, instead of being perceived as distinctive interactional processes, are all seen as unidirectional exercises of state power. Contract is perceived, not as a source of "law" or social ordering in itself, but as something that derives its whole significance from the fact that

---

21. R. F. Barton, *Ifugao Law* (Berkeley: University of California Press, 1969), p. 87. (The first edition of this work was published in 1919.)

22. Max Gluckman, *Politics, Law and Ritual in Tribal Society* (Chicago: Aldine, 1965), pp. 211–16. Henderson's study of the history of conciliation in Japanese law is instructive for its analysis of the way in which roles familiar to us were combined and intermixed in Japan. Dan F. Henderson, *Conciliation and Japanese Law—Tokugawa and Modern* (Seattle: University of Washington Press, 1965). See especially chapter 3, "The Tokugawa Concept of Law and the Role of Law in Tokugawa Society," pp. 47–62.

the courts of the state stand ready to enforce it. Custom is passed over in virtually complete silence by sociologists and is viewed by legal scholars as becoming worthy of attention only when it has been recognized by the courts and thus been converted into "law." Only mediation seems to resist this tendency to subsume every kind of ordering under the rubric of "power" or "authority." Perhaps the attempt made in this essay—tentative and imperfect as it is—to analyze the forms and functions of mediation may help in some small measure to stimulate a more general interest in the analysis and comparison of the competing forms of social ordering.

The Implicit Laws of Lawmaking

Editor's Note

One of Fuller's most famous mythopoeic devices is the story of the hapless king, Rex, who attempts with noble intentions to make laws for his subjects and fails. The failure is instructive, for each of the eight ways in which Rex bungles the job involves a violation of what Fuller calls "the internal morality of law" or "the morality that makes law possible." The canons of this morality may be summarized as follows: (1) there must be general rules; (2) the rules must be promulgated; (3) the rules must typically be prospective, not retroactive; (4) the rules must be clear; (5) the rules must not require contradictory actions; (6) the rules must not require actions that are impossible to perform; (7) the rules must remain relatively constant over time; and (8) there must be a congruence between declared rules and the acts of administrators. Only by adhering to these canons will a legislator be successful at his enterprise, subjecting human conduct to the governance of rules.

However, even if one accepts the claim that these canons, or some set closely resembling them, are necessary conditions of success in the legislative enterprise, one might still contest the proposition that these canons are "internal" to the law—or, as one might say, part of the nature of law. For example, a law that is unclear, or retroactive, or specific rather than general, would still seem to be a law by ordinary criteria. Also, one might question the claim that the canons constitute a "morality," at least in a sense sufficiently important to assert a necessary connection between law and morality. After all, one would hardly call the conditions of success in most enterprises—for example, the making of automobiles—a "morality." In order to grasp the force of Fuller's argument, one has to understand that the "internal morality" is an enumeration of the moral duties that attach to the role of legislator, and underlying the definition of that role is a special conception of the legislator's task. In Fuller's view, the only permissible form of legislation is the sort that lets individuals plan their own lives. Simply put, legislative enactments are baselines for self-directed conduct by citizens, providing the minimal restraints necessary for continuing interaction. Legislation properly conceived permits citizens to order their own affairs, to pursue their own good in their own way (in the words of John Stuart Mill). In this respect legislation differs fundamentally from what Fuller calls managerial direction, which provides detailed regulations for accomplishing objectives set by a political superior. To the contrary, legislation involves complete deference to citizens' powers of self-determination and so can be said to promote their autonomy. Thus, Rex's failure to make "laws" is a special affront to the dignity of citizens as autonomous agents.

The eight canons are internal, then, in the sense that they attach to the particular task the legislator is called upon to perform. (Other political offices will have comparable canons which may partly overlap the legislative set.) And the canons constitute a morality in the sense that they characterize the responsibility of legislators in the exer-

cise of their authority. In this selection from Anatomy of the Law, *Fuller provides his most artful account of the canons of the internal morality—or the implicit laws of lawmaking, as he calls them here. This selection is reprinted with permission of Frederick A. Praeger Publishers.*

In analyzing implicit elements in made law we have so far identified those elements as they affect the interpretation of statutes and the reconciliation of statutes when they are inconsistent with one another. The problem runs deeper, however, and touches the very meaning of law itself. Every exercise of the lawmaking function is accompanied by certain tacit assumptions, or implicit expectations, about the kind of product that will emerge from the legislator's efforts and the form he will give to that product. A somewhat bizarre illustration may serve to make this point clear. Suppose that in a newly created nation a written constitution has been adopted after lengthy consideration. This constitution has been drafted with great care and every precaution has been taken to state clearly *who* can make law and by what *rules* the lawmaking authority must proceed if it is to make laws that will bind the citizen. The new constitution, we shall suppose, provides that the supreme lawmaking power shall be vested in a legislature, the members of which are to be selected by balloting procedures clearly set forth in the constitution itself. All of these rules are followed faithfully. When the new legislature meets, its first act is to pass a resolution that all laws enacted by it shall be kept secret from the citizenry. There is in this act no violation of the language of the constitution, for it says nothing whatever about the publication of laws, being in this respect like the Constitution of the United States.

Surely, it will be said, there is implicit in the very notion of a law the assumption that its contents will, in some manner or other, be made accessible to the citizen so that he will have some chance to know what it says and be able to obey it. But to say this is to assert, in effect, that the lawmaking process is itself subject to implicit laws. This is obviously not an assumption that will appeal to those who insist that all true law is made law. Nor does the difficulty end with unpublished laws. What shall we say of the wholly unintelligible law? The statute with an internal contradiction such that it appears to nullify itself? The law that purports to impose a duty to perform some act that lies beyond human capacities? The retrospective law declaring illegal an act that was perfectly lawful when performed?

It may be said that the possibility of such legislative aberrations is ruled out by common sense and ordinary conceptions of decency. History, however, offers little support for this assurance. Retrospective criminal statutes, for example, have made their appearance down through the centuries and in a great variety of human contexts. To be sure, if your object in making law is to lay down rules by which people may guide their conduct, then your laws will operate prospectively and will govern only those actions which take place after their enactment. But if you possess the lawmaking power, and you wish to get rid of an enemy who has violated no law now in the books, what expedient is more apt to occur to you than to enact a "law" declaring what he did last week to be a capital offense?

Abuses of this sort reached a grotesque climax during the Nazi regime in Germany. The ordinary expectations that accompany lawmaking were violated by Hitler's government on an unprecedented scale. Special military courts trying citizens accused of subversive acts often reached convictions in complete disregard of the provisions enacted by the Nazis themselves for the decision of such cases, thus making it pointless for the German citizen to study the Nazi statutes to see what he could and could not do under the new regime. Retrospective legislation was freely employed. It is said that many "secret laws" were passed, though it is not easy to know to what extent this occurred, for the Nazis were extremely casual about giving any publicity to their "laws." There are scholars who have insisted that, though the statutes enacted under Hitler were thoroughly evil in their objectives, they were nevertheless just as much laws as were those enacted in England or Switzerland. In terms of the analysis presented here, such a view implies that the lawmaking power, once accepted as such, can contain no implicit limitations—there are no implicit laws of lawmaking. If this view were consistently maintained it would mean that a whole book of laws enacted secretly and locked in a vault would be "just as much law" as a compilation of rules put in the hands of every citizen and expressed in the plainest vernacular of the people to whom it was applicable.

In many countries there are, of course, written constitutions which regulate and control the making of laws. Such a constitution may prescribe the form a statute must take in order to be valid; in other words, the constitution may lay down in advance rules for determining what kinds of legislative acts shall count as laws. Where such a constitution exists, it may seem there would be no occasion for the courts to resort to any implicit understanding about the nature of law, the constitution itself being a variety of made law—a kind of man-made "higher law" fully capable of answering the question whether a given legislative act is entitled to be called a law.

But there are at least four reasons why failure must attend any such attempt to rescue made law from dependence on implicit or inherent "laws of lawmaking." *First*, the most grotesque aberrations from ordinary conceptions of what law means are precisely those which the constitutional draftsman is most likely to leave out of account. One of the most obvious things about a law is that there ought to be some way for the citizen to find out what it says, yet the Constitution of the United States contains no provision requiring the publication of laws. The explanation for this kind of omission is suggested in the following passage from the philosopher Wittgenstein:

> Someone says to me: "Shew the children a game." I teach them gaming with dice, and the other says, "I didn't mean that sort of game." Must the exclusion of the game with dice have come before his mind when he gave me the order?[1]

Certainly the one who gave the order would be entitled to reply: "Obviously I did not mean to include gambling with dice, and the proof of this is not that I consciously excluded it, but that such a 'game' did not even remotely enter my mind as a possibility; in my conscious calculations there was simply no occasion to direct my mind toward such a bizarre outcome."

Had there been a written constitution in Imperial Rome it is certainly doubtful whether the draftsmen could have anticipated that the Emperor Caligula would appoint his horse as consul or that he would circumvent a requirement that laws be publicly posted by putting his own in such fine print and hanging them so high that no one could read them.

The writing of constitutions becomes impossible unless the draftsman can assume that the legislator shares with him some implicit notions of the limits of legal decency and sanity. If the draftsman were to attempt to forestall in advance every conceivable aberration of the legislative power, his constitution would resemble a museum of freaks and monsters. It is certainly difficult to imagine such a constitution serving an educational function or offering a suitable object for a pledge of allegiance.

There is another, and in our sequence, *second*, reason why a written constitution cannot successfully control legislation entirely by principles that have themselves been previously legislated. This lies in the fact that a purported statute that seems in one context inconsistent with the very idea of law, in another context may serve the cause of legal decency. The retrospective statute is a good example.

If a law is to guide the conduct of the citizen subject to it, then it seems obvious that it must operate *prospectively*, that it must tell the citizen what he should do *after* its enactment and not what he should have done before it went into effect. To this sober common sense the draftsmen of the Constitution of New Hampshire added a note of moral indignation when they inserted in their charter of lawmaking (1784) the following language: "Retrospective laws are

---

1. [Ludwig Wittgenstein, *Philosophical Investigations*, trans. G. E. M. Anscombe (New York: Macmillan, 1953), p. 33e.]

highly injurious, oppressive, and unjust. No such laws, therefore, should be made, either for the decision of civil causes, or the punishment of offenses."

This would seem to take care of the matter and to convert into an explicit, made rule what was previously only implicit in ordinary ways of thinking about law. But trouble lay ahead for the courts charged with applying this provision. What shall we say of a situation like this: A legislature enacts a law providing that henceforth no marriage shall be valid unless the person performing the ceremony fills out a form provided by the state and returns it to a central bureau within five days of the ceremony. Shortly before the statute goes into effect, a fire destroys the state printing office, and for six months it is impossible for the state to provide the required forms. Meanwhile the legislature has adjourned and there is no lawful way of repealing the statute or postponing its effective date. Before the legislature can meet again hundreds of couples go through the marriage ceremony, and since the required forms could not be filled, their marriages are, by the relevant statute, legally invalid and any children born of their union illegitimate. When the legislature meets again its first act is to pass a statute retrospectively curing the defect in the marriages that have meanwhile taken place.

The New Hampshire Supreme Court was in fact confronted with the necessity of passing on the constitutional validity of curative measures of this sort, though to be sure in a somewhat less dramatic context than that just supposed. They faced the embarrassment of having to decide that the Constitutional provision did not, despite its categorical language, really mean what it said and that some kinds of retrospective legislation were not only not "highly injurious, oppressive, and unjust" but were innocent and beneficial.

This experience might suggest converting the perceived implicit necessity for retrospective legislation in certain situations into an explicit, made rule of constitutional law. Why not, for example, amend the provision against retrospective laws by adding the words: " . . . but this provision shall not apply to laws intended to cure defects of legal form"?

But this would never do. Suppose a citizen accused of murder is tried, convicted, and sentenced to be hanged at a trial presided over by a man who appeared to hold the office of judge, but who, as the result of some "irregularity," did not lawfully hold that position. Surely before considering a law that would retrospectively validate the purported judge's authority we would want to know more about the "irregularity" affecting his position. And to be reminded of the monstrous things that can be done in the name of curative legislation we need only make another short visit to that chamber of legal horrors, Hitler's Germany. In 1934 trouble was brewing in the Nazi party, the dissident elements apparently grouping themselves about Ernst Röhm in Munich. When Hitler got wind of this development, he and his followers made a hasty trip to Munich where they shot down Röhm and some seventy of his supporters. On his return to Berlin Hitler declared that in taking this measure he had acted as "the supreme judicial power of the German people." The fact that he had not lawfully been appointed to any such office, and that no trial had ever been held of the condemned men—these "irregularities of form" were promptly rectified by a statute retrospectively converting the shootings into lawful executions.

The example of retrospective laws illustrates how difficult it is to convert the implicit demands of legal decency into explicit constitutional limitations. It will be useful to consider briefly another example of this difficulty. It is ancient wisdom, tracing back at least as far as the Roman taboo against the *privilegium*, that laws ought to be *general*, they ought to be addressed, not to particular persons, but to persons generally or to classes of persons (say, "all householders"). Accordingly, a number of American states have inserted in their constitutions prohibitions against "private or special" statutes. These have given rise to endless difficulties.

The trouble is that the private or one-man statute, like the retrospective statute, can only be judged in its specific context. We have already given an example of an innocent and beneficial "private law," a *privilegium* that served, rather than disserved, the cause of legality. A bribed judge improperly holds a patent invalid. Seven years go by before his perfidy is discovered; the case is reheard by a reconstituted court, which declares the patent valid. This gives the injured party back his patent, but does nothing about the seven years during which he was deprived of the profits he would otherwise have obtained from it. This is an injustice the courts are powerless to correct; they have no authority to grant or extend patents; the issuing of patents rests with the Patent Office acting under an act of Congress. The cure for the situation was found in a special act of Congress extending the life of the patent for seven years. No constitutional difficulty arose, for it happens that the Constitution of the United States contains no general provision against special or private legislation, an omission which has historically, in turn, facilitated abuses that would not be possible under many state constitutions.[2]

It will be well to recall that we are now discussing the extent to which a written constitution can dispense with the necessity for resorting to what may be called implicit laws of lawmaking or limitations on governmental power resting in generally received conceptions of what is meant by a regime of order founded on law. We have pointed out, first, that it is impossible (and would probably be undesirable) for the constitutional draftsman to attempt to forestall all the more bizarre ways in which the expectations that normally accom-

2. [See Joseph Borkin, *The Corrupt Judge* (New York: Potter, 1962), pp. 23–93.]

pany exercises of governmental power may be violated; a provision requiring that the consulship be held by a human being, and not a horse, would make strange reading in any constitution. We have further observed, secondly, that certain departures from the usual practices of lawmaking, such as those involved in retrospective and special or one-man statutes, though thoroughly objectionable in most contexts, may in some cases actually serve the ends of legality and fairness.

A *third* limitation on constitutional foresight lies in the difficulty of anticipating possible situations of emergency and of foreseeing what modifications in normal practices may be required in meeting them. One of the most obvious things about a law is that it ought to be published and made available to those subject to it. A natural way of meeting this desideratum in a written constitution is to prescribe some form of publication, with a stipulation that no statute shall go into effect until, say, one week after its first publication, thus allowing time for the word to get around, as it were. This delay, beneficial under normal circumstances, may become disastrous under the conditions of a sudden national emergency. At the same time, under such conditions it may be pointless to delay the statute's effective date; with everyone watching and listening to learn what the legislature will do, news of the enactment is likely to spread very rapidly.

As is well known, some constitutions have granted to the government a power to declare the existence of a state of national emergency; during this officially declared emergency certain constitutional restraints on governmental power are suspended. The experience with such provisions has not been a happy one. Paradoxically, it may conceivably be better to rest departures from constitutional restraints on an implicit necessity, readily perceived by the overwhelming majority of citizens, rather than on an explicit grant of authority which may serve to give despotism words on paper to point to as proof of its legality.

There is a *fourth* and final reason why a written constitution cannot dispense with the need for a resort to implicit or unwritten principles of legal decency and orderly government. This lies in the simple fact that before they can be applied, the words of a constitution require to be interpreted. In our discussion so far we have been assuming that the vital task of interpretation will be taken over by the regular courts of law, as it has been in the United States. There are nations, however, with written constitutions whose interpretation is entrusted to special constitutional courts or is even left with the legislature itself, which is thus assigned the task of interpreting the limits of its own power. For our present purposes it is enough to observe that, whatever the agency charged with the task of interpretation, that task—when approached conscientiously—remains much the same and presents essentially the same problems.

We have previously pointed out how fallacious it is to suppose that in interpreting a statute the judge simply draws out of its text a meaning that the legislature has put there. In the case of a hypothetical statute prohibiting vehicles from entering a park we noted that in determining the effect of the statute the court would have to ask itself: What are parks for anyway? The answer to this question must largely be drawn from what may be called implicit sources, from the attitudes and practices of the community, and some shared conception of the most beneficial use of park areas. The considerations that make it vain to suppose that a statute can be cut loose from the developing life into which it is projected apply with a vengeance to the interpretation of constitutions.

In the United States the best illustration of this touches the central feature of the whole constitutional system, namely, the power of the courts to declare statutes unconstitutional. This all-important power is nowhere explicitly conferred on the judiciary by the words of the Constitution. At best it can be seen as an oblique implication of words primarily addressed to other subjects. The most secure foundation for the power does not, however, rest on the text of the Constitution, but lies rather in a necessity implicit in the whole frame of government brought into existence by the Constitution. This last consideration is most persuasive in those cases where, the laws of the federal Congress and those of a state legislature being in conflict, the court determines the jurisdictional boundaries that separate state and federal powers. Without this particular judicial power it is difficult to see how the American federal system could have functioned at all. The power had to be and therefore was.

Any modern governmental structure involves a complex system of interrelated and complementary powers. By some means or other these powers must be kept in jibe with one another. The obvious and tempting way to accomplish this is to bring them all under a central despotic power. This solution would mean, of course, the end of constitutionalism. On the other hand, no constitutional draftsman can foresee what points of rub and friction will develop in the future as the structure he has created feels the strain of new and novel demands. The solution must be found in an interpretation of the constitution that will respect not merely its words but the implicit ideals of orderly and decent government those words attempted to express.

Reflecting on the complexity of modern constitutions and their tragic dependence on the integrity, judgment, and insight of those who must interpret and administer them, one may almost be inclined to yearn for the simpler days of the absolute monarch. In those days what the ruler said *was* law and that was an end of it. Then was the heyday of made law, when human fiat could bring law into existence pure and undefiled by any contamination of "laws of lawmaking," whether written or unwritten. Or so it may seem from our perspective. The reality was much more complex.

We have already pointed out that Maine's last stage in the evolution of law, that of legislation, by no means came into existence overnight.[3] The first ventures into this field were tentative and fragmentary. The "absolute" monarch might be able to order a commoner to give up his wife to him, but it did not follow that he would be able, or that he would suppose he would be able, to command a fundamental revision in the general laws of marriage. Furthermore, if he felt any inclination toward broad legislation of this sort, there would be learned men and priests about him ready to tell him what he might do and not do "lawfully" in the way of lawmaking.

The most important "unmade" limitation on the monarch's lawmaking lies, however, in the fact that his reign must sooner or later come to an end. If he is lucky enough to hold the throne until his death, there must be some way of designating his successor. The principle most consonant with the theory that all true law is made law would be, of course, a rule by which the lawmaker himself had the power to name his successor. In the course of history a rule of this sort has from time to time emerged, but it has never achieved secure acceptance, since men in their full powers do not like rivals, even of their own choice, and men whose powers are waning seldom make good kingmakers, even assuming, as is improbable, that they will recognize that the time has come to designate a successor.

In actual practice, succession is commonly made to depend on some defined relationship to the departing monarch. If the relationship is simple (say, that of being the eldest son) the rule may default because the designated successor does not exist or is incompetent. If the rule is complex, covering a wide range of relationships, it can easily give rise to disputes and civil war. But, whatever the rule of succession may be, it can never be simply a *made* or enacted rule. It must rest on a perceived need for some institutional backstop against chaos, and its terms will normally be found not in enactment, but in a received tradition reinforced by a general conviction of its essential rightness.

The monarchical principle of lawmaking suffers its most serious crisis when the monarch is displaced before his death. This displacement, or the threat of it, may come about in a variety of ways. A self-appointed council of elder statesmen, acting perhaps without the support of precedent, declares the monarch incompetent; a rival to the throne discloses an apparent flaw in the title

3. [The reference is to Sir Henry Maine, *Ancient Law: Its Connection with the Early History of Society and Its Relation to Modern Ideas*, 10th ed. (London: John Murray, 1884), chapter II.]

of the occupant and claims the throne for himself; a rebellious faction seeks by armed force to oust the reigning sovereign. Historians are likely to construe such events in terms of a sheer struggle for power. But these struggles are seldom unaccompanied by claims of rightfulness; both sides will normally make some pretense to the support of implicit law. There is usually much that is specious in these claims. But the fact that such claims are made, and that action is taken in the name of them, tends, when the dust has settled, to restrain the victorious party. Having achieved its position in the name of law, it has taken on itself an obligation toward the principles of legal morality; it has, in effect, entered a tacit agreement with its subjects to make its laws with due regard to what we have here termed the implicit laws of lawmaking.

One final problem deserves brief consideration before we quit the subject of implicit elements in made law. This is the problem presented by a situation like the following. An established government is overthrown by violence; the rebellious party holds power for six months, during which time it repeals many laws of the old regime and enacts new ones in their stead; the old regime then returns to power. What laws now govern events that occurred during the six months while the rebels held the reins of government? Do we make bastards of all the children of marriages contracted under new marriage laws enacted by the intervening regime and now repealed by the returning government? If we declare these marriages legally valid, do we also uphold every confiscation of property accomplished under laws enacted by the now deposed regime?

These are perplexing problems, and they have arisen historically in a great variety of contexts. The predicament of postwar Germany in liquidating the abuses of law that occurred under Hitler serves to remind us of how agonizing these problems can be. On the other hand, the German experience may easily mislead us into thinking that it is only some monstrous distortion of ordinary moral values that can give rise to such problems. This is far from being the case.

Toward the end of World War II, as the German troops were being driven out of France, a vacuum of governmental power was left behind that had to be filled in some manner. Impromptu governments were put together by the French people. Men volunteered themselves for the office of mayor or judge, much as during some emergency an ordinary citizen might on his own initiative take over the role of traffic officer. Improvised courts were set up for trying persons charged with improper collaboration with the occupying troops. Most of what happened during this period was probably well intentioned, though of course abusive exercises of power were bound to occur. When a more orderly government was established, it faced the task of sifting through the legal debris left behind, confirming this act despite its irregularity, nullifying that act despite, perhaps, its outward respect for legal form.

During the 1840s the state of Rhode Island underwent a somewhat similar experience. In a little-remembered civil war known as Dorr's Rebellion, that tiny commonwealth for a time enjoyed the doubtful blessing of having two rival governments, each with its own written constitution and both voted into power, though at different times and by differently qualified electorates. When the dispute was finally resolved, the legal entanglements left behind were like those that follow any period during which it is not possible to say clearly who has the authority to make law and who does not. The fact that in Rhode Island little blood was shed, and that no really deep-dyed villains appeared on either side, hardly made those problems simpler.

Reflection on historical incidents like these, falling as they do outside the ordinary range of human experience, can impart important lessons about law. There are at least three: (1) Normal processes for making law can fail, or fall into confusion, from a variety of causes; human perfidy is only one of these. (2) In leading a society back to a condition where legality is a realizable ideal, no guidance can be obtained from a philosophy which asserts that the only true law is made law; this philosophy is a luxury to be enjoyed after the return trip is over. (3) The legal measures necessary to accomplish this return will of necessity include some that would be thoroughly reprehensible under normal conditions. The most indispensable of these measures is the retrospective statute, condemned by the New Hampshire constitution as "injurious, oppressive, and unjust." To paraphrase Walter Bagehot, we may say that the bottom steps of the ladder leading back to legality are very steep.[4]

4. [See Walter Bagehot, *Physics and Politics* (Boston: Beacon Press, 1956), p. 106.]

The Role of Contract in the Ordering Processes of Society Generally

Editor's Note

Fuller is best remembered by his former students as a teacher of contract law. Although he taught a great range of subjects within the law school curriculum at one time or another during his career, contracts became his principal area of expertise. Two articles of his made a permanent contribution to the development and understanding of the field: "The Reliance Interest in Contract Damages" (1936–37, coauthored with his student at Duke University Law School, William R. Perdue, Jr.) and "Consideration and Form" (1941). The success of his casebook, Basic Contract Law *(1947; 2d edition with Robert Braucher, 1964; 3d edition with Melvin Eisenberg, 1972), helped to carry his influence to classrooms other than his own.*

Fuller considered his approach to contract law as "something akin to [the method of] 'natural law.'" It was a form of internal criticism, identifying the underlying policies or rationale of the contractual process and then employing them as standards to assess the contribution of particular judicial decisions and legislative enactments. In "Consideration and Form," for example, he described three functions served by the formalities that produce binding contracts: the evidentiary function (attesting to the existence and purport of a contract), the cautionary function (deterring unreflective action), and the channeling function (facilitating the execution of a plan of action and making it socially effective). Judicial treatment of breaches of contract which fail to enhance these functions become suspect to that degree.

In addition, Fuller described several "substantive" bases of contractual liability, the most important of which are reliance and individual autonomy. To introduce reliance as a basis of liability is to recognize that the breach of a promise may work an injury to a party who has changed position in the expectation that the promise will be fulfilled. (This is distinct of course from appealing to reliance as a measure of a promisee's recovery.) The principle of autonomy, on the other hand, focuses attention on the fact that contracting parties, within limits, set the law of their relationship. Fuller's preoccupation with contract law was in large part, I think, an expression of his concern with the conditions of individual freedom. Thus he noted: "The problem generally discussed in this country under the heading 'freedom of contract' is the problem of the limits on private autonomy." This perspective made him especially sensitive to heteronomous elements in contractual relations, such as result from a gross inequality of bargaining power between parties or from judicially-declared rules that specify obligations attaching to statuses (for example, master and servant) independently of the wishes of the parties.

In the present essay, Fuller is concerned more with sketching the social contexts in which contract is an apt, or conversely an inept, form of ordering. He also describes more or less systematically the relation of contract to other forms (or "principles" as he calls them here). The enumeration of forms of ordering which he offers is the longest and the last to occur in any of his writings. "The Role of Contract" was written specially for the third edition of Basic Contract Law *and is reprinted with permission of West Publishing Co.*

The present chapter may be said to represent an excursion into the sociology of contract. It asks what specific functions contract performs in the ordering of human relations generally. It is a commonplace of anthropology that explicit contractual arrangements are a rarity among primitive peoples. What do such peoples miss by not employing the contractual form in regulating their relations with one another? Or, one may also ask, what do they gain by not imposing this particular kind of harness on themselves? Again, though in modern society contract serves a pervasive and important ordering function, it is plain that there are many relationships that do not lend themselves to regulation by contract. What are those relationships? Why is contract an inept device for putting them in order?

I

In attempting some answer to questions of this sort we shall begin by listing nine distinct principles of social order. The sequence in which these nine principles are listed does not pretend to any logical neatness and certainly does not purport to reflect, item by item, the historical order of their emergence in human affairs. The primary purpose in listing these principles is the practical one of facilitating a comparison of their respective capacities and limitations, with, of course, special reference to the principle of contract.

Nine principles of social ordering

1. The coordination of expectations and actions that arises tacitly out of interaction; illustrated in "customary law" and "standard practice"
2. Contract
3. Property
4. Officially declared law
5. Adjudication
6. Managerial direction
7. Voting

8. Mediation
9. Deliberate resort to chance; "tossing for it"

The list just offered leaves out many nuances and combinational forms. It does not mention, for example, the principle of kinship or the influence of the charismatic leader; these may perhaps be subsumed under other headings, such as legislation, managerial direction, and adjudication—all operating, in some measure, within the framework of customary law. Again, money is not listed, but it may be regarded as a particularly flexible kind of property. Historically "bread and circuses" have provided an expedient for stilling discontent but can hardly be regarded as providing an affirmative ordering principle. Finally, any concentration on order as an overriding desideratum may obscure the function of conflict in articulating and bringing into the open discords that may then be compromised or reconciled.

The last of the nine listed principles of order—"deliberate resort to chance"—may seem too trivial a device to deserve a place in an analysis devoted to the basic ordering principles by which a society is enabled to function. We should remember, however, that this device is used to select those who must risk their lives in military service as well as those who, as jurors, must decide the fate of others. According to the Scripture, land was divided among the tribes of Israel by lot. (It should be observed that the word *allot* contains itself a tacit reminder of this use of chance as an ordering principle.) The significance of the lot in social processes is certainly not underesteemed in the following passage from Proverbs (18:18): The lot causeth contentions to cease,/and parteth between the mighty.

The practice of deciding important issues by a resort to chance is not only of some importance itself, but it serves also to illustrate how the various principles of order may be interrelated and combined. The use of the lot in particular situations may be prescribed by tradition (that is, by customary law), by legislative enactment, or by a contract of the affected parties. It may also appear as an adjunct to managerial direction, as where a military commander might employ it to decide which squad should undertake a particularly dangerous mission. (It will be noted that "managerial direction" as used here carries a very broad connotation. It extends the concept of management beyond the usual context of economic activity to include, say, a direction and coordination of efforts to achieve military or therapeutic ends. Managerial direction understood in this sense cannot, for obvious reasons, proceed by laying down the relatively stable rules of duty and entitlement characteristic of a legal system.)

Returning to the social uses made of a deliberate resort to chance, it should be observed that though the lot has been found appropriate to quite diverse situations this does not mean that it offers an all-purpose device ready to solve any kind of problem. Its use to choose the judge who will resolve a particular controversy may be quite acceptable and is not unknown in practice; for the judge himself to decide the case by a throw of the dice represents an absurdity of a magnitude sufficient to insure an enduring place in literary history for Rabelais' Judge Bridlegoose, who not only employed but extolled the virtues of this expedient.

II

In discussions of ordering processes a distinction is often taken between order imposed from above and order achieved through reciprocal adjustments on a horizontal plane. On this basis officially declared law and managerial direction would seem to represent a vertical ordering, while contract and customary law would appear as obvious illustrations of a horizontal ordering. There are, however, difficulties with this distinction, difficulties that derive from the inherent complexity of the social processes involved. Thus, if we take officially declared law as the archetypal expression of rules imposed from above, complications appear so soon as we examine the legislative process itself. In a democracy many horizontal adjustments of opposing interests take place in the course of drafting and enacting laws. Even the lawmaking of a dictator commonly undergoes some accommodation to demands tacitly expressed in rumbling discontents. These are, of course, trite observations. What is not so evident is that there enters a certain contractual element into any ordering of human relations by declared and published rules. If the lawgiver wants his subjects to accept and act by his rules, he must himself display some minimum respect for those rules in his actions toward his subjects, say, in distributing awards and imposing punishments. This means that the publication of a code of legal rules carries with it a tacit commitment by government to abide by those rules in judging the citizen. If this commitment is grossly disregarded a regime of "officially declared law" will not be achieved, though society may continue after a fashion to function by other principles.

If there is, then, commonly a horizontal element in systems that appear to represent order vertically imposed, the reverse is equally true, that is, the forms of ordering which are thought of as reflecting a horizontal accommodation may in fact be shaped by a downward thrust of control that is all the more powerful for its tacit mode of operation. Thus, a written contract between *A* and *B*, though taking the verbal form of a reciprocal adjustment of their respective interests, may have been in fact wholly drafted by *A* and imposed by him on *B*.

This phenomenon is commonly analyzed in terms of an "inequality of bargaining power." But this is a loose way of putting the issue. A noted actor, enjoying a sensational public acclaim, may possess great "bargaining power" in negotiating with a theatrical producer; the actor may be, as we say, almost in a position to write his own contract. But this bargaining advantage derives from the fact that the actor has attained something (lawfully we are supposing) that his producer wants badly; the actor's bargaining power is as much a function of the producer's needs as it is of the actor's special capacity to satisfy those needs. And the advantage enjoyed by the actor still leaves room for bargaining; at some point his demands may reach a point where the producer will bid him goodbye.

Henningsen v. *Bloomfield Motors, Inc.*,[1] presents a quite different situation. It appeared in that case that the National Automobile Manufacturers Association employed a standard purchase order to be signed by the buyer of any automobile made by its members; this order stated in effect that the dealer selling the car should not be liable for any physical injuries suffered by the purchaser in driving the car, even though the accident causing the injuries was due to a defect in the car. The court held that the purchaser was not bound by this disclaimer of the dealer's liability. The court observed that, though it could be said that there was in such a situation a disparity in bargaining power, the fact was that the purchaser was really "not permitted to bargain at all." By a kind of legislative fiat of the Automobile Manufacturers Association a contract was imposed that excluded any claim for personal injuries.

III

In the fragmentary analysis just concluded enough has been said to suggest the pervasive nature of the problem of distinguishing between, on the one hand, imposed order and, on the other, order that is, broadly speaking, "contractual" in nature. The complexities and ambiguities presented by this distinction pervade every branch of thought affecting our conception of society and social order. In confronting perplexities of this sort there is a natural tendency for the mind to seek out simplistic formulas that will shape our language, and with it our thought, in ways offering some reassurance that things

---

1. *Henningsen* v. *Bloomfield Motors, Inc.*, 32 N.J. 358, 161 A. 2d 69 (1960).

are not, after all, utterly chaotic or so complicated as to be inaccessible to analysis.

Perhaps the most famous of these formulas of reassurance is that represented by the theory of an original Social Compact, which reached the height of its influence during the seventeenth and eighteenth centuries. There has always been some obscurity as to whether this notion assigning a contractual origin to all government was intended as a description of historical fact or as the expression of a political ideal. The temper of modern thought is apt to regard this theory as false if presented as an historical fact, though perhaps suggestive if proposed as a model.

What of present-day theory? In our efforts to analyze the forms of social ordering do we see things clearly as they are without distorting fictions and prejudgments? There is serious reason to doubt that our thinking has achieved quite this degree of liberation from the shackles of language and tacit presupposition. Today, it may be suggested, there runs through legal thinking an assumption that all social ordering is, directly or indirectly, imposed from above. Thus, though contract and property rights serve to organize the relations of citizens to one another, they are thought of as doing this solely because they are recognized and enforced by "law," that is, by state-made rules imposed from above. Probably no one has had more influence on our modern ways of thinking about law than Jeremy Bentham. He declared: "Property and law are born and must die together. Before the laws there was no property: take away the laws, all property ceases. . . . No bargain is void in itself—no bargain is valid of itself: it is the law which in each case gives or refuses validity." [2]

Certainly it is clear that contracts and property were in some measure functioning social institutions before state-made laws existed or were even conceived of. Today many human relations are effectively organized by contracts that neither party would dream of taking to court; as for property, even wild animals often display some sense of respecting the other fellow's territory. Yet Bentham's assertion that contract and property rights exist because, and to the extent that, the law of the state enforces and protects them reflects a general predisposition of thought which is today shared by lawyers and laymen alike.

There is in this connection an interesting quirk of linguistic usage as it affects contract. When we speak of "the law of contracts" we mean the law *about* contracts not the "law" contained *in* a contract; indeed any suggestion that a contract could of itself create "law" would seem bizarre indeed. Yet what shall we say of Article 1134 of the French Civil Code declaring that a

2. Jeremy Bentham, *Works*, ed. John Bowring (Edinburgh: W. Tait, 1859), vol. 1, pp. 309 and 333.

contract "serves as law" between the parties? ("Les conventions légalment formées tiennent lieu de loi à ceux qui les ont faites.") If the form of expression seems odd it remains perfectly clear that legal rights and duties, enforceable through judicial procedures, may derive from the words of a contract just as they may from the provisions of a statute.

International law is another source of embarrassment to the conception that all law is imposed from above. The "law of nations" is a law deriving primarily from contractual arrangements called treaties and the tacit adjustments that give rise to customary law. Curiously enough this departure from the conception of law as something imposed from above seems to have little influence on the usages associated with ordinary law, that is, state-made law. Here the assumption that all law in the strict sense is imposed from above remains largely intact.

It may be objected at this point that nothing of consequence hinges on the way we *talk* about law or contracts; the question is not what we *say* but what we *do*. That contracts which are unenforceable through court action can nevertheless serve as sources of social order may be interesting as a kind of sociological aside, but it has no significant bearing on the law of contracts; that law is made by legislatures and courts.

But to accept this view is to underestimate the influence of language in shaping our general approach to legal questions. The judge who keeps firmly in mind that the principle of contract can, without his aid, serve as a source of social ordering will approach his task in a spirit different from that of the judge who tends to suppose that the influence of contract in human affairs derives entirely from the state-made law of which he is the official custodian and expositor. The first judge will see himself as one whose task it is to facilitate a form of ordering that could function, in some measure, without his intervention; he will accordingly seek to understand the special role that contract plays in the ordering processes of society and will strive to shape his decisions by the perception thus obtained.

IV

It will be well at this point to attempt a somewhat systematic analysis of the ways in which the principle of contract is related to the other "principles of social order."

With the first of the listed principles—that of *customary law*—the difficulty is not in discerning some relation between it and contract, but in drawing a

clear distinction between the two. Customary law may, indeed, be described as
the inarticulate older brother of contract. We may describe customary law in
general terms as consisting of the reciprocal expectations that arise out of
human interaction. It is illustrated when A and B, as the result of past encounters, begin to shape their conduct toward each other by patterns perceived as
emerging from their past interactions. As with language, these patterns will
tend to "jell" and to spread from one context to another. Customary law may,
indeed, be aptly described as a *language of interaction.*

In many situations it may be difficult to distinguish between contractual
obligations and those imposed by customary law. This is particularly true in
the area of commercial transactions where repetitive dealings tend to create
standardized expectations. Thus, if problems arise which are left without verbal solution in the parties' contract these will commonly be resolved by asking
what "standard practice" is with respect to the issues in question. In such a
case it is difficult to know whether to say that by entering a particular field of
practice the parties became subject to a governing body of customary law or
to say that they have by tacit agreement incorporated standard practice into
the terms of their contract.[3]

The meaning of a contract may not only be determined by the area of practice within which the contract falls but by the interactions of the parties themselves after entering their agreement. If the performance of a contract takes
place over a period of time, the parties will often evidence by their conduct
what courts sometimes call a practical construction of their agreement. The
interpretation of the contract reflected in the parties' acts may control over the
meaning that would ordinarily be attributed to the words of the contract itself.
The meaning thus attributed to the contract is, obviously, generated through
processes that are essentially those that give rise to customary law.

On a more radical level the courts may imply a contract entirely from the
conduct of the parties; though no verbal exchange has taken place the parties
may have conducted themselves toward one another in such a way that one
can say that a tacit exchange of promises has taken place.[4] Here the analogy
between contract and customary law approaches identity; indeed, the only
reason for hesitancy about applying the second term derives from a customary
law of language itself, namely, that it is not a common linguistic practice to
speak of "law" as governing a two-party relationship even though a statute,
coming from "above," would hardly be denied the designation *law* simply
because it happened to regulate the relations of two state officials toward one
another.

3. See the items reprinted in Lon L. Fuller and Melvin Aron Eisenberg, *Basic Contract Law*,
3d ed. (St. Paul, Minn.: West Publishing Co., 1972), pp. 277–80.
   4. See the cases reprinted, ibid., pp. 389–94.

The prevailing tendency to regard all social order as imposed from above has led to a general neglect of the phenomenon of customary law in modern legal scholarship. Outside the field of international law and that of commercial dealings legal theorists have been uncomfortable about the use of the word *law* to describe the obligatory force of expectations that arise tacitly out of human interaction. The most common escape from this dilemma is to downgrade the significance of customary law and to assert that it has largely lost the significance it once had for human affairs. Another and more radical way out was that taken by Austin and followed explicitly or tacitly by many writers since his time.[5] This is to assert that what is called customary law becomes truly law only after it has been adopted by a court as a standard of decision and thus received the imprimatur of the state. This linguistic expedient, it should be noted, would deny the designation *law* to a custom so firmly rooted and so plainly just and useful that no one would waste his time taking it to court to be tested for its right to be called law.

The fact is that the operation of a system of state-made law is itself permeated with internal customary practices that enable it to function effectively by facilitating a collaboration among its constituent elements. Thus, for example, the drafting and enactment of a statute is a task assigned to the legislature; its interpretation is left to the judiciary. Plainly these two functions must be coordinated by reciprocal expectations displaying some stability. In achieving their goal, the legislative draftsmen have to ask themselves, "What will the court make of our statute? What standards of interpretation will they apply to our literary creation?" If the courts of the state have generally displayed a decided inclination toward "literalness" in the interpretation of laws, the legislative draftsmen will take this "standard practice" into account in phrasing their statute. On the other hand, if the courts have displayed a tendency toward a broadly purposive interpretation, a quite differently phrased statute, and, perhaps, a much shorter one, will result from the efforts of the drafting committee. The effective functioning of the total law-making and law-applying process depends, then, upon a kind of customary law that lies behind enacted law and enables it to achieve its goals effectively. And plainly this customary law contains a strong consensual element, something like a tacit "meeting of minds."

Turning now to the ordering principle of *property*, it is apparent that there is a close affinity of function between it and contract. Much of what is normally conceived of as property in fact consists essentially of contract claims— e.g., bank accounts, insurance policies, bonds, and, for most practical pur-

5. John Austin, *Lectures on Jurisprudence*, 4th ed. (London: John Murray, 1879), vol. 1, p. 105.

poses, corporate stock. On another level, where a man has property that can be assigned to another, he is in a position to commit himself by contract to make this assignment. Conversely, where a man can contract to give something to another, this means that he has command over a value that can in a broad sense be called property, though, to be sure, a contract for the rendition of personal services stretches this usage to the point of metaphor (e.g., outfielder *A* is the property of baseball club *X*).

Of *adjudication* it has often been asserted that its historical origins lie in consensual arrangements; two parties, being in dispute and wishing to avoid open warfare, agree on a third person to settle their controversy. This, it is said, is how adjudication got its start as a principle of social ordering. Certainly there is ample evidence that this voluntarily accepted mode of settlement was often adopted in putting an end to the "blood feud" between families. Whether, however, it can be asserted that in all societies adjudication had its origin in contract is not clearly established.

Certain it is that adjudicative procedures today are often established by agreement of the litigating parties. The most familiar example is to be found in the common practice of submitting commercial and labor disputes to arbitration, both the selection of the arbitrator and the rules by which he is to proceed often being determined by an agreement between the parties to the dispute. Today with our crowded court dockets, the trial of cases is often speeded by stipulations of counsel dispensing with the formal proof of relevant facts and generally simplifying the procedures of trial in the interest of a speedy decision. Even in the criminal law it is notorious that most convictions are the result of "plea bargaining."

It should also be observed that much of the law of procedure remains uncodified and derives from a tacit adjustment of expectations of the sort that create customary law. For example, in the trial of an ordinary law suit (say, for breach of contract) a private conversation concerning the case between the judge and one of the litigants out of the presence of the other would involve a gross violation of the tacit expectations that surround the whole judicial process. Yet, curiously, though there are long chapters of complicated rules concerning procedure, an explicit prohibition of this practice is generally not to be found among them; it is so patently violative of the judicial proprieties that no one has thought to spell it out and put it down in the books.

Turning now to *managerial direction*, it will be well to begin by setting aside for the moment the managerial functions of government in order to direct our attention to private contracts of employment. In entering such a contract the employee will normally in some measure subject himself to the lawful orders of his employer. Suppose he is directed to perform some task and it turns out that his skills are insufficient to enable him to perform it satisfactorily. Though his services have been engaged for a year he is discharged forthwith or assigned to a different task carrying a lower salary. If the employee sues for damages, the question will be stated formally in terms of an interpretation of his contract. What level of skill did the contract explicitly or implicitly stipulate as being reasonably expected of the employee? Here contract serves as the principle for defining the limits of managerial direction.

In turning to the managerial functions of government we are not concerned with its position as an employer (which would not be radically different from that of a private employer) but chiefly with its function in distributing scarce resources—for example, in allocating television channels, air routes, welfare funds, irrigation waters, etc. In this broad area there is a constant struggle between those who want to keep these functions free from the restraints of fixed legal rules and those who want to "judicialize" and "legalize" them.

There is a close affinity between this issue and that we have previously discussed concerning the commitment implied in enacting and publishing rules of law. We suggested that the lawgiver is properly regarded as promising to judge the citizen's actions by rules he has announced in advance as governing those actions. In the case of allocative functions, the citizen subject to them tends to read into the actions of government tacit rules of law; he wants to receive what is assigned to him as of right and not as a matter of grace. So it may come about that the disadvantaged applicant will feel that government has cheated on its own rules while the allocative agency will conceive of itself as discharging a function that simply cannot be rule-bound but requires a broad discretion to meet shifting contingencies and changed conditions.

At first glance the ordering principle of *voting* seems to offer no entry for the principle of contract. One cannot hold a meaningful election without at least three voters; a contract ordinarily involves only two parties. Yet there is a kind of consensual arrangement that can be said to involve a two-man voting system. Suppose that at the outset of a law suit the judge proposes to counsel an expedient that will speed the trial by dispensing with some of the usual procedural steps. The judge asks the parties if they will agree to it; if either objects, he will follow the book, if both consent the short cut will be adopted. Though we might hesitate here to speak of a contract or a bargain, there is certainly a consensual arrangement or agreement with significant operative effect. This phenomenon is worthy of mention because we tend to identify contract with the notion of a trade or exchange, and it is well to remember that there are consensual arrangements from which the element of "trade-off" is absent.

That there is a close connection between *mediation* and the ordering principle of contract certainly requires no demonstration here. One of the most common tasks of the mediator is to facilitate the negotiation of complicated contracts, though it should be observed that his services are also sometimes employed in reaching an agreement to rescind a contract.

With respect to the relations between *the lot* and the principle of contract it is obvious that a resort to chance may result from a contract; finding no better way to solve their differences the parties may agree "to toss for it."

The discussion just concluded was primarily concerned with the interrelations between the principle of contract and the various other forms of social ordering. In the course of this exposition it should have become clear that the function of the lawyer is not simply that of telling laymen "what the law is." The lawyer is constantly engaged in fitting into some workable design the relations of men to one another. His task as a social architect can demand creative imagination of a high order.

There is in the books a relatively ancient illustration of the role ingenuity can play in solving problems of interpersonal relations. A father dies, leaving all his property to two sons "in equal shares." The estate consists of a miscellany of items: furniture, valuable paintings, a cellar of alcoholic beverages, three horses, shares of stock in an adventurous mining company, etc. How shall the division "in equal shares" be accomplished? The classic solution is as follows: Let the older son divide the property into two parts, let the younger son take his pick. (Would it be better to draw lots to see who should make the division?)

V

So far we have been chiefly concerned with contract as a principle supplementing and interacting in various ways with other principles of social ordering. It is time now to attempt a general appraisal of contract itself; to examine what it can and cannot do, to inquire for what tasks it is a suited instrument and when its employment may do more harm than good.

Let us begin by supposing the following case. Two neighboring farmers share a dirt road—a private way not maintained by public authority—which provides the only access to their farms. During a heavy rainstorm a large stone rolls down a hillside and completely blocks the road. Neither farmer would be capable of removing the stone without the help of his neighbor. The two farmers meet, discuss their predicament, provide themselves with crowbars, and join forces to remove the obstructing boulder.

Now it is hard to imagine that in this situation, before undertaking the removal, either farmer would propose to the other anything like a contractual commitment. It is extremely unlikely that one would say to the other, "I propose a deal. If you will promise to work hard with your crowbar, I will work hard with mine." If any such proposal were advanced the most charitable interpretation its addressee could make of it would be that it was intended as a rather sick joke.

Notwithstanding the seeming triviality of this illustration it will be useful to analyze with some care just why in such a situation the parties would be unlikely to think of expressing their relationship in contractual terms. First, the parties have no need of a contract. The self-interest of each, combined with the inescapable necessity for their collaboration, provides a motivation for joint action that no contract could augment. Second, if a contract were seriously insisted on by one of the farmers as a condition precedent to his lending his hand to the effort, it would imply a distrust damaging to the relationship that must obtain between close neighbors. Third, if a contract were in fact drawn up and written down it would be largely lacking in any significant prescriptive or directive function. It would be hard to imagine a law suit in which the plaintiff alleged simply that "the defendant didn't try hard enough." If one of the farmers, after signing the agreement, defaulted altogether and failed to make any appearance at the appointed time, one might imagine a successful law suit against him, though in such a case the disapproval of his neighbors would scarcely be any different from what it would have been had he refused from the outset to have anything to do with the job of removal. Once the two farmers had begun the joint task of removing the boulder any outside judgment of the parties' respective performances would be rendered difficult by the intensely collaborative nature of the task; each farmer would have to adjust his efforts in such a way as to reinforce and supplement the efforts of the other. Indeed, it is possible that the best contribution one farmer might make would be to stand off at some distance, where he could obtain an overview of the operation, and direct his perhaps more muscular neighbor how and where to apply his efforts with the crowbar.

Let us assume that the two farmers will be sensible enough to see that they need no contract covering their joint efforts to remove the stone and ask how this particular cooperative endeavor might fit into the larger configuration of their relations over a period of time. It is almost certain that there would be other occasions for joining forces, as, for example, in the routine upkeep of their shared roadway. Again, each might look after the other's property while the other was away on a trip; in the event of an emergency, like getting a crop in on time, a helping hand would be forthcoming from the neighbor. At the end of the year, there might be a rather even balance between these voluntary contributions. If there was a serious imbalance an effort would probably be made by the advantaged party to correct it by some gratuitous offering. At no time would there be likely to enter into their relations any contractual commitment or any explicit exchange of one performance against another, though no doubt tacit expectations would develop that would carry with them a certain sense of obligation.

Early in this chapter the statement was made that it is a commonplace of anthropology that explicit contractual arrangements are a rarity among primitive peoples. The situation just discussed suggests why this should be so. Where the basic physical necessities of life—food, shelter, weapons, some covering for the body—are all produced through the cooperative efforts of the extended family, human beings will generally find themselves in the situation of our two farmers. The members of a small, self-sufficient group are all parts, one of another; all are bound together by a complex network of reciprocal renditions and expectations. In such a human situation any attempt at an explicit verbalized definition of each party's expected performance, and the price to be paid him for it, would certainly not produce order and might produce chaos. The ineptitude of contract as an organizing principle in this type of case becomes especially clear when we take into account the shifting contingencies affecting such a group: storms, droughts, sudden attacks by enemy tribes, and the like. No contractual foresight would be equal to providing in advance what should be done in these emergencies or prescribing how the contribution of each member of the group should be fitted in with that of others, though again accustomed roles and expectations generated by past actions would serve some directive and coordinative purpose.

In discussing social contexts in which contract is likely to be an inept ordering principle we have so far been considering situations radically removed from the usual commercial relationship in which contract plays its accustomed and often indispensable role. It should be observed, however, that even between business firms intent on maximizing their individual profits a relationship of heavy and complex interdependence can develop that may impair the utility of contract as an instrument for defining their rights and duties toward each other. Suppose, for example, that A is the manufacturer of a piece of electronic equipment; B makes a component part essential to the functioning of the device made by A. The field is one of rapid technological advance; an unanticipated improvement in the design of A's machine may require on short notice a redesign of the component part made by B. Conversely a significant improvement in the component part may require a redesign of the equipment made by A and at the same time greatly enhance its sales appeal. It may be impossible to foresee in advance whether and when such technological improvements will be made. Plainly there is here some difficulty in drafting a contract that will specify delivery dates, design specifications, and prices by standards that will remain constant over a set period of time. Nor would it be easy to specify in advance by what standards changes in the contract should be made when a sudden improvement in design becomes necessary to keep ahead of competition. Here fidelity to explicit contractual commitments must be tempered by a sense of reciprocal dependence and a willingness to meet unexpected developments in a spirit of cooperation.

It is worthy of observation that all contracts, and indeed all rules of law, presuppose some stability in external conditions. This is true even of property rights. Suppose, for example, that X and Y own separate farms on either side of a river; X's thirty-acre tract is described in his deed as bounded on the east by the river, while the river marks the west boundary of Y's ten-acre holding. Suddenly, as the result of a seismic disturbance, the river shifts its course, removing ten acres from X's land and adding five to Y's. Who now owns what?

The law of contracts is similarly dependent for its integrity upon some stability of external conditions. Suppose, for example, A agrees to sell Blackacre to B for $10,000, delivery of the deed to take place one year from the time of the signing of the contract. Before the time for performance arrives a drastic monetary inflation has taken place, so that the purchasing power of the dollar is a fraction of what it was when the contract was entered. Does B get Blackacre for ten thousand greatly depreciated dollars? If not, how much should he be required to pay, and, if the inflation continues, as of what date shall the reevaluation be made? In situations like this the courts have had to rewrite contracts against a shifting economic situation offering little that could serve as a secure baseline for even-handed justice.[6]

A famous historical instance of the wholesale rewriting of contracts occurred as a result of the Great Fire of London in 1666, a fire which consumed in three days more than thirteen thousand buildings. Many of the buildings were occupied by tenants and the practice of the time was to provide in the lease that the tenant was bound to repair any damage suffered by the property during his occupancy. (This may seem a harsh provision, but it should be recalled that this was before the institution of fire insurance, which indeed took its origins in the lessons of the London Fire.) With the wholesale destruction that occurred and with normal business suspended indefinitely, it was essential to make some adjustment in the leases. A special Fire Court was instituted, its judges being drawn from the ordinary common law courts. Proceeding partly by mediation, with a reserved power of imposing a decision if mediative efforts failed, the judges of the Fire Court in effect rewrote hundreds of leases. In some cases, where the lease had only a short time to run, the lessee was ex-

---

6. See, for example, John P. Dawson, "Effects of Inflation on Private Contracts: Germany, 1914–1924," *Michigan Law Review* 33, no. 2 (1935): 171–238; and John P. Dawson and Frank E. Cooper, "The Effect of Inflation on Private Contracts: United States, 1861–1879," *Michigan Law Review* 33, no. 5 (1935): 706–57.

cused from the rent in return for a surrender of the premises to the landlord. In other cases, adjustments were made whereby the landlord and tenant would share in varying proportions the cost of rebuilding. Some very "unlegal" considerations were often drawn into account; for example, if during the fire a tenant showed great bravery and selflessness in helping his neighbors fight the fire threatening their homes, this service "beyond the call of duty" was thought to entitle him to special consideration in the apportionment of the loss between him and his landlord.[7]

VI

So much for the limitations that affect the institution of contract and that may, in special circumstances, impair its efficacy as an ordering principle. It is time now to turn to the opposite side of the coin and to explore the special contribution contract can make to human relations—benefits it can confer that are not to be derived, or are not to be derived so readily, from other principles of social ordering.

The special virtue of contract lies in its capacity to increase human satisfactions through an exchange, as where A has something B wants, B has something A wants, and an exchange will increase the satisfactions of both A and B; in Bentham's quaint language, "the sum of enjoyment . . . is augmented by the transaction." Bentham continues:

> If there be an exchange, there are two alienations, each of which has its separate advantages. This advantage for each of the contracting parties is the difference between the value which they put upon what they give up, and the value of what they acquire. In each transaction of this kind, there are two new masses of enjoyment. In this consists the advantage of commerce.[8]

Bentham's statement suggests a trade or exchange of commodities. But the reciprocal and separate gains that can result from a carefully negotiated contract are by no means confined to physical objects.[9] . . . As illustrating [this] point we may mention the negotiation of a collective bargaining agreement between an employer and a labor union. We are apt to suppose that the central

7. See Philip E. Jones, ed., *The Fire Court* (London: W. Clowes, 1966), vol. 1.
8. Bentham, *Works*, vol. 1, p. 331.
9. [A long quotation from Chester Barnard has been deleted here. It is repeated in "Mediation—Its Forms and Functions," p. 136 of this volume.]

issue under discussion would be wage rates, but this is not necessarily so. The issue most ardently pressed by the union may be a demand for a change in seniority provisions, while the company may demand a rephrasing of the clause on management prerogatives. Issues of this sort are not unrelated to monetary costs and benefits, but the relationship may be quite indirect. That the issues are not directly convertible into monetary terms does not mean, however, that the final result of the negotiations will not involve some element of trade-off. The company may accept a rewriting of Article V in return for the union's consent to a rephrasing of Article XII. Both parties may feel that they have gained from this "trade" though each would have been happier if he could have achieved this gain without having to accept language he would be glad to see stricken from the agreement.

It is apparent from what has just been said that the creation of a complex contractual relationship through explicit negotiations requires a certain attitude of mind and spirit on the part of the participants; they must share a common conception of the nature of the game they are playing. Each must seek to understand why the other makes the demands he does even as he strives to resist or qualify those demands. Each must accept the other's right to work for a solution that will best serve his own interests.

Explicit bargaining involves, then, an uneasy blend of collaboration and resistance. This explains why it does not fit readily into either extreme of the spectrum of human relationships running from intimacy to open hostility. Within the close-knit family, demands for a contractual spelling out of obligations will seem to imply an inappropriate distrust. Between parties openly hostile to one another, the element of cooperation essential for effective bargaining will be absent. Curiously enough, at the two extremes of the spectrum where men cannot bargain with words, they can often half-bargain with deeds; tacit understandings arising out of reciprocally oriented actions will take the place of verbalized commitments. This is true within the close-knit tribal community; it is also often true of the relations between hostile tribes, where tacit restraints on hostility, or on specific ways of expressing hostility, are common. (It should be observed that today much of the customary law of international relations has the same quality.)

So far we have been emphasizing the influence of "the social context" on the aptness of explicit contract as a principle of social ordering. But personal inclinations and dispositions, the "life style" or *Weltanschauung* of the individual, may also play a role. There are those who love to bargain and take pride in the skill and insight they bring to the enterprise; there are those who find the whole process distasteful.

One strategically located personal inclination of this sort has had profound influence on human history. Karl Marx expressed in his writings a deep aversion for relations of explicit exchange. This aversion found its most eloquent expression in the youthful "alienation theme." In 1843 Marx wrote of a man as leading a double life; "a life in the *political community* in which he recognizes himself as a *communal being*, and a life in bourgeois society [that is, in a trading society] where he acts as a private person, who regards others as means, reduces himself to the level of a means and becomes the plaything of alien forces." [10]

Explicit defenses of the contractual principle are not common, no doubt because it is generally accepted as an inevitable ingredient in a functioning economy. Perhaps the circumstance that he began his career as a Unitarian minister explains why the famous economist, Philip Wicksteed, felt the need to offer some defense of the principle of exchange as expressed in explicit contractual arrangements:

> . . . over the whole range of exchangeable things we can usually act more potently by the indirect method of pursuing or furthering the immediate purposes of others than by the direct method of pursuing our own. . . . We enter into business relations with others, not because our purposes are self-ish, but because those with whom we deal are relatively indifferent to them, but are (like us) keenly interested in purposes of their own, to which we in our turn are relatively indifferent. . . . There is surely nothing degrading or revolting to our higher sense in this fact of our mutually furthering each other's purposes because we are interested in our own. . . . The economic nexus [that is, the nexus of exchange] indefinitely expands our freedom of combination and movement; for it enables us to form one set of groups linked by community of purpose, without having to find the "double coincidence" which would otherwise be necessary. [11]

VII

In closing this account it may be well to return briefly to mediation and its role in assisting contracting parties to reach a satisfactory and viable agreement. Some of the contributions a mediator can make to the negotiations are fairly obvious. The mere presence of a third person may tend to put the parties

10. See Robert Tucker, *Philosophy and Myth in Karl Marx* (Cambridge, U.K.: Cambridge University Press, 1961), p. 105. [Fuller has altered the translation somewhat.]

11. Philip H. Wicksteed, *The Common Sense of Political Economy*, ed. Lionel Robbins (London: Routledge and Kegan Paul, 1933), vol. 1, pp. 156, 179–80.

on their good behavior and generate in them a desire to take positions that will seem fair to an impartial observer. If the mediator is a person with creative imagination, who can draw on a considerable experience in contractual negotiations, he may be able to offer expedients that will resolve differences which on the surface seem intractable to solution.

The mediator's most fundamental and often indispensable function relates, however, to the basic principle that makes possible what have here been called the gains of reciprocity—the principle that enables both parties to profit from an agreement because each gives up what he values less in exchange for what he values more.[12]

. . . .

12. [Two concluding paragraphs dealing with mediation have been deleted. In the interest of clarity, it may be worth repeating that, in this chapter, Fuller refers to as *principles* of social order what he elsewhere calls *forms* of social order. If one were to render Fuller's usage more consistent than it is, *principle* would be used only for association by reciprocity (horizontal ordering) and association by common aims (vertical ordering). The *forms* of social order listed on pp. 170–71 would then be seen as embodying these two principles.]

Irrigation and Tyranny

Editor's Note

Unlike the preceding essays in this section, "Irrigation and Tyranny" does not describe in detail the features of a single form of social ordering. Rather it develops and applies to a specific social phenomenon (systematic irrigation in agricultural societies) a broad theme which runs through all the essays: that the existing state of social invention limits the availability of institutional forms of decisionmaking and thereby determines the manageability of social problems. Although Fuller emphasizes climatic, geographic, and technological factors in accounting for emergent forms of social organization, he shies away from a commitment to cultural materialism. Human inventiveness is spontaneous and unpredictable, and though the success with which particular models of decisionmaking will find institutional expression depends crucially upon contextual matters it is not independent of shared ideals of justice in the distribution of benefits and burdens.

Nonetheless, "Irrigation and Tyranny" touches most directly on the form of social ordering that Fuller called managerial direction. He nowhere provided, to my knowledge, a complete and explicit characterization of this form of ordering, which may indicate a failure to come to terms fully with the growth of administrative law in this century. The principal feature of managerial direction seems to be the authoritative issuance of directives to subordinates for accomplishing tasks or ends set by a superior. Thus the term is used to cover not only despotism, as discussed in the present essay, but also various types of corporate authority and bureaucratic regulation, including the administrative reallocation of goods (from an initial distribution determined by other processes, such as contract). A simple and benign example offered by Fuller is the position of a baseball manager, who decides such matters as which team members will play which positions, when a pitcher is to be relieved, etc., and issues orders accordingly. In contrast to legislation which, in Fuller's conception, provides guideposts for self-directed activity by citizens, managerial direction operates within a hierarchical structure and is valued when efficiency or a convergence of people's aims is considered desirable.

Whether, in the end, managerial direction is intelligible as a single and distinctive form of social ordering is a question independent of the particular insights of this essay about the limits of despotic power and the social conditions that foster or inhibit its growth. "Irrigation and Tyranny" appeared in the Stanford Law Review *(volume 17, 1965) as part of a festschrift for J. Walter Bingham, one of Fuller's teachers at Stanford Law School. It is reprinted with the permission of the* Stanford Law Review.

Karl A. Wittfogel's *Oriental Despotism—A Comparative Study of Total Power*[1] is a book with a thesis of devastating simplicity. That thesis is this: as one surveys the history of mankind and examines the archeological evidence from prehistoric times, one will find that irrigation is normally accompanied by tyranny. If we were to discover, for example, in some hitherto unexplored area of the world the remains of the dams, canals, and conduits essential for an agriculture based on irrigation, we could conclude with considerable assurance that the political system of the people inhabiting that area was one of despotism.

Thus, if acquaintance with Wittfogel's book had sharpened the perceptions of Shelley's traveler from an antique land he would not have concluded so hastily, after viewing the shattered visage of Ozymandias with its sneer of cold command, that "nothing beside remains." Looking about in the surrounding desert sands he might well have discovered some primitive ditchdigging tool or some fragment of an ancient sluice gate.

In taking Wittfogel's thesis as an object of scrutiny in this chapter I shall make no attempt to appraise the historical and archeological evidence on which he bases his conclusions. This is a task that lies beyond my competence. It is, in any event, a task that has already been accomplished, with compendious documentation, by others.[2]

My concern here is not with the evidence Wittfogel adduces, but with the principles he applies in interpreting that evidence. His book furnishes, in fact, an excellent occasion for an examination of certain fundamental problems of method and of theory that are shared by law, sociology, economics, political science, and social psychology. It is to these problems that I shall address myself here.

I should say, however, that in my case these problems of social theory cannot be wholly divorced from an interest in what might be called the sociology of irrigation. I spent most of my childhood and youth in a reclaimed desert area wholly dependent on water brought from the Colorado River across many intervening miles of arid sands. Though this area—the Imperial Valley in the southeast corner of California—is counted as one of the most productive in the United States, it has only about two inches of rainfall a year, most

---

1. (New Haven: Yale University Press, 1957; paperback ed., 1963). For indispensable aid in preparing this essay I am deeply indebted to my secretary, Mrs. Julianne Levit. Without her patient and imaginative work of bibliographical research I would not have had the courage to venture into so complex a field.

2. S. N. Eisenstadt, Book Review, *Journal of Asian Studies* 17 (1958): 435–46; O. H. K. Spate, Book Review, *Association of American Geographers Annals* 49, no. 1 (1959): 90–95; Arnold J. Toynbee, Book Review, *American Political Science Review* 52, no. 1 (1958): 195–98.

of which seemed to us to come down in one torrent. Many of the most vivid memories of my childhood are connected directly or indirectly with irrigation and flooding. For a while we lived, or thought we lived, under the threat that the Colorado might decide to turn back into the valley, instead of emptying safely into the Gulf of California. The ugly scars of its past misbehavior were everywhere around us, interrupting the fertile fields with miniature badlands. Following the heavy earthquakes of June 1915, there were persistent reports that new tremors might destroy our canal system or cause a sinking of the delta that protected us from the waters of the Gulf. I can remember being impressed at an early age by a foreign-sounding word that stood for a strange and important person, the *zanjero*. I never saw a *zanjero* but I pictured him as a kind of biblical figure, dividing the waters and quieting the alarms of farmers whose crops could be destroyed in a few days by a lack of moisture. It was only later that I learned there was an English term for this official, the water-master, and that the Mexicans themselves called him by the more approachable name of *canalero*.

In all this there was nothing remotely suggesting tyranny or autocratic government. Instead there was a strong sense of community such as I have never experienced since. The political issues under most earnest discussion were those affecting the Irrigation District, and everyone had a sense of participating in the affairs of the district. We were all parts, one of another, and we knew it. One who has had this sort of experience will be left, as I have been, with a lasting skepticism toward the notion that the frontier was a place of "individualism" where every man faced nature by himself. One does not conquer a desert—nor, I suspect, a forest—alone.

Before quitting this personal vein I may perhaps be permitted to suggest that there is a certain appropriateness in an article on the sociology of irrigation as a contribution to an issue of the *Stanford Law Review* honoring Professor Bingham. Water law has been one of his principal interests, and in the fall of 1925 I myself took his course in this subject. Candor compels the admission, however, that for us students this course, like everything he taught, was less a course in its specific subject than it was in Walter Bingham. And I may add most emphatically, it was none the worse for that.

Wittfogel's Conception of the Hydraulic Society

Wittfogel does not, of course, argue for any such absurd position as that any practice of irrigation, however restricted, contains within itself the germs of tyranny. He himself describes the development of his thought and the kind of society with which he was ultimately concerned in these words:

> For three decades I studied the institutional settings of Oriental despotism; and for a considerable part of this time I was content to designate it "Oriental society." But the more my research advanced, the more I felt the need for a new nomenclature. Distinguishing as I do between a farming economy that involves small-scale irrigation (hydroagriculture) and one that involves large-scale and government-managed works of irrigation and flood control (hydraulic agriculture), I came to believe that the designations "hydraulic society" and "hydraulic civilization" express more appropriately than the traditional terms the peculiarities of the order under discussion. The new nomenclature, which stresses human action rather than geography, facilitates comparison with "industrial society" and "feudal society." And it permits us, without circumstantial reasoning, to include in our investigation the higher agrarian civilizations of pre–Spanish America as well as certain hydraulic parallels in East Africa and the Pacific areas, especially in Hawaii. By underlining the prominent role of the government, the term *hydraulic*, as I define it, draws attention to the agromanagerial and agrobureaucratic character of these civilizations.[3]

Critics have complained about the curious use Wittfogel makes of the word *hydraulic*. This usage does indeed comport badly both with the normal use of the term in English and with its derivation. In Wittfogel's usage the word *hydraulic* seems in fact intended as a translation of the German *Wasserbau*, "water-construction," by which of course he would have in mind large-scale and governmentally controlled water-construction. In any event, in this discussion I shall adopt Wittfogel's nomenclature as a convenient shorthand for discussing his thesis.

The situation envisaged in Wittfogel's book then comes to this: successful irrigation requires constructions on a scale so large that no one can accomplish them but the government. The government, accordingly, brings into being and then itself operates the whole vast machinery of dams, canals, and aqueducts by which water is collected and then brought to the cultivated fields. This is the situation in which Wittfogel asserts that we may normally expect the government to be despotic.

But one step in the demonstration seems lacking. How does power over canals convert itself into power over people? The answer that suggests itself at once is that since the government controls access to water, the most indispensable commodity in the community, it has a stranglehold on the whole

3. Wittfogel, *Oriental Despotism*, pp. 2–3.

economy. It can favor its friends and punish its enemies by the manner in which water is allocated. The dissenter or rebel can be brought quickly to terms by the simple process of shutting off his water.

Though this explanation seems on its face plausible, it is in fact no explanation at all, for it constitutes a definition of hydraulic despotism rather than a statement of its causes. It presupposes a government free to furnish or refuse water at its whim—a government that possesses, in other words, despotic powers. To treat it seriously as a demonstration that irrigation necessarily creates tyranny would be like arguing that since in a democracy access to polling places and the counting of votes rests with public authorities, any democratic government, once elected, is certain to be despotic since it is in a position to perpetuate itself through its control over election procedures.

Whether the question be the allocation of water or the supervision of elections, we plainly cannot treat the possibility of abuse as a demonstration that abuses occur and, still less, that they occur on a large scale. We must enter into a more exacting scrutiny of the problems of actual administration and the general moral atmosphere within which administration takes place.

If our concern is with possible despotic abuses of the power of water allocation we should have to consider questions like the following: What rules of law or custom control, or purport to control, the allocation of water among competing users? What sanctions lie back of those rules? Is there anything resembling a democratic participation in their administration? Do the rules of water allocation provide for the emergency of a severe shortage, and if so, what reallocation do they contemplate in such a situation?

On questions like these there is an immense literature, describing the most diverse and often picturesque practices that prevail or have prevailed in different parts of the world.[4] Though in the decades of research Wittfogel devoted to hydraulic societies he must have become familiar with this literature, it is passed over in his book with the most casual mention.

Only one section of Wittfogel's book is explicitly devoted to the law and practice of water rights. This section is, characteristically, headed "Hydraulic Management."[5] At a later point Wittfogel casually mentions that it was not uncommon for governments to set the taxes levied on irrigation farmers as a share of their crops.[6] Such an arrangement would seem to create an overlapping of interest between the government and the farmer that might put some brake on tyrannical abuses. But no appraisal of this aspect of the matter is attempted by Wittfogel, who is content to observe that the taxes levied by the hydraulic despot, like taxes everywhere, were subject to unanticipated in-

4. Some references to this literature will be found in notes 30–34 *infra*.
5. Wittfogel, *Oriental Despotism*, pp. 52–54.
6. Ibid., pp. 71–72.

creases. Beyond these brief indications his book gives virtually no account of the rules that might govern water allocation or payment for water.

What is the reason for this offhand dismissal of the law of waters in a book that deals with the connection between irrigation and governmental lawlessness? The explanation is, I think, that Wittfogel accepts, and is here applying, the distinction, not uncommonly made by other writers,[7] between "formal" and "real" power. Rules of law, property rights, all the formal aspects of social structure, have to do with a fragile and derivative kind of control called "formal" power. "Real" power lies in the background, pulling the strings and setting the forms through which merely formal power expresses itself.

Where, then, lies the real power that creates hydraulic despotism? Wittfogel's answer is that it lies in a governmental monopoly of managerial skill arising from the necessities of large-scale irrigation. It is not a monopoly of water that counts, but a monopoly of the managerial and engineering competence necessary to accumulate and deal with water. This competence constitutes real power, since it inheres in human beings, and not in the fragile forms of legal or political entitlement.

The monopolistic concentration of managerial skill characteristic of hydraulic society is assumed by Wittfogel to attract to itself (through means not analyzed) a labor force sufficient to accomplish the heavy works of irrigation. Once assembled, this labor force, consisting of slaves or conscripted labor (the "corvée"), or a combination of the two, can be employed for undertakings foreign to its original purpose. Thus, Wittfogel explains the monumental style of architecture characteristic of hydraulic civilizations—stately pleasure domes that to be built require only to be decreed, spacious walled-in gardens, impressive temples designed more to inspire awe than to provide places of worship. Finally, there are, of course, the pyramids. A stalwart American socialist, Walter Clark, Chief Justice of North Carolina from 1903 to 1924, once raised the question why the British bondholder (then the "real" ruler of Egypt) did not erect pyramids to cover his remains. Clark could find no answer but an unfathomable aesthetic preference—the "pet vanity" of the British bondholder "does not happen to be a pile of rock in the desert as a tomb."[8] Wittfogel's theory brings the explanation within a more tangible sphere. (To be sure, some difficulty remains. Why did not the accomplished Egyptian hy-

---

7. One is not at all surprised to see this theme expounded in, or derived from, such writers as Marx, Pareto, and Mosca, but it comes as something of a shock to see it expounded so uncompromisingly by John Chipman Gray, *The Nature and Sources of the Law*, 2d ed. (New York: Macmillan, 1921), pp. 121–25, and Melville M. Bigelow, *Centralization and the Law* (Boston: Little, Brown, 1906). There is also, plainly, a strong flavor of this view in Oliver Wendell Holmes, Jr., and Learned Hand.

8. Walter Clark, "Old Foes With New Faces," *Virginia State Bar Association Reports* 16 (1903): 163.

draulic engineer build a pyramid for his own remains instead of one commemorating some ignorant Pharaoh, who presumably knew nothing of hydraulic or funerary architecture? In terms of what we ordinarily expect in government structure, the answer may not be difficult; it is certainly not to be found in Wittfogel's analysis.)

In his preface Wittfogel remarks that though the results of his analysis have aroused considerable interest, no corresponding interest has been shown in the method he pursued in reaching those results. This method he describes as "the use of big structured concepts for the purpose of identifying big patterns of societal structure and change." This "macroanalytic" method is, Wittfogel asserts, "largely responsible for whatever insights the inquiry achieved."[9]

Wittfogel is quite mistaken, I believe, in thinking that the method of reasoning exemplified in his book departs in any radical way from that generally pursued in the social sciences today. What is novel in his book is not the basic method underlying it but the drastic manner in which that method is applied. With him the macroanalytic approach becomes "macro" with a vengeance, not only in the mode by which his conclusions are developed, but in the dramatic nature of the conclusions reached.

It is precisely because he presses familiar modes of reasoning to an extreme that Wittfogel's book is worthy of careful study. In the three sections that follow, I shall attempt to deal in succession with three basic errors of method I believe to be exemplified in Wittfogel's book. They are:

First, a loose conception of the distinction between real and formal power which overlooks the structural elements (based on an implicit reciprocity) present in real, no less than in formal, social power.

Second, a failure to recognize that the institutional procedures of social decision are limited in number, and that their availability depends upon the existing state of social invention within the society in question.

Third, a failure to recognize that the specific tasks or responsibilities undertaken by a given society may vary drastically in what may be called their "manageability."

In a final section, "Irrigation and Distributive Justice," I shall advance reasons (particularly connected with the third point just stated) why Wittfogel may be right in his ultimate conclusion, though mistaken in the arguments he advances to support that conclusion. That is to say, there are, I believe, solid grounds for anticipating a certain tendency toward despotism in any government that undertakes, particularly under relatively primitive conditions, the construction and administration of large-scale irrigation works.

9. Wittfogel, *Oriental Despotism* (paperback ed.), p. iii.

Power and Reciprocity

The thesis concerning power that I shall maintain here asserts that every kind of social power, whether designated as formal or real, is subject to an implicit constitution limiting its exercise. When we say that *A* has power over *B* we do not mean simply that it lies within *A*'s capacity to destroy *B*; even a lunatic with an axe may have this pointless power. When we speak of power as an aspect of social relations, we mean that the power-holder, *A*, while allowing *B* to continue to function in some sense as a human being, has the capacity to control *B*'s actions in certain respects. In other words, *A* is in a position to take advantage of *B*'s capacity for self-direction and to shape *B*'s exercise of that capacity for purposes of his own, which may of course include that of benefiting *B*. The fact that *A* must leave in the addressee of his power some remnant at least of his capacity for self-direction introduces into every power relation an element of interaction or reciprocity, though the reciprocity in question may be most unwelcome to *A* and so attenuated as to afford *B* little consolation for his position of subservience. Nevertheless, this element of reciprocity is always present and may under changing conditions grow in force.[10]

Let us test this view by a case of the most direct physical power imaginable, that of the highwayman who has his victim at the point of a gun. If the highwayman shoots his victim down and then removes the purse from his dead body, we would hardly regard the highwayman's actions as an exercise of power in any sense relevant to social theory. Is the case different if he says, "Your money or your life," and demands that the victim himself hand over the purse?[11] Certainly the highwayman may if he sees fit accept the innocent traveler's purse and then kill him. But this course of action would not be without its inconveniences and risks. If our highwayman follows armed robbery as a profession and it becomes known that he shoots his victims down in spite of the fact that they surrender their purses to him, the practice of his profession may become more dangerous, since his future victims will have little to risk in opposing his demands. Furthermore, if he is a member of anything like a high-

---

10. It is the great service of the sociologist Simmel to have discerned the pervasive influence of reciprocity (*Wechselwirkung*) in human relations, even in those where it seems most obviously absent. See *The Sociology of Georg Simmel*, trans. and ed. K. Wolff (New York: Free Press, 1950); Simmel, *Conflict and The Web of Group-Affiliations*, trans. K. Wolff and R. Bendix (New York: Free Press, 1955); *Georg Simmel, 1858–1918, A Collection of Essays*, ed. K. Wolff (Columbus: Ohio State University Press, 1959).

11. I am, of course, abstracting here from any mental calculations the highwayman might make in response to the formal source of social power represented by the criminal code.

wayman's guild, he may conceivably be called up for disciplinary action for needlessly endangering the lives of the other members of his guild.

Turning from the threat of direct physical violence as a source of power, let us now consider briefly a more indirect, and perhaps more sordid form of power, that of the blackmailer. Some disgraceful incident in the life of the victim, B, gives A, the blackmailer, the power to extort money from B. A, we say, "has B at his mercy." But plainly A's power is subject to an intrinsic limitation, for it ends when B or someone else makes a public disclosure of the incident that was the source of A's power. The possibility of this disclosure puts a limit to A's extortions. One can indeed imagine an earnest discussion between A and B in which B communicates to A his resolution to tell all, while A pleads with him for the sake of his family not to do so foolish a thing, promising for himself to be more reasonable in his future exactions.

I need hardly say that the two illustrations just discussed have not been offered here as making of themselves any serious contribution to social theory. I have used them merely to drive home the point that informal or real power is subject to intrinsic limitations even in its most direct and brutal manifestations. In more complex situations, as, for example, where we inquire into the degree of real power held by some profession within the structure of society as a whole, the limits of power become more complex and subtle. But even here the holder of power will find himself hedged in by a network of reciprocities that trace the limits of his control. In a quite literal sense his power is subject to constitutional restraints, though these restraints may serve the public interest only accidentally and may be such as would scarcely be incorporated in an explicit constitution. In any event and despite the subtitle of Wittfogel's book, there is no such thing as total power.

The general tendency to put informal and formal power in stark opposition to one another has obscured not only the analysis of informal power but that of formal power as well. It has led to the view that the only structural or pattern-revealing limitations on formal power are those that are explicitly planned and formalized. Thus, in the literature of jurisprudence, law is generally defined as consisting of those rules that emanate from some human source that is itself regarded as formally authorized to enact or declare law. In the absence of explicit constitutional limitations, this human source can enact anything it sees fit into law. Its laws may be wise or foolish, intelligible or obscure, just or unjust, prospective or retrospective in effect, general or specific in their coverage, published or unpublished, etc. In all this variety, it is assumed, there is no structural constancy, except that imposed by the formal rule which identifies the authorized source of law. But this view overlooks the fact that there are what may be called informal limitations implicit in any attempt to subject human conduct to the control of general rules. For example, if rules are to be followed they must in some manner or other be published or made available to their addressees. Again, if control by rules is to be established there must be at least some general rules, and not a haphazard and patternless rain of discrete interventions by government in the lives of its citizens.[12] (Neither of these informal compulsions, it may be remarked, finds any explicit expression in the formal charter of our national government, the Constitution of the United States.)

When we view the processes of society as a whole, then, we do not see two distinct kinds of power—formal and real—competing for dominance in men's lives. Instead we are confronted with an intertwining of many strands of control. In this intertwining, formal power reshapes and redirects itself in accordance with the intrinsic but informal demands of the tasks it undertakes. Informal power, on the other hand, finds itself hedged about by intrinsic necessities more resistant than words on paper can ever be. Against such a view, we can see how essentially unreal is any attempt to define the real power in a hydraulic society as inhering in a governmental monopoly of managerial skill.

It requires no very subtle analysis to see certain obvious difficulties in Wittfogel's demonstration. In one place he acknowledges his indebtedness to the thesis developed in *The Managerial Revolution* and asserts, "Social science is indebted to James Burnham for pointing to the power potential inherent in managerial control."[13] In the same context he intimates a like indebtedness to Thorstein Veblen. But Veblen and Burnham saw the control of American corporations as shifting from the owners to the managers, while Wittfogel sees the power of the hydraulic manager as reinforcing that of the hydraulic "owner," the political ruler. The two lines of thought seem to move in exactly opposed directions.

Other aspects of his argument are equally mystifying. Among the special qualities he attributes to hydraulic society is that of a strong tendency toward theocracy.[14] But in crude vernacular terms, if the real power lies in a concentration of managerial skill, what incentive has the manager to cut the priest in on his racket?

In many interstitial ways Wittfogel's own description of the hydraulic society belies the thesis suggested by his subtitle, "A Comparative Study of Total

12. I have attempted an analysis of the "informal" compulsions that are implicit in "the enterprise of subjecting human conduct to the governance of rules" in *The Morality of Law* (New Haven: Yale University Press, 1964; rev. ed., 1969), pp. 33–94 passim.

13. Wittfogel, *Oriental Despotism*, p. 48n. [The reference is to James Burnham, *The Managerial Revolution* (New York: John Day, 1941).]

14. Ibid., pp. 90–100.

Power." Though he makes very little of the restraints of law, in one place he asserts: "The most elementary considerations of rationality require that even those who make—and change—laws onesidedly and despotically should emphasize their validity by not abrogating them unnecessarily."[15]

At another crucial juncture he recognizes another intrinsic restraint on despotic power. This lies in what he calls "the law of diminishing administrative returns."[16] At some point in the imposition of despotic controls the cost begins to exceed the return. Even if the hydraulic despot could control every single aspect of his subject's life, the administrative effort required to accomplish this would at some point cease to pay for itself. Hence there are respects in which even the hydraulic despot may be expected to leave his subject alone.

One wonders why at this point Wittfogel does not grant to his hydraulic despot the capacity to perceive that a relaxation of administrative controls may set in motion a law of increasing returns. Why not accord to the subject (normally a farmer) a secure position of entitlement to land and water and thus put him in a position to develop his full capacities free from hampering restraints? By a share-crop arrangement the despot would then be able to enjoy a portion of this increased productivity. To answer this question we have to draw into consideration factors that lie completely beyond the scope of Wittfogel's analysis, that are, in other words, foreign to his conceptions of social theory.

The Forms of Social Order and Their Availability Within a Given Society

By "the forms of social order" I do not refer to the inert, traditional forms by which men's relations are often supposed to be structured, where conformity is assumed to take place automatically without any awareness of an alternative. Rather I have in mind those active processes of social decision by which deficiencies and conflicts are removed, and a stable foundation for future relationships is established. Elsewhere I have tried to give some account of the significance and interplay of these procedures;[17] in particular I have attempted a fairly thorough analysis of adjudication as a form-setting device of social

15. Ibid., p. 293.
16. Ibid., p. 110.
17. Lon L. Fuller, "American Legal Philosophy at Mid-Century," *Journal of Legal Education* 6, no. 4 (1954): 473–81; "Freedom—A Suggested Analysis," *Harvard Law Review* 68, no. 8 (1955): 1305–25.

decision.[18] For present purposes it will be enough to discuss briefly two such forms: (1) deliberate resort to chance and (2) explicit reciprocity or contract.

The casting of lots is an ancient device for resolving conflicts. Its social function is thus described in the Bible: "The lot causeth contentions to cease, and parteth between the mighty." [19]

Volumes could be devoted to the historical and legendary uses that have been made of the lot, under the most diverse social conditions. Moses is reported to have apportioned land among the tribes of Israel by lot;[20] the occupants of certain ecclesiastical offices among the Hebrews were selected by lot;[21] the man who should join the eleven apostles as a successor to Judas was chosen by lot.[22] The ancient Greeks selected public officials by lot, and we still pursue the same method in selecting jurors.

Ancient as it is, the lot obviously represents a fairly high level of social invention. A perception of its utility demands a considerable capacity for abstract thought, as does the design of a mechanical device that will reliably invoke pure chance. Numberless primitive peoples had to survive without its aid. In order to resolve disputes among his followers no doubt many a tribal chieftain had to assume arbitrary powers (had to play the tyrant, if you will) because he did not have available to him this less personal way of causing contentions to cease.

If the lot is one of the most ancient modes of creating social order, contract or explicit reciprocity is, in its more sophisticated forms at least, one of the most recent. The simple idea of trading one thing for another is for us today an expedient so obvious as to require no explanation at all. If there are two tribes on one island, a coastal tribe engaged in fishing and an island tribe engaged in raising yams, nothing would seem more obvious than that both tribes could gain a more varied diet by arranging some exchange of their respective products.[23] But in the actual development of social arrangements this insight was long in coming. Scattered through history, along the tortuous routes that have led to what now seems an extremely simple idea, there appear many twisted and ambiguous forms of reciprocity: Gifts rendered with the expectation of a return—a transaction pregnant with misunderstanding, as the expression "Indian giver" reminds us even today; barter distorted from its

18. Lon L. Fuller, "Adjudication and the Rule of Law," *American Society of International Law Proceedings* 54 (1960): 1–8; "Collective Bargaining and the Arbitrator," *Wisconsin Law Review* 1963: 3–46.

19. Prov. 18:18.

20. Num. 26:55.

21. Neh. 10:34.

22. Acts 1:26.

23. The actual "trading" that developed in a situation like this is described in Bronislaw Malinowski's classic, *Crime and Custom in Savage Society* (London: Routledge and Kegan Paul, 1926).

obvious function by the desire of each trader to show that he is more powerful and wealthy than the other by giving more than he receives; silent and hostile trade, in which one party places articles in some traditional spot and retires to safety, whereupon the other makes his proposal by displaying his offering in the same location, after which he in turn retires beyond the reach of his co-trader's spears, and so on. Even ordinary commercial trade was, in many parts of the world, carried on for centuries only in certain places and during certain periods of the year, as it still is today among many primitive peoples.

With these considerations in mind we are now in a position to deal with the question raised at the end of the last section: Why did not the hydraulic despot enjoy increasing economic returns, both for himself and his subject, by granting to his subject a secure position of legal entitlement to water and land, and then entering into a contractual relationship with him by which water was traded for a fixed share of his crop? An answer sufficient to our present purposes may be that such an arrangement simply did not enter into his vocabulary of possible responses. Though trading was not unknown to early hydraulic societies, it consisted mostly of external trade conducted by the government itself.[24] Furthermore, the concept of a contract between government and subject is, of all contractual notions, one of the most recent to develop and one which even today occupies in most societies a curious twilight zone between legal entitlement and political concession.

The point of these observations is that we cannot deal intelligently with such a question as that of hydraulic despotism without asking what alternatives to despotism were made available by the state of social invention within the community in question. Today we have at our disposal a considerable number of what my colleague Henry M. Hart has called procedures of institutional settlement: contractual arrangements, adjudicative procedures, various methods of voting and of parliamentary decision. These routes to social order are enriched and made more flexible by various mixed forms. With all this institutional abundance there are social problems that remain intractable to solution by any of them. But if our institutional resources are insufficient to our needs, those of more primitive societies were often so meager that, with respect to certain crucial issues, they may have left no real alternative to direct, personal rule—in other words, to despotism.

At this point it may be objected that despotism is a moral phenomenon that has nothing to do with institutional forms. A kindly ruler will treat his subjects benevolently without having to strike bargains with them, and certainly without having to cast lots to decide what to do with them. The evil ruler, on the

---

24. Rosemary Arnold, "A Port of Trade: Whydah on the Guinea Coast," in *Trade and Market in the Early Empires*, eds. Karl Polanyi, et al. (New York: Free Press, 1957), p. 155; John A. Wilson, *The Burden of Egypt* (Chicago: University of Chicago Press, 1951), p. 81.

other hand, will always find outlets for his iniquity despite institutional barriers. Questions of morals are entirely distinct from those of social procedures, since morals have to do with ends, while procedures are merely means to ends.

Though a view like that just stated has become a commonplace of moral philosophy, it is, I believe, based on a profound misconception of the relation between morality and social forms. Today converging streams of ethical philosophy have nearly obliterated the notion of an institutional or procedural morality. Among the influences that join in this work of destruction we may mention such apparently diverse philosophies as utilitarianism, noncognitive and emotive theories of moral preference, and Kant's solitary ethical soliloquizer, impartially legislating for all mankind, including himself. What is lacking in all these philosophies is the simple picture of human beings confronting one another in some social context, adjusting their relations reciprocally, negotiating, voting, arguing before some arbiter, and perhaps even reluctantly deciding to toss for it.

When Piaget studied the moral growth of the child he found a certain circular relation between the playing of games and the moral attitudes necessary to play them successfully. To enjoy a game the child must have the moral insight to see the necessity for rules and must possess the self-control that will enable him to abide by the rules, even in defeat. These are qualities obviously lacking in the very young child. Yet the only way he can acquire them is to start playing games. When he does, working within the institutional forms of the game generates the moral qualities necessary to make the game playable.[25]

In a similar vein Bagehot observes that tolerance "is learned in discussion and, as history shows, is only so learned."[26] He might well have added, "And this despite the fact that unless tolerance is present discussion is useless."

The development of moral insight through participation in institutional procedures is nowhere more clearly revealed than in the negotiation of complex agreements, such as those involved in treaties or collective bargaining contracts. The good negotiator in such a case must not only make a genuine effort to understand the declared aims of the opposing party, but must be capable of some sympathetic participation in those aims. If he takes the demands of the opposing party at face value and makes no real effort to understand their underlying motivations, he may easily overlook the possibility of some hitherto undiscussed arrangement that will let both parties have what they want without undue cost to either. To serve his principal well he must identify himself with the opposing party. To win the game of negotiation he

25. Jean Piaget, *The Moral Judgement of the Child*, trans. M. Gabain (London: Routledge and Kegan Paul, 1932), pp. 91–93.
26. Walter Bagehot, *Physics and Politics* (Boston: Beacon Press, 1956), p. 119. This volume was first published in 1872.

must in some measure help his opponent to win what he wants of that game. In this reconciliation of altruism and self-interest there is revealed, I believe, a more mature conception of morality than that expressed in Mill's famous dictum that the true utilitarian must be indifferent between his own happiness and that of other men.[27]

So, if humanity has over the centuries shown some slight capacity to outgrow its inclination toward and its dependence upon despotism, this growth reflects not only the increasing availability of social alternatives to despotic rule, but also an increasing moral disposition, nurtured by actual experience, to employ these alternatives.

The Manageability of Social Tasks

In the section just concluded we were concerned with the institutional means available for performing certain social tasks. We now turn to the intrinsic difficulty of the tasks themselves, to what Michael Polanyi has called their "manageability."[28] Since the problems of operating an irrigation system are essentially economic in nature, we shall be concerned with the comparative manageability of economic undertakings. Obviously nothing like a comprehensive analysis can be ventured here. It is possible, however, to discern several crucial factors.

The first of these lies in the relative stability of the external conditions that impinge on the undertaking in question. The significance of this factor may be revealed by a comparison of agricultural production with ordinary manufacturing operations. In a market economy both the farmer and the manufacturer are supposed to plan their production by a comparison of the anticipated price for which their products will sell and the cost of bringing them into existence. Thus guided, the manufacturer can usually set a target for the volume of his production and look forward with some confidence to achieving at least an approximation of it. No such assurance is granted to the farmer. The size of his crop is determined by a host of conditions that lie beyond his control: weather conditions of moisture, heat, light, and wind; insect invasions; a possible epidemic of plant diseases; etc. Some of these variable factors have been partly tamed by irrigation, long-range weather forecasts, insecticides, and

27. John Stuart Mill, *Utilitarianism*, ed. Oskar Piest (New York: Liberal Arts Press, 1957), p. 22.
28. Michael Polanyi, *The Logic of Liberty: Reflections and Rejoinders* (Chicago: University of Chicago Press, 1951), pp. 154–200.

chemical means of preventing infection. But with all these aids the farmer (along with the hunter and fisherman) is left to a significant degree at the mercy of Nature's caprices. In some areas of agricultural production a bumper crop may still be disastrous for the farmer growing his share of it by plunging the price so low that he must leave his fields unharvested. Though the farmer knows from sad experience that this sort of thing can happen to him, there is no way open to him by which he can plan against it.

This means that farming has never fitted well into the economist's picture of the ideal market in which a host of relatively dependable calculations by individuals are combined to maximize the public good. But the vagaries that make farming inconvenient for control by market forces make it even less tractable to central planning. The planned quotas, with bonuses for exceeding them, that have been a feature of the economies of the Soviet bloc, have worked badly as a substitute for the index of profit even in manufacturing operations. But plainly they were fated to work even more disastrously in farming operations.

A second consideration affecting the manageability of economic tasks is the degree to which it is possible to predict with confidence, and to take into advance account, the repercussions that will follow some contemplated intervention in a given state of affairs. A project for building a dam and hydraulic power station will ordinarily have certain quite foreseeable consequences: an increase in the population of the community served, an enhanced demand for household electrical devices, etc. But, though we may foresee that the project will destroy the beauty of a waterfall, it is not easy to know how many persons will actually feel this loss, or how the resulting aesthetic deprivation will affect future generations. Nor is it possible, perhaps, to foresee and calculate in any precise way what dangers the dam may create, or how the whole project may turn out to inconvenience some future more comprehensive use of the river system affected.

It is of course true that no human activity is accompanied by a complete anticipation of all of its consequences, immediate and remote. But the degree to which the future consequences of a particular economic project can be foreseen may determine whether it is manageable within acceptable limits. Furthermore, the institutional framework within which a project is undertaken may affect the extent to which any unfavorable repercussions of it may be offset or compensated.

It is at this point that one of the chief advantages of socialism is discerned. A factory, let us say, makes a useful product but spreads a pall of smoke over the countryside. Obviously this smoke represents a social cost of operating the factory, though of diffuse and varying incidence. In an economy of private enterprise, unmitigated by public restraints, the factory owner has no occasion to include this cost in his reckonings; indeed, his calculations are simplified by the fact that he does not have to worry about the housewife's dirty sheets or her children's clotted lungs. Under socialism, it is contended, all such social costs can be included in the reckoning and will be taken into account in planning production. In this particular case it happens that there is a measure short of socializing industry that may effectively solve the problem. This consists of a legal requirement that the manufacturer install a device for reducing the volume of smoke discharged from his factory; the added cost of this device will then be reflected in the price paid by consumers of the factory's output. This solution may, to be sure, present some difficulty in knowing when the cost of an increasingly stringent reduction of smoke ceases to pay for itself—when, in other words, the law of decreasing returns begins to apply to the purification of the atmosphere. But at least this solution avoids the government's having to assume responsibility for operating the factory.

The argument for socialism goes further, however, and asserts that not all the social costs of an economic enterprise can thus be projected into the price of the products manufactured, but require for their alleviation the broader social controls possible only when there is an assumption of public responsibility for the entire economy. An example would be the social cost involved in the brutalizing or degrading effect on the worker of certain kinds of labor. Under socialism it is said that costs of this kind, indeed all social costs, will be taken into account and prevented or offset. But as the responsibility for social costs expands, so also do the uncertainties of causal connection. Perhaps the allegedly degrading effect of the work in question is not really intrinsic to the work itself, but results from mistaken social attitudes that inflict on the worker a false sense of inferiority. In this case the remedy would be to improve education, or perhaps, if the incorrect attitudes result from "Western influence," to reduce intellectual exchange with the capitalist countries.

These considerations make it clear that in judging what constitutes acceptable manageability in a social task we must take into account not only the degree of control that may be exercised but the public expectations that accompany that control. Furthermore, the question is not one of the brute quantum of control that is possible, but of its mode and manner, or the point in the total situation at which intentional direction makes itself felt. This is well illustrated in discussions of the possibility of controlling the weather.

When cloud-seeding experiments were first performed it was suggested that the time might come when man could actually achieve a control over the weather. A fervent hope was expressed by some that such a time should never arrive, for it would involve the assumption of responsibilities that could never be discharged in a satisfactory manner. But this would depend on the kind of control that was established. If this took the form of stabilizing the weather—for example, by equalizing the rainfall, season by season, over a wide area—it might be quite feasible and desirable to assume such a control. There would be some disruptions: relative land values might be altered, some movement of population might occur, favored locations for certain crops might change, and so forth. But the gradual imposition of this kind of weather control might turn out to be something generally desirable and approved.

It would, however, be an entirely different matter if the control in question should take the form of being able to set the course of a death-dealing tornado or of determining on which particular farms a cloud system should release its moisture on soil parched by a long drought. Here indeed a government faced with responsibilites of this sort might well wish it had never acquired the ability to assume them.

Against the background of these considerations we are now finally ready to deal with hydraulic despotism. I think it will be found that the pieces of the Wittfogelian puzzle will fall rather rapidly into place.

Irrigation and Distributive Justice

The explanation here offered for hydraulic despotism may be briefly stated in these terms: The early hydraulic societies tended toward despotism because they took on too difficult a social task too soon. They took on the task too soon because the existing state of social invention did not make available to them the institutional means that might have facilitated a solution of their problems—that might, in other words, have offered workable alternatives to despotism. The task was too difficult because by its nature it is a perplexing one for any society, whatever the state of its advancement.

Irrigation, it may be said, brings down to earth a part of the weather—that affecting the transfer of moisture to the soil—and places in human hands the responsibility for directing the available moisture to the proper places. But in this transfer downward one aspect of Nature's caprice—the most important one, that determining the total supply of moisture—remains wholly untamed and unmitigated. Nature in effect says to the hydraulic ruler: "Here is all the water I can give you for this season. I realize that this will not satisfy the needs of your country. In the old days, before you built your canals, I used to decide whose crops would be saved and whose left to dry in the sun. Now this is your job."

The risk of a water shortage may be regarded as a normal feature of economies based on irrigation, located as they are in arid or semiarid regions. A successful irrigation project may be expected, under primitive conditions, to produce a considerable increase in population. The resulting pressure on existing resources is likely, in turn, to suggest an expansion of irrigation facilities. As this expansion occurs the margin of safety against critical water shortages becomes progressively narrowed. To arrive, therefore, at the conclusion that hydraulic societies will show a strong tendency toward despotic forms of government we need only make the almost trite assumption that recurring conditions of crisis present the dictator with a kind of standing invitation to take over.

The relation between conditions of crisis and the necessity for drastic and often arbitrary controls is evident to those whose memories include the experience of this country during the two world wars. More disquietingly, one whose memory stretches so far back will also recall that after hostilities ceased some sensitive and public-spirited citizens looked back on those controls with a sort of nostalgia, expressing regret that they were not continued into peacetime when they might have been used "for the public good."

In judging the sociological implications of recurring crises it should be recalled that it is virtually impossible to lay down in advance fixed rules to be followed in the event of a crisis. No two crises are ever exactly alike. One year a water shortage may occur at a time when one crop is about to mature; in a second year a different crop altogether may be put in peril. During a single crisis the directions for water allocation may have to be changed as the drought deepens, with perhaps a final priority given to those uses of water that are absolutely essential for human survival.[29]

The emphasis here put on conditions of crisis should not be interpreted to suggest that under normal conditions the allocation of irrigation waters is a simple and obvious matter, presenting no difficulties that might invite the despot to take over. In actual practice, over the world and through history, the most diverse rules have been applied to the allocation of irrigation waters. These rules express every conceivable standard of distributive justice: First

29. The somewhat idyllic picture I have presented above of my own experience of living in a hydraulic society may reflect the circumstance that the Imperial Valley has never suffered from actual shortage of water, though it has often lived under the threat of one. Under such circumstances the problems of allocation largely relate to the timing of the delivery and to managing deliveries so as to balance the flow of water in the canal system. My colleague Arthur Maass, who visited the area recently, reports that in the newly developed irrigation systems south of the border in Mexico shortages are a real problem. Working rules for a kind of proportionate sharing have been adopted, and during a severe shortage a representative elected by the affected farmers works with the canalero, this arrangement being designed "to keep the canalero honest."

come, first served;[30] to each according to his contribution;[31] to each according to his needs;[32] to each according to the needs of society;[33] to each according to the luck of the throw.[34]

The diversity of these rules is a tribute to human ingenuity. It may also be a tribute to the difficulty of the task human ingenuity sets for itself when, instead of leaving the distribution of moisture to the chance play of winds and clouds, it assumes that task itself.

If the explanation for hydraulic despotism that has been offered here is accepted, most of the difficulties of Wittfogel's thesis disappear. We no longer have any problem of explaining how a concentration of managerial skill enhances the power of a political ruler who is himself unlikely to know anything about irrigation engineering. If the essential problem lies in the deep-cutting nature of the questions to be answered, and the lack of obvious answers to them, it is understandable that they should be referred to the Big Decider himself.

Any difficulty of explaining the tendency of hydraulic societies toward a theocratic form of government also disappears. It may be said of priests that in every society they are specialists in solving unsolvable problems. Further-

30. This is of course the prior appropriation doctrine familiar to the western states in the division of natural waters. On irrigation under Islamic law, see Ann Lambton, *Landlord and Peasant in Persia* (London: Oxford University Press, 1953), p. 211 (the land first cultivated has priority to water over land later cultivated; land nearer the source has priority over land lower down).

31. Near East: waters reach the fields by channels that the community has constructed. V. Gordon Childe, *Man Makes Himself*, rev. ed. (London: Tavistock, 1941), p. 109. Hawaii: the quantity of water allocated was proportional to the time spent by the cultivator and his family in building and maintaining the ditch and dam furnishing the water. E. S. C. Handy, *The Hawaiian Planter—His Plants, Methods and Areas of Cultivation* (Bernice P. Bishop Museum Bulletin, 161, 1940), Vol. 1, p. 36. Water is divided among the chiefs in proportion to the contributions of manpower they have made to the creation and maintenance of the irrigation system. Perry, "Hawaiian Water Rights," *Hawaiian Almanac and Annual* (Thrum, 1913), p. 92.

32. Persia: water distributed according to the needs of the crop sown; the *mirab* (watermaster) is not strictly bound by the rules of allocation but may give rice, for example, a little more water than needed, provided not more than the stipulated amount has been sown. Ann Lambton, "The Regulation of the Waters of the Zāyande Rūd," *Bulletin of the School of Oriental Studies* 9 (1938): 669.

33. Persia: "The king orders the floodgates to be opened toward the country whose need is the greatest, and lets the soil drink until it has had enough; after which the gates on this side are shut, and the others are unclosed for the nation which, of the remainder, needs it most." Wittfogel, *Oriental Despotism*, p. 53 (quoting Herodotus). Egypt: the waters having to pass the holdings of different cultivators in succession, a social sense of cooperation became necessary and moral precepts were much concerned with one's duty to one's neighbor in this respect. Frederick W. Robins, *The Story of Water Supply* (London: Oxford University Press, 1946), p. 35.

34. India: Maine reports that water made available by British governmental projects was allocated within the Indian villages by lot. Henry Maine, *Village Communities*, 5th ed. (London: John Murray, 1887), pp. 109–10. Islamic Law: lots are used to assign priority in the division of water shares, each shareholder's right lasting for sixteen days. Lambton, *Landlord and Peasant*, p. 219.

more, anthropological theories of the function of magic help to explain why their presence is especially welcome in the hydraulic society:

> [A]s far as his knowledge goes, as far as he can safely rely on experience, reason and technical ability, the native [in primitive society]—whether in his gardening or fishing, in the building of craft, in warfare or sailing—does not use magic. . . . Only where, in spite of knowledge and effort, the results still turn unaccountably against him, only when forces completely beyond his mental grasp and practical control baffle him—in dealing with garden pests, with the supply of fish and animals, in securing wind and weather . . . does the savage resort to supernatural means of filling the lacunae in his practical power.[35]

If the function of magic in primitive society is indeed to serve as a kind of tranquilizer, as a means of reducing anxieties, then it is no mystery that the hydraulic ruler, as well as his subjects, should have need of it.

The stately pleasure domes require, of course, no separate explanation. If the despot cannot within wide limits set his own rate of compensation, he is scarcely a despot. Moreover, whenever an attempt is made to formalize the standards for compensating an occupation, the degree of responsibility assumed by the practitioner of that occupation is commonly listed as something to be taken into account. In judging his own case the hydraulic despot can be counted on to give a generous weighting to this factor. (Wittfogel is no doubt right in supposing that certain kinds of monumental architecture, such as the pyramids, were facilitated by the availability of work forces and engineering skills trained in the heavy construction works of irrigation.)

Finally, the analysis presented here may serve, I believe, to explain some apparent exceptions to the rule that hydraulic societies tend toward despotism. These exceptions largely concern flood controls. Flood controls rather regularly accompany irrigation, since irrigated lands, being normally below the level of their water supply, are generally subject to flooding. The technological problems of flood control and irrigation are similar, and both require the same concentration of engineering and managerial skills. Furthermore, the intractable questions of distributive justice that irrigation generates are also characteristic of flood controls. If a river is left without dikes, no one assumes responsibility for the precise point where flood waters break through. If, however, the public undertakes a system of embankments to hold the river in its course, *A*, whose land is flooded, may complain that the dikes protecting his

---

35. Bronislaw Malinowski, "Functionalism in Anthropology," in *Sociological Theory*, ed. Lewis Coser and Bernard Rosenberg. (New York: Macmillan, 1957), p. 529. This article first appeared in *Encyclopaedia Britannica* (Supp. vol. 1, 1936), pp. 132–39. The article on magic in the current *Britannica* is by another author.

land were less well maintained than those protecting B's. Worse yet, if A's land is upstream and is deemed less valuable than B's, which is downstream, the question may arise whether the dikes protecting A's ought not to be opened deliberately to save B's land. Or, again, if this procedure is explicitly rejected, then B may complain that in effect his land was sacrificed to save the less valuable land of A. These perplexities may be counted among the diffuse social costs of a system of flood controls. The lack of clear answers to them may also tend to favor some system of authoritative decision that will dispense with the need for clear answers.

These considerations might seem to support the conclusion that extensive flood controls would favor a despotic form of government, even in the absence of irrigation. History, however, lends little support to this conclusion, as the outstanding example of Holland at once suggests. Perhaps the explanation for this anomaly is to be found in the public attitudes that accompany the relief of distress as compared with the conferring of benefits. The economist may declare that the removal of a disutility is indistinguishable from the rendition of a utility; the engineer may likewise declare that stopping waters from wreaking destruction is not a different task from directing them to places where they are wanted. Yet the disbursement of public funds for the alleviation or prevention of disaster is never subject to the same accounting that is expected when benefits are explicitly and directly conferred. Impulses of charity and mercy have gained in human practice a kind of prescriptive right to transcend the demands of distributive justice.

This is not to say, of course, that flood controls present no problems of distributive justice. I am told that in Holland the just and proper allocation of the expenses involved in maintaining that country's elaborate system of dikes constitutes a perennial issue of politics. The earliest decisions in England in the field we now call administrative law related to similar questions.[36] We may indeed describe the law relating to the control of waters as the most ancient branch of administrative law. If this designation is apt, it may certainly be said of this branch of law that it had a hard start in life.

Many details of the presentation just concluded would, I am sure, undergo modification if the issues discussed were subjected to a more thorough study. The final demonstration may seem to some, perhaps with justice, a little too pat. Nevertheless, I am convinced that the mode of analysis exemplified is fundamentally sound.

That mode of analysis is relevant to questions extending far beyond those presented by the public control of waters. It has a bearing, for example, on the

36. Edith G. Henderson, *Foundations of English Administrative Law* (Cambridge, Mass.: Harvard University Press, 1963), pp. 28–35.

problems involved in the economic, political, and legal development of the newly emerging nations. It may offer some help in understanding the internal problems of the communist countries by revealing that those problems are much more like our own than we commonly suppose. Finally, it has relevance to the future development of administrative law in this country and its possible expansion into new fields.

Meanwhile, there is no lack of material for reflection in problems directly relating to water supply. An article in the *Stanford Law Review* effectively conveys some of the urgency of these problems in the West.[37] In the claims and counterclaims there reported one discerns slight intimations of violence backed by metaphysical arguments about who "owns" the thing in dispute— a danger signal in any society. Today there seems to be an increasing tendency to subject our most difficult problems to some form of adjudicative solution. When things go wrong we are more and more inclined to run to the judge. This is, I believe, an escapist solution. Problems concerned with the sharing of water supplies and the joint utilization of river systems are inherently unsuited to adjudicative solution, involving as they do a complex interplay of diverse interests. Only those who know those interests intimately, who can feel their way toward the best reciprocal adjustment of them, are competent to find a truly satisfactory solution. If this is not the easiest way to hydraulic peace, it is surely the best.[38]

---

37. B. Abbott Goldberg, "Interposition—Wild West Water Style," *Stanford Law Review* 17 (1964): 1–38.

38. [For further discussion of managerial direction as a form of social ordering, especially in contrast to legislation, see Fuller, *The Morality of Law*, pp. 207–13.]

Human Interaction and the Law

Editor's Note

In The Concept of Law, *H. L. A. Hart characterizes as "primitive" and "prelegal" societies which lack certain official agencies: an agency for making authoritative identifications of obligatory rules, an agency for changing the rules (a legislature), and an agency for determining when violations of the rules have occurred (a court or adjudicative body). These agencies, in turn, are constituted by sets of rules ("secondary rules") which define their powers and procedures. When a society establishes agencies of the requisite sort it moves "from the pre-legal into the legal world." Without such agencies, a society is ruled by "custom," that is, shared standards of conduct toward which the community as a whole is favorably disposed.*

Hart's distinction between a customary and a legal order is used to mark a stage in the historical development of societies. Anthropologists have employed similar criteria in deciding whether a given society can be said to have laws, sometimes insisting on the strong condition of the existence of a state (that is, an agency with the exclusive and legitimate authority to enforce rules by the threat of physical coercion) or the weaker condition of a court (an agency engaged in the resolution of disputes between contending parties, particularly by reasoned application of established rules). As a consequence, many societies were discovered to be devoid of law.

Fuller saw in such accounts, I think, a failure to recognize important continuities between our familiar legal institutions and alternative forms of social ordering. He regarded such a conception of law as too narrow and parochial, having the ironic consequence of hiding from view some pervasive features of our own institutions and thus rendering us unable to draw upon common experience in making cross-cultural comparisons. For example, the stress on explicit, "made" law slights the tacit understandings and mutual accommodations that emerge from the interaction of social members. In this sense, Fuller considered "customary law" to be as much a factor in the complex and highly formalized procedures of developed societies as in the apparently informal and non-rule-bound mechanisms of so-called primitive communities.

In many instances, with legal institutions being no exception, the formal description of an agency in terms of its constitutive rules is the least enlightening aspect of its character as an ongoing social phenomenon. More can be learned from the purposes it is being made to serve and the resources at its disposal (including authoritative rules as one element). Stress on the "official" character of an agency tends to overestimate its autonomy. In Fuller's view, the practices of countless interacting individuals that underlie official conduct at any moment are what give the latter its shape and force. If made law is divorced from its context, it may be projected upon a social terrain incapable of supporting it, in which case tacit modifications or outright evasions of the law will ensue. (One thinks of the many informal practices in our society which are not in accord with written law, and often inconsistent with it, but are otherwise sanctioned.)

In its fullest sense, then, "the law" does not consist only of discrete and readily identi-
fied sets of official declarations but is continuous with conventions and understandings
that are partly inchoate and evolving.

In "Human Interaction and the Law," Fuller offers his most persuasive defense of
this broader picture of legal institutions. The essay was originally an address to the
thirteenth annual meeting of the Board of Editors of the American Journal of Jurisprudence, *September 26, 1969. It appeared in the* Journal *the same year (volume 14) and*
is reprinted with permission.

As it is used in my title, I mean the word *law* to be construed very broadly. I
intend it to include not only the legal systems of states and nations, but also
the smaller systems—at least "law-like" in structure and function—to be
found in labor unions, professional associations, clubs, churches, and universities. These miniature legal systems are, of course, concerned with the member's duties and entitlements within the association itself. They find their most
dramatic expression when the erring member is called up to be tried for offenses that may lead to his being disciplined or expelled.

When the concept of law is given this broad coverage, it becomes apparent
that many of the central issues of today are, in this extended sense, "legal" in
nature. The pressure of our present predicament pushes us—as we have not
been pushed for a long time—toward an effort at comprehension. We must
come to perceive and understand the moral and psychological forces that underlie law generally and give it efficacy in human affairs.

1. *The Nature and Significance of "Customary Law"*

If in search of this understanding we turn to treatises on jurisprudence, we
shall find that they commonly begin by distinguishing two kinds of law. On
the one hand, there is enacted or authoritatively declared law—what may be
called made law; on the other hand, there is what is known as customary law.
Customary law is not the product of official enactment, but owes its force to
the fact that it has found direct expression in the conduct of men toward one
another.

As between these two kinds of law the treatises commonly devote almost
their entire attention to enacted or declared law, to the law that can be found
in statutes, judicial decisions, bylaws, and administrative decrees. The discussion of customary law is largely confined to the question, Why should it be
thought to be law at all? After some discussion along this line, and some treat-

ment of its function in primitive societies, customary law is generally dismissed as largely irrelevant to advanced civilizations. It tends to be regarded as a kind of museum piece offering an object for serious study only to anthropologists curious about the ways of tribal peoples.

This neglect of the phenomenon called customary law has, I think, done great damage to our thinking about law generally. Even if we accept the rather casual analysis of the subject offered by the treatises, it still remains true that a proper understanding of customary law is of capital importance in the world of today. In the first place, much of international law, and perhaps the most vital part of it, is essentially customary law. Upon the successful functioning of that body of law world peace may depend. In the second place, much of the world today is still governed internally by customary law. The newly emerging nations (notably in India, Africa, and the Pacific) are now engaged in a hazardous transition from systems of customary law to systems of enacted law. The stakes in this transition—for them and for us—are very high indeed. So the mere fact that we do not see ourselves as regulating our conduct toward fellow countrymen by customary law does not mean that it is of no importance to us as world citizens.

The thesis I am going to advance here is, however, something more radical than a mere insistence that customary law is still of considerable importance today. I am going to argue that we cannot understand "ordinary" law (that is, officially declared or enacted law) unless we first obtain an understanding of what is called customary law.

In preparing my exposition I have to confess that at this point I encountered a great frustration. This arises from the term "customary law" itself. This is the term found in the titles and the indices, and if you want to compare what I have to say with what others have said, this is the heading you will have to look under. At the same time the expression is a most unfortunate one that obscures, almost beyond redemption, the nature of the phenomenon it purports to designate. Instead of serving as a neutral pointer, it prejudges its subject; it asserts that the force and meaning of what we call customary law lie in mere habit or usage.

Against this view I shall argue that the phenomenon called customary law can best be described as *a language of interaction*. To interact meaningfully men require a social setting in which the moves of the participating players will fall generally within some predictable pattern. To engage in effective social behavior men need the support of intermeshing anticipations that will let them know what their opposite numbers will do, or that will at least enable them to gauge the general scope of the repertory from which responses to their actions will be drawn. We sometimes speak of customary law as offering an unwritten code of conduct. The word *code* is appropriate here because what is involved is not simply a negation, a prohibition of certain disapproved actions, but also the obverse side of this negation, the meaning it confers on foreseeable and approved actions, which then furnish a point of orientation for ongoing interactive responses. Professors Parsons and Shils have spoken of the function, in social action, of "complementary expectations";[1] the term *complementary expectations* indicates accurately the function I am here ascribing to the law that develops out of human interaction, a form of law that we are forced—by the dictionaries and title headings—to call customary law.

Pursuing the comparison with language, let us suppose we were to open a treatise on linguistics and were to encounter the following statement as the first paragraph of the book:

> A spoken language consists of certain patterns of sound men make with their mouths. The forms of these patterns of sound are set by custom and tradition; such is the force of habit that within any given culture men will always be found to make the same general set of sounds that their ancestors did, with at most minor modifications and additions.

Surely, our reaction would be, this is a most curious way to open a discussion of language. We would be apt to say:

> But this statement does not tell us what language is *for*. Plainly its purpose is *communication*. If that is its purpose, why then of course men will go on using generally the same sounds their fathers did and that their neighbors do now: the reason they do this is simply that they want to be *understood*.

Yet in spirit and thought this imaginary introduction to linguistics is not far from what we find about customary law in treatises on jurisprudence. It will be well to turn briefly to some appraisals of customary law taken from the existing literature.

A much-quoted discussion is to be found in Holland's *Elements of Jurisprudence*. He asserts that the characteristic which marks customary law is that "it is a long and generally observed course of conduct." He goes on to explain:

> No one was ever consciously present at the commencement of such a course of conduct, but we can hardly doubt that it originated generally in the conscious choice of the more convenient of two acts, though sometimes doubtless in the accidental adoption of one of two indifferent alternatives; the choice in either case having been either deliberately or accidentally repeated till it ripened into habit.

The best illustration of the formation of such habitual courses of action

---

1. Talcott Parsons and Edward Shils, eds., *Toward a General Theory of Action* (Cambridge, Mass.: Harvard University Press, 1951).

is the mode in which a path is formed across a common. One man crosses the common, in the direction which is suggested either by the purpose he has in view, or by mere accident. If others follow in the same track, which they are likely to do after it has once been trodden, a path is made.

Before a custom is formed there is no juristic reason for its taking one direction rather than another, though doubtless there was some ground of expediency, of religious scruple, or of accidental suggestion. A habitual course of action once formed gathers strength and sanctity every year. It is a course of action which every one is accustomed to see followed: it is generally believed to be salutary, and any deviation from it is felt to be abnormal, immoral. It has never been adjoined by the organized authority of the State, but it has unquestioningly been obeyed by the individuals of which the State is composed.[2]

Now in the whole of this lucid passage there is to be found, I submit, no hint that customary law originates in interaction or that it serves the purpose of organizing and facilitating interaction. Indeed, the picture of the lonely pathmaker seems almost deliberately chosen to rule out the complications involved when men attempt to achieve a reciprocal orientation of their actions.

In the first edition of the *Encyclopedia of the Social Sciences* the article on customary law begins by citing Holland, borrows his figure of the lonely pathmaker, and ends its first paragraph by explaining the role played by customary law in primitive societies as being due to "the force of habit" which "prevails in the whole early history of the race."[3]

Let me now quote briefly a passage from an author generally more favorable to—and, I would say, more perceptive about—customary law than those I have just quoted. Salmond in his *Jurisprudence* discusses the question, What reasons can justify a court in adopting customary practice as a standard of decision? One of these reasons he sees as consisting of the fact that

custom is the embodiment of those principles which have commended themselves to the national conscience as principles of truth, justice, and public utility. The fact that any rule has already the sanction of custom, raises a presumption that it deserves to obtain a sanction of law also. . . . Speaking generally, it is well that courts of justice, in seeking those rules of right which it is their duty to administer, should be content to accept those which have already in their favor the prestige and authority of long accep-

---

2. Thomas Holland, *The Elements of Jurisprudence*, 8th ed. (New York: Macmillan, 1896), pp. 50–51.

3. *Encyclopedia of the Social Sciences* 4 (1930): 662. There is no entry under the heading "Customary Law" in the 2d edition of the encyclopedia.

tance, rather than attempt the more dangerous task of fashioning a set of rules for themselves in the light of nature.[4]

There is, of course, much wisdom—as well as a considerable measure of conservatism—in these remarks. But as touching the nature of customary law the notion expressed seems to be that, just as a society may have rules imposed on it from above, so it may also reach out for rules by a kind of inarticulate collective preference. Men are seen as directing their interactions by a law that their society has, in some silent way, told them is just and proper. What is missing is any inquiry into the actual social processes through which this law came into being and by which it is sustained.

I might add other quotations from the literature of jurisprudence, but they would not introduce any substantial change in tone or substance into those I have just discussed. The point I wish to make here relates, in any event, not so much to what the writers say about customary law, but to what they do not say. They ask nearly every question that can be asked about customary rules except this one: What are the processes by which these rules are created? They ask, What should we do about inherited customary law? but not such questions as, What functions did that law serve among those who brought it into being? Do the same functional needs exist in our society, and if so, how are we ourselves meeting them? Do we have processes going on around us that are similar to those which before state-made law existed brought customary rules into being?

These are questions to which I shall return later. Meanwhile, I should like to consider certain objections that may be raised against the proposal to view customary law as a language of interaction. In the process of answering these objections I may succeed in clarifying somewhat the view I am defending.

The first of these objections is that customary law in primitive societies may lay down rules that have nothing to do with human interaction. There may be offenses against deities and spirits; a man may be punished, even by death, for an act committed out of the presence of other persons where that act violates some taboo. The answer to this is, I suggest, that animistic views of nature may vastly extend the significance one man's acts may have for his fellows. There is a passage in Walter Bagehot that is very much in point here. Bagehot observes that the "notion that the bad religion of *A* cannot impair, here or hereafter, the welfare of *B* is, strange to say, a modern idea."[5] The extent to which one man's beliefs and acts will be seen as affecting his fellows will depend upon the degree to which men see themselves as parts, one of another,

4. John Salmond, *Jurisprudence*, 7th ed. (London: Sweet & Maxwell, 1924), pp. 208–9.
5. Walter Bagehot, *Physics and Politics* (Boston: Beacon Press, 1956), p. 117. This book was first published in 1872.

and upon their beliefs about the intangible forces that unite them. Within the extended family the distinction between other-regarding and self-regarding acts will assume an aspect very different from what it has in our own society, composed, as that society is, largely of strangers with a strong disbelief in the supernatural.

A further objection to the conception of customary law as a language of interaction may be stated in these terms: Any such conception is much too rationalistic and attributes to customary law a functional aptness, a neatness of purpose, that is far from the realities of primitive practice. Customary law is filled with ritualistic routines and pointless ceremonies; these may cater to a certain instinct for drama, but they can hardly be said to serve effective communication or the development of stable expectations that will organize and facilitate interaction.

In answer I would assert, on the contrary, that a significant function of ritual is precisely that of communication, of labelling acts so that there can be no mistake as to their meaning. Erik Erikson has a fascinating discussion of the ritualism that develops in the interactions of a mother with her infant child:

> The awakening infant conveys a message to his mother and immediately awakens in her a whole repertoire of emotive, verbal, and manipulative behavior. She approaches him with smiling or worried concern, brightly or anxiously voicing a name, and goes into action: looking, feeling, sniffing, she ascertains possible sources of discomfort and initiates services to be rendered by rearranging the infant's condition, by preparing food, picking him up, etc. If observed for several days (especially in a milieu not one's own) it becomes clear that this daily event is highly formalized, in that the mother seems to feel obliged (and to be not a little pleased) to repeat a performance arousing in the infant predictable responses, which encourage her, in turn, to proceed.[6]

Erikson goes on to observe that the formalization of this performance, the ritualistic element in it, is much more readily perceived by strangers to the participants, that is, by those who do not belong to the family, or the class, or the culture within which it develops. He ends by concluding that the purpose of the performance is to express a *mutuality of recognition*; its essential function is, in other words, *communication*. He refers to studies of ritualistic behavior among animals which indicate that such behavior has developed to "provide an unambiguous set of signals so as to avoid fatal misunderstand-

6. Erik Erikson, "Ontogeny of Ritualization," in Rudolph M. Loewenstein, *Psychoanalysis—A General Psychology—Essays in Honor of Heinz Hartmann* (New York: International Universities Press, 1966), p. 603. (I am indebted to my colleague Alan Stone for this reference.)

ings," and concludes that with man "the overcoming of ambivalence is an important aim of . . . ritualization." Certainly among a people who have no state-kept official records to show who is married to whom, the elaborate wedding ceremonies found in some customary systems can be said to serve a purpose of communication and clarification.

To illustrate the points I have been making with regard to ritualism, and, more generally, with regard to the communicative function of customary practices, I should like to refer briefly to a development that appears to be occurring in the diplomatic relations of Russia and the United States. Here we may be witnessing something like customary law in the making. Between these two countries there seems to have arisen a kind of reciprocity with respect to the forced withdrawal of diplomatic representatives. The American government, for example, believes that a member of the Russian embassy is engaged in espionage, or, perhaps I should say, it believes him to be *over*engaged in espionage; it declares him *persona non grata* and requires his departure from this country. The expected response, based on past experience, is that Russia will acquiesce in this demand, but will at once counter with a demand for the withdrawal from Russia of an American diplomatic agent of equal rank. Conversely, if the Russians expel an American emissary, the United States will react by shipping back one of Russia's envoys.

Here we have, for the time being at least, a quite stable set of interactional expectancies; within the field covered by this practice each country is able to anticipate with considerable confidence the reactions of its opposite number. This means that its decisions can be guided by a tolerably accurate advance estimate of costs. We know that if we throw one of their men out, they will throw out one of ours.

It should be noticed that the practice is routinized and contains (at least latently) ritualistic and symbolic qualities. Suppose, for example, that the American authorities were confronted with this dilemma: the Russians have declared *persona non grata* a high-ranking member of the American embassy in Moscow, and it turns out to be difficult to find an appropriate counterpart for return to Russia. We may suppose, for example, that the Soviet representatives of equal rank with the expelled American are persons Washington would like very much to see remain in this country. In this predicament it could cross the minds of those responsible for the decision that they might, in order to preserve a proper balance, return to Russia five men of a lower rank than the expelled American, or perhaps even that the expulsion of ten filing clerks would be the most apt response.

Now I suggest that any responsible public official would reflect a long time before embracing such an alternative. Its danger would lie in the damage it would inflict on the neat symbolism of a one-to-one ratio, in the confusion it might introduce into the accepted meaning of the acts involved. This is a case where both sides would probably be well-advised to stick with the familiar ritual since a departure from it might forfeit the achieved gains of a stable interactional pattern.

The illustration just discussed may seem badly chosen because it represents, one might say, a very impoverished kind of customary law, a law that confers, not a reciprocity of benefits, but a reciprocity in expressions of hostility. But much of the customary law of primitive peoples, it should be recalled, serves exactly the same function. Open and unrestricted hostilities between tribes often become in time subject to tacit and formalized restraints and may, in the end, survive only as a ritualistic mock battle.[7] Furthermore, in the diplomatic practice I have described here there may be present a richer reciprocity than appears on the surface. At the time of the *Pueblo* incident it was suggested that Russia and the United States may share an interest in being moderately and discreetly spied on by one another. We don't want the Russians to pry out our military secrets, but we want them to know, on the basis of information they will trust, that we are not planning to mount a surprise attack on them. This shared interest may furnish part of the background of the ritualistic and patterned exchange of diplomatic discourtesies that exists between the two countries.

I have already recorded my distress at having to employ the term *customary law* so frequently in this discussion. Both ingredients of the expression, the adjective and the noun, offer difficulties. I shall take up shortly the embarrassments created by the noun. Meanwhile it would be well to explore more carefully than I have so far the problems involved in finding a satisfactory substitute for "customary." As I have already observed, the principal objection to this word lies in its suggestion that the mere repetition of some action by *A* will create in others a right that *A* shall repeat this action, with an added implication that the strength of this claim will vary directly with the duration in time of *A*'s repetitive behavior. Of course, no theorist of customary law in fact embraces any such absurdity, however much the language employed may seem at times to suggest the contrary. My neighbor might for years have arisen every morning precisely at eight, yet no one would think that this settled practice could create any obligation toward me unless it entered into some coordination of our activities, as it might if I had come to depend on him to drive me to work in his car. Instead, therefore, of speaking vaguely of an obligation arising through mere custom or repetition, it would be better to say that a sense of obligation will arise when a stabilization of interactional expectancies

---

7. There is thus less paradox than might at first appear in the title of Paul Bohannan's anthology, *Law and Warfare—Studies in the Anthropology of Conflict* (New York: Natural History Press, 1967).

has occurred so that the parties have come to guide their conduct toward one another by these expectancies.

The term *interactional expectancy* is itself, however, capable of producing difficulties. We shall be misled, for example, if we suppose that the relevant expectancy or anticipation must enter actively into consciousness. In fact the anticipations which most unequivocally shape our behavior and attitudes toward others are often precisely those that are operative without our being aware of their presence. To take an example from a somewhat trivial context, experiments have shown that the distance people stand from one another in carrying on ordinary conversations varies predictably among cultures and between individuals. At the same time most people would not be able to state, without some preliminary testing, what they themselves regard as a normal conversational distance. My inability to define offhand a proper distance would not prevent me, however, from finding offensive the action of someone who projected his face uncomfortably close to mine, nor would it relieve my puzzlement and distress at the conduct of someone who kept retreating when I approached what seemed to me a normal speaking distance. Our conduct toward others, and our interpretations of their behavior toward us, are, in other words, constantly shaped by standards that do not enter consciously into our thought processes. The analogy of language is once again useful; often we only become aware of rules of grammar when they are broken, and it is sometimes their breach that leads us to articulate for the first time rules we had previously acted on without knowing it.

Any analysis in terms of "interactional expectancies" must also confront the problem of the man who is in some sense an outsider to the expectancies that organize the life of a particular group. He may be literally an outsider, a trader, for example, coming from a distance to sell his wares among a tribal people. Or, though born and raised within the group, he may be "alienated," too imperceptive to understand the system, or perhaps too perceptive to accept some of its built-in absurdities and anomalies. It would, of course, be impossible to undertake here any adequate analysis of the problems suggested. A guess may be hazarded, though, that it is to the intrusion of the true outsider—"the stranger" in Simmel's famous essay[8]—that we owe, not only the invention of economic trade, but the more general discovery that it is possible for men to arrange their relations with one another by explicit contract.

Now for the difficulties produced by the noun in the expression *customary law*. If we speak of a system of stabilized interactional expectancies as a more adequate way of describing what the treatises call customary law, we encounter the embarrassment that many of these expectancies relate to matters that

8. *The Sociology of Georg Simmel*, ed. K. Wolff (New York: Free Press, 1950), pp. 402–8.

seem remote from anything like a legal context. For example, rules of etiquette fully meet the suggested definition, yet one would scarcely be inclined to call rules of this sort rules of law.

This raises the question, How much of what is called customary law really deserves the epithet *law*? Anthropologists have devoted some attention to this question[9] and have arrived at divergent responses to it, including one which asserts that the question is itself misconceived, since you cannot apply a conception interwoven with notions of explicit enactment to a social context where rules of conduct come into existence without the aid of a lawmaker. Among those who take the question seriously the answer proposed by Hoebel has perhaps attracted the most attention; it will repay us to consider it for a moment. Hoebel suggests that in dealing with stateless or primitive societies "law may be defined in these terms: A social norm is legal if its neglect or infraction is regularly met, in threat or in fact, by the application of physical force by an individual or group possessing the socially recognized privilege of so acting." [10]

There are, I suggest, a number of difficulties with this solution. First, it seems to define "law" by an imperfection. If the function of law is to produce an ordered relationship among the members of a society, what shall we say of a system that works so smoothly that there is never any occasion to resort to force or the threat of force to effectuate its norms? Does its very success forfeit for such a system the right to be called by the prestigious name of "law"?

Again, can it always be known in advance whether the infraction of some particular norm will be visited with forceful reprisal? The seriousness of the breach of any rule is always in some measure a function of context. One might be inclined to hazard a guess that few societies would regularly punish with violence infractions of the rules of etiquette. Suppose, however, that a peacemaking conference is held by delegations representing two tribes on the verge of war; a member of one delegation uses an insulting nickname in addressing his opposite number; the result is a bloody and disastrous war. Is it likely that his fellow tribesmen would be content to visit on the offender some moderate measure of social censure? If this illustration seems contrived, it may be observed that in our free society it is an accepted legal principle that a man incurs no liability for expressing to another a low opinion of his intelligence and integrity. If a lawyer trying a case in court were to take advantage of this freedom in addressing the judge, he might very well find himself escorted forcibly from the courtroom to serve a jail sentence for contempt.

9. References to most of the literature on this subject will be found in Max Gluckman, *The Judicial Process among the Barotse of Northern Rhodesia*, 2d ed. (Manchester, U.K.: Manchester University Press, 1967), chaps. 5 and 9.

10. E. Adamson Hoebel, *The Law of Primitive Man* (Cambridge, Mass.: Harvard University Press, 1954), p. 28.

Perhaps the basic objection to Hoebel's proposal is that it ignores the *systematic* quality of primitive law. The law of the tribe or extended family is not simply a chart of do's and don'ts; it is a program for living together. Some parts of the program may achieve articulation as distinct norms imposing specially defined sanctions. But the basic logic of customary law will continue to inhere in the system as a whole. Lévi-Strauss may seem at times to drive this quality of primitive social orders to the point of caricature,[11] but if so, his efforts have provided a wholesome antidote to the tendency to assume that any customary system can be reduced to a kind of code book of numbered paragraphs, each paragraph standing forth as a little law complete in itself.

A recent controversy among anthropologists is worthy of consideration in this connection. In his famous book, *The Judicial Process among the Barotse of Northern Rhodesia*, Max Gluckman suggested that a key element of Barotse legal reasoning lay in the concept of "the reasonable man." The fact that this concept also plays a role in more "advanced" systems argued, so Gluckman concluded, for a certain unity in legal reasoning everywhere. This conclusion was rather emphatically rejected by a number of his professional colleagues.[12]

Perhaps it may help to clarify the issues by considering a rule of law, familiar to every reader, that is at least customary in origin. I refer to "the rule of the road" by which (over most of the world) one passes the oncoming vehicle on the right. Now it would seem redundant and even absurd to introduce into this context anything like the concept of the reasonable man; I pass on the right, not because I am a reasonable man, but because it is the rule. But suppose a situation is encountered in which the presuppositions underlying the rule no longer hold. For example, one is driving in a parking lot, without marked lanes, where other vehicles are coming and going, backing and turning. Or, driving on a regular highway, one encounters an approaching vehicle careening back and forth across the road apparently out of control. In situations like these what is demanded is plainly something like the judgment and concern of "the reasonable man"; in such a context the rule of the road can furnish at most a kind of presumptive guide as to what to do when other factors in the situation offer no clear solution.

Primitive society, like vehicular traffic, is run by a system of interlocking roles. When one man steps out of his role, or a situation arises in which a familiar role forfeits some or all of its meaning, then adjustments will have to be made. There can be no formula to guide these adjustments beyond that of reasonableness—exercised in the light of the demands of the system as a

---

11. See Claude Lévi-Strauss, *The Savage Mind* (Chicago: University of Chicago Press, 1966).
12. Gluckman, *Judicial Process*, pp. 82–162, 387–98. (Gluckman's answer to critics on this point will be found in the second reference.)

whole. It is, therefore, no accident that Gluckman should report that he first perceived the significance of "the reasonable man" for Barotse law as he reflected on a controversy he designates as "The Case of the Biassed Father." [13]

Before proceeding to other matters it may repay us to pursue a little further the analogy between primitive legal systems and the laws of traffic. To that end, perhaps the reader will extend his indulgence to a somewhat uninhibited exercise in fantasy. We begin by supposing that an earthling is being interviewed by a visitor from outer space. In his astral home this visitor follows a profession we would designate as that of legal anthropology. In the pursuit of his specialty he has become fascinated with the earthly laws of traffic, a subject wholly unfamiliar to him because on his planet the movement of goods and living beings is accomplished automatically under the guidance of a computing center. He begins by asking what the rule is when two vehicles approach each other from opposite directions. The response is that each driver keeps to the right. The astral visitor asks, "Why to the right? Why not to the left?" The earthling replies that there is no special reason for the one rule or the other and that in some automotive cultures the rule is indeed that one keeps to the left. (At this point the anthropologist records in his notebook that the earthlings seem singularly incurious about the basic principles of their legal systems and are content to follow rules simply because they have been told they are the proper rules to follow.)

The interview is resumed, and the anthropologist asks, "What about the rule when you overtake another vehicle? I would suppose it would be the same, that is, that you pass on the right; this would keep the law simple and understandable." To the surprise of the astral visitor the earthling replies that the rule in this case is that you pass on the left. But why this anomaly? The earthling replies that it is not an anomaly at all, but a logical corollary of the rule that you pass the oncoming vehicle on the right. At this point the anthropologist begins to lose his patience and demands that the earthling give him some simple, easily understood reason why the rule that you overtake on the left is the appropriate rule to go with the rule that you pass the oncoming vehicle on the right. Those of us who feel we might have some difficulty in producing a prompt response to this demand may take some consolation in the reflection that this incapacity of ours may help us to understand the difficulties natives sometimes have in explaining to outsiders the internal logic of their legal orders, particularly with respect to complex systems for reckoning kinship.

Some reflection on problems of traffic regulation may also be useful in another connection, that is, in helping us to understand the impact of "social

13. Ibid., pp. 37–45.

change"—urbanization and industrialization, for example—on peoples used to ordering their lives by customary law. As every experienced driver knows, the old simplicity of "pass on the right, overtake on the left" has undergone substantial modification in accommodation to modern highway conditions. These changes reflect themselves in lengthy and largely unread paragraphs in the traffic code. Overtaking on the right may, for example, be permitted when driving on multilaned, divided highways, on one-way city streets, or when the driver ahead signals for a left turn. But these qualifications introduce their own special crop of uncertainties. Are you permitted to overtake on the right when on a very wide, multilaned highway that is not divided into two unidirectional sections? Again, the driver ahead signals for a left turn, you start to pass him on the right, then discover (before he does) that he is not permitted to turn left. Or, driving on a one-way street you are about to take advantage of your privilege of overtaking on the right when you suddenly realize that the street is about to become two-way. The American driver caught in these perplexities is in a position to understand something of the plight of the African tribesman who tries conscientiously to live in town by one set of rules, in the country by another, and has some trouble at times in keeping the two systems apart.

II. *The Interactional Foundations of Contract Law*

The brief account of contract law that follows has been included here primarily for the light it may shed on customary law, which is often and properly said to contain a consensual element. In this shared aspect contract law and customary law are indeed near-cousins, and a study of either will help to understand the other. In the course of the analysis that follows, I shall have occasion to revisit from a somewhat different perspective some of the questions already discussed, particularly that of knowing how to determine when patterns of interaction can properly be said to have created an obligation to persist in them.

In keeping with the general objective just outlined we shall be concerned here with contract as a source of social order, as one means for establishing "stable interactional expectancies." As it is used in the heading for this section, the term *contract law*, therefore, refers primarily, not to the law *of* or *about* contracts, but to the "law" a contract itself brings into existence. This employment of the word *law* represents, of course, a considerable departure from the conventions we ordinarily follow in using the term.

Our reluctance to apply the word *law* to the obligation created by a contract is, however, in many ways an anomaly. In enforcing contracts courts purport to derive the legal rights and duties of the litigants from the terms of their agreement, much as if a statute were being applied. The Romans did not hesitate, at least in certain contexts, to apply the word *lex* to contractual provisions, and the Latin word seems indeed to have taken its origin in a contractual context. Today international lawyers list treaties as the prime source of their kind of law. Though the term *customary law* has been regarded by some legal theorists as an abuse of language, today most writers seem to have overcome any qualms about that expression; the acceptance of customary law and the rejection of contractual law are all the more remarkable since, if what is associated with law is something like an explicit legislative process, the contract comes much closer to fitting that model than do the silent processes through which customary law comes into being. Finally, as proof that lawyers do not reject the expression *law of the contract* because it conflicts with any basic demand of legal logic, I cite their readiness to accept the thought contained in the expression, provided it comes decently clothed in paraphrase. Thus, I doubt if any lawyer would be deeply perplexed (though he might be slightly intrigued) by the statement contained in Article 1134 of the French Civil Code that a contract "serves as law" between the parties. (*"Les conventions légalment formés tiennent lieu de loi à ceux qui les ont faites."*)

If we permit ourselves to think of contract law as the "law" that the parties themselves bring into existence by their agreement, the transition from customary law to contract law becomes a very easy one indeed. The difficulty then becomes, not that of subsuming the two kinds of law under one rubric, but of knowing how to draw a clear line of division between them. We may say of course (using the jargon I have inflicted on the reader here) that in the one case the relevant interactional expectancies are created by words; in the other, by actions.

But this is too simple a view of the matter. Where words are used, they have to be interpreted. When the contract falls within some general area of repetitive dealings, there will usually exist a body of standard practice in the light of which verbal ambiguities will be resolved. Here, in effect, interactional regularities in the world outside the contract are written into the contract in the process of interpretation. In commercial law generally it is often difficult to know whether to say that by entering a particular field of practice the parties became subject to a governing body of customary law or to say that they have by tacit agreement incorporated standard practice into the terms of their contract.

The meaning of a contract may not only be determined by the area of practice within which the contract falls, but by the interactions of the parties themselves after entering their agreement. If the performance of a contract takes place over a period of time, the parties will often evidence by their conduct what courts sometimes call a practical construction of their agreement; this interpretation by deeds may have control over the meaning that would ordinarily be attributed to the words of the contract itself. If the discrepancy between the parties' acts and the words of their agreement becomes too great to permit the courts to speak of a practical construction, they may hold that the contract has been tacitly modified or even rescinded by the manner in which the parties have conducted themselves toward one another since entering the agreement.

Generally we may say that in the actual carrying out of a complex agreement between friendly parties, the written contract often furnishes a kind of framework for an ongoing relationship, rather than a precise definition of that relationship. For that definition we may have to look to a kind of two-party customary law implicit in the parties' actions, rather than to the verbal formulations of the contract; if this is true of contracts that are eventually brought to court, it must be much more commonly so in situations where the parties make out without resort to litigation.

If the words of a contract have to be interpreted in their interactional context, or in the light of the actions taken under them by the parties, the actions that bring customary law into existence also have to be interpreted sometimes almost as if they were words. This problem of interpretation is at once the most crucial and most neglected problem of customary law; intrinsically difficult, it is made more so by inept theories about the nature of customary law, such as those explaining it as an expression of "the force of habit" that "prevails in the early history of the race."

The central problem of "interpretation" in customary law is that of knowing when to read into an act, or a pattern of repetitive acts, an obligatory sense like that which may attach to a promise explicitly spelled out in words. All are agreed that a person, a tribe, or a nation does not incur an obligation—legal or moral—simply because a repetitive pattern can be discerned in his or its actions. All would probably also agree that the actions which create customary law must be such as enter into *inter*actions, though a complication ensues when we recall that under some circumstances inaction can take on the qualities of action, as when it becomes appropriate to call it acquiescence or forbearance. Beyond this we encounter almost a vacuum of ideas.

Into this vacuum there is projected at least one articulate attempt at formulating a test. This is found in the doctrine of *opinio necessitatis*. According to this principle (which still enjoys some esteem in international law) customary law arises out of repetitive actions when and only when such actions are motivated by a sense of obligation, in other words, when people behave as they do, not because they want to, or because they act unreflectively, but because they believe they have to act as they do. This seems a curiously inept solution. In clear cases of established customary law, it becomes a tautology; in situations where customary law is in the process of being born, it defaults.

One might suggest that a better approach could be found in the principle contained in Section 90 of the American Law Institute's Restatement of Contracts. As formulated to fit the problem at hand this principle would run along these (unfortunately somewhat complex) lines: Where by his actions toward B, A has (whatever his actual intentions may have been) given B reasonably to understand that he (A) will in the future in similar situations act in a similar manner, and B has, in some substantial way, prudently adjusted his affairs to the expectation that A will in the future act in accordance with this expectation, then A is bound to follow the pattern set by his past actions toward B. This creates an obligation by A to B. If the pattern of interaction followed by A and B then spreads through the relevant community, a rule of general customary law will have been created. This rule will normally become part of a larger system, which will involve a complex network of reciprocal expectations. Absorption of the new rule into the larger system will, of course, be facilitated by the fact that the interactions that gave rise to it took place within limits set by that system and derived a part of their meaning for the parties from the wider interactional context within which they occurred.

The familiar phenomenon of the spread of customary law from one social context to another suggests a further distinction between customary law and contract law that deserves critical examination here. It may be said that a contract binds only the parties to it, while customary law normally extends its rules over a large and at times somewhat unclearly defined community. The first observation is that while this spread of customary law is a common occurrence it is by no means inevitable. Something that can be called two-party customary law can and does exist; it is, again, only linguistic prejudice that makes us hesitant about this employment of the word *law.*

Where customary law does in fact spread we must not be misled as to the process by which this extension takes place. It has sometimes been thought of as if it involved a kind of inarticulate expression of group will; the members of Group B perceive that the rules governing Group A would furnish an apt law for them; they therefore take over those rules by an act of tacit collective adoption. This kind of explanation abstracts from the interactional processes underlying customary law and ignores their ever-present communicative aspect. Take, for example, a practice in the field of international relations, that of offering a twenty-one-gun salute to visiting heads of state. By a process of imitation this practice seems now to have become fairly general among the nations. One may say loosely that its appeal lies in the appropriateness of a resounding boom of cannon as a way of signalizing the arrival of a distinguished visitor. But why twenty-one guns, instead of sixteen or twenty-five? It is apparent that once the pattern of twenty-one became familiar, any departure from it could generate misapprehension; spectators would spend their time, not in enjoying the grandeur of cannon roar, but in counting booms, attributing all sorts of meanings—intended and unintended—to any departure from the last allocation. Generally we may say that where A and B have become familiar with a practice obtaining between C and D, A is likely to adopt this pattern in his actions toward B, not simply or necessarily because it has any special aptness for their situation, but because he knows B will understand the meaning of his behavior and will know how to react to it.

As for the proposition that a contract binds only those who made it, who actively and knowingly assented to its terms, a mere glance at modern contracting practice is sufficient to reveal how unreal and purely formal this proposition can become. Only a tiny fraction of the "contracts" signed today are actually negotiated or represent anything like an explicit accommodation of the parties' respective interests. Even contracts drafted by lawyers, and in theory specially fitted to the parties' situation, are apt to be full of traditional or standard clauses borrowed from other contracts and from general practice. These clauses are employed for a great variety of reasons—because the lawyer is in a hurry, or because he knows from the precedents how courts will construe them, or because the interests at stake are insufficient to justify the fee that would be appropriate to a more careful, specially tailored phrasing.

But the realities of contracting practice are much farther removed from the picture of a "meeting of minds" than is suggested by a mere reference to standard clauses. In fact, the overwhelming majority of contracts are embodied in printed forms, prepared by one party to serve his interests and imposed on the other on a take-it-or-leave-it basis. In recent years American courts in dealing with such contracts have increasingly exercised the right to strike out clauses they regard as oppressive or grossly unfair. This practice stands in contrast with that of the homeland of the common law, where the courts are much more conservative in this matter, being inclined generally to enforce the contract "as written," that is, as printed from boiler plate. There is a certain irony in this, for from the time of Lord Coke the English courts have freely claimed the right to refuse enforcement to customary law deemed unreasonable and repugnant to the ordinary sense of fairness. If we were to search about in modern society for the nearest counterpart to the "repugnant" customary law of Coke's time, we might well find it in the standardized, printed contract, drafted by one party and signed unread by the other.

There remains for discussion one further distinction that can be made between contract law and customary law. This lies in the notion that a contract comes into effect at once, or when the parties stipulate it shall, while custom becomes law only through a usage observed to have persisted over a considerable period.

This is, again, too simple a view of the matter. The notion that customary law comes into effect gradually and only over a considerable period of time comes about, in part because of mistaken implications read into the word *customary*, and in part because it is true that normally it takes some time for reciprocal interactional expectancies to "jell." But there are circumstances in which customary law (or a phenomenon for which we have no other name) can develop almost overnight. As an authority in international law has observed, "A new rule of customary international law based on the practice of States can emerge very quickly, and even almost suddenly, if new circumstances have arisen which imperatively call for regulation—though the time-factor is never wholly irrelevant." [14] (The assertion sometimes encountered that to be accepted as law a custom must have existed "from time immemorial" is directed to a very special question, that is, When should custom be regarded as overriding provisions of the general law? This obviously can be something quite different from asking when custom should control an issue previously not regulated by law at all. The doctrine of *opinio necessitatis* probably originated in the same context, for it may make good sense to say that a man should not be held to have infringed at least some kinds of general law where he acted in the belief that a special or local customary law obligated him to conduct himself as he did.)

As for the notion that a contract binds at once, and before any action has been taken under it, this is again a misleading simplification, especially when the matter is viewed historically. It is, of course, dangerous to attempt generalizations about the historical course of legal development in all societies. Nevertheless, it is reasonably safe to say that the legal enforcement of contracts first emerges in two contexts. The first of these is that of the ritualistic promise, the promise accompanied by some traditional oath or the recital of a set verbal formula, for example. Here, indeed, the contract binds at once and without proof of any action under it. But the very formality of this process of "binding," or the distrust implied by an insistence on it, has no doubt always inhibited its use, as it does today in the case of its modern counterparts.

The second early legal manifestation of the contract principle involves the situation of the half-completed exchange. *A* delivers fish to *B* in return for *B*'s promise of a basket of vegetables. *B* keeps the fish but refuses to deliver the vegetables. Plainly there is nothing mysterious about the fact that in this situation legal redress became available at an early period in history. It should be

---

14. Judge Fitzmaurice, quoted in Clive Parry, *The Sources and Evidences of International Law* (Manchester, U.K.: Manchester University Press, 1965), p. 60n.

noted, however, that the obligation enforced rests not on mere words, but primarily on the action (and inaction) that followed the words.

It appears likely that in all legal systems the enforcement of the executory bilateral contract is a development that comes quite late. This is the situation where *A* and *B* agree on the exchange, let us say again, of fish for vegetables; when *A* comes to deliver the fish, *B* refuses his offering and repudiates the agreement. The recognition that *A* has a legal claim in this situation seems generally to have occurred contemporaneously with the development of something like a market economy. But in such an environment there is likely to be action, at least in the sense of forbearance, in the very act of entering the contract. *A*, in seeking for a chance to trade his fish for vegetables, foregoes, when he strikes his bargain with *B*, the chance to enter a similar trade with *C*, *D*, or *E*. So here once again the agreement becomes enforceable because its words have been underscored, as it were, by reliance on them—in this case, by an inferred neglect of other opportunities once the contract in question had been concluded.

Finally, it should be recalled that the promise of an outright gift retains to this day a somewhat uncertain legal status. There may exist cumbersome legal forms for making such promises enforceable, and the courts have sometimes shown remarkable ingenuity in finding tacit elements of exchange in what appears on its face as an expression of sheer generosity. In the United States there has emerged a doctrine (now known generally as the Section Ninety Principle) whereby the promise may become enforceable when the promisee has seriously and reasonably taken its anticipated performance into account in the arrangement of his own affairs. As I have previously suggested, this principle is not far removed from one that underlies customary law generally.

III. *The Interactional Foundations of Enacted Law*

Early in this chapter I stated my intention to advance a thesis more radical than a mere insistence that customary law is still of considerable importance today: namely that we cannot understand ordinary law (that is, officially declared or enacted law) unless we first obtain an understanding of what is called customary law. The time has come to attempt some fulfillment of the commitment implied in this statement.

In the pages that have gone before I have treated both customary law and contract law as interactional phenomena. I have viewed them as arising out of interaction and as serving to order and facilitate interaction. Can anything like this be asserted of enacted law, as typified, for example, by the statute? Can we regard enacted law itself as dependent on the development of "stable inter-actional expectancies" between lawgiver and subject? Does enacted law also serve the purpose of ordering and facilitating the interactions of citizens with one another?

It cannot be said that there are no traces of ideas like these in the literature. What can be said is that it requires some diligence to find them. As for the general purpose of enacted law, the standard formula—in both jurisprudence and sociology—is to the effect that law serves as an instrument of social control. Sometimes this conception is coupled with the notion that the necessity for law arises entirely from man's defective moral nature; if men could be counted on to act morally, law would be unnecessary. As for the way law is conceived to come into existence, it is by an exercise of authority and not from anything like an interplay of reciprocal expectancies. The law does not invite the citizen to interact with it; it acts upon him.

Let us test the question whether enacted law serves to put in order and facilitate human interaction by inquiring how this conception applies to some actual branches of the law. First, consider the law embraced under the follow-ing headings: contract, agency, marriage and divorce, property (both private and public), and the rules of court procedure. All of these vital branches of the law serve primarily to set the terms of men's relations with one another; they facilitate human interaction as traffic is facilitated by the laying out of roads and the installation of direction signs. To say that these branches of law would be unnecessary if men were more disposed to act morally is like saying that language could be dispensed with if only men were intelligent enough to com-municate without it. The fact that the branches of law just listed include re-straints as well as enabling provisions detracts in no sense from their facilita-tive quality; there is no more paradox here than there is in the proposition that highway traffic can be expedited by signs that read, No Left Turn, or Stop, Then Enter.

An interactional theory of law can hardly claim acceptance, however, sim-ply because it seems apt when applied to certain branches of the law, such as contracts, property, agency, and marital rights. The law of crimes, for example, presents a quite different test, for here an interactional view encounters an environment much less congenial to its premises. There would, for example, be something ludicrous about explaining the rule against murder as being in-tended to facilitate human interaction by removing from men's confrontations the fear that they may kill one another. Murder, we are likely to say, is prohib-ited because it is wrong, not because the threat of it can detract from the potential richness of man's relations with his fellows.

Viewed from a historical perspective, however, the matter assumes a very different aspect. Students of primitive society have seen the very inception of the concept of law itself in limitations on the blood feud. A member of family *A* kills a member of family *B*. In a primitive society the natural response to this act is for the members of family *B* to seek revenge against family *A*. If no limits are set to this revenge, there may ensue a war to the death between the two families. There has, accordingly, grown up in many primitive societies a rule that blood revenge on the part of family *B* must, in the case supposed, be limited to one killing, though the injured family is regarded as being entitled as of right to this degree of counterkill. A later development will normally prohibit blood revenge and require instead compensation in the form of "blood money" for the life of the man whose life was taken. Here, plainly, the law of murder serves to regulate interaction and, if you will, to facilitate interaction on a level more profitable for all concerned than killing and counter-killing.

Today the law against murder appears on the surface to have become entirely divorced from its interactional origins; it is seen as projecting its imperative, "thou shalt not kill," over the members of society generally and without regard to their interrelations. But what has in fact happened is that interactional issues that were once central have, as the result of legal and moral progress, been pushed to the periphery, where they remain as lively as ever. The most obvious example is offered by the plea of self-defense; a man is still legally privileged to kill an aggressor if this is necessary to save his own life. But how shall we interpret "necessary" in this context? How far can we expect a man to run some risk to his own life in order to avoid taking the life of another? Again, there is the question of reducing the degree of the offense when a man kills in "hot blood," as when he comes upon another making love to his wife. Finally, there are the disputed issues of killing to prevent a felony or to stop a fleeing felon. In all these much-debated cases the rule against homicide may be modified, or punishment reduced, by a reference to the question, What can reasonably be expected of a man in these interactional situations?

I trust it is clear that I am not advancing here the thesis that law, in its actual formulation and administration, always serves exclusively the purpose of ordering and facilitating human interaction. There are, certainly, some manifestations of law which cannot readily be forced into this frame of thought. Perhaps the most significant of these lies in that portion of the criminal law relating to what have been called "crimes without victims." Included here are laws forbidding the sale of intoxicants and contraceptive devices, the use of marijuana, homosexual practices, prostitution, and gambling. Assuming that those involved are of sound mind, and that there is no deception—the roulette wheel has not been rigged, for example—these laws, far from facilitating interaction, have as their purpose preventing forms of interaction desired by the participants and not directly designed, at least, to injure others.

It is no accident, I think, that it is in this area—the area precisely where legal restraint appears most unequivocally as an "instrument of social control"—that the grossest failures of law have everywhere occurred. It is an area characterized by corruption, selective and sporadic enforcement, blackmail, and the open tolerance of illegality. There is no need to argue here that this body of law requires critical reexamination. The problem is to know by what guiding principle to direct that reexamination.

We should begin by asking ourselves why the law fails so notably in this general area of crimes without victims. The usual answer is that you cannot enforce morality by law. But this is not so. Keeping promises may be a moral obligation, yet the law can and does successfully force people to keep their promises. Not only that, but the legal enforcement of promises, far from weakening the moral sense of obligation, tends to strengthen it. Suppose, for example, a situation where men associated in some business enterprise are discussing whether they ought to perform a disadvantageous contract. Those who believe they are morally bound to do so are in a position to remind their less principled associates that if the contract is broken they will all be brought to court and will subject themselves, not only to the cost, but also to the opprobrium of an adverse judgment. There are areas of human concern, then, where the cliché that you can't make men act morally by law does not hold. These are, I believe, precisely the areas where the law's sanctions reinforce interactional expectancies and facilitate a respect for them.

In dealing with primitive systems a distinction is sometimes taken between wrongs and sins.[15] A wrong is an act that inflicts a palpable damage on the fabric of social relations; a sin is thought to work a more diffuse harm by spreading a kind of corruption. Typically in primitive societies wrongs and sins are dealt with by different standards and different procedures, formalized "due process" being not uncommonly relaxed in the case of sins. While I would not recommend a resort to sorcery or ostracism as a way of dealing with modern sins, I think we might profitably borrow from primitive society some of the wisdom displayed in the basic distinction between wrongs and sins. Perhaps we might also add to that wisdom the insight that the best way for the law to deal with at least some modern sins is to leave them alone.

In this discussion of "the interactional foundations of enacted law" I have so far been chiefly concerned with the question whether enacted law can properly be regarded as putting in order and facilitating human interaction. It is time now to turn to what may seem the more basic question: Does enacted

15. E.g., Henry Maine, *Ancient Law*, 10th ed. (London: John Murray, 1884), pp. 359–61.

law itself depend for its existence on the development of "stable interactional expectancies" between lawgiver and subject?

To answer this question in the affirmative, as I shall here, is to run counter to an assumption now generally accepted in jurisprudence and sociology, the assumption, namely, that the essential characteristic of law lies simply in the fact that it is an exercise of *authority*. But we must ask, authority to do *what*? Many men enjoy authority without being empowered to make law. Both an army colonel and the director of a government printing office have authority in that they are thought of as rightfully exercising a control over those committed to their direction. They are not, however, considered to make law. How, then, do we distinguish between the functions performed by, let us say, a boss and those performed by a lawgiver? These two figures plainly represent distinct kinds of social control. But how do we define the difference between them?

An ancient answer to this question—rather lost from view in contemporary discussions—is that the basic characteristic of law lies in its *generality*. Law lays down *general* rules. Managerial direction may proceed by specific orders: "Here, do this," "*A*, change places with *B*," or "Report tomorrow at eight-thirty." The difficulty here is that managerial direction also often proceeds by general rules or standing orders. Would a managerial director so gifted with foresight and a capacity for apt phrasing that he never had occasion to issue anything but general orders become by that token a lawgiver?

To perceive the distinction between the office of boss and that of lawgiver we have to go behind the quality of generality and ask *why* it has been thought that law must take the form of general rules. The answer is a relatively simple one: The law does not tell a man what he should do to accomplish specific ends set by the lawgiver; it furnishes him with baselines against which to organize his life with his fellows. A transgression of these baselines may entail serious consequences for the citizen—he may be hanged for it—but the establishment of the baselines is not an exercise in managerial direction. Law provides a framework for the citizen within which to live his own life, though, to be sure, there are circumstances under which that framework can seem so uncomfortably lax or so perversely constrictive that its human object may believe that straightforward managerial direction would be preferable.

If we accept the view that the central purpose of law is to furnish baselines for human interaction, it then becomes apparent why the existence of enacted law as an effectively functioning system depends upon the establishment of stable interactional expectancies between lawgiver and subject. On the one hand, the lawgiver must be able to anticipate that the citizenry as a whole will accept as law and generally observe the body of rules he has promulgated. On the other hand, the legal subject must be able to anticipate that government will itself abide by its own declared rules when it comes to judge his actions, as in deciding, for example, whether he has committed a crime or claims property under a valid deed. A gross failure in the realization of either of these anticipations—of government toward citizen and of citizen toward government—can have the result that the most carefully drafted code will fail to become a functioning system of law.

It is a curious fact of history that although the older books are full of discussions of the principle that law implies general rules, there is almost no explicit recognition that the enactment of general rules becomes meaningless if government considers itself free to disregard them whenever it suits its convenience. Perhaps there is here illustrated a phenomenon already discussed,[16] that the anticipations which most firmly direct our actions toward others are often precisely those that do not rise to consciousness. Such anticipations are like the rules of grammar that we observe in practice without having occasion to articulate them until they have been conspicuously violated. Perhaps there is also operative here a confusion arising from the fact that we realize that normally a lawgiver can change any one of his laws simply by repealing it and providing a quite different law for the governance of events thereafter happening. It seems curious that the agency that can rewrite the whole book of laws should be held to respect the most insignificant of its enactments in judging events that occurred while it was still in effect. There is the paradox here, in Simmel's words, of "interaction within an apparently one-sided and passive submission."[17] Yet without that paradox the notion of enacted law would become empty and meaningless.

What are the practical implications of the twin requirements that law be expressed in general rules and that government abide by its own rules in acting upon the citizen? The short answer is that these implications are subtle and complex, so much so that they cannot be adequately explored in the present context. Certainly there is no intention here to suggest that the ordinary citizen should go about with a code book in his hand ascertaining whether government is conforming to its own rules. Normally, and by and large, the citizen must of necessity accept on faith that his government is playing the game of law fairly. But precisely because this faith plays so important a role in the functioning of a legal system, a single dramatic disappointment of it, or a less conspicuous but persistent disregard of legality over a whole branch of law, can undermine the moral foundations of a legal order, both for those subject to it and for those who administer it.

In speaking here of the moral aspects of the problem, there is no intention to imply that the preservation of legality does not make demands on the intel-

16. See p. 220.
17. *The Sociology of Georg Simmel*, p. 186.

lect as well as on good intentions. For example, a legislature passes a law authorizing the construction of a park in the city of Zenith. Does this enactment violate the principle that laws must be general in form? We may dismiss this problem as involving nothing more than a pun on the word *law*, but in other cases, since government normally exercises managerial and administrative functions as well as legislative ones, the problem can become more perplexing. Again, suppose the absurd situation of a government that has only one law in the books: "Do right and avoid evil." Here the rule is general in a way that undermines legality more thoroughly than any number of special laws could do. These examples can only suggest some of the complexities that arise in the actual realization of the rule of law.[18] When these complexities are taken into account the task of creating and administering a legal system will be seen as a very different kind of enterprise than is suggested when it is described simply as an exercise of authority for the purpose of effecting social control.

In the analysis now being concluded three distinct kinds of law have been passed in review: customary law, contract law, and enacted law. This list omits a fourth expression of law, namely, adjudicative law as exemplified in the Anglo-American common law. It is fashionable nowadays to consider the common law as being simply a form of enacted law, differing from statutory law only in its authorship, a statute being enacted by a legislature, a rule of common law being declared by a court. This view ignores the special qualities exemplified by the common law, qualities that once led men—with much justification—to speak of it as a form of customary law. For the common law, by virtue of its special way of making law case by case, projects its roots more deeply and intimately into human interaction than does statutory law— though, to be sure, in the country of its origin it seems to be losing the qualities that once distinguished it, perhaps because its judges have finally begun to conform their practice to the pattern legal theory has been ascribing to it for more than a century.

If we view law as serving the purpose of putting in order and facilitating human interaction, it is apparent that the making of law involves the risk that we may be unable to foresee in advance the variety of interactional situations that may fall within the ambit of a preformulated rule. A statute that reveals itself as a patent misfit for situations of fact that later come to court—situations plainly covered by the language of the statute, but obviously misunderstood or not foreseen by the draftsman—such a law certainly has no special claim to praise simply because it is clear in meaning and announced in ad-

18. I have attempted to deal with these complexities in my book, *The Morality of Law*, rev. ed. (New Haven: Yale University Press, 1969), especially chaps. 2 and 5.

vance. The virtue of the common law is that, proceeding case by case, it can fit and refit its prescriptions to the configurations of life as they reveal themselves in litigation. What the common law lacks in the way of clear advance formulation, it may more than make up for by its capacity to reshape and reword its rules in the light of the actual situations that offer themselves for decision.

The common law presents, then, a complex amalgam of lawmaking forms, intermixing explicit legislation with the tacit adjustments characteristic of customary law, sometimes expressing the best qualities of both systems, and, on rare occasions, displaying the worst qualities of both.[19]

iv. *Interactions Between Law and Its Social Context*

Implicit in all that has gone before in this discussion is the view that law and its social environment stand in a relation of reciprocal influence; any given form of law will not only act upon, but be influenced and shaped by, the established forms of interaction that constitute its social milieu. This means that for a given social context one form of law may be more appropriate than another, and that the attempt to force a form of law upon a social environment uncongenial to it may miscarry with damaging results.

This presents the problem of knowing how to define and distinguish the various kinds of social contexts. On this matter, the literature of sociology provides an uncomfortably extensive vocabulary of relevant terms: *Gemeinschaft* and *Gesellschaft*; organic and mechanical solidarity; social space; social distance; familistic, contractual, and compulsory relations; the folk-urban continuum; the primary group; and a host of related terms attempting to describe the varying textures, patterns, and densities displayed by the social fabric.[20]

For present purposes I shall employ simply the notion of a spectrum or scale of relationships, running from intimacy, at the one end, to hostility, at the other, with a stopping place midway that can be described as the habitat of friendly strangers, between whom interactional expectancies remain largely open and unpatterned. As typifying the intimate relationship, I shall take the

19. In my book *Anatomy of the Law* (New York: Praeger, 1968) I have undertaken an analysis of the special virtues and defects of the common law system, pp. 84–112.

20. A useful summary of the ways in which sociologists have attempted to distinguish different forms of the social bond will be found in Ferdinand Tönnies, *Community and Society*, trans. C. P. Loomis (East Lansing: Michigan State University Press, 1957), pp. 12–29.

average American family, with no servants, young children in the home, household chores to be apportioned, and members who are on reasonably good terms with one another. At the other end of the spectrum, I have in mind, not two individuals who are enemies, but two hostile nations not under the control of a superior political power that might constrain their tendencies toward overt hostile action.

In attempting here to test the different forms of law against varying social contexts I shall begin with contractual law, by which, the reader will recall, I mean the "law" of the contract itself, not the state-made law *of* or *about* contracts. The reason for choosing contractual law as a starting point is that, in a sense, it stands halfway between customary law and enacted law, sharing some of the qualities of both. On the one hand, contractual law is like customary law in that its prescriptions are not imposed on the parties by some outside authority; they make their own law. On the other hand, contractual law resembles legislation in that it involves the explicit creation of verbalized rules for the governance of the parties' relationship.

If we start with the "intimate" end of the scale, it is apparent that contract is an instrument ill-suited to ordering the relations within a functioning family. We are apt to put this in affective terms, saying that people united by affection would have difficulty in negotiating with one another and that any attempt to do so might disturb the harmony of the home. But the problem also has what may be called an operational aspect; the allocation of household responsibilities is affected by shifting and unpredictable contingencies: someone becomes ill, one of the children falls behind in his schoolwork, father has to be away on a trip, etc. No degree of contractual foresight would be equal to dealing in advance with all these permutations in the internal affairs of the family.

It seems a safe guess that not many married couples have attempted to arrange their internal affairs by anything like an explicit contract. In the few reported cases in which judicial enforcement of such contracts has been sought, the courts have denied relief. One court observed that "judicial inquiry into matters of that character, between husband and wife, would be fraught with irreparable mischief." [21] Another court remarked that if the parties were able to enter binding contracts regulating their internal relations this would "open an endless field for controversy and bickering and would destroy the element of flexibility needed in making adjustments to new conditions. . . ." [22]

If we move to the opposite end of the spectrum and consider contracts between parties standing in what I have called a social relation of hostility, a

---

21. *Miller* v. *Miller*, 78 Iowa 177, 182, 42 N.W. 641, 642 (1889).
22. *Graham* v. *Graham*, 33 Fed. Supp. 936, 938 (E. D. Mich. 1940). [Cf. the references in notes 10 and 12, "Mediation—Its Forms and Functions."]

contractual regulation becomes, once again, not only difficult to negotiate, but also often an inept device for achieving the end sought. The simple way of explaining this is to say that hostile parties don't trust one another, and mutual trust is essential for both the negotiation and the administration of a contract. But the problem, once again, has what may be called an operational aspect. The negotiation of a contract of any complexity will involve an intricate fitting together of diverse interests. This, in turn, means that in the course of negotiations—in the stand he takes for or against some demanded concession—each party is compelled to make some disclosure of the internal posture of his own interests. This disclosure may be disadvantageous to him, especially if negotiations fall through. Thus, suppose that in negotiations looking toward a reduction in armaments between two hostile countries, country *A*, to the surprise of country *B*, seems quite ready to agree to a broad limitation on the production and use of weapon *X*. Country *B* at once begins to ask itself such questions as, Why is that? Are they aware of some limitation on the effectiveness of weapon *X* we don't know about? Or do they want us to give up producing weapon *X*, which they fear, and divert our resources to weapon *Y*, against which they perhaps have developed an adequate defense? This necessity for some disclosure in order to achieve a successful fitting together of the parties' diverse interests is often inhibitive, not only in international relations, but in other fields as well, sometimes even in business deals. Perhaps the ultimate cure for it lies in the gradual and patient establishment of multiple ties of association between the parties, so that their social bond is not concentrated in one negotiation or one document. When that happens, however, the organizing principle of the parties' relationship is apt to cease to be contractual and become essentially one of customary law.

I should like now to turn to the middle ground of the spectrum of social contexts, the area I have previously described as the habitat of friendly strangers, between whom interactional expectancies remain largely open and unpatterned. This is precisely the area where contractual law is most at home and most effective; it is also here, without much doubt, that the very notion of explicit contracting was first conceived.

We are prone to suppose that as we move away from relations of intimacy our freedom of expression and action becomes progressively restricted; with strangers we are ill at ease; it is only with close friends that we are free to say what we think and declare what we would like to have. But in fact, in dealing with intimates we are, often quite without knowing it, restrained by a host of unarticulated expectations—compelled, as it were, to act out roles tacitly assigned to us in previous encounters. As Simmel points out, it is often precisely the stranger who receives "the most surprising openness—confidences which would be carefully withheld from a more closely related person."[23] It is this openness of the relations between strangers that facilitates negotiation in a manner that would be impossible (and probably inadvisable) within an intimate group like the family.

All over the world the intimacies of the extended family, the tribe, and the country village have proved an obstacle to the establishment of dealings on a straightforward commercial basis. It is hard, for example, to hold a relative or a close friend to prompt payment of his account. Mair reports a general anthropological observation that the "pressures to give easy credit on a man setting up a store in his own village are apt to be so great that he cannot make a success of his business."[24] An enterprising American Indian tribe in the state of Washington is said to have encountered a similar frustration in attempting to engage in business enterprises on the Reservation.[25] Perhaps the most interesting observation of this sort is contained in *The Irish Countryman*, by Conrad Arensberg. According to Arensberg the practice in rural Ireland is for the customer of the local shopkeeper virtually never to pay off his account in full; indeed this is something he would do only in a fit of anger. The standing unpaid account, reduced from time to time by partial payments, is regarded as symbolizing a bond of mutual trust—the customer gives his patronage, the shopkeeper extends his credit.[26] Many Americans have observed a similar phenomenon: when one makes a purchase at the local store and instead of charging it, as he usually does, offers to pay cash, this may be resented by the storekeeper. When one considers how common this tendency is to shy away from a purely impersonal businesslike relationship, it is no wonder that the pioneering merchants and traders seem everywhere to have been outsiders— the Jews in Europe, the Parsees in India, the Indians and Lebanese in Africa, the Chinese in the Pacific, and perhaps one could say, in the early days, the Yankees in North America. As some of the items on this list suggest, it might even appear that a difference in religion may at times facilitate the achievement of the kind of social distance essential for purely contractual relations.

It might be worth remarking here that sometimes the very success of a contractual relation has the effect of supplanting it by something akin to a two-party customary law. Those who renew contracts year after year, and who thus become intimates, are likely to have increasing difficulty in preserving an atmosphere of open negotiation; they become prisoners of the expectations

23. *The Sociology of Georg Simmel*, p. 404.

24. Lucy Mair, *An Introduction to Social Anthropology* (London: The Clarendon Press, 1965), p. 181.

25. A study by E. Colson reported in Max Gluckman, *Politics, Law, and Ritual in Tribal Society* (Chicago: Aldine Press, 1965), pp. 296–99.

26. Conrad Arensberg, *The Irish Countryman*, rev. ed. (New York: Natural History Press, 1968), pp. 155–62.

created by past practice. This is, of course, especially likely to occur where a situation has developed in which it is not easy for the parties to find alternative sources for filling their needs, a situation approaching that of "bilateral monopoly." [27]

So much for the interactions between contractual law and its social context. Turning now to customary law, the first observation is that this form of law is at home completely across the spectrum of social contexts, from the most intimate to those of open hostility. That the family cannot easily organize itself by a process of explicit bargaining does not mean there will not grow up within it reciprocal expectancies of the sort that, on a more formal level, would be called customary law. Indeed, the family could not function without these tacit guidelines to interaction; if every interaction had to be oriented afresh and *ad hoc*, no group like the family could succeed in the discharge of its shared tasks. At the midrange, it should be observed that the most active and conspicuous development of customary law in modern times lies precisely in the field of commercial dealings. Finally, while enemies may have difficulty in bargaining with words, they can, and often do, profitably half-bargain with deeds. Paradoxically the tacit restraints of customary law between enemies are more likely to develop during active warfare than during a hostile stalemate of relations; fighting one another is itself in this sense a social relation since it involves communication.

That customary law is, as I have expressed it, at home across the entire spectrum of social contexts does not mean that it retains the same qualities wherever it appears. On the contrary, it can change drastically in nature as it moves from one end of the spectrum to the other. At the terminal point of intimacy customary law has to do, not primarily with prescribed acts and performances, but with roles and functions. The internal operations of a family, kinship group, or even tribe, may demand, not simply formal compliance with rules, but an allocation of authority, and a sense of trusteeship on the part of those who make decisions and give directions. In the middle area, typified by arm's length commercial dealings, customary law abstracts from qualities and dispositions of the person and concentrates its attention on ascribing appropriate and clearly defined consequences to outward conduct. Finally, as we enter the area of hostile relations, a decided change in the general flavor of customary law takes place. Here the prime desideratum is to

---

27. The thesis of the study by Lawrence Friedman, *Contract Law in America* (Madison: University of Wisconsin Press, 1965), might be stated as the tendency of contractual relations to convert themselves into something like customary law. However, Friedman's study does not, in my opinion, take sufficient account of the special qualities of the economic background of the phenomena studied; it should definitely have been called Contract in Wisconsin, not Contract in America. Another valuable study is Stewart Macaulay, "Non-Contractual Relations in Business: A Preliminary Study," *American Sociological Review* 28 (1963): 55–67.

achieve—through acts, of course, not words—the clear communication of messages of a rather limited and negative import; accordingly there is a heavy concentration on symbolism and ritual.

The influence of social context should be borne in mind, I suggest, in weighing against one another the sometimes conflicting views of anthropologists as to the nature of customary law. It is interesting in this connection to compare two works that have become classics: Malinowski, *Crime and Custom in Savage Society* (1926), and Gluckman, *The Judicial Process Among the Barotse of Northern Rhodesia* (1955, 2d ed. 1967).

Malinowski sees the central principle of customary law in a reciprocity of benefits conferred; he even suggests, in one incautious moment, that the sanction which insures compliance with the rules of customary law lies in a tacit threat that if a man does not make his contribution, others may withhold theirs. Though Gluckman is for the most part careful in limiting his generalizations to the particular society he studied, he seems to see as a central concept of customary law generally that of "the reasonable man." The reasonable man, for Gluckman, is the man who knows his station and its responsibilities and who responds aptly to the shifting demands of group life. Simplifying somewhat we may say that the central figure for Malinowski is essentially a trader, albeit one who trades on terms largely set by tradition rather than by negotiation. For Gluckman it is the conscientious tribesman with a sense of trusteeship for the welfare of the group.

When we observe, however, the internal economic and kinship organizations of the two societies studied, it becomes apparent why the two scholars should arrive at such divergent conceptions of the model of man implicit in customary law. Malinowski begins his account by observing that the human objects of his study, who live dispersed on different islands, are "keen on trade and exchange." The first concrete situation he discusses involves two village communities on the same island at some distance from each other, the one being located on the coast, the other inland. Under a standing arrangement between the two, the coastal village regularly supplies the inland village with fish, receiving in return vegetables. The trade between the two is not, of course, the product of explicit bargaining, and indeed at times each of the villages will seek, not to give short measure, but to put the other to shame by outproducing it.

Among Gluckman's Barotse, on the other hand, economic production and consumption are organized largely on a kinship basis. The cases before the *kuta* studied by Gluckman were chiefly cases that might be described as involving the internal affairs of an extended family, though those affairs included some property disputes. Something of the range of the cases studied is suggested by a sampling of the titles Gluckman assigns to them: "The Case of the

Cross-Cousin Adultery," "The Case of the Wife's Granary," "The Case of the Urinating Husband," "The Case of the Headman's Fishdams (or) the 'Dog-in-the-Manger' Headman." The atmosphere of the arguments and decisions, reported so vividly by Gluckman, reminds one of what might be expected in a court of domestic relations, mediating the tangled affairs of the family and, occasionally and reluctantly, exercising a power to put them straight by judicial fiat.

The two systems of customary law studied by Malinowski and Gluckman operated, it is plain, in quite different social contexts, though this does not mean that a Malinowski might not find elements of reciprocity or exchange among the Barotse, or that a Gluckman could not find apt occasion to apply the concept of "the reasonable man" among the Trobrianders. I would suggest generally that if we seek to discover constancies among the different systems of customary law we shall find them in the interactional processes by which those systems come into being, rather than in the specific product that emerges, which must of necessity reflect history and context. I would suggest further that if we look closely among the varying social contexts presented by our own society we shall find analogues of almost every phenomenon thought to characterize primitive law.

Resuming our analysis of the effects of social context on the different forms of law, there remains for consideration enacted law as exemplified in a statute. At the outset it is apparent, I think, that the "home ground" of enacted law coincides largely with what we have already found most congenial to the organizing principle of contract, that is, with the middle area on the spectrum of social contexts—the region populated by friendly strangers, whose relations with one another generally stand open in the sense of not being prestructured by bonds of kinship or the repulsions of a shared hostility.

If enacted law and contractual law are alike in finding especially congenial the midpoint on the spectrum of social contexts, they also share an ineptitude for attempting anything like an internal regulation of the family. If a contract of the parties themselves is too blunt an instrument for shaping the affairs of a family, the same thing could be said with added emphasis if any attempt were made to impose detailed state-made regulations on the intimate relations of marriage and parenthood.[28]

Yet, as I have observed here, much of customary law serves—and often serves well—the function of putting in order the relations of kinsmen. What is the explanation for this special quality of the customary law of family affairs? I think it is to be found in the fact that customary law does not limit itself to

28. I am not at this point, of course, referring to such problems as child abuse, compulsory education, and the like.

requiring or prohibiting precisely defined acts, but may also designate roles and functions, and then, when the occasion arises, hold those discharging these roles and functions to an accounting for their performances. This conception does not conflict with the analysis of customary law presented at the beginning of this essay. Stable interactional expectancies can arise with reference to roles and functions as well as to specific acts; a language of interaction will contain not only a vocabulary of deeds but also a basic grammar that will organize deeds into meaningful patterns.

It is important to observe that the very qualities of enacted law that make it an inept instrument for regulating intimate relations are precisely those which lend to it a special capacity to put in order men's interactions within the larger impersonal society. Within that wider context the basic necessity is to impose rules that will serve to set the limits men must observe in their interactions with one another, leaving them free within those limits to pursue their own goals. This in turn means that the law must deal with defined acts, not with dispositions of the will or attitudes of mind. The rule of law measures a man's acts against the law, not the man himself against some ideal perceived as lying behind the law's prescriptions.

What is involved here may be expressed as a distinction between judging the person and judging the act.[29] In the ordinary affairs of life these two forms of judgment are in constant interaction. We judge what a man is by the way he acts; we evaluate his acts as expressions of what he is. We know that a man sometimes has to act as he does "because that's the sort of person he is"; we also know that over a lifetime a man, to some extent at least, makes himself the kind of person he is by a multitude of decisions as to how to act in specific situations.

Primitive systems of law, including the common law of England in its early period, accept without qualms this commonsense view of the matter and show but little concern to preserve a distinction between the man and his act. The jury was originally selected from the immediate vicinage so that they might know the litigants personally and perhaps even be acquainted with the facts of the controversy itself. Included in the criminal law were what have been called crimes of status—the crime, for example, of "being a common scold."

All of this has, of course, changed drastically. In a criminal trial today personal acquaintances of the defendant would normally be excluded from the jury, evidence of past misconduct is inadmissible, and it is unthinkable that a witness, however well acquainted he might be with the defendant, would be

29. I have attempted to apply some of the implications of this distinction to the internal legal systems of voluntary associations in my article, "Two Principles of Human Association," *Voluntary Associations*, ed. J. Roland Pennock and John Chapman (New York: Atherton Press, 1969), pp. 3–23, especially pp. 17–19. [See this volume, pp. 81–83.]

allowed to tell the jury what kind of person he considers him to be.[30] The task of the jury is to determine as best it can just what act or acts the defendant committed and then to measure those acts against the prescriptions of the law.

This picture of a lean and sparing justice, deliberately averting its gaze from the man himself, becomes considerably clouded, however, when we consider what happens before and after the confrontation that takes place in open court. Before the case is brought to court the defendant has to be arrested, and it would certainly be a rare policeman who routinely—and without taking into account the nature and circumstances of the offense—arrested every person he believed to have committed a crime. Certainly in dealing with minor offenses the police officer uses, and is expected to use, "judgment"; this judgment is inevitably affected by his perception of the kind of person the suspected party seems to be. When the case is brought to the prosecutor he in turn is influenced in some degree by similar considerations in deciding whether to prefer charges. If he has the case set for trial there will, in many routine cases, ensue a process that has come to be called plea bargaining. This is a procedure by which the prosecutor and the defense attorney will attempt, with court approval, to reach an agreement by which the defendant will plead guilty to a lesser charge than that asserted to be justified by those representing the state. The outcome of this process is inevitably affected by opinions about the basic dispositions of the defendant. If the case goes to trial and the accused is found guilty, the question of the appropriate sentence has to be decided. In deciding that question the judge will take into account what is known about the defendant himself, his past, and his probable future propensities. Similar considerations will, of course, determine the granting of parole or a pardon. When, finally, we consider that probably less than ten percent of the criminal charges filed ever come to trial, the emphasis placed in open court on the act, rather than the person of the defendant, will shrink in significance to the point where it may seem only a kind of symbolic tribute to the principle of judging the deed and not the man.

This symbolism is, however, of vital importance. If it were ever completely lost from view the principle of legality, the rule of law, would become an empty sham. The apparent contradictions within the total processes of the criminal law are tolerable because it is generally perceived, at least by those directly concerned, that distinctive institutional roles are played by those who arrest, prosecute, defend, try, sentence, parole, release, and pardon—all of these roles being directed toward the discharge of differing functions. Whether these distinctions are always perceived by the public or by the accused himself is doubt-

---

30. I am not attempting to deal here, of course, with expert testimony concerning the sanity of the defendant. It might be suggested, however, that the modern legal uses of psychiatry present some difficult problems when viewed in the light of the person-act dichotomy.

ful. There is, however, no question that any such elaborate division of function would be impossible within an intimate society; it presupposes large and impersonal processes.

When we view the matter in this light it becomes apparent that in a complex modern society enacted law and the organizational principles implicit in customary law are not simply to be viewed as alternative ways of ordering men's interactions, but rather as often serving to supplement each other by a kind of natural division of labor. Generally we may say that enacted law will default in complex relations of interdependence that cannot be organized by set rules of duty and entitlement; these situations are by no means confined to such as we would call intimate in any affective sense.[31] That they cannot be put in order by statutory enactment does not mean that they cannot, and do not in our own society, receive an effective ordering by silent processes which, manifested in a primitive society, would be called customary law.

Much that is written today seems to assume that our larger society is enabled to function by a combination of the individual's moral sense and social control through the threatened sanctions of state-made law. We need to remind ourselves that we constantly orient our actions toward one another by signposts that are set neither by morals, in any ordinary sense, nor by words in lawbooks. If this chapter has served to rekindle some appreciation of this fact I shall be content.

---

31. I have tried to show the inadequacies of formal legal rules and processes of adjudication for dealing with "polycentric" problems in "Collective Bargaining and the Arbitrator," *Wisconsin Law Review* 1963: 3–46, and "Irrigation and Tyranny," *Stanford Law Review* 17 (1965): 1021–42. [See this volume, pp. 111–21 and 202–10.]

III. *Legal Philosophy, Legal Education, and the Practice of Law*

The Needs of American Legal Philosophy

Editor's Note

The four items in this section were not written for publication. Three are addresses delivered to special gatherings in the 1940s and 1950s, and one is extracted from mimeographed materials distributed to students in Fuller's jurisprudence class. The formulation of ideas or the choice of arguments in these pieces might not be what they would have been had Fuller intended them for a more general audience. Nonetheless, I have included them in this volume because they complement the published essays so well. Although there is some repetition, in many ways these pieces clarify the themes developed in the published essays or extend them to topics not otherwise touched upon.

"The Needs of American Legal Philosophy" was one of two major presentations at a conference of legal scholars organized by the Rockefeller Foundation in 1952 as a way of obtaining advice about the foundation's plan to support research in legal philosophy. Fuller served subsequently as a member of a special advisory committee to the foundation and reviewed individual requests for funding.

In responding to the initial invitation to deliver this address, Fuller said he found himself in a quandary: "If I talk about what I think is truly important in this field and what I think ought to be done, I will seem to some of the participants to be expressing personal predilections. . . . [T]hey may have the uncomfortable feeling that they have been brought together to comment on Fuller's idiosyncratic stuff." If he instead tried to cover all the aspects of legal philosophy as traditionally defined, however, he thought he would turn out to be more of a "wet blanket" than the "spark plug" he was expected to be. Characteristically, he followed the idiosyncratic path.

"The Needs of American Legal Philosophy" is a clear anticipation of the eunomics program formulated in "Means and Ends." It is devoted largely to identifying factors that, in Fuller's view, have inhibited legal philosophy from taking such a route in the past. The last part sketches briefly the sorts of questions that would be posed in a eunomic approach to adjudication as one form of social ordering.

1. Introduction

In attempting to outline briefly what seem to me to be the needs of legal philosophy in this country, I start with a pragmatic conception of the function of philosophy. As I see it, the object of legal philosophy is to give an effective and meaningful direction to the work of lawyers, judges, legislators, and law teachers. If it leaves the activities of these men untouched, if it has no implications for the question of what they do with their working days, then legal philosophy is a failure. Judged by this standard I don't think we can claim that the last quarter of a century has been a fruitful one for legal philosophy in this country—certainly not in terms of immediate yield.

In analyzing the causes of this condition, I want to start by describing what seem to me to be the influences that have inhibited legal philosophy in this country. I do not do this—or at least I hope I do not do this—because of any personal preference for negations. I begin in this way because by describing first what I think we should rescue ourselves from, I shall be in a better position to describe later what I think we ought to embrace; the rejections I recommend will, I hope, clarify the affirmations to come. But first, the rejections.

As I see it, for several decades American legal philosophy has been retarded, and kept from significant tasks, by three main influences. Though these influences, or currents of intellectual fashion, are close cousins among themselves, they may nevertheless be separately formulated in something like the following terms. The first of these influences is a conception that defines the lawyer's lifework entirely in terms of state power, which treats him as a technician whose special aptitude is that of predicting and influencing the impact of state power. The second influence is one that identifies itself with the demands of scientific method and, in the name of science, ropes off and erects barriers before fruitful lines of inquiry that should be open to legal philosophy. The third inhibitive influence—in some ways the most significant—consists of a false severance of the problem of ends from that of means.

2. *The Lawyer as an Expert in Predicting and Influencing the Ways in Which State Power Will Be Exercised*

This view has a distinguished ancestry. It started with Holmes and Gray. With them it represented in part a reaction against the introverted logic of Christopher Columbus Langdell and his brothers in method, and in part a reaction against the historical mysticism symbolized by James Coolidge Carter.

The revolt begun by Holmes and Gray was continued and sharpened in the movement called American Legal Realism.[1] With the Realists the proper func-

1. [See Lon L. Fuller, "American Legal Realism," *University of Pennsylvania Law Review* 82, no. 5 (1934): 429–62, and O. W. Holmes, Jr., "The Path of the Law," edited with commentary by Lon L. Fuller, in *American Primer*, ed. Daniel Boorstin (Chicago: University of Chicago Press, 1966).]

tion of the lawyer and legal scholar became that of charting the behavior patterns of judges and other state officials. In its later phases the Realist movement exemplifies the historical truism that in every governmental or intellectual upheaval there are those for whom revolution becomes so much a habit that they find it difficult to take up constructive tasks once the revolution has been brought to successful completion. In this negative sense the Realist movement is still very much alive today, even though little is now being written in explicit advocacy of the Realist viewpoint.

It does not take long to demonstrate the inadequacies for legal philosophy of a view that has nothing more to say of the lawyer than that he is a person knowledgeable in the ways and prevailing dispositions of state power. One familiar objection to that view must, however, be qualified at the outset. It is often said that this conception of the lawyer's work is wholly without ethical implications. I believe, on the contrary, that it has an important ethical implication which is none the less significant because it is negative. The view that identifies law and the work of the lawyer with state power contains within itself the assertion that law is made by men for men. It does not derive law from logical compulsions supposed to be implicit in the nature of legal reasoning, nor does it see law as the inevitable product of blind evolutionary forces. It treats law as something capable of being shaped to meet human needs and to increase human satisfactions, and there is conveyed the implication that it should be so shaped. So much of ethical affirmation is certainly contained in the school of Holmes, Gray, and the Realists.

This school of thought seems to me, however, to suffer from serious deficiencies. The first lies in the obvious fact that it does not offer any principle that would assist us in deciding what the law should be or how state power ought to be organized and directed. If the theory does not obstruct an inquiry in that direction, it also does nothing to assist, guide, or advance such an inquiry.

Furthermore, it is not quite true to say of the school of Holmes, Gray, and the Realists that it leaves wholly unobstructed the path of inquiry that leads to the question of what ought to be. This school does not, to be sure, erect so obvious and conspicuous a roadblock as does evolutionary determinism or the dogmatic branches of the natural-law theory. It does, however, interpose its own more subtle impediment. If the distinguishing characteristic of the lawyer lies in his ability to predict where, and under what conditions, state power will strike, he ceases to be a lawyer when he concerns himself with any other question. This means that if he ventures into questions of what the law ought to be he leaves behind him the comfortable shelter of prestige-filled words like *lawyer*, *professional competence*, *jurisprudence*, and perhaps even *legal philosophy*. He is put strictly on his own with nothing to support him but a private call and a shaky belief in the validity of his own insight.

The school of Holmes, Gray, and the Realists does not tell the lawyer that he can have no opinions about what the law ought to be, or how government should be organized and conducted, but it tells him something almost as inhibitive, that he steps out of his role as lawyer when he expresses such opinions. The lawyer is thus cut off from a device open to the sociologist or economist, who, when he has reached personal conclusions about how things could be rearranged for the benefit of mankind, is always able to support these conclusions with the prestige of his own science. When he conveys those conclusions to the world, it is indeed usual for him to make very broad claims for the special competence of his profession to deal with the issues at stake. Since these claims relate to the method and not to the man applying it, no immodesty is seen in them but only a just pride in one's calling. The spiritual comfort of this literary form, and the protective coloration it confers, are denied to the lawyer who prescribes remedies for the ills of society, that is, they are denied to him if his only claim to special competence lies in his ability to fend off or invoke established state power, or to chart the regularities implicit in its exercise.

The conception that identifies the lawyer's work with state power is also responsible, I think, for a point of view closely related to that I have just been describing. This is the notion that strictly speaking there is no such thing as a legal end or objective. To borrow the mistranslation applied as a title to Jhering's famous book,[2] law is merely a means to an end; it is a way of implementing objectives that originate outside itself. It is therefore assumed that the ends which law serves must be those set by other sciences, such as sociology and economics, law being itself merely a technique or way of getting things done. The grounds for this assumption are generally left unexamined. The reason they are left unexamined is, I think, largely to be found in a conception of the lawyer's work as concentrating on the point where the canalized power of the state emerges, thus removing from his concern and his special competence all that lies behind that point.

But I have not yet stated the most serious deficiency in the view that identifies the lawyer's work with established state power. This lies in the fact that it falsifies and distorts the services that lawyers are actually rendering in our society. It is essentially a litigational conception of the lawyer's competence, and yet we know that the number of lawyers directly concerned with litigation is every day decreasing and constitutes today a minority of the profession as a whole.

It may be answered that the lawyer who never goes to court—the office

2. [The reference is to a translation by Isaac Husik of the first volume of the fourth German edition of *Der Zweck im Recht* by Rudolph von Jhering (Boston: Boston Book Co., 1913).]

lawyer, the business counsellor, the negotiator, the go-between, the drafts-man—that this kind of lawyer is also ultimately concerned with litigation and state power, though in an indirect way. When a lawyer drafts a contract, for example, he has his eyes on possible future litigation; he is seeing to it that the right words go down on paper so that his client's interests will be protected if things should later come to a law suit. There is no question that the competent lawyer renders this service, and charges a portion of his fee for it. But it would be a serious mistake to say that the lawyer's chief concern, or that his chief competence is exhausted in battening down the hatches against possible future litigation. His chief job is to devise a framework of dealings that will function between the parties, that will produce the results desired, and that will not give rise to disputes. A former colleague of mine has expressed this function of the lawyer by saying he is an expert in structure.[3] He is a man who is called in to design a formal structure into which the parties' respective interests can be accommodated fairly, comfortably, and safely. In performing this service the lawyer who drafts a contract, let us say a long-term supply contract, exercises a function analogous to that of the author of a constitution. He is like one charged with the responsibility of organizing and setting up governmental power; he is the architect of a charter that will govern the parties' future deal-ings and relations.

The lawyer's function as an expert in structure is most clearly seen in those frequent cases where he is called upon to draft an agreement known to be legally unenforceable, as for example where both parties have reserved a power of cancellation, or where the intervention of state power is expressly excluded in favor of a settlement of disputes by arbitration. In the latter case the lawyer's responsibility includes working out a kind of private system of adjudication, so that his task is like that of the draftsman of those articles of a constitution that define the judicial power of the state.

The conception of the lawyer as an expert in established state power cannot be stretched to include his special competence as an architect of social struc-tures. On the other hand, the view that sees him primarily as an expert in structure can be interpreted to embrace his activities as an advocate in litiga-tion. In that case he is a participant, and a needed participant, in a process of adjudication that is directed toward the establishment of just and workable relationships among men; he is a partisan collaborator in an enterprise di-rected toward achieving through governmental power an end that can also be achieved, and often is achieved, through private settlement.

This conception of the lawyer as an expert in structure dissipates at once the view that there is no such thing as a legal end or an end that is the special

3. [Milton Katz, professor of law at Harvard Law School, 1940–1950, 1954–1978.]

concern of lawyers. When, for example, a public utility enters a long-term contract with a mine for the supply of coal needed to operate its plant, there are two sets of objectives. One has to do with problems familiar to economies, the avoidance of waste, price savings, procedures for readjusting prices to fluctuating business conditions, etc. The other set of objectives is legal in the sense that it represents the special responsibility of the lawyer. These objectives include, for example, drafting an arbitration clause that will function effectively and fairly in the event of dispute, anticipating possible sources of trouble and devising procedures that will put out the fire of controversy while it is still manageable, and generally constructing a satisfactory framework for the parties' future dealings.

3. Barriers to Fruitful Inquiry Erected in the Name of "Science"

Frank Knight, in commenting on the methodological disputes that have wreaked such havoc in the social sciences, once observed that it would be hard to conceive of such disputes arising in a practical science like law or medicine.[4] The main argument in the social sciences, as to whether the objective is welfare or betterment, on the one hand, or understanding and scientific description, on the other, would make no sense, he suggested, as applied to any science faced with immediate problems. In medicine, for example, it is apparent that the objective is at once betterment and understanding, and that the two go hand in hand.

I hope he is right about medicine, but I have to report that he was mistaken about law, at least about what might be called law professors' law. (I do not mean that he was wrong in saying the debate makes no sense in law; I mean he was mistaken in assuming it would not in fact arise in the legal field.) During the last twenty-five years we have seen in American legal theory not only a repetition of all the debates about method that have occurred in, say, sociology, but also many of the taboos and restrictions on inquiry that have been set up in the other social sciences in the name of scientific method. As in sociology, it has been affirmed that we cannot *prescribe* until we have exhaustively *described* what actually goes on in the legal field; the patient must be given no treatment until we know everything about the structure and workings of his body.

---

4. [See Frank H. Knight, *The Ethics of Competition and Other Essays* (New York: Harper & Bros., 1935), chap. 11.]

I am not going to spend much time on the influence of this particular conception, because what has happened in the legal field is not essentially different from what has happened in, say, economics and sociology. I will content myself with a few general observations.

As J. W. N. Sullivan has pointed out in his book, *The Limitations of Science*, it was essential in the physical sciences to assume that physical events were not the expression of some purposive intervention by God.[5] This was necessary not only to rid the field of speculative theories but also to summon the intellectual energy necessary to a solution of scientific problems. So long as men assumed that a stone fell to the ground in response to some divine purpose, the really interesting and challenging problem was to determine the nature of that purpose; *how* the stone fell, the precise manner of its falling and its rate of acceleration, were insignificant and boring details. Sciences could not get started until interest shifted from the *why* to the *how*. In the words of Bertrand Russell, ". . . 'purpose' is a concept that is scientifically useless."[6] Being useless, it obstructs fruitful inquiry so long as it clutters men's minds and absorbs their interest.

By and large the social sciences have attempted to pattern their methods as closely as possible after those of the physical sciences. In some cases, as in behavioristic psychology, the attempt to exclude purpose is explicit. In other cases, the attempt is to reduce the role of purpose as much as possible, and when it gains admission it is under some kind of linguistic disguise, like "dynamic tendency," "on-going process," "conation," "value-oriented behavior," and the like. While one may criticize verbal manipulations that let purpose in without admitting what they are doing, still there can be no criticism of the social sciences' attempt to follow the methods that have proved so successful in the physical sciences.

But at this point there enters what seems to me to be a gross confusion of thought. It is assumed that in searching out the regularities and interconnections involved in social behavior, one must disregard the fact of purposive intervention by men, one must assume that no such intervention takes place. Now there is nothing like this in the physical sciences. Indeed, if one identifies scientific method with experiment, then the essence of science consists in measuring the effects of a purposive intervention by man in the events of nature. If the physical scientist followed the example of the social scientist, in reporting an experiment he would say to himself, "I will disregard the fact that this retort was twenty degrees hotter than that one, because that came about be-

5. [J. W. N. Sullivan, *The Limitations of Science* (New York: New American Library, 1949), p. 11.]

6. [Bertrand Russell, *The Impact of Science on Society* (New York: Columbia University Press, 1951), p. 9.]

cause my assistant turned up the burner, and I cannot be scientific if I take into account such an interference with the course of nature."

Now of course in society purposive human intervention is constant and pervasive. People are always adding chemicals to the social test tubes and turning the heat up or down under the retorts. To say that all this must be disregarded makes no sense at all in terms of scientific method. If this exclusion is justified in the name of social determinism, then it should be presented not as science but as metaphysics, a metaphysics that, applied to the physical sciences, would lead to the conclusion that experiment is impossible.

It is no accident that some of the most promising work in the social sciences has been done by men like Lewin and Bavelas, who, in their studies of group dynamics, so-called, have attempted to determine experimentally the effects of different types of purposive intervention in the organization of group behavior.[7]

For social philosophy the crucial question is, What can be obtained through a purposive intervention in human affairs? For legal philosophy it becomes, What can be obtained through a purposive intervention that gives some particular formal structure to human relations? In my opinion, that inquiry will be most profitably pursued if it cuts across all kinds of social structure, including not only those incorporated in government, where law shares the field with political science, but also those structures which result from negotiation and voluntary settlement.

Obviously, the inquiry cannot be profitably conducted in terms of a philosophy that systematically disregards or discounts the effects of any purposive intervention in social affairs.

4. The Severance of the Problem of Ends from That of Means

Here I shall begin by stating my own halting and imperfect analysis of this difficult problem before analyzing the conception that seems to me to be inhibiting legal philosophy.

As I see it, means and ends are complementary concepts; neither make sense without the other. Both presuppose that human resources, in the form of time, energy, and accumulated goods, are in limited supply. If we could imagine a being able to enjoy all pleasures at once, that could be in two places at

7. [See, for example, Kurt Lewin, *Field Theory in Social Science: Selected Theoretical Papers*, ed. Dorwin Cartwright (New York: Harper and Bros., 1951), and Alex Bavelas, "A Method for Investigating Individual and Group Ideology," *Sociometry* 5 (1942): 371–77.]

the same time, that could have its cake and eat it too, then we would have to say that for such a being there are neither ends nor means. If a flood of simultaneous effortless satisfactions constantly poured over this creature, he could not be said to have ends, for ends presuppose some organization of resources, some direction of energies, some choice among alternative forms of effort that exclude one another.

The concept that underlies the means-end relation not only assumes a limited supply of resources, but the possibility of directing those resources, of making a choice among competing ways of organizing them. Without this assumption, neither ends nor means have any significance. If the only way of moving our bodies from one place to another were by walking, it would make no sense to say that walking was a means of getting from one place to another, and the means-end relation would not come into play at all. It is only when we have a choice among different modes of locomotion that the end of getting from one place to another becomes a constant in comparison with the variable means of achieving it.

As I see it, the means-end relation may be described as a subjective category by which we orient choice. We cannot exercise choice over the whole field at once; we are incapable of embracing so vast and complex a problem in one mental effort. Accordingly, we proceed by taking as given a particular direction of effort, which we call the end. Treating this assumed or tentative direction of effort as a constant, we then explore the interrelation of our resources and our possible satisfactions, so as to see what can be obtained by the proposed line of effort and what the costs of obtaining it will be. This is the part of the process that has to do with means.

If this analysis is right, then a good many alleged truisms about the means-end relation are by no means of obvious truth.

First of all, since the means-end relation is merely a device of the internal economy of our minds by which we orient choice and avoid a futile attempt to decide everything at once, the concept of an "end" is just as relative as the concept of a "means." All of our ends are themselves means to other ends; they are severed from these ends only provisionally and as a step in the process of choosing what to do with our time and energies. This is true even of so-called ultimate ends, such as life or survival. We eat to live, but we also live to eat in the sense that eating is part of what makes life worth living. The same relationship could be established among all the other so-called ultimate or final ends. Indeed the idea of ultimates is here out of place, since it assumes that our means and ends are organized in a kind of tandem fashion. The truer picture would be that of an electronic circuit with interacting units, with both a "feed through" and a "feed back" of electric current, with vacuum tubes connected not in parallel but in a push-pull relationship.

It also follows that if the analysis I have presented is right, ends cannot be intelligently selected in abstraction from means. To assume that ends could be so selected would be to assume boundless supplies of human energy and material resources, which would mean that there would really be no problem of choice at all. In the limited world in which we live, we have to find out what things cost before we know whether we want them, and this is just as true for law and ethics as it is for economics. Because it proceeds upon unreal assumptions, a view that attempts to choose ends without reference to means easily drifts, on the one side, toward "absolute values" and "ultimates," and, on the other, to the view that all ethical judgments are fathomless expressions of personal predilection. It is as if scientists sat around discussing endlessly where an improvement in our control over nature was "most needed." Some would say that it lay in neutralizing gravity, others in eliminating biological aging, still others in discovering whether there is an extrasensory realm of being. Various schools of thought would arise to wrangle with each other and to support their competing absolutes. Meanwhile, no one would be finding out what can in fact be done and what the cost of doing it is.

To avoid misunderstanding, I want to make it clear that in talking about the cost of achieving an end I do not have in mind primarily material costs. In the field of social organization, these costs arise in part from the fact that society cannot be organized in inconsistent ways at the same time. For example, if you wish a particular field of human relations to be governed by adjudication or by a rule of judges, rather than, say, majority vote, you must accept the limitations that go with the adjudicative process, and not expect it to accomplish what can only be attained by other forms of social organization.

Another conclusion that seems to me to flow from the analysis I have presented is this: In assessing the relative role of rational calculation in human choice, we cannot assume, as is so often done, that ends are set by nonrational and emotional factors, while it is only in the selection of means that reason can become operative. To make an assumption of this sort is to ignore the interaction of means and ends and the fact that all ends are in part means to other ends. In saying this I have no intention of embracing the absurdity that human choice is entirely governed by rational calculation. What I am asserting is that we cannot simplify a difficult problem by assigning reason to the choice of means and by excluding reason from the choice of ends. This is to falsify the whole significance of the means-end relation, and to convert what is in fact only an internal convenience of thought into a pretended objective reality.

A further and final conclusion derives from the views I have been expressing here. It is not true to say that no intelligent discussion of means is possible until the end has been precisely and clearly defined. The clarity of any end is always a relative matter. Because of the interrelation of ends and of means and ends, to demand complete clarity in the definition of an end is, in effect, to demand complete clarity in all the elements that enter into the total process of choice, a demand that if taken literally would make it impossible ever to get started in that process at all. It is like asking an electrician to define the precise function of an electronic element without saying anything about the interacting system of which it is a part.

Often the best way to conduct the process of choice is to start with a vaguely conceived end and then to begin at once considering what means might be devised for the attainment of that end. In this way we learn not only how desirable the end really is, but we also often attain in the process a clarification of what it is we are aiming at; the obscurity of the end begins to clear up as we consider the various things that might be done to achieve it.

Let me clarify these abstract remarks by a couple of examples. The first of these relates to the problem of drawing up rules for a game. Nothing is more obscure than the question of the end of sport or play. Why do human beings play? Many theories have been advanced. Some say play is practice for the serious business of life, often assumed to be that of killing other men. Some say it is recreation, a way of restoring the body when the work necessary to survival has been done. Others say it is an expression of the aesthetic impulse, and perhaps even its highest expression, so that Schiller could declare, "Der Mensch ist nur ganz Mensch, wo er spielt." One might easily conclude that it is impossible to devise any means for giving expression to the end of play since we do not know what that end is. Or, worse yet, that we would have first to adopt some "theory of play" before we could start designing ways of playing.

Of course this is not so. People utterly ignorant of the "theory of play" can not only devise games and draw up complicated rules for them, but can also pass meaningful judgment on the rules of existing games by asking whether they yield "a good play." Though our objective may be difficult to articulate, it is clear enough to light our way toward the satisfaction we seek. Furthermore, it is by comparing means that we get the most direct insight into what it is we are really aiming at.

A second example may reinforce this point. The concepts of "equality" and "fairness" are easy marks for the skeptic, who has little difficulty in demonstrating that we really don't know what they mean. Yet suppose one is compelled to make a "fair and equal distribution" of an estate between two sons. The estate consists of many incommensurables having no definite market value: Heirlooms, works of art, lands and buildings of different qualities, speculative investments, etc. The task is hard and the objective difficult to define. This does not prevent us, however, from seeing the aptness of the classic solution that calls for having one son divide the property into two lots and then allowing the other to take his pick. Here again some reflection on the reasons for the appeal of this device will help us to see what it is we aim at when we seek an equal division of goods radically different in kind.

Now I believe that all of what I have been saying is contrary to notions now generally current. According to these notions it is futile to discuss means unless one can define precisely the end sought; the determination of ends is not, however, a rational process but something controlled by emotions, instinct, or social conditioning; the only point where rational calculation can become operative is where means are being chosen for ends already adopted and clearly formulated; since means are a mere adjunct to ends, it is obvious that one cannot advance the proper choice of ends by starting with a discussion of means. The inhibitive effect on social philosophy of this combination of views is clear. Two simple conclusions become immediately evident: (1) there is only one subject worth discussing, namely, ends; (2) ends cannot be discussed because they lie beyond the reach of the rational faculty.

In the remaining part of my discussion, I want to proceed chiefly by presenting to you an example of the kind of inquiry that seems to be fruitful. I am taking as my example the process of adjudication, but I should like for you to keep in mind that it is only an example. Generally, the function of legal philosophy ought to be, I think, that of understanding the full implications of the various ways in which human relations may be shaped or given formal structure. From this point of view, adjudication is only one way of organizing the relations of human beings to one another, though it happens to be the one that seems to me most apt as an illustration for purposes of this discussion.

5. *Adjudication as an Object of Inquiry for Legal Philosophy*

Adjudication is a process that is resorted to in many different contexts. We have adjudication by courts and administrative tribunals clothed with governmental authority and power. We have it in the home when father hears the case of Mary v. John for the replevin of one rubber ball. We have it as a voluntary measure in labor relations, and as a means of settling disputes among nations. G. D. H. Cole recommends that in a socialist economy which has no labor market, wages should be set by arbitrators.[8] President Conant suggests some kind of arbitration to determine what research programs should be given priority under a general program of scientific research subsidized by the government.[9]

8. [G. D. H. Cole, *Socialist Economics* (London: Victor Gollancz, 1950), pp. 96–97.]
9. [James B. Conant, *Science and Common Sense* (New Haven: Yale University Press, 1951), pp. 337–38.]

In all of these contexts adjudication retains certain constant features. To take an obvious example, it cannot be successful unless there is a chance for both sides to be heard; this is just as true in the home when father decides between Mary and John as it is in the Supreme Court. An even more obvious proposition is that adjudication cannot achieve its purpose if the adjudicator is bribed by one party. That in some countries judges habitually receive bribes no more disproves this proposition than the fact that some savages use wooden shovels shows that in their peculiar culture there exists a value judgment that wooden shovels are better than steel shovels. There are good and bad ways of conducting adjudication that are independent of cultural influences, just as there are good and bad shovels that are similarly independent. The optimum conditions for the operation of adjudication are never fully achieved, and in borderline cases there may be difficulty in stating just what those conditions are. But this does not mean that adjudication does not contain a solid core of purpose that defines in general how it should and should not be conducted.

What I am suggesting is that legal philosophy can take adjudication in its various contexts and ask questions like the following: What kinds of human relations are best organized and regulated by adjudication, and what kinds are better left to other organizational procedures, such as negotiation and voluntary settlement, majority vote, or expert managerial authority? What are the consequences where adjudication is given problems inappropriate to its capacities, and how can the damage done be minimized? What are the procedural limitations which adjudication must respect if it is to be effective, not only in the sense of reaching an apt and intelligent decision, but also in retaining the respect of the losing party?

There is very little discussion of questions of this sort in the Anglo-American literature. Indeed, it may be said that we lack anything that could be called a coherent philosophy of forensic procedure generally. I attribute this lack to the three inhibiting influences I have tried to describe, and I want to take a few minutes to show how those influences affect the example of adjudication.

The conception that identifies the lawyer's work with state power would draw a sharp and false line between adjudication by a judge, clothed with governmental authority, and adjudication by an arbitrator appointed by the parties. The one is "law" and a proper concern of lawyers, the other is neither. The sharp line of division drawn by this view obscures the elements that are common to adjudication in all contexts and discourages anything that might be called a comparative study, crossing freely over the line that marks the boundary of state power. Within the field of governmental adjudication, the view I am discussing would discern as the primary consideration the fact that the judge is an agent of the state, and that his decision is backed by the coercive power of the state. Such a view would not consider, for example, how the judge ought to proceed in order to secure the maximum respect for the whole process of adjudication, so as to preserve its moral force, thus reducing the need for a resort to coercion.

If we break down the sharp line between official and nonofficial adjudication, then there are valuable insights that can be carried over from the nonofficial field into that of state power. For example, to take a very practical issue, is it advantageous to arrange adjudication on tripartite lines, so that a neutral arbiter is flanked by two other arbiters, one representing each of the interests opposed in the controversy? There are certainly advantages in such an arrangement. It means that if the decision involves some intervention in a complex network of interests—as in drawing an international boundary, or in drafting a set of job descriptions in a labor dispute—there will be informed guidance for the tribunal as to the exact posture of those interests right up to the time the award is drafted. This improves the chance that the losing party will accept and conform himself to the verdict, and it also makes for a more intelligent verdict. It not only sugarcoats the pill but means that the pill will be more likely to be compounded in a way to meet the patient's actual needs. On the other hand, there are serious disadvantages to the tripartite arrangement, the most obvious of which is that it converts what was intended to be adjudication into a bargaining process. I could spend a half hour discussing the pros and cons of this issue, and also the question whether there are ways here of having your cake and eating it, that is, whether there are arrangements that will procure the advantages of the tripartite system without its disadvantages. But the point I wish to make is that the only active discussion of such issues is to be found where adjudication is still in the process of securing acceptance, where its forms have not yet had a chance to jell. That means, in the field of labor relations and in international law. Now it seems to me clear that the lively insights that can be obtained in those fields could lead us to rethink and reevaluate the whole process of adjudication by state officials, which we now take for granted as if it were something the forms of which were either ordained by nature or by some arbitrary legislative fiat.

The self-consciously "scientific" attitude of mind would of course see nothing to be gained by an inquiry such as I have suggested. Since that inquiry calls for an appraisal of the effects of a particular kind of purposive intervention in human affairs, its issues would lie beyond the scope of a method that excludes consideration of any such intervention as a matter of principle. At the most a view that seeks only nonpurposive regularities in human society, or nonpurposive evolutionary stages of society, might ask such questions as the following: Under what social conditions does adjudication arise? How does adjudication differ from one culture to another?—the anticipated conclusion being that adjudication displays no general or universal features. Finally, within a given culture, what are the actual patterns of adjudication as contrasted with the current rationalizations and the explanations given by those who adjudicate?—the anticipated conclusion being of course that the discrepancy between practice and theory would be very wide.

The view that abstracts ends from means would say of the inquiry I have proposed that it would be at once trivial and futile. It would be trivial because the really important thing about adjudication is not how it is organized, but what kind of a decision it reaches, what principles the judge or adjudicator applies in deciding the case. A view that concentrates on ends would say that the end of adjudication is decision, and that unless we know what value-judgments, what conceptions of justice, shape the decision, there is no use wasting time on the mechanical details of organization. A discussion of organizational forms and modes of procedure is a waste of time, because you cannot, so it would be said, discuss means until you have defined ends. Hence you cannot talk about how adjudication should be organized until you know toward what criteria of decision it is ultimately aimed. Since no one can articulate clearly in any field the ultimate criteria of decision, there is really nothing to talk about. The only subject worthy of discussion is incapable of being discussed.

In opposition to this sad conclusion, I have already expressed my conviction that adjudication, as a means for organizing human relations, can be discussed intelligently even though we are unable to define with precision its assumed end, namely, justice. I have also suggested that we can arrive at a better understanding of the aim we call justice if we discuss critically the various means by which it is imperfectly realized. Such a program at least allows us to get under way. It does not tell us we must hold up our exploration until we already know the things we seek to learn through exploration.

The Lawyer as an Architect of Social Structures

Editor's Note

In 1957, Fuller was asked by the Harvard Law Record, *a student publication, to provide a brief account of his course in jurisprudence. He emphasized the practical character of his concerns. "I try to relate the course as closely as I can to the work of the practicing attorney. I try to present the lawyer . . . to borrow a phrase from my colleague Milton Katz, as 'an expert in structure.' I try to uncover the common thread of insight into the problems of human organization that run through all of the lawyer's work, whether he is acting as judge or arbitrator, arguing a case, drafting a statute, or negotiating a contract." But while the concerns were practical, they were not purely instrumental. "As I see it, the whole of legal philosophy should be animated by the desire to seek out those principles by which men's relations in society may be rightly and justly ordered."*

"The Lawyer as an Architect of Social Structures" approaches the subject matter of eunomics from the point of view of the practicing attorney. It describes the role of the lawyer as a creator and manager of forms of social ordering. It also, incidentally, identifies some of the social scientific literature that Fuller considered to be of assistance in carrying out a eunomic analysis of legal institutions. These remarks were distributed as supplementary reading to Fuller's class in jurisprudence. The copy in my possession is dated 1952–53.

The analysis presented in this volume is primarily concerned with what may be called the order-creating process. It attempts to discern the principles that underlie the bringing into existence of legal, political, economic, and social order. The scope of the inquiry is, therefore, by no means confined to "law" in the usual sense of the word, nor solely to those problems that normally fall within the professional competence of the lawyer. Nevertheless it may be helpful, in order to convey some preliminary understanding of what is here being attempted, to begin by relating the present inquiry to the actual work of the practicing attorney.

By the necessities of his profession the lawyer is frequently called upon to become the architect of social structure. This is true not only where great affairs of state are involved and constitutions or international treaties are being brought into existence, but in the most commonplace arrangements, like working out a contract for a two years' supply of paper towels for the rest rooms of a chain of service stations. In a sense, every contract, every testament, every lease—in short, every legal instrument is a kind of constitution establishing a framework for the future dealings of the affected parties.

Common sense tells us, of course, that the success of a contract is not guaranteed merely because the lawyers who drafted it gave the most fitting formal structure to the parties' relations. Many other factors will affect the success or failure of an agreement—habits and attitudes built up in previous dealings, the degree to which the interests of the parties in fact overlap or conflict, the personal compatibility of those who have to deal with one another under the agreement. But to say that the structure imposed on the parties' relations by their contract is not all-important is not to assert that it is unimportant. On the contrary, in many situations it is very important, and often the other factors mentioned above (for example, a growing personal antagonism between the parties) are aggravated by bad design in the contract itself and could have been obviated or neutralized by better draftsmanship.

When we speak of the lawyer as an architect of social structures it should not be supposed that the social structure for which he is responsible is necessarily represented entirely by words on paper. It has been remarked by experienced attorneys that when a contract has been carefully negotiated and drafted it can usually be filed away and forgotten. During the negotiation and drafting of an agreement, the parties, by being compelled to work out together the framework of their future relations, come to share an understanding of the problems each of them faces in the performance of his side of the undertaking. This understanding is often itself the source of a set of reciprocally adjusted expectations that functions as a basis of order between the parties without reference to the written contract, and often better than the written contract would. In other words, a certain accommodation of interests takes place during the negotiation and drafting of a contract, and even if the contract itself were then thrown away, the structure of that accommodation might well govern the parties' actions and prevent disputes. The experienced lawyer, realizing this, assumes a responsibility for bringing about this informal, and to some extent tacit, accommodation as well as that formalized in the terms of the written agreement. He sees to it that the parties have reached common ground as well as common language.

The illustration of the contract has been used here simply because it is a familiar and pervasive legal transaction. What has been said of the contract can be applied, however, to any kind of legal arrangement worked out by negotiation between or among the affected parties or in consultation with them by some rule-making authority. The list of possible illustrations would be very long and would include such diverse transactions as a statute, the charter of a corporation, an administrative regulation, the bylaws of the local of a labor union, and a consent decree.

With some modification the comments about the structure-creating function of the contract could also be applied to unilateral legal acts, such as the testament, or the deed of real estate. Any of these will normally establish a framework of human relations, and any of them may fail to provide a workable arrangement capable of achieving the results intended even when it is completely "litigation-proof."

Though the illustrations so far given have been drawn from areas where the participation of lawyers is expected and even welcome, the lawyer has no monopoly over the process by which social structure is created. Where the choice among competing ways of arranging the relations of the parties concerns methods of compensation, for example, the problem is generally considered to be an economic, not a legal one. Under schemes of "compulsory health insurance" or "socialized medicine" it is generally recognized that there are three methods of paying for medical services: (1) physicians are paid a salary directly by the state; (2) payment is on a "fee-for-service" basis; (3) the physician assumes responsibility for the care of a "panel" of patients and is paid an annual sum for each patient. Choice among these methods of payment is essentially a problem of social structure or order. The choice has broad implications for such questions as the anticipated "overhead" costs of the scheme, the likelihood of inflated claims or of malingering, the freedom of the patient to select his physician, the freedom of the physician to reject unwelcome patients.

The problems that are the traditional concern of political science, such as the choice among different methods of electing public officials, are, within the meaning of this analysis, questions of the forms of social order. So, too, are problems of business and public administration that touch on formal structures, even though these structures be quite without legal force and are thought of as expressions of internal administrative policy. For example, a problem of choosing among principles of order is involved even in the familiar question of the relative merits of the "stenographic pool" as compared with a system that assigns stenographers to individual executives.

The Social Sciences and the Order-Creating Process

From what has been said it is apparent that the ambitions of the present discussion transcend the boundaries of any particular "social discipline," and especially those of legal study as it has been generally conceived. Perhaps the most appropriate designation for what is here attempted would be to call it an essay in general sociology.

This designation would not be taken to imply, however, that the analysis has been primarily based on the writings of professional sociologists and anthropologists. Unfortunately, with some notable exceptions, these writers have very little to say about the order-creating process. By and large sociologists and anthropologists have been so busy trying to discern and chart continuities in social behavior that they have almost completely neglected the problem of social change, or a comparative study of the methods of bringing about social change.

Now it is apparent that a literature oriented in the directions just indicated cannot serve as a satisfactory guide to the man who actually finds himself a participant in the order-creating process, who is called upon, for example, to negotiate and draft a treaty or a collective labor agreement. He is not greatly assisted by being told that what he proposes to do is impossible. Nor is he helped much more if he is told that he is free to do whatever he likes, provided only he respects the essential irrationality of human nature. He knows that some arrangements work out properly and produce satisfaction, while others (probably the great majority of those of any complexity) fail in some measure in achieving their objectives. He knows that the failures cannot all be attributed to a mistaken belief in the rationality of the human animal. What he wants is an analysis of the causes of success and failure in attempts to create social order. Since the existing literature of sociology and anthropology is not generally directed toward that problem, it can at best offer him only an indirect assistance. Of this it can, to be sure, offer a good deal, particularly in the form of a caution against a naively optimistic view of man's capacity to shape his life in society by verbal resolutions.

For assistance in understanding the order-creating process, we have to turn to the more active, problem-solving directions of thought and research. Some studies in business administration will be found valuable, particularly the pioneering work of Chester I. Barnard, who virtually created the field of study he calls "the sociology of organization."[1] Experimental studies in group behavior by men like Lewin and Bavelas will also be found pertinent and helpful.[2] Political science has, fortunately, always had an orientation toward problems of choosing among alternative structures or procedures, and within the

1. [See Chester Barnard, *The Functions of the Executive* (Cambridge, Mass.: Harvard University Press, 1942), and *Organization and Management: Selected Papers* (Cambridge, Mass.: Harvard University Press, 1948).]

2. [See Kurt Lewin, *Field Theory in Social Science: Selected Theoretical Papers*, ed. Dorwin Cartwright (New York: Harper and Bros., 1951), and Alex Bavelas, "A Method for Investigating Individual and Group Ideology," *Sociometry* 5 (1942): 371–77.]

somewhat narrow range of issues indicated by the adjective *political* it has studied the order-creating process, with a view both to accurate description and sound prescription. Studies of the relative merits and demerits of proportional representation are, for example, directly relevant to our subject.

Economics has, for our purposes, the advantage that it has generally dealt with its central problem as being that of choice, that is, choice in the disposition of scarce resources. Unfortunately, however, it has tended to neglect the structure and institutional framework within which economic choice is exercised and has confined itself to choice as applied to goods and services, treating the rendering of these goods and services as if it occurred in a completely unorganized or "unstructured" social situation. When an attempt was made in this country to redress the balance, in so-called institutional economics, there was a tendency to swing over to the passive observational point of view characteristic of sociology and anthropology. Though these are the defects, from our point of view, of the literature of economics generally, there is much to be learned from individual economists and from sociologists and anthropologists who have concerned themselves with economic organization. One may mention in particular the names of Frank H. Knight, John R. Commons, Emile Durkheim, Max Weber, Bronislow Malinowski, A. S. Diamond, H. I. Hogbin, and Raymond Firth.[3] The combination of the concept of choice implicit in economic analysis and the "institutional" conceptions of sociology and anthropology is, for our purposes, an ideal one.

One familiar with the early history of this country would naturally suppose that an active interest in the order-creating process would be a prominent characteristic of American legal scholarship. The draftsmen of our national constitution accomplished something that had often been (and still often is) declared to be impossible—they brought a nation into existence and gave it a form of government that was at once new and workable. During the period Pound calls the Formative Era of our law there was a lively debate whether we should adopt the French system of comprehensive codification or allow our rules of law to develop through precedents after the English model.[4] Until about the middle of the nineteenth century almost everything written by law-

3. [See, for example, Frank H. Knight, *The Ethics of Competition and Other Essays* (New York: Harper and Bros., 1935); John R. Commons, *Institutional Economics* (New York: Macmillan, 1934); Emile Durkheim, *The Division of Labor in Society*, trans. George Simpson (New York: Free Press, 1933); Max Weber, *On Law in Economy and Society*, ed. Max Rheinstein (Cambridge, Mass.: Harvard University Press, 1954); Bronislaw Malinowski, *Crime and Custom in Savage Society* (New York: Routledge and Kegan Paul, 1926); Arthur S. Diamond, *Primitive Law* (London: Longmans, Green & Co., 1935; 2nd ed., Watts & Co., 1950); Herbert Ian Hogbin, *Law and Order in Polynesia* (London: Christophers, 1934); and Raymond Firth, *Elements of Social Organization* (London: Watts & Co., 1951).]

4. [See Roscoe Pound, *The Formative Era of American Law* (Boston: Little, Brown, 1938), chap. 4.]

yers was filled with the spirit of choice, not simply among substantive rules of law, but among ways of law-making and among forms of government, great and small. Writing in 1859, John Stuart Mill could still describe Americans as being expert "in every kind of civil business; let them be left without a government, every body of Americans is able to improvise one, and to carry on that or any other public business with a sufficient amount of intelligence, order, and decision."[5] Though Mill does not say so, it was of course primarily the American lawyer who supplied this special competence in organizing and carrying on "public business."

Gradually, however, this creative spirit faded. By the 1870s the lawyer was no longer thought of as having any special concern with the order-creating process. Instead, he was considered to be an expert in the necessary implications of certain basic legal concepts: for example, whether an offer "by its nature" is revocable. These concepts were regarded as compulsions more or less inherent in the nature of legal thinking. The primary concern of the legal scholar was with what the Europeans call problems of construction, that is, problems of finding some technical rationalization, within the framework of accepted doctrine, for rules or results deemed desirable. The articulation of the grounds of their desirability was not regarded as a proper concern of legal scholarship. The question asked by the lawyer of every proposed rule or decision was, Can it be reconciled with legal theory?

A reaction against the abstract and verbal nature of this direction of legal thought began at the turn of the century with Holmes and Gray. By the 1920s it had assumed the proportions of a "movement" which came later to be called American Legal Realism. Unfortunately this reaction did not redirect the lawyer's concern to the basic order-creating process. Instead, with Holmes and Gray the lawyer became an expert in predicting and influencing the incidence of state force. In the language of the Realists his task was to study and chart the "behavior patterns" of judges and other state officials. Insofar as the Realist movement broadened its interest beyond problems of legal theory (where it sought chiefly to demonstrate the question-begging nature of most legal rationalizations) it tended to accept the inhibitions of method so many sociologists and anthropologists had seen fit to impose on themselves. Its methodology, in other words, not only did not include the problem of choosing among alternative social structures, but tended to stigmatize any concern with this kind of problem as "unscientific," "metaphysical," and a matter of personal predilection.

There was, to be sure, a kind of reformist tendency implicit in the Realist

5. [John Stuart Mill, "On Liberty," in *The English Philosophers from Bacon to Mill*, ed. E. A. Burtt (New York: Random House, 1939), p. 1039.]

movement insofar as it rejected the compulsions on the basis of which certain rules and principles had been supposed to be "necessary." Realism considered that rules of law are not possible or impossible, but wise or unwise, expedient or inexpedient. This was a great advance. But Realism did not, any more than the Conceptualism against which it revolted, take as an object of direct concern any search for principles of social order or any articulation of the grounds on which legal rules may be deemed to be wise or unwise. As with most directions of social thought that become self-consciously preoccupied with being "scientific," Realism considered that this area of inquiry lay beyond its jurisdiction. A neglect of this area tended, in turn, to encourage extreme positions about social change; on the one hand, a belief that society is a thing wholly man-made that may be shaped in any direction desired, on the other, a determinism denying any creative role to the human will. Realism did not, in other words, recognize the middle ground where man creates within the limits of compulsions he cannot remove but must understand.

Fortunately, there are minds too active to accept for long the restraints of any methodological orthodoxy. Men like Karl N. Llewellyn and Jerome Frank, though identified originally with the Realist movement, turned in their later writings to problems of the order-creating process and wrote much that is valuable to our inquiry.[6]

6. [See Karl N. Llewellyn, *The Bramble Bush*, 2nd ed. (New York: Oceana, 1951); Jerome Frank, *Courts on Trial* (Princeton: Princeton University Press, 1949).]

On Legal Education

Editor's Note

If lawyers are indeed architects of social structures, they ought to receive a training appropriate to their vocation. Fuller believed there were two ways in particular that the law school curriculum could be more suitably designed to prepare law students for the tasks they would be called upon to perform after graduation. First, legal education should provide students with an understanding of the processes in which lawyers actually participate, and, second, it should be oriented toward the examination and resolution of problematic situations, involving both legal and extralegal factors.

Fuller observed that since the adoption of the case method the traditional focus of legal education has been only one aspect of the adjudicative process, the reasoning of appellate courts. This focus, he thought, offers a very incomplete picture of the lawyer's work in arguing cases and settling disputes. For example, the factual records utilized in appellate decisions are incapable of conveying to students the subtle issues involved in gathering and substantiating facts. Furthermore, the case method results in an almost total neglect of other legal processes, such as legislation and mediation. These processes involve the lawyer as "planner, negotiator, and draftsman," whether the task be public rule-making or writing a contract. Fuller believed that a more direct examination of these processes could also improve students' understanding of the adjudicative process.

> *I have found in teaching Contracts that those of my students who have had some practical experience in what may generally be called negotiation bring to problems of interpretation a much more mature insight than those who lack this experience. Recently I tried the experiment of beginning my course with an exercise in negotiation and draftsmanship. My object was to convey, by a kind of vicarious or staged experience, the insight that comes from participation in the act of bringing an agreement into existence.... Students do actually draw on their experience in the drafting exercise in discussing judicial decisions that interpret agreements. The observable improvement in their insight and judgment tends to confirm a prejudice I have entertained for some time, namely, that no judge should sit on the interpretation of a contract who has himself never negotiated one. ["What the Law Schools Can Contribute to the Making of Lawyers" (1948), p. 194.]*

This passage indicates that Fuller was an early advocate of simulation in teaching. It also reflects his penchant for a curriculum structured around problematic situations. In contrast to the case method, the virtues of the problem method are, first, that it begins with a broader conception of the facts which are potentially relevant to the satisfactory resolution of a controversy and, second, that it is oriented to the social or institutional contexts within which controversies arise, and hence is more sensitive to the ramifications of alternative decisions. On both counts it is clear that the tasks of the lawyer, according to this conception, involve many factors of which existing legal rules are often only a part. Consequently the lawyer must be prepared to bring to bear the learning achieved in the social sciences, especially economics and psychology. An education which initiated students into this conception of the lawyer's job would lead them to make decisions, as Fuller expresses it, not simply about "what legally can be done" but about "what should be done, all things considered."

Fuller wrote many articles on legal education, but no one of them offers a comprehensive statement of his views. I have selected the present item, "On Legal Education," for this volume both because it touches on the principal theme of the whole collection and because it is a fine example of Fuller's wit. "On Legal Education" was an address delivered to the Yale Law School Forum on Legal Education, December 4, 1946. At the time of the address, Fuller was chairman of the Committee on Legal Education, which was reexamining Harvard Law School's offerings. Part of the address was published under the title "Objectives of Legal Education" in The Record of the New York City Bar Association, *vol. 2, no. 3 (1947) and is reprinted with permission.*

I

In preparing my case for presentation before this tribunal, my chief difficulty was to know what it was I was expected to prove, or even what it was I was expected to talk about.

The prospect of presenting a critique of legal education as it is conducted at Yale was an appealing one, particularly since it was one on which I would not be handicapped by any great knowledge of the facts. In this respect I enjoy the same advantage as Fred Rodell when he talks about Harvard.[1]

As I reflected on the matter, however, I decided that after all I knew too much about Yale to talk about "the Yale approach." There was no point in reviving old issues, such as might once have centered about names like Hohfeld and Beale.[2] Today, these are only a little bit more alive than those that once surrounded, say, Langdell and Baldwin, who quarreled about the case method.[3] As I surveyed the professors alive and now practicing their craft in New Haven, the list seemed to add up to a very wholesome and fertile variety and not to a single ideology I could pin up on the wall and throw darts at. My conviction that this was so was increased by my visiting six classes today, where I found six different methods of instruction being employed.

So far as making a comparison of the Yale and Harvard Law Schools was concerned, I had several difficulties. In the first place, I have the same trouble with Harvard that I have with Yale, that is, in defining "the Harvard ap-

1. [Fred Rodell (1907–1980), professor of law at Yale University, 1933–1974.]

2. [Welsey N. Hohfeld (1879–1918), professor of law at Yale University, 1914–1918; Joseph H. Beale (1861–1943), professor of law at Harvard Law School, 1890–1938.]

3. [Christopher Columbus Langdell (1826–1906), professor of law at Harvard Law School, 1870–1900, and Dean, 1870–1895; Simeon Eben Baldwin (1840–1927), professor of law at Yale University, 1869–1919.]

proach." We have, I think, quite a nice assortment of biases ourselves, and our usual method of arriving at agreement is that hallowed in American democratic practice: to hold a faculty meeting so long that most of the members go home. Without doubt, the Langdellian strain is a little thicker in Cambridge, for quite understandable reasons.

There's another very sound reason for not attempting to conduct this discussion in terms of a comparison of Yale and Harvard. It would be taking both schools much too seriously. I suppose it's essential to satisfaction in life to think what you are doing is much more important and much more significant than the things other people are doing. As a rank outsider, however, I must say that it seems to me there's an overdose of this both in Cambridge and in New Haven. I suppose the Yale faculty, or some of it, gets a great titillation out of the conviction that it is sending out "key policy moulders" destined, because of their unique training, for positions of great influence. Harvard likes to think it is giving men the *hard, intelligent discipline* that will later make them capable of doing almost anything, from running a war to drafting a label for Scotch-type whiskey that will get by the Alcohol Tax Unit. Actually, the quality of the men who come to both institutions is, by and large, such that we couldn't ruin them if we tried. We could give them their legal education out of the Koran or the collected works of Elbert Hubbard[4] and still many of them would be able to do the things that their professors like to take credit for.

So far as the reform of legal education is concerned, both institutions seem to me to be at present in a state of suspended animation, and the only really concrete programs for reform that have developed recently have come out of the distant city of Chicago.

Ruling out institutional comparisons, therefore, as possibly embarrassing for both of us, I considered for a while concentrating my fire on a 93-page article, "Legal Education and Public Policy: Professional Training in the Public Interest," by Professors Lasswell and McDougal—certainly the longest, the most documented, and the most widely ranging article ever written on legal education.[5] I set the whole of Thanksgiving Day aside for a close study of this article.

I found in it many things of interest, including a good many with which, unfortunately for this forum, I had to agree. Toward the end of the article, I found a good deal that promised to be directly and personally helpful in grooming myself for this appearance.

---

4. [Elbert Hubbard (1856–1915) founded the Roycroft Press in East Aurora, New York; wrote a series of biographical sketches, beginning with *A Little Journey to the Home of George Eliot* (1894), and several books, including *Life of Ali Baba* (1899) and *The Man of Sorrows* (1908); and published two magazines, *Philistine* and *Fra*.]

5. [*Yale Law Journal* 52, no. 2 (1943): 203–95.]

You may recall that beginning on about page 280 the authors point out that one of the glaring deficiencies of present day legal education is that it does not *train law students how to judge men*. The authors proceed to make good this deficiency. They lay down the rules to follow in making yourself a judge of men and of human character. Knowing how fast things move at Yale, I knew that these rules must be part of the curriculum by now and that I could count on you gentlemen applying them to me.

This was a great comfort, because it removed one of the major hazards of advocacy. In my few appearances as an advocate before tribunals—in my own experience they were always of the impure variety known as administrative tribunals—in those appearances I was never worried too much about what they would think of my case and my arguments. There were rules about that, and I have always retained a naive faith that rules have something to do with the decision, and even if they don't, at least they're handy in explaining to the client how you came to lose the case. So I wasn't worried about what they would think of the *case*, but I was worried about what they would think of *me*. There were no rules about that, and I was left uncomfortably floating around on an uncharted sea.

Now this has all been fixed up by Lasswell and McDougal and we have rules for that too. Since I knew I would be tested by these rules, the thing to do was to learn them, follow them, and be judged accordingly.

You can imagine, therefore, with what interest I read these rules. The law student is advised first to observe "in an unobtrusive way, some of the specific acts" of the person being judged. "Where does he focus his gaze? Does he look the other person in the eye, or does his gaze wander up and down and around the room? . . . Physicians have found that shifty eyes are a useful clue of neurotic instability."

When I read that I knew that Langdell and Beale were right after all. Life really is simpler and nicer when you have rules to go by. The thing for me to do was to put my eyes on dead center and keep them there.

Unfortunately, however, I read on in Lasswell and McDougal: "We must beware of the 'over-compensatory' reaction of keeping the eyes riveted on the other person; this is found in slick, bold imposter types."

There I was right back where I started. I couldn't keep my eyes still, and I couldn't keep them shifting. Apparently I had to keep them gently rolling around in a relaxed way, just as if I had never heard of any rules. These new Yale rules were as bad as the rules of Langdell and Beale; they went around traveling in opposite pairs with no way of choosing between them.

Discouraged, I nevertheless read on, encountering some useful admonitions against "fingering the nose" (the authors were speaking literally) and against using a "quick stereotyped smile" that would reveal "an inner uncertainty."

Then I really hit pay dirt. This was the part of the article that tells you how to rise above your middle-class origins in appearing before tribunals. It recommends "an upper-class manner of gracious detachment that is difficult for the middle or lower-class individual to acquire." That is, difficult without the aid of Messrs. Lasswell and McDougal, for they continue:

> The clue to a genuinely aristocratic attitude is that the aristocrat has no compulsion to allow himself to be measured in terms of proficiency in any particular skill. He secures respect just because he exists, not because he is "good for something." Part of the code is to maintain an air of imperviousness to the trials and tribulations of the moment; the ego must appear to remain unruffled and uncontaminated by the momentary acts of fate. Even enemies must be treated with ceremoniousness. In negotiations, as well as before some of the higher courts, the near-aristocratic benignity may be a more powerful instrument than the "huffing and puffing" of the "over-zealous" middle-class derivative.

This was, of course, exactly what I wanted, and I could see again the advantages of following rules instead of groping, of applying principles instead of hunches. However, once again I made the mistake of not stopping, and I read on, encountering this disturbing passage: "When tribunals are made up of middle-class personnel, however, certain accents and demeanors may be resented, especially if the person in question is suspected of being 'really' middle-class himself."

There I was with my illusions shattered again. Two competing rules and no way to choose between them. I must be aristocratic, but not too much so; I must be impervious, but also a little pervious; I must keep my eyes moving but not too rapidly. I was like a student cramming for an examination and finding that every rule he crammed in was cancelled out by a subsequent rule that had also to be crammed in.

Finally, I gave the whole thing up and decided to get back to legal education. I decided I would try to outline for you, briefly and in general terms, my own views about legal education. Not legal education at Harvard or Yale, but American legal education generally.

II

My starting point in any thinking about legal education is the legal profession itself. I believe in that profession and in its usefulness to mankind. The best definition I ever heard of a lawyer was that given by the young daughter of a friend of mine. A neighbor's child asked her what her father did. She said, "He's a lawyer." "What's a lawyer?" "A lawyer is a man that helps people."

That definition has always been a good one. It seems to me that it is gaining a new meaning and a new depth in the era in which we are now living. People need help as they never did before. They need help in meeting each other on common ground, in finding ways of living together.

Some years ago I wrote that I thought we had lost a valuable insight when we threw away, sometime around the middle of the last century, the notion of a "law of nature." [6] I still think this, and the intervening years, if anything, have strengthened this conviction. We need the notion that there is something to law besides judicial behavior patterns and legislative fiats. We need it because it points the lawyer toward the most essential part of his task.

I can best illustrate my meaning by a metaphor. Imagine that you hold in your hand about twenty small pieces of cardboard, cut in irregular shapes. Each of these represents a human being, with his own particular capacities, desires, and interests. The pieces are irregular and varied because men are that way. Before you on a table lies a circle within which you must place all of these pieces. This circle represents the total means of satisfying human desires and realizing human capacities. If you allow the pieces of cardboard to drop within the circle in random order you will find that many of them will be stacked on top of one another, leaving blank spaces in which there are no pieces—unused space, in other words. By experimenting and patiently rearranging the pieces you will find that it is possible to reduce radically the instances in which the pieces overlap and push against one another. There is, in other words, a law already given by the dimensions of this circle and by the dimensions and shapes of these pieces, which determines in some measure how they must be arranged to utilize the available space to the fullest advantage and with the least overlapping.

I know that there are many things wrong with this simple figure. In actuality, the circle is not a circle but something irregular itself; it is not fixed but expanding and contracting. The actual pieces are not individual human beings but a complex of human beings and human institutions, which also change shape constantly. Furthermore, our task is not to arrange the pieces so that they may lie inertly alongside one another but so that they may work together.

But none of these variables and qualifications affects the basic proposition that there is a significant task to be performed in so arranging and ordering

6. [Lon L. Fuller, *The Law in Quest of Itself* (Evanston, Ill.: Northwestern University Press, 1940), pp. 101–4.]

the pieces that they will least interfere with one another. This is the insight Immanuel Kant expressed in his ideal of "a community of free-willing men."[7] We want every one to be as free as possible, and the task of the law is to discover the ways in which this can be accomplished. On this view the primary task of the lawyer is not to expound the fiat of some sovereign, nor to predict which way judges will jump, but to search for truth.

Because I view the lawyer's task in these terms, I must confess I am out of sympathy with the general tone of the article by Lasswell and McDougal, with its talk about "upper, middle, and lower classes," about the "total power process," about "persons whose power position in the world entitles what they say to particular consideration," about "influential policy makers" bent on "extending their special values."

I don't think that either of these gentlemen really conducts his life by slogans and symbols like this. The trouble with them, particularly with Lasswell, is that they have read too much Pareto, Weber, Mosca, and Sorel. They're overprimed with power, and they have forgotten the most useful job the lawyer can do.

Perhaps I can make clearer my conception of the lawyer's task by a more concrete reference. In the field of labor relations, there often seems to be an irreconcilable conflict between two interests: the interest of management in industrial efficiency (which is also an interest of society), and the interest of the worker in human dignity and the right not to be pushed around. (This interest is also one of society as well as of the worker.) Here the circle seems definitely too small for the pieces that have to go into it, and conflict seems inevitable.

However, with patience, with insight, with hard intellectual labor, one will find that there is an arrangement that will avoid the overlapping or conflict of the pieces or will reduce it to negligible proportions, without breaking the circle. The worker can be protected against indignities in ways that do not reduce, too much, industrial efficiency; there are ways of promoting industrial efficiency which do not involve pushing the worker around.

This is the kind of job in which the lawyer, properly trained, excels. He it is who has the detachment that is the first essential for the task. With this he combines the imagination and the capacity for analyzing the factors in the situation that are equally indispensable. Lawyers representing both management and labor have made important contributions to this task.

I believe that the fundamental objective of legal education should be that of

7. [Immanuel Kant, *Selections*, ed. T. M. Greene (New York: Chas. Scribner's Sons, 1929), pp. 334–50.]

training lawyers for this kind of job, not simply in the field of labor relations, but throughout our whole social and economic order.

III

If you ask, What reforms are needed in legal education? I think you can most quickly and surely obtain the answer by asking in turn, During the last two or three generations, what changes have taken place in the nature of the demands made on the legal profession? You will then have the clue to the inadequacies in our present system of legal education.

For it is a fairly safe generalization that education lags behind the needs of the tasks for which it is preparing. This is particularly apt to be true where education seems on the surface successful, and certainly legal education in this country during the last forty years can be counted, in comparison with education generally, a very successful enterprise. One of my most astute colleagues has often said that the greatest handicap of the Harvard Law School has been its success. I think we can extend that observation to the case method and to American legal education as a whole.

The secret of the success of American legal education, in comparison, say, with undergraduate instruction, lies in the fact that it centers about problems. The intellectual challenge of this method is such that it has succeeded remarkably well without basic changes for decades. It has succeeded so well, indeed, that those who employ it have often forgotten to ask whether the problems they are dealing with correspond to the tasks for which they purport to train men.

The case method originated in 1870 when Langdell came to Harvard as dean. That was about thirty years before it became the exclusive method of instruction at Harvard. It was still an issue during the first decade of the twentieth century, but by the time of World War I it had ceased to be a debatable question. We may take 1900, therefore, as the approximate turning point, as the time when the mold of present legal education was set.

If we compare the work of the legal profession in 1900 with the tasks it performs today, I think we can make the generalization that *the scope of the lawyer's responsibility has greatly expanded.* As I see it, this expansion of his responsibilities has two aspects.

In the first place, he now has typically a different responsibility with respect to facts. In 1900 the lawyer was typically an advocate or a strictly legal adviser. As an advocate, he was dealing with facts, not the way an administrator does, but with forensic facts, with facts as they get into a written record. When he gave advice, he was usually permitted to hedge against any responsibility for facts. His formal opinion letter started out by stating that, *on the assumption* that the facts were X, Y, and Z, then legal consequence A would follow.

In the intervening half-century a change has occurred in the responsibility typically assumed by the lawyer. Today, whether he is in private practice or a government lawyer, his responsibility for facts is generally that of an administrator. He is no longer dealing with *forensic* facts but with *managerial* facts.[8]

Yet, by and large, legal education centers on the facts of a written record, or worse still the tendentiously reported skeleton of the facts found in an appellate decision. This is a serious deficiency, because in my opinion one of the greatest contributions a lawyer can make in any situation is to get at the facts. It is remarkable how many people in this world (people who in Lasswell and McDougal's terms occupy "high positions of influence in the power hierarchy")—how many of these people go about deciding things with only the slightest notion of what it is they are really deciding.

If we are to get our irregularly shaped pieces inside the circle without too many clashes, somebody has got to stand to one side and study the actual shape of these pieces and the actual size of the circle in which they have to fit. This is, in my experience, a job that lawyers must perform if it is to get done. It is the responsibility of the law schools to prepare them for this job, and I don't think any of us is doing too good a job of it now.

Going back to the changes that have occurred in the responsibilities of the legal profession during the last half century, I think the second great change lies in the fact that the lawyer today has, typically, a responsibility for what may be called the total decision. Almost any decision, whether arrived at by private interests or government agencies, involves a synthesis of legal and ex-

---

8. [In a subsequent essay, Fuller drew this distinction somewhat differently:

Though, as I have said, the legislative and adjudicative processes are closely related, each of them represents a distinct set of problems and a distinct set of postures of mind, so that neither can be taught as an unplanned by-product of teaching the other. The essential distinction between the two processes can be seen if we consider the different way each views facts.

Adjudication has to do with forensic facts. If we are dealing with appellate decisions, the facts reported have been filtered through the rules of evidence and purged of their natural ambiguities by presumptions and rules about the burden of proof. Even in the most informal administrative hearing or arbitration, however, facts assume a new character when presented in a context of litigation. . . .

Legislation, on the other hand, deals not with forensic facts but with what may be called managerial facts. It is not the task of the lawyer acting as planner, negotiator, and draftsman to reduce the facts to a neat pattern but to see them whole, in all their disorder, in all their ambiguity. He must gear his decision to a range of factual probability and must devise a plan that will anticipate, and absorb without disruption, future changes in the facts. "What the Law Schools Can Contribute to the Making of Lawyers," *Journal of Legal Education* 1 (1948): 194–95.]

tralegal factors. In simpler days, when interests were less complex, the lawyer had ingenious ways of ducking responsibility for extralegal considerations. These he no longer has. Today he has to be capable of making his own synthesis of legal and extralegal considerations; he must be able to make a responsible contribution to the "total decision."

Here the second greatest inadequacy of American legal education becomes apparent. We do not give the student training in this process by which the total decision is arrived at. A number of us were interested very much in the way Professor Gellhorn[9] expressed the objectives of his seminar in administrative law. He stated that the shift is from the question, "What *can* be done?" to the question, "What *should* be done, all things considered?" This expresses neatly a shift in emphasis that many of us in many American law schools have had in mind for a long time. The shift has by no means been completed.

The general formula I would prescribe for bringing American legal education up to date would read something as follows: We must retain the problem method implicit in the case method. We must continue to concentrate on real issues, as they arise in real human contexts, and not get lost in abstract theories. At the same time, we must expand these issues in two directions: *first*, so as to include live facts and not the frozen facts of a written record; *second*, so as to include the extralegal considerations that bear on the final decision.

At this point our conservative colleagues on all faculties speak up and say: You are attempting the impossible. You can't spread legal education out without making it thinner. We must concentrate on straight thinking. You can't do this without fixed points of reference. If legal education is allowed to roam all over the map, it becomes a mere windy exchange of attitudes and biases.

On this issue, I count myself somewhat to the left of center. I agree with Lasswell and McDougal that much of the so-called rigor of traditional legal thinking is merely disguised tautology and consists of putting rabbits in the hat with one hand and pulling them out with the other. On the other hand, I am convinced that the conservatives have a real point. As confirmation for this conclusion, I can refer to an experience I have encountered several times. A student trained in literature or history enters the law school and conceives very rapidly a strong distaste for legal reasoning. He complains that it is narrow, question-begging, and tautological. As one very sensitive student of mine expressed it, "It seems to me that when a question becomes really important, it ceases to be a legal question." After trying law school for a year or so, such a student gives up the law as a bad job and goes back to his first love, which may have been history or psychology—typically one of the humanities. Then he finds, lo and behold, that he has become a man without a country. His legal

9. [Walter Gellhorn (1906–), professor of law at Columbia University, 1945–1974.]

training has done something to him. He can no longer abide the vague and loose methods of his instructors and fellow students. And strangely he is convinced that he has become a better thinker and a more effective person generally, as a result of the legal training he fought so hard against when he was getting it.

As I see it, the basic dilemma of American legal education is well expressed by the following statement made by a committee on the reform of engineering education:

> Again and again the professional engineer must deal with problems that involve indeterminate values, intangible factors, and the making of alternative and even speculative hypotheses. Yet in dealing with such problems, he must apply the same thoroughness and orderliness of thought that applies to problems subject to mathematical solution. This is an extremely difficult and important thing to learn how to do well.

Teaching men how to do this is a problem that can never be solved by one man or one school alone. Yet I think it is vital that it be solved.

We live in a world that is threatened by international and internal chaos. In my opinion, this threat comes not from wicked intentions (neither of the Russians nor John L. Lewis) but from our inability to reach a real understanding of one another's problems. I believe that there is a profound truth in the statement that the injustices and cruelties of this world are done, not with the fists, but with the elbows. What we need is someone with the imagination, the patience, and the skill to work out a seating arrangement that will put us all within reach of the banquet, but that will keep our elbows from knocking against one another. Only the lawyer is capable of doing this job. It is our responsibility to train him for it.

Philosophy for the Practicing Lawyer

Editor's Note

Fuller once remarked that he thought legal education needed to become both more practical and more philosophical.

In speaking of the practicality of legal education, he was referring to its adequacy in preparing students for the actual tasks and responsibilities they would assume as modern lawyers. By this measure he thought there were three respects in which legal education was deficient: (1) in training students in the process of gathering, sifting, and organizing facts; (2) in preparing students to draw on the contributions of experts in different fields (such as accounting, economics, psychology) for the proper disposition of problems; and (3) in orienting students toward "legal planning," that is, the job of giving legal form to desired goals and policies, rather than simply defending the validity or propriety of actions already taken. Each of these reforms, of course, would serve better to acquaint students with the variety of legal processes.

A practical legal education, however, must also be philosophical. Far from these two aspects being incompatible, Fuller thought they require each other. A philosophical perspective focuses on processes of law as purposeful human activities and keeps the lawyer from adopting an overly formalistic approach to legal issues.

> *In recommending a philosophic approach for legal education, I do not mean that we should increase our pretensions to cosmic understanding. I mean merely that we need to become aware of, and reflective about, the ends of law and government, and that we need to relate specific rules of private and public law to those ends. We need to recapture some of the intellectual spirit of the early days of the Republic, when lawyers fought for and planned a new form of society and were thoroughly aware that every aspect of their professional lives touched, in one way or another, the governance of men.*
>
> *We need a philosophic awakening that will put law in its proper place in the human struggle to achieve order and justice and will see it as a part of the eternal quest for those principles that will enable us to live and work together in harmony. This philosophic quest should, I believe, dominate the law school curriculum from the beginning to the end. [From an untitled, undated address.]*

"Philosophy for the Practicing Lawyer" describes the contribution that philosophy can make toward realizing this conception of the lawyer's role in society. It was an address to law students delivered, so far as I have been able to determine, some time in the late 1940s.

My assignment is to discuss with you briefly what philosophy has to offer the young practicing attorney, and in what sense he himself should seek to become a philosopher.

Now, of course, the word *philosophy* means different things to different men. If we are to reach any kind of understanding, we shall have to discriminate among the various uses of the term. There is one modern sense of the word *philosophy* that I want to set definitely to one side, since, far from recommending the thing it stands for, I want to warn you against it. I refer to the conception that identifies philosophy with position-taking, that condemns, as "lacking a philosophy," those who do not claim to have any simple, abstract formula by which they measure life.

The devastation that can be wrought by "philosophy" in this sense is illustrated in an incident drawn from the political history of Germany between the two wars, an incident related by a recent visitor from the University of Marburg. There was under discussion in Germany during the thirties a proposal to improve the legal situation of the illegitimate child, it being argued that the existing law was inadequate for his protection and unjustly discriminated against him.

Political leaders, eager to expound their divergent "world-views," seized upon this homely legislative issue as a kind of sounding board for their philosophies. Each of the major parties tried to prove its right to exist by demonstrating that it had a special, ready-made attitude toward this question, as it did toward all the other great and small problems of law and government.

The Communists asserted that the plutocrats of a decadent capitalism were debauching the daughters of the workers and should be made to pay for their crimes. They pictured the bourgeoisie in shining limousines driving by night into the slums of the German cities on errands of lechery. At the opposite extreme from the Communists were those, of both Catholic and Protestant faith, who purported to take their political principles directly from the precepts of religion. For them the proposal to improve the legal status of the child born out of wedlock was an attack on the institution of marriage, a step toward reducing man to an animal level, a measure designed to wipe out the distinction between holy matrimony and living in sin. In another corner, the Nazis added their own strident notes to the discord. The birth rate of Germany was dropping because of the corrupting influence of capitalism and Marxism. The Fatherland needed soldiers. The woman fortunate enough to have a baby of pure German blood should be given an honorable citation, an extended vacation with pay, and a purse to meet all the expenses of rearing her child.

These abstract prejudgments of the problem gave rise, inevitably, to abstract solutions—"lebensfremd," as the Germans say, "unrelated to life." Some proposed, as a way of removing the stigma of bastardy, to give the child a legal right to take his father's name. Others brought forth the ingenious suggestion that in cases where the *exceptio plurium* was allowed (that is, where more than one man was cohabiting with the mother at the time of conception so that it was impossible to say who the father was) *all* of the possible fathers should be compelled to join in supporting the child.

This discussion proceeded with great heat and oratory and to the immense personal satisfaction of the participants. Meanwhile no one really thought about the unfortunate creature whose plight was at stake or tried to find out what his actual situation and needs might be. When the facts were examined, it was discovered, first of all, that illegitimate children are almost always born of parents belonging to the same general social and economic class; there was in reality no question of class conflict involved. As for destroying the institution of marriage, most erring couples, between whom there is the slightest affection, are likely to get married, if no impediment exists, as soon as it is discovered that the woman is pregnant. Where such a marriage does not take place, it is a good indication that no tolerable life in common is possible. Furthermore, the plight of the child and its mother is so unhappy and afflicted, no one could seriously suppose that the reality of the institution of marriage would be impaired by a measure increasing the rights of illegitimate children. As for the cannon-fodder argument, an examination of the facts would show that the social disruption, misery, and crime caused by illegitimacy was so expensive to the Fatherland as to render insignificant any possible gain in military manpower—so that even the brutally realistic cost accounting of the Nazis was as naive in its way as the views to which it was opposed.

As for the proposed cures, a right to his father's name is the last thing an illegitimate child needs. This linking of him with the name of a man unknown to his friends and neighbors would merely disclose to the world the irregularity of his origin. More practicable was the proposal to permit his mother to add "Mrs." to her own name and to have schools and hospitals cease asking for the name of the father on routine applications and forms. The proposal to make all possible fathers chip in was abandoned when the child sought to be helped by this arrangement was nicknamed the "corporation baby," and it was realized in what a ludicrous light the proposal placed its intended beneficiary.

It is a commentary on current intellectual fashions that the banner-waving, slogan-shouting kind of argument with which this discussion began would today be described without irony as a dispute about "philosophies of life," and the participants would be treated as reaching their conclusions, not through sheer ignorance of the facts and a stirring toward vocal activity, but through the guidance of their special "philosophies."

How remote this conception is from the "philosopher" of popular tradition! He was a tweedy, pipe-smoking kind of fellow, not easily excited, who approached life relaxed and with his guard down. He was a man who could discern some truth in all honest contentions, who could absorb reversals of fortune gracefully and go down to defeat without screaming recriminations. This philosopher of the popular tradition was tolerant, broad, disinclined toward any sort of prejudgment.

I am afraid that we have come a long way from this conception. Today the term *philosophy* is apt to be associated, not with "being a philosopher," but with "having a philosophy." "To have a philosophy" is often understood to mean something almost the opposite of the genial figure I have just sketched. It means approaching life with your intellectual muscles taut, with your tactics calculated and planned before the battle begins. It means position-taking and having "definite values," as they are called, by which the world can be judged and a good part of it rejected.

Why has this shift in the connotations of the word *philosophy* occurred? I suspect that the reason lies in the notion—now so widespread as to be commonplace—that all "value judgments" are inherently subjective. During most of history it was thought that what we now call, following Nietzsche, questions of value were to be decided by a complicated process that included, first, securing by meditation as much clarity as possible about what men want of life, then seeing how, and to what extent, these wants can be satisfied under the limiting conditions of human existence, and then, finally, modifying our aims in the light of what was thus revealed. In this way, "values" were defined by reflection and experience, acting and reacting upon one another. Man humbly inquired what could be had of the world, before telling it what it must give him.

Today, there is a tendency to think of values as having a kind of spontaneous origin within the individual psyche, expressing the peculiar emotional structure of the person entertaining them. These values inside-the-skin are wholly unrelated to the external world, except insofar as the accidental experiences of the individual may have helped to shape them.

One might suppose that a man who admitted the subjectivity of his values would be a more tolerant fellow, easier to get along with, than one who pretends to obtain his conceptions of what is good from a reality that extends beyond himself. Strangely enough, it works out just the other way, for two reasons. In the first place, if values are in fact formed spontaneously inside the psyche, then no one has any excuse not to have a complete set of them ready to apply to every issue. Indeed, not to have a complete kit of prefabricated values may be taken as a sign that one is, in some obscure and slightly shameful manner, internally incomplete. To say, "I have not yet arrived at a complete understanding of what is right and what is wrong, but I am working my way toward it," sounds as naive as if one were to say, "I do not yet have a complete set of teeth, but I am at work growing them."

If the theory that all values are subjective makes every man want to claim that he is provided with a complete set of them, it also makes the values which he affirms less vulnerable to the attack of inconvenient fact. That which does not seek to demonstrate itself cannot be demonstrated to be wrong. Not purporting to be derived from the world, the subjective value is ready to reject as an irrelevance any part of the world that seems to contradict it.

I take it I have by now made clear my aversion to the notion that identifies philosophy with a capacity for prejudgment, that conceives of the philosopher as the navigator who screws down the needle of his compass before the voyage begins. I condemn this view not only in the name of common sense but in the name of my profession. Of all men the lawyer should be able to suspend judgment until the evidence is in. One of the finest services our profession renders lies in its ability to get beneath slogans and facile catch-phrases to uncover and define the actual areas about which men are in fact agreed and disagreed. If we have to be "unphilosophic" by modern acceptations to accomplish this end, then I am willing to accept whatever stigma attaches to that description.

But I think that philosophy can have a more constructive meaning for the lawyer. First, a word about the technical literature of philosophy. I believe that lawyers will profit from a study of the works of the great philosophers. I think, however, that it is a great mistake, likely to engender disillusionment, to search these writings for some principle or formula that may be applied directly to solve the problems that confront a lawyer in his practice and in planning his life. What should be sought is not a principle that will exclude and render irrelevant the disturbing parts of reality, but an enlargement of view, an opening up of areas of meaning that have been lost from sight. Approached in this spirit, I think one can learn something from nearly any philosopher, whether he be Plato, St. Thomas, Dewey, Hegel, Carnap, Sartre, Korzybski, or Schweitzer—and I have intentionally included some in this miscellaneous list that I find personally uncongenial.

Somewhat closer to the lawyer's work is the literature of jurisprudence and legal philosophy. I recommend to you the short books of Roscoe Pound, especially *An Introduction to the Philosophy of Law*, *The Formative Era of American Law*, and *Law and Morals*.[1] I trust that you have all read Cardozo's *Nature of the Judicial Process*[2] and, if you have not, that you will do so at the first opportunity. Gray's *Nature and Sources of the Law*[3] is sprightly and pro-

---

1. [Roscoe Pound, *An Introduction to the Philosophy of Law* (New Haven: Yale University Press, 1922; rev. ed., 1954); *The Formative Era of American Law* (Boston: Little, Brown, 1938); *Law and Morals* (Chapel Hill: University of North Carolina Press, 1924; 2d ed., 1926).]

2. [Benjamin Cardozo, *The Nature of the Judicial Process* (New Haven: Yale University Press, 1921).]

3. [John Chipman Gray, *The Nature and Sources of the Law* (New York: Columbia University Press, 1909; 2d ed., New York: Macmillan, 1921).]

vocative but filled with hidden premises that must be uncovered if one is to put the work in its proper perspective. The best current general treatises on jurisprudence are all by men now teaching in Australia—Professors Stone, Paton, and Friedmann.[4] One may read with profit the treatises of any of this trio.

I hope that you will find time in your practice for some reading among books of the kind I have just described. Whether you do or not, however, I urgently recommend to you one form of philosophic activity that I consider indispensable. However preoccupied you may be with your professional and personal affairs, however confident you are that all is well and that your work as a lawyer meets the highest requirements of professional tradition, I urge that from time to time you engage in the imaginative exercise of standing off and looking at yourself and what you are doing with eyes as completely disinterested and candid as you can make them. This is a hard thing to do. It requires both powers of mind and of will. Without it, however, you will lose the most profound satisfaction that any man can have in his work, and that is a real understanding of what he is doing.

Let us go through the steps of such an exercise hypothetically. We shall suppose a young lawyer out of school for five or six years. He is working in an office with at least, let us say, six other lawyers—perhaps with as many as a hundred or more. To make our case typical, we shall suppose that he is engaged in private practice, though our analysis would not have to be changed in any essential if he were working in a government office.

Our young lawyer has made a good start and, judged by his performance so far, has already established himself as a success in his chosen career. This means, of course, that he is very busy and probably, in consequence, quite happy.

When he was in law school he used to worry that he might be called upon by his office to advocate causes in which he did not personally believe. He finds that this is not a real problem. Apparently people do not generally ask lawyers to represent them in outrageous positions, or at least they do not come to his firm when they seek that kind of legal assistance. Then, things are not quite so black and white as he had anticipated, there are more shades of gray, and it is difficult to judge in advance who is right and who is wrong. In those instances where he had some doubts about the client's case at the beginning, these doubts evaporate after he has worked on the case for a few days; his client's cause then comes to seem at once logical and just. He worries a little

---

4. [Wolfgang Friedmann, *Legal Theory*, 2d ed. (London: Stevens and Sons, 1949); George W. Paton, *A Textbook of Jurisprudence* (London: The Clarendon Press, 1946); Julius Stone, *The Province and Function of Law* (London: Stevens, 1947).]

that he might have experienced the same conversion had he been working on the other side, but this slight concern does not detract from his zeal or his desire to advance his client's interests.

In short, he finds that advocacy, instead of being a problem, is a tremendous stimulus and release. It is fun to have a cause and with it a clear-cut goal to work toward, even if it is the cause of someone else or, rather, especially since it is the cause of someone else.

He finds that law practice involves to a greater degree than he had anticipated the elements of a game, played vigorously but, for the most part, honorably. He is surprised that in general the game goes on so good-naturedly, considering that the stakes are high and that what one side gains the other loses, though he reflects that this is not always so, since he has seen that an apparent deadlock of opposed interests can often be resolved by the lawyer's ingenuity in devising a procedure that will let both parties have what they want.

One moral issue bothers our young lawyer occasionally for which he was not prepared when he entered the profession. He is worried that he may allow himself to become too completely identified with his client's interest. This is not a fear that he may be drawn into unethical practices. He would act honorably if he acted in his own interest, and the situation is no different where he feels an identity of interest between himself and his client. No temptation to impropriety is created by that identity of interest. Furthermore, the logic of his situation seems to call for this identification. His obligation of loyalty to his client pulls in that direction, as does the spirit of the game in which he is engaged. And yet in an obscure way he feels that it is wrong not to preserve some detachment from his client, not to keep a certain wall of separation between himself and his client's interests. He wishes he had time to think these things through.

At this point we shall give him a week off with pay and instruct him to go through the exercise I have recommended. He is asked to detach himself intellectually and emotionally from his work and to look at what he is doing as if he were a complete stranger to it.

From the perspective of this new detached point of view, what does he see? Does the game he enjoyed so much while playing it now seem a sordid trifling with the public interest, a waste of taxpayers' and clients' money? Does his eagerness to identify himself with his client's cause show that he has undergone a moral disintegration so complete that such desire for detachment as remains is stifled by a guilty conscience that dares not look facts in the face? Does the comradeship that persists between lawyers who are fighting one another hard lose its wholesome appearance and acquire some of the sinister quality of a

Daumier cartoon, recalling the augurs of ancient Rome, who were said to smile furtively at one another as they passed in the streets?

I don't think our young lawyer will experience any such disillusionment about his profession. Looking at his work from this outside vantage point, I think he will, on the contrary, come to see that a profound morality justifies what may be called, in the broadest sense, the adversary system and the game-like spirit that goes with that system.

Let me explain in very simple terms why I think this is so. I begin with the trite observation that life is complicated, and that this is especially so of the problems with which lawyers have to deal, which generally involve situations where things have become badly entangled and snarled, or threaten to become so. Men do not readily summon the energy necessary to deal properly with problems of this sort unless they have what psychologists call adequate motivation. Digging up facts, thinking up arguments, tracing out the full implications of proposed solutions—all of these things are very hard work. This is where the game spirit comes in. Without it work that is vital in the public interest would not get done.

We had a beautiful illustration of this during the [Second World] War when the War Labor Board was functioning. Some complicated issue, say involving piece rates, would arise between the management of a company and the union which represented its employees. A series of conferences would be held to settle the matter. Questions would constantly come up that could not be answered. The union would want to know some technical fact, obtainable, say, from the time-study department. The president or personnel manager handling the negotiations would reply that he didn't know the answer but would try to have it in time for the next meeting. Sometimes he had it by then and sometimes he did not. The company would inquire whether this or that solution was worthy of consideration. The union would reply that it would have to consult the members more immediately affected before it could give an answer. Weeks dragged on, and listless, loose-ended discussions took hours of everyone's time.

Finally it was decided to submit the thing to the War Labor Board. Attorneys were called in, everybody got busy, found out what the facts were, and began thinking seriously about the impact of the various possible solutions that might be reached. The excitement of the coming formal hearing put everyone on his toes. The case was set for argument, briefs were written and filed, and a whole morning was spent in spirited dispute before the hearing officer of the board. Then, strangely enough, it was found that the parties had no real need for a decision by an outside tribunal; they were ready to settle the case by negotiation. The parties now knew for the first time what the facts, in all their complexity, actually were; they had a chance to gauge the force of their opponents' position; they had finally thought through the full meaning to them of the various solutions proposed for the problem. The case was quickly closed by a settlement reasonably satisfactory to everyone.

This kind of thing happened repeatedly. We argued in the morning, negotiated in the afternoon while the Hearing Officer stood by, and reached an agreement without his aid before the day was over. All of this could have been done without lawyers, without a hearing, without arguments—that is, it could have been done if men were disinterested angels with an insatiable thirst for work, which of course they are not.

Viewed in this light the zeal of advocacy is one of those tricks of nature by which a man is lured into serving the public interest without knowing it, by which he is made to work and think harder than he really wants to. The process I have described is, in a less dramatic way, manifest throughout the profession. It is the zeal of advocacy, for example, that supplies the court with the facts and the thinking without which an intelligent decision is impossible.

Does all this mean, then, that our young lawyer will return from his trip beyond the periphery of his daily activities smug and complacent, unaltered by the experience of seeing himself as others might see him? I think not. I believe, on the contrary, that his conception of his work will have undergone a very considerable change.

Without losing any of his zest for the game, he will want to play it now in a somewhat different manner. In negotiation, instead of seeking primarily to gain some advantage for his client, he will see his most important task as that of searching out those procedures by which apparently conflicting interests can be reconciled. In arguing cases before the courts, he will see his job, not as one of mere persuasion, or of a facile manipulation of legal doctrine, but as one of conveying to the court that full understanding of the case which will enable it to reach a wise and informed decision.

Our young lawyer will do these things, not because of any newly acquired moral prudery, but simply because by playing the game this way he will gain that double satisfaction that comes from serving both his client and the public interest. He will also have learned, incidentally, why it is essential that he keep some sense of detachment toward his client's cause even in the very thick of battle, because without that detachment the satisfaction I have described is impossible.

I believe that when lawyers have come generally to view their work in this manner we shall have a society in which philosophers are kings, even though we live in a democracy and even though few of our citizens pretend to be students of the technical literature of philosophy.

Appendix

Letter from Lon L. Fuller to Thomas Reed Powell

Editor's Note

The following letter to Thomas Reed Powell, a colleague at Harvard Law School, has been placed in this collection as an appendix because it does not speak directly to the central theme of the essays. Yet it is, in part, the most revealing statement of general philosophical viewpoint that I have found among Fuller's papers.

Powell had written a much longer letter in criticism of Fuller's The Law in Quest of Itself. *(Neither letter is dated, at least on the copies preserved in the Harvard Law School archives, but references in Powell's letter indicate it was written after the appearance in 1941 of reviews of Fuller's book by Myres McDougal and Morris Cohen.) Though Fuller's response is intelligible by itself, it may help the reader if I identify two issues Powell constantly recurred to in his letter.*

First, he expressed considerable scepticism regarding Fuller's claim that the legal realists were committed, perversely, to a "rigid separation" of the law that is *and the law that* ought *to be. Powell thought rather that the realists held (and certainly ought to have held, if they in fact did not) a more moderate view: that the distinction between* is *and* ought *is intelligible, that it is often useful in understanding legal phenomena, and indeed that it is essential "for those who must deal with a system which has conventions about precedent." A theorist who distinguishes the law that* is *and the law that* ought *to be, he added, is not compelled to insist that judges are not (or ought not to be) influenced by moral considerations. It is important only to be clear that the nature of law is independent of its sources.*

Second, Powell believed that Fuller's book revealed a strong animus against governmental administration and regulation of the economy. More specifically, he thought Fuller failed to grasp the moral foundation of federal intervention as a way of curbing the deleterious power of "private government." Thus: "You seemed to me to be almost completely callous to what to increasing numbers of enlightened people are the most pressing moral issues of our time. And this in the name of infusing ethics and moral ideals into the law." In an ad hominem remark characteristic of the letter as a whole, Powell declared Fuller's views to be in harmony with those of Calvin Coolidge.

Whatever the merits of the second issue, Fuller's claims for the necessary intermingling of the law that is *and the law that* ought *to be won him, over the years, the scorn of a veritable parade of philosophers, beginning with Morris Cohen's review which carried the stinging title, "Should Legal Thought Abandon Clear Distinctions?" This review was collected in a volume of Cohen's essays,* Reason and Law *(Free Press, 1950; Collier paperback, 1961), a copy of which was in Fuller's library. At the conclusion of the review, Fuller had penned: "I must have written a bad book to have given rise to so bad a review as this." He also had noted in the margin the page numbers of several passages in another essay by Cohen, "Absolutisms in Law and Morals." One of these passages is especially illuminating for understanding Fuller's response to the review. The passage begins with the remark:*

> The craving for greater simplicity and definiteness than our material naturally offers shows itself also in the desire for clear-cut absolute divisions. Now the simplest mode of division is that into two mutually exclusive parts such as we have when a line divides a surface into two mutually exclusive areas. This type of division (dichotomy) is especially prominent in the law. . . .

Cohen then illustrates his point by reference to the troublesome distinction between criminal and civil law. In conclusion he says:

> . . . the point I am making is that the existence of such differences [as between criminal and civil actions], like the existence of the varieties of a species, does not necessarily establish a rigid dichotomous division. Similar considerations hold in regard to the dichotomous divisions between public and private law, between substantive and procedural law, between judicial and administrative law.
>
> We may carry over this distrust of dichotomous division to the distinction between what is and what is not law. Looking at the matter externally after the courts have decided, we can say what is and what is not the law in the given case. But can we be so certain as to the cases not yet decided? . . .

I am certain that what puzzled Fuller, as he compared this passage to the scathing attack on his own effort to reject the rigid dichotomy (especially in judicial decision-making) between is *and* ought, *is Cohen's failure to appreciate their common aim.*

Dear Reed:

Let me begin my comments on your letter by saying that I think some of your criticisms of my book are quite justified. My book *is* too polemic. I was, at times, a little carried away by my desire to make out a case, and I said some things which I would not say again if I were rewriting the book. In the third chapter, particularly, I made criticisms of "positivism" generally, which either do not apply to the realists or apply only with qualifications which I did not make explicit. I agree with you also that too many things are treated as if they turned entirely on the natural law-legal positivism issue, when as a matter of fact they have other facets. With some of your specific criticisms of my treatment of the realists I would be inclined to disagree rather sharply, as I would also with your report of some of the things I am alleged to have said, particularly about bureaucracy. I may point out incidentally that you are quite incorrect in saying I did not name the realists whose conception of law I was criticizing. They were Bingham, Frank, Llewellyn, and Cook, with Holmes and Gray as forerunners (see pages 48–53).

My object in writing this letter is not, however, to defend myself on matters of detail, but to make some contribution toward clarifying our differences. In your letter you do not quarrel, very much, with the *answers* I give to the issues I raise. Rather you deny the reality of the issues themselves. You say, "If you are right that there is a vital problem of choosing between two competing directions of legal thought, it is one that I have never appreciated." The burden placed on me is, therefore, that of proving not that I was right about my answers, but that I was right about my questions. Is the issue of natural law versus legal positivism a real issue, or is it a "phony" which I cooked up in order to have something to talk about?

At no place in your letter do you really quarrel with the basic premise of my book, the "metaphysical inseparability" of *is* and *ought*. You say, in effect, "But what is all the shouting about? Didn't we all know that before?" You seem to assume not only that you knew it, but that all the realists knew it and took it for granted. Specifically you write on page 8, "I would need proof that 'the realists' have assumed that a 'rigorous' separation is possible, and that one may study law 'in isolation from its ethical context.'"

Since the rules of the game seem to require that I cite chapter and verse and am not entitled to rely on "general tendencies," to meet this challenge adequately I would have to present a detailed analysis of some dozen or more articles. Unfortunately my present commitments to the Absolute Is-Ought do not allow me the time required for this task. I will call your attention, however, to a passage in Llewellyn's article in the *Harvard Law Review*,[1] in which he agrees with Felix Cohen that Pound could be cited for all the planks of the realist platform, except perhaps "the rigorous temporary severance of Is and Ought." I know of no passage in Llewellyn's writings in which there is recognition that this severance involves any difficulties whatever. Cook has asserted repeatedly that the legal scientist studies judicial behavior as the physicist studies the behavior of atoms. I am not aware that he has ever recognized any limitations on the aptness of this analogy, except to say that *after* the legal scientist has found out how *his* atoms were behaving, he might try to talk them into behaving in some other way. When I wrote my book I reread all the relevant writings of Llewellyn, Cook, Bingham, and Frank, and I found no recognition that the severance of Is and Ought ever involves any violence to the subject matter severed or pain to the severer.

It is true that I can point to no passage where a realist has said in so many words, "*It is possible* to separate the is and the ought rigorously." But are you fair in asking for that? If Jones says, "I urge that we visit Smith tonight," am

---

1. [Karl N. Llewellyn, "Some Realism About Realism—Responding to Dean Pound," *Harvard Law Review* 44, no. 8 (1931): 1255.]

I not justified in thinking that Jones considers a visit to Smith possible? To justify this inference must I prove that Jones said, "I urge that we visit Smith tonight, and *I may observe parenthetically that it is possible for us to do so*"?

Perhaps you will say in answer to all this that I am talking, not about the practice of the realists, but about their *professions* when they were in an evangelizing mood. You may consider that their philosophic professions have as little significance as my own. This puts upon me the burden of proving that philosophy and evangelizing about general "tendencies" have any significance.

I can only say that it seems to me to be a plain fact that there have been in the past shifts in the "general tendency" of legal thought. The books which formed the mainstay of legal instruction in 1820—Vattel, Grotius, Ahrens, Burlamaqui, Pothier, Pufendorf—are today almost completely forgotten. *Something* has happened to give men's minds a new direction. What is it that has happened? I do not pretend to have the whole answer. I only assume that conscious human purpose has had *some* part in giving direction to legal thinking, and that men's metaphysical assumptions, in turn, have had *some* influence on their choice of the things which they attempt to accomplish in a short life.

Do you really deny that shifts in the prevailing bent of legal thinking have occurred in the past? I don't think you do. You say that it is necessary to train students to make an effort to separate *is* and *ought* when those students "must deal with a system which has conventions about precedents." By implication you recognize that the "system" might have a different set of "conventions," and that if it did then it would not be necessary to insist on such a strict severance of *is* and *ought* in legal instruction. I take it that you will concede that the law's "conventions about precedents" have changed in the course of history, and that today they are not quite the same in Massachusetts as they are in New York, for example. Are you then assuming that the prevailing attitude toward precedents is something which you and I must accept but which we cannot influence? Or is it your assumption that we can influence this attitude only in our treatment of case law, and that general professions and "philosophy" are so much "airy drool"? If so, then why has the "philosophy" of realism had such a potent influence during the last ten or twenty years?

You say that I am wise to disavow concurrence with any particular system of natural law, for I am thus in a position to praise something "vague and amorphous" and have "an exit readily available when a specific folly appears." What I was advocating in my book was not a *system* of natural law but the natural-law *method*. As to vagueness, I have written two articles about specific problems of private law which seem to me to exemplify the legal method I recommend in my book of sermons. They are "The Reliance Interest in Contract Damages" and "Consideration and Form."[2] These articles represent the result of a good deal of internal striving after the "right" legal method. Now that I feel enough confidence of my own methodology to want to write about private law, I can only say that the method *seems to me* to be closer to that of Pothier than to that of Llewellyn, Cook, Williston, or Langdell. Maybe I wholly misjudge my own legal method; probably I overestimate its novelty. But surely there exist *some* differences in legal method, and surely it is desirable that the practitioner of a particular method should try to explain in general terms the premises which seem to him to underlie it.

The quality of the legal method I am advocating may be illustrated in the way comparative law is used. One may study comparative law for its own sake, of course. Or again, one may study it to see in what ways our own law could be improved. For example, one sees that in Germany an offer stated to run for a certain time is irrevocable without consideration; on the basis of this, one may propose a statute "changing our law" to make it accord with "the German law." Both of these approaches stay within the positivistic approach. But a quite different approach is to treat the foreign law and our own as a kind of common undertaking in solving common problems. When foreign law is used this way it bears not only on the *improvement* of our law but on its *interpretation*, and the blending of interpretation and improvement is, of course, a blending of *is* and *ought*. Now I do not deny that others have used comparative law in the way I have just described. But the use has in recent decades been a sparing one, quite different from the general and generous use made in, say, 1800.

I want to devote the rest of this letter to some discussion of your frequently repeated intimation that back of my whole philosophy lies an unavowed economic royalism (not to use an uglier word) which makes me indifferent to the plight of hungry people and puts me on the side of plutocrats and swindlers.

A possible source of misunderstanding between us on this point may lie in the fact that in my last chapter I am concerned with a problem which so far as I can see has no existence for you at all. This I may call the problem of *absorbing* reform. I think of society as an organism which can absorb and survive only so much surgery. I find congenial many parts of the philosophy of Burke, which conceives society to be founded on institutions and conventions which are not wholly rational and which conceives of progress as a gradual

---

2. [Lon L. Fuller and William R. Perdue, Jr., "The Reliance Interest in Contract Damages," *Yale Law Journal* 46, nos. 1 and 3 (1936–37): 52–96, 373–420; Lon L. Fuller, "Consideration and Form," *Columbia Law Review* 41, no. 5 (1941): 799–824. For a brief description of the "natural law method," see the Editor's Note to "The Role of Contract in the Ordering Processes of Society Generally" in this volume.]

improvement of those institutions and conventions in the direction of greater rationality. This view emphasizes that our present state of society, however imperfect, represents an acquisition, an encroachment of reason on chaos, if you will. I *think* I was brought to this conservative philosophy by my experiences in Germany and France,[3] though of course you are free to attribute it to an increasing salary and a general hardening of the categories.

You, on the other hand, seem to me to be blind both to the conception of society as a living organism, and to the notion that our present economic and political structure represents itself an acquisition. I cannot otherwise explain the fact that it seems wholly irrelevant to you that a particular form of government does not "go down well" with those who have to be governed. You seem to me to fit Ortega y Gasset's description of the modern man who supposes the rule that next year's automobile will be better than this year's to be a law of nature.[4] You take our present state of society as a going concern and assume that it has something inherent in it which makes it go, and that all you and I have to concern ourselves about is to see that the hungry are fed and that the intellectual phonies are shown up for what they are.

I argued that the Hobbes-Austin theory, which makes of the sovereign will a kind of artificial reason to take the place of a defaulting natural reason—I argued that this theory lost its persuasiveness at a time when "the sovereign's most conspicuous activity consists in redistributing wealth." To your mind, this was a "cheap" remark. If my heart had been in the right place, I would have spoken not of "redistributing wealth," but of "redistributing poverty" or "preventing starvation." Once again, you simply fail to recognize the existence of the issue I was concerned with. Dealing as I was with the problem of "absorbing" reform, I naturally assumed that those who were being fed would be happy about it, and that the discontent would be on the part of those who were having things taken away from them. The people who put Hitler in power were not those who were feeding off the Weimar Republic, but those who decided, rightly or wrongly, that it was feeding off them. The side that won in Spain was not that of the recently enfranchised, but that of the dispossessed, who took back with bombs what they thought was being taken away from them by the law.

One of the bases for your inference that I am guilty of covert Bourbonism rests on my defense of an "autonomous order." Since this order includes an existing distribution of economic power, in defending it I am defending the interests of my economic class—that seems to be your reasoning. I do not deny that the existing "autonomous order" includes economic, as well as political

3. [Fuller is referring to personal visits abroad in the late 1920s and early 1930s.]

4. [Jose Ortega y Gasset, *The Revolt of the Masses*, trans. anon. (New York: Norton, 1932), p. 63.]

and ethical relations. But I cannot follow your argument that a preference for non-governmental control of men's affairs rests on a fear of chance and a wish to oppress the underprivileged. After all, the Communists, with their desire to see the state and the law "wither away," go much further than I do in championing "autonomous order." Harold Laski, another advocate of natural law, also goes considerably beyond my conceptions.[5] The question is not whether change shall occur, but *how* it shall occur.

Let us recognize frankly that the modern factory owner is in a position comparable to the judge who bought his office in the reign of Louis XIV. The factory owner exercises functions which affect the lives of other people; he has powers which can be abused. Those powers have been abused at times by men lacking ordinary human decency; at other times factory owners have been forced by the system under which they operated to take decisions which were harsh in their effects on others. What shall we do about this situation? Shall we throw the factory owner out and substitute an elected or appointed commissioner in his place? Shall we leave him in office (that is, "with his property") and subject him to legal regulations? Shall we try to develop a common morality which will check him and lead him to conceive of his position as that of a fiduciary? These problems seem to me to be hard to answer, and there are disadvantages in any course we take. All I have contended is that, if we are to preserve our present system as a going concern, then it is wise to accomplish as much as we can of the reforms needed through the "autonomous order."

It has been said that the practice of buying and selling judicial office in France before the Revolution was probably in the main a more wholesome institution than would have been a system of appointing judges. The judge's office, being *property*, gave him an independence which enabled him to fight off the encroachments of royal power. That a man may buy his job and work faithfully at it is shown by the case of Samuel Pepys, who wore himself and his eyes out on a job that he had bought. The reason why I am in favor, in general, of preserving the system of buying and selling the office of factory manager is not so much a fear of autocratic interference with the bureaucrat who might take his place (though *that is a factor*), but a desire to preserve the fluidity and flexibility of our economic structure, which is likely to be lost under "bureaucratic" (neutral sense) control. But if we are to keep the man who bought his job in office, we shall have to develop as rapidly as we can a body of morality which will keep him from abusing his office. I believe that the development of this body of morality can be influenced favorably through the judicial process.

In my review of Pound's book on the Formative Era I reported Pound's

5. [See Harold Laski, *The State in Theory and Practice* (New York: Viking, 1935), pp. 78–79.]

assertion that he had changed his mind about the creative power of legislation. My comment was: "At a time when legislative reform is usurping some of the best creative energies of the profession, any disparagement of the reformative power of enacted law may seem ill-timed. Yet I think the author's view can be justified. Declared law and taught law have in the past proved themselves tougher than made law. They probably remain so today. The great accomplishments in legislative reform of recent years, such as the Securities Exchange Act and the National Labor Relations Act, will probably not be firmly established until the philosophy which underlies them has gone over into and become a part of the common law. In the long run men are ruled by accepted beliefs, not by legislative fiat."[6]

I think this passage should be modified by pointing out that the problem of "absorbing reform" does not exist where what appears formally as a "legislative reform" actually reflects a change which has already taken place in the field of "autonomous order." In the case of both of the statutes cited I think it can be said that to a considerable extent they did reflect such a change; the majority of men had come to see, in both cases, that the existing state of affairs could not continue and that some new order would have to take its place. But where the problem of absorbing reform really exists in a significant sense, then I think that there are advantages in the judicial process which it is desirable to point out, *particularly at a time like the present when our best efforts have been concentrated on legislative reform.* Even in the case of the National Labor Relations Act there was plenty of friction on the edges—not simply friction where selfish people's interests were touched, but friction in the sense that there were elements in the act—the compulsion to negotiate, for example—which ran counter to conceptions of what was fittin' and proper held by many men who at least felt themselves to be disinterested. That their doubts on these points were inconsistent with other views which they accepted only proves that man is not a wholly rational animal.

I read somewhere that early in the present century a French judge compelled an employer to negotiate with a labor union. Can it be seriously doubted that the reform of the Labor Relations Act would have been better accomplished if it had come through "sweet reason and reasonableness broadening slowly down through the [decades] from judicial precedent to judicial precedent," to use your own description of my point of view? You say at once, "But that was impossible." But *why* was it impossible? Very considerable revolutions in human affairs have in the past been brought about through judicial decisions. Is

---

6. [Lon L. Fuller, "The Formative Era of American Law" (a review), *Illinois Law Review of Northwestern University* 34 (1939): 373.]

the possibility of such revolutions not affected by the prevailing legal philosophy? Is that philosophy not affected somewhat by the philosophers?

My general conclusion from your letter is that you are by no means as free from philosophic preconceptions as you conceive yourself to be. Indeed, I do not hesitate to pin an awful label on you, that of "positivist," though let me add a wholly ineffective caveat that I would not say all the mean things about you that I say about "the positivists" in my book. Your conception of judge-made law is essentially Austinian. You do not think of judge-made law as a cooperative search for the right result, with many little miscarriages by individual judges on the way. You do not see it as the product of the interaction of men's minds, in which the effects of individual prejudice and stupidity are gradually cancelled out. Rather you see the judge as a petty little sovereign "laying down the law." Viewing him in that light, you can see no reason why his "law" is any better than that of a commissioner.

Your statement that "from a practical standpoint there is governmental fiat in governmental abstention as well as in governmental regulation" is certainly reminiscent of a famous assertion that "what the sovereign permits he impliedly commands." In *International News Service* v. *Associated Press* (248 U.S. 215) the question was whether the News Service should be enjoined from filching, for use in the West, news published by the Associated Press in New York. The majority granted the injunction; Brandeis dissented on the ground that this was a case where the court should not "make law," but should leave the problem to the legislature. Cook criticized Brandeis sharply for this, pointing out that the poor fool didn't seem to realize that a court "made law" just as much in deciding for the defendant as in deciding for the plaintiff. Cook said in effect, "There is judicial fiat in abstention as well as in intervention." Though Brandeis did not act according to my ideal of the legislator-judge in this case, I submit that he was right in thinking that there is a great difference between assuming responsibility for control over a realm of human activity and refusing to assume control over it. I think that he was also right in thinking that there is a problem of choosing the best kind of control for the particular activity in question. I think also that Cook's blindness to these distinctions and problems was produced by a methodology which abstracted legal issues from their total context. And I am frank to say that your refusal to recognize the existence of the problems dealt with in my book seems to me to come about in a similar way. I cannot criticize this. One of the assumptions of my book is that it is necessary to reject some things, that there are positions which must be taken, and that the taking of these positions necessarily causes us to lose something we could otherwise have had. What I *do* criticize is the assumption you seem to take that those who decline the name of philosopher do not let philosophic premises affect their thinking, and that they see reality as it is, whole. I do not claim to see reality whole. What I claim is that I have given some thought to the problem: what aspects of reality is it best for me and my generation to concentrate on? In doing this I have tried to keep in mind an ancient truth which seems to me to be pretty well slurred over in your philosophy: *Ars longa, vita brevis est.*

After finishing the above, I read your "Additional Notes." I do not deny that legislation helps to shape morality. In introducing this whole topic, I spoke (p. 135) of "the extent to which law, *particularly judge-made law*, shapes common morality." In the note on the same page I called attention to a passage in Timasheff which described the effect on morality of Soviet legal reforms, which were, of course, effected through legislation. All I said was that, as between the two kinds of law, judge-made law has a better chance of effecting permanent changes in morality, of "passing over into" the realm of autonomous order. I stand by that; indeed, it seems to me a matter of common sense. In putting their stuff over, judges enjoy various advantages over legislators. They work in an atmosphere of ritualistic impartiality. They avoid a too active and direct intervention in men's affairs. They assume, as far as they can, the position of umpires over a dispute. This is not only true today, but has always been true. Jhering says that the primitive judge was merely a referee in a procedure by which the plaintiff obtains relief through self-help.[7] The common-law courts always refused to assume a too conspicuously active role. Thus, they refused, when debt was the only remedy for simple contract, to evaluate damages and insisted on a "sum certain." They have refused to enter conditional judgments, which would require supervision; they refused specific performance for the same reason, and even today courts of equity do not specifically enforce construction contracts. The common-law courts also refused to enter declaratory judgments, a procedure which would have made their law-making power too conspicuous. When they overruled previous decisions, they did it not as legislators, but on the theory that the law had always been what they now declared it to be. Some of these inhibitions on judicial action are stupid, others are hypocritical. But underlying them there is, I submit, a sound political instinct which realizes that there is a problem of making government "go down well." In Pareto's terms, the judges have realized that they have to govern as foxes and not as lions.

On the other hand, legislative reform often appears, to the man who feels the pinch, as a direct intervention in his affairs; he also often knows exactly where the pinch came from. He may know the history of a particular piece of

---

7. [Rudolph von Jhering, *Geist des römischen Rechts* (Leipzig: Breitkopf & Härtel, 1924), vol. I, pp. 169–70.]

legislation, who conceived it, and how it was put across. The lumber dealers know, for example, that it was the bankers' association which got through at the last meeting of the legislature the statute which curtailed the effect of the materialman's lien. They know it, and they resent it; and they wait for a chance for revenge.

Naturally, this distinction is a matter of degree, and an attempt by judges to revolutionize the common law would be likely to forfeit for them some of their advantage in "shaping common morality." Furthermore, the judge must play his part in the drama; as David Cavers said in criticism of the Hutcheson Case, the desire to *épater le bourgeois* is scarcely appropriate on the Supreme Court.[8]

But as things now stand, and as they seem likely to stand in the future, it seems to me that the advantage in this respect is still with judge-made law.

These last remarks may raise a question which I had expected you would put in your letter: Is this fellow saying that his concept of the natural-law method is right, or is he saying that it is politically expedient? Is he trying to be a Grotius or a Machiavelli?

I should say in answer that I am trying to be a little of both. I *do* believe that the natural-law method is, at the present juncture, politically expedient. But if I felt merely that it was a useful "phony" I would feel more discomfort in advocating it than I do. I feel also that it is metaphysically defensible. I believe that if we are freed from the inhibitions of positivism, which has taught since Hobbes that fiat must largely take the place of reason in regulating human relations—I believe that if we are freed from this restraint we shall find that reason has capacities we had not suspected in it. I believe that there is a possibility of discovery in human relations as in natural science. All I want is an intellectual atmosphere in which men are free to attempt that discovery.

8. [David F. Cavers, professor of law at Duke University School of Law, 1931–1945, and at Harvard Law School, 1945–1969.]

Bibliography of the Published Writings of Lon L. Fuller

Compiled by *Kenneth I. Winston*
and *Stanley L. Paulson*

Books

The Law in Quest of Itself. Evanston, Ill.: Northwestern University Press, 1940; Boston, Mass.: Beacon Press, 1966.
Basic Contract Law. St. Paul, Minn.: West Publishing Company, 1947; 2d ed., with Robert Braucher, 1964; 3d ed., with Melvin Aron Eisenberg, 1972. Teacher's Notes, 1948, 1965.
The Problems of Jurisprudence. Temporary ed., Mineola, N.Y.: Foundation Press, 1949.
The Morality of Law. New Haven: Yale University Press, 1964; rev. ed., 1969.
Legal Fictions. Stanford: Stanford University Press, 1967.
Anatomy of the Law. Chicago: Britannica Perspectives, 1968; New York: Praeger, 1968; New York: New American Library, 1969; Westport, Conn.: Greenwood Press, 1976.

Articles

"Adverse Possession—Occupancy of Another's Land under Mistake as to Location of a Boundary." *Oregon Law Review* 7 (1928): 329–39.
"Legal Fictions." *Illinois Law Review* 25 (1930–31): 363–99, 513–46, 877–910. Reprinted as *Legal Fictions.* Stanford University Press, 1967.
"The Legal Mind." *Atlantic Monthly* 152 (1933): 85–94.
"What Motives Give Rise to the Historical Legal Fiction?" In *Recueil d'etudes en l'honneur de François Gény* 2 (1934): 157–76.
"American Legal Realism." *University of Pennsylvania Law Review* 82 (1934): 429–62. Reprinted in *Proceedings of American Philosophical Society* 76 (1936): 191–235.
"Special Nature of the Wage-Earner's Life Insurance Problem" (symposium). *Law and Contemporary Problems* 2 (1935): 10–48; also "Foreword" 1–2.
"The Reliance Interest in Contract Damages" (with William R. Perdue, Jr.). *Yale Law Journal* 46 (1936–37): 52–96, 373–420.
"Williston on Contracts." *North Carolina Law Review* 18 (1939): 1–15.

"My Philosophy of Law." In *My Philosophy of Law: Credos of Sixteen American Scholars.* Boston: Boston Book Co., 1941.

"Consideration and Form." *Columbia Law Review* 41 (1941): 799–824.

"Reason and Fiat in Case Law." *Harvard Law Review* 59 (1946): 376–95. An earlier version was published for limited circulation, New York: American Book—Stratford Press, 1943.

"Objectives of Legal Education." *Record of New York City Bar Association* 2 (1947): 120–27.

"What the Law Schools Can Contribute to the Making of Lawyers" (conference). *Journal of Legal Education* 1 (1948): 189–204.

"The Place and Uses of Jurisprudence in the Law School Curriculum" (roundtable). *Journal of Legal Education* 1 (1948): 495–507.

Introduction. *The Jurisprudence of Interests*, ed. by M. Magdelena Schoch. 20th Century Legal Philosophy Series, vol. 2. Cambridge, Mass.: Harvard University Press, 1948.

"The Case of the Speluncean Explorers." *Harvard Law Review* 62 (1949): 616–45.

"Pashukanis and Vyshinsky: A Study in the Development of Marxian Legal Theory." *Michigan Law Review* 47 (1949): 1157–66.

"On Teaching Law." *Stanford Law Review* 3 (1950): 35–47.

"What is the Bar Examination Intended to Test?" (panel). *Bar Examiner* 20 (1951): 111–20.

"Legal Education and Admissions to the Bar in Pennsylvania." *Temple Law Quarterly* 25 (1952): 249–300.

"American Legal Philosophy at Mid-Century." *Journal of Legal Education* 6 (1954): 457–85.

"Some Reflections on Legal and Economic Freedoms—A review of Robert L. Hale's 'Freedom through Law.'" *Columbia Law Review* 54 (1954): 70–82.

"Role of the Lawyer in Labor Relations" (panel). *American Bar Association Journal* 41 (1955): 342–45.

"The Philosophy of Codes of Ethics." *Electrical Engineering* 74 (1955): 916–18.

"Freedom—A Suggested Analysis." *Harvard Law Review* 68 (1955): 1302–25.

[A memorandum on the teaching of law] in *On the Teaching of Law in the Liberal Arts Curriculum*, edited by Harold J. Berman. Mineola, N.Y.: Foundation Press, 1956.

"Human Purpose and Natural Law." *Journal of Philosophy* 53 (1956): 697–705. Reprinted in *Natural Law Forum* 3 (1958): 68–76.

"A Rejoinder to Professor Nagel." *Natural Law Forum* 3 (1958): 83–104.

"Positivism and Fidelity to Law—A Reply to Professor Hart." *Harvard Law Review* 71 (1958): 593–672.

"Professional Responsibility: Report of the Joint Conference" (with John D. Randall). *American Bar Association Journal* 44 (1958): 1159–62, 1216–18.

"Governmental Secrecy and the Forms of Social Order." In *Community*, Nomos II, edited by C. J. Friedrich. New York: Liberal Arts Press, 1959.

"Adjudication and the Rule of Law." *American Society for International Law Proceedings* 54 (1960): 1–8.

"The Academic Lawyer's 'House of Intellect.'" *Journal of Legal Education* 14 (1961): 153–63.

"The Adversary System." In *Talks on American Law*, edited by Harold J. Berman. New York: Vintage Books, 1961.

"Collective Bargaining and the Arbitrator." *Wisconsin Law Review* 1963: 3–46.

"Christopher Columbus Langdell." *Encyclopaedia Britannica* 13: 689, 14th ed., 1963 printing.

"La Philosophie du Droit aux États-Unis." Translated into French by Mme. Van Camelbeke in *Les Études Philosophiques* (1964): 559–68.

"Irrigation and Tyranny." *Stanford Law Review* 17 (1965): 1021–42.

"Jurisprudence." *Encyclopaedia Britannica* 13:149, 14th ed., 1965 printing.

"A Reply to Professors Cohen and Dworkin" (symposium). *Villanova Law Review* 10 (1965): 655–66.

"Afterword: Science and the Judicial Process" (symposium). *Harvard Law Review* 79 (1966): 1604–28. Reprinted in *Social Science Approaches to the Judicial Process*. New York: Da Capo Press, 1971.

"Oliver Wendell Holmes, Jr.: *The Path of the Law*." Edited with commentary in *An American Primer*, edited by Daniel Boorstin. Chicago: University of Chicago Press, 1966.

"Freedom as a Problem of Allocating Choice" (symposium). *Proceedings of the American Philosophical Society* 112 (1968): 101–6.

"Some Observations on the Course in Contracts" (roundtable). *Journal of Legal Education* 20 (1968): 482–84.

"Some Unexplored Social Dimensions of the Law." In *Path of the Law from 1967*, edited by Arthur E. Sutherland. Cambridge, Mass: Harvard University Press, 1968.

"Two Principles of Human Association." In *Voluntary Associations*, Nomos XI, edited by J. Roland Pennock and John Chapman. New York: Atherton Press, 1969.

"The Law's Precarious Hold on Life." *Georgia Law Review* 3 (1969): 530–45.

"Human Interaction and the Law." *American Journal of Jurisprudence* 14 (1969): 1–36. Partially reprinted as "Law and Human Interaction" in *Sociological Inquiry* 47 (1977): 59–91, special issue nos. 3 and 4.

"Mediation—Its Forms and Functions." *Southern California Law Review* 44 (1971): 305–38.

"The Justification of Legal Decisions." *Archiv für Rechts- und Sozialphilosophie*, Beiheft Neue Folge Nr. 7 (1972): 77–89. Read at the 1971 World Congress for Philosophy of Law and Social Philosophy.

"Law as an Instrument of Social Control and Law as a Facilitation of Human Interaction." *Archiv für Rechts- und Sozialphilosophie*, Beiheft Neue Folge Nr. 8 (1974). Read at the 1973 World Congress for Philosophy of Law and Social Philosophy and reprinted in *Brigham Young University Law Review* 89 (1975): 89–96.

"Law and Morality," a contribution to "Moral Choices in Contemporary Society: Newspaper Articles for the Sixth Course by Newspaper." N.E.H. project coordinated by Philip Rieff, University of California, San Diego, 1976.

"Some Presuppositions Shaping the Concept of 'Socialization.'" In *Law, Justice and the Individual in Society*, edited by June L. Tapp and Felice J. Levine. New York: Holt, Rinehart and Winston, 1977.

"The Forms and Limits of Adjudication." *Harvard Law Review* 92 (1978): 353–409. Posthumously published; originally presented to a group of Harvard Law School faculty in 1957 and subsequently revised in 1959 and in 1961.

Book Reviews

Kaden, *Bibliographie der rechtsvergleichenden Literatur* (1930). *Illinois Law Review* 26 (1931): 481–85.

Friedmann, *Die Bereicherungschaftung im angloamerikanischen Rechtskreis in Vergleichung mit dem deutschen buergerlichen Recht* (1930). *Illinois Law Review* 26 (1931): 481–85.

Ogden, *Bentham's Theory of Fictions* (1932). *Harvard Law Review* 47 (1933): 367–70.

Llewellyn, *Präjudizientrecht und Rechtsprechung in Amerika* (1933). *University of Pennsylvania Law Review* 82 (1934): 551–53.

Rheinstein, *Die Struktur des vertraglichen Schuldverhaltnesses im angloamerikanishen Recht* (1932). *Columbia Law Review* 35 (1935): 140–44.

Hall, *Readings in Jurisprudence* (1938). *University of Pennsylvania Law Review* 87 (1939): 625–27.

Pound, *The Formative Era of American Law* (1938). *Illinois Law Review* 34 (1939): 372–74.

Bodenheimer, *Jurisprudence* (1940). *Columbia Law Review* 41 (1941): 965–67.

Jones, *Historical Introduction to the Theory of Law* (1940). *Harvard Law Review* 55 (1941): 160–63.

Adler, *A Dialectic of Morals: Toward the Foundations of Political Philosophy* (1941). *University of Chicago Law Review* 9 (1942): 759–61.

Buckland, *Some Reflections on Jurisprudence* (1945). *Harvard Law Review* 59 (1946): 826–29.

Paton, *A Textbook of Jurisprudence* (1946). *Harvard Law Review* 61 (1948): 383–85.

Brown, *Lawyers, Law Schools and the Public Service* (1948). *Harvard Law Review* 62 (1948): 155–58.

Reuschlein, *Jurisprudence—Its American Prophets* (1951). *Louisiana Law Review* 12 (1952): 531–35.

Viehweg, *Topik und Jurisprudenz* (2d ed., 1963). *Natural Law Forum* 10 (1965): 236–38.

Schwartz and Skolnick (eds.), *Society and the Legal Order* (1970). *Harvard Law Review* 85 (1971): 523–26.

Translations

H. Mankewicz, "German Law of Alimony Before and Under National Socialism." *Law and Contemporary Problems* 6 (1939): 301–18.

This bibliography does not include translations (unless original publication was in the foreign language) or editions published in countries other than the United States.

Index

Adjudication, 86–124, 260–63; as model of social order, 27, 28, 29, 34, 89–90; in administrative agencies, 88, 107–8, 117–18, 119–20; distinguishing characteristic of, 92, 94; and rationality, 92–98; and rule of law, 98–103; and impartiality, 104, 178, 261, 302; and retrospective decisions, 109–10; two sources of power in, 110–11; polycentricity in, 111–21; opposed to mediation, 147; and contract, 178; and forensic facts, 279n

Administrative law. *See* Adjudication, in administrative agencies

Ahrens, Heinrich, 296

American Arbitration Association, 97, 106

Anthony v. *Syracuse University*, 69n

Aquinas, St. Thomas, 56

Arbitration: and reasons for decisions, 106, 107–8; tripartite, 113–14, 262; and allocative tasks, 119; perverted forms of, 121–24. *See also* Adjudication

Arensberg, Conrad, 240

Arnold, Rosemary, 200n

Austin, John, 13, 298, 301; conception of law, 18; account of legal obligation, 19–20; on anarchy of natural law, 20n; on customary law, 177

Automobile Manufacturers Association, 173

Bagehot, Walter, 168, 201, 216

Baldwin, Simeon Eben, 272

Barnard, Chester, 136n, 267

Barton, Ralph F., 156

Bavelas, Alex, 256, 267

Beale, Joseph H., 272

Bentham, Jeremy, 12n, 61–63, 174, 184

Berlin, Isaiah, 53

Bigelow, Melville M., 193n

Bingham, J. Walter, 188, 190, 294, 295

Black, Duncan, 57n

Blackstone, Sir William, 19, 20

Bohannan, Paul, 219n

Bonham's Case, 40

Borkin, Joseph, 163n

Braithwaite, Richard B., 117n

Brandeis, Louis, 301

Burke, Edmund, 143, 297

Burlamaqui, Jean Jacques, 296

Burnham, James, 197

Camus, Albert, 19n

Cardozo, Benjamin, 286

Carroll, Lewis (Charles Dodgson), 57

Carter, James Coolidge, 250

Case method, 127, 278–81

"Case of the Speluncean Explorers," 16–18

Cavers, David F., 303

Childe, V. Gordon, 207n

Church disputes, 73–75

Civil Aeronautics Board, 88

Clark, Walter, 193

Cohen, Felix, 295

Cohen, Morris R., 293–94

Coke, Sir Edward, 40, 228

Cole, G. D. H., 109, 260

Collective bargaining. *See* Arbitration; Mediation

Colson, Elizabeth, 240n

Common aims, as principle of social order, 67

Commons, John R., 268

Conant, James B., 118, 260

Contract, 170–87; as model of social order, 27, 28, 34, 199–200, 224; as formal expression of reciprocity, 67, 91; test of rationality in, 94–95; and polycentric problems, 116–17; and adjudication, 122–24, 178; functions of formalities in, 169; and autonomy, 169; inequality of bargaining power in, 173; and theory of Social Compact, 174; law *about* and law *in*, 174–75, 224–25; in relation to other legal processes, 175–80, 186–87; limits of, 180–84, 238–39; appropriate contexts for, 184–86, 239–41; interactional foundations of, 224–30; and Section 90, 227, 230

Cook, Walter Wheeler, 294, 295, 297, 301

Customary law, 212–24; as model of social order, 27; conception of, 27n, 176, 211, 219–21; and contract, 175–77, 224–30, 238; as language of interaction, 176, 213–14, 216–18; in international relations, 218–19; and "the reasonable man," 222–23, 242; and doctrine of *opinio necessitatis*, 226–27, 229; and common law, 236–37; appropriate contexts for, 241–43. *See also* Made law; Primitive society

Dawson, John P., 183n

Del Duca, Louis, 37n

Despotism, 188–210 passim. *See also* Managerial direction
Dewey, John, 18
Diamond, A. S., 268
Divorce, law of. *See* Marriage
Dorr's Rebellion, 168
Due process of law, 68–70, 79, 80–81, 83
Durkheim, Emile, 268
Dworkin, Ronald, 31n, 33n, 39n

Elections: as model of social order, 27, 91–92; as formal expression of organization by common aims, 91; manner of participation in, 94, 95; and polycentric problems, 117; and contract, 179
Enacted law. *See* Made law
Equality, 61–64
Erikson, Erik, 217
Eunomics, 12; defined, 14, 48; principal concerns of, 14–15, 29n, 261

Fallers, Lloyd, 26n
Federal Communications Commission, 88, 119–20
Firth, Raymond, 268
Fitzmaurice, Sir Gerald, 229n
Forms of social order: vertical and horizontal, 172–73, 174–75, 187n; availability of, within given society, 198–202. *See also* Legal processes
Frank, Jerome, 270, 294, 295
Freedom, 59–60
Frege, Gottlob, 93
Friedman, Lawrence, 241n

Game theory, 117, 137n, 140
Gellhorn, Walter, 280
Generality of laws, 163, 234–36
Gluckman, Max, 156, 221n, 222, 223, 242–43
Goldberg, B. Abbott, 210n
Górecki, Jan, 151
Graham v. *Graham*, 149n, 238n
Gray, John Chipman, 96, 103, 193n, 250–52, 269, 286, 294
Great Fire of London, 183
Grotius, Hugo, 296

Hall, Jerome, 56n
Hamilton, Alexander, 101
Hampshire, Stuart, 81n
Hand, Learned, 193n
Handy, E. S. C., 207n
Hart, Henry M., Jr., 126, 128, 200
Hart, Herbert L. A., 15, 33n, 75n; account of legal obligation, 20–23; on step from prele-gal to legal world, 21, 211; and internal point of view, 21–22; on "core of good sense" in natural law, 24; on purpose in law, 37
Hart, Samuel, 57n
Hayek, Friedrich A., 39n, 101
Henderson, Dan F., 156n
Henderson, Edith G., 209n
Henningsen v. *Bloomfield Motors, Inc.*, 173
Heyman, Ira M., 81n
Hitler, Adolf, 298. *See also* Nazi law
Hobbes, Thomas, 24–25, 298, 303
Hoebel, E. Adamson, 105n, 221
Hogbin, H. I., 268
Hohfeld, Wesley N., 272
Holland, Thomas, 214–15
Holmes, Oliver Wendell, Jr., 193n, 250–52, 269, 294
Huxley, Aldous, 52–53

Internal morality of legislation. *See* Legislation, internal morality of
International News Service v. *Associated Press*, 301
Interpretation of laws, 164–65
Irrigation: and mediation, 152–54; and tyranny, 189, 191–92, 206, 208–9; and theocracy, 207–8; in Holland, 209
Ivanov, Georgii, 124

James, William, 27
Javert, Cart T., 149n
Jhering, Rudolph von, 252, 302
Jones, Philip E., 184n
Judge: constraints on, 14, 22, 42; sources of authority of, 22–23, 41, 110–11; and essence of adjudication, 92–93; role of, in initiating suits, 103–6; and reasons for decisions, 106–9; Powell's view of, 301
Judicial review: of church quarrels, 73–75; of university expulsions, 84; of constitutionality of laws, 165
Jurisprudence, division of studies in, 29n. *See also* Legal philosophy
Justice: distributive, in irrigation, 205–10; as end of adjudication, 263

Kant, Immanuel, 38n, 201, 277
Katz, Milton, 253n, 264
Kelsen, Hans, 29n, 36–37, 75
Knight, Frank H., 254, 268
Kuhn, Thomas, 72

Laird, John, 81n
Lambton, Ann, 207nn
Landis, James M., 88

Langdell, Christopher Columbus, 97, 250, 272, 278, 297
Lange, Oskar, 116n
Laski, Harold, 299
Lasswell, Harold, 57n, 273–75, 277, 279, 280
Law: criteria of a conception of, 17–18, 30–33; conception of, as generous, 17, 30, 73, 211–12; as purposive and problem-solving, 17–18, 31–32, 214–16, 231–32, 267, 278–81, 282; as normative, 18–23, 32–33, 42–44, 231, 264, 282, 293–95, 297–98; as instrument of social control, 221–22, 232–33; and its social context, 237–46. *See also* Legal processes
Lawyer: as architect of social structures, 12–13, 253–54, 264–66, 276–77; effects of, as advocate, 58, 289–90; role of, in adjudication, 108, 301; realist conception of, 250–54, 269; assistance for, from social science, 266–70; expansion of responsibility of, 278–81; what philosophy offers the, 283–90
Legal education, 271–81, 282
Legalism, 67, 79–85, 154
Legal morality. *See* Legislation: internal morality of
Legal naturalism, 29n
Legal obligation: Austin on, 19–20; H. L. A. Hart on, 21–23; Fuller on, 35–36, 40, 41–42
Legal philosophy: object of, 249–50, 260, 264; inhibiting influences on, 250–60
Legal positivism, 13, 294, 298, 303; on moral neutrality of law, 13, 75; on normativity of law, 19–23; subject matter of, 29n; on purpose in law, 36–37; on criteria of judicial review, 41–42; and comparative law, 297
Legal processes: as models of social order, 26–29; principal types of, 27, 34, 127, 155, 170–71; principal elements of, 28, 34, 91; and relation to actual institutions, 28–29; and distinctively legal ends, 251–52. *See also* Adjudication; Contract; Elections; Legislation; Lot; Managerial direction; Mediation; Property
Legal realism, 250–52, 269–70, 293, 294–96
Legislation: as model of social order, 27, 28, 34; internal morality of, 33–42, 75n, 158–68, 172, 196–97; purpose of, 36–40; traditional liberal conception of, 38; and mediation, 146–47; as last stage in evolution of law, 166; and managerial facts, 279n; and "autonomous order," 298–300, 302–3
Leontief, Wassily, 116
Lévi-Strauss, Claude, 222

Lewin, Kurt, 256, 267
Lindsay, A. D., 89
Llewellyn, Karl, 105, 270, 294, 295, 297
Lot: as a model of social order, 27, 171–72, 199; and contract, 180
Lyons, David, 28n, 33n

Maass, Arthur, 206n
Macaulay, Stewart, 241n
McDougal, Myres S., 57n, 273–75, 277, 279, 280, 293
McDowell, Banks, 149n
Mackenzie, W. J. M., 92n
Made law: implicit elements in, 159–68, 177; opposed to customary law, 211, 212–13; interactional foundations of, 230–37; appropriate contexts for, 243–46; opposed to declared law, 300. *See also* Legislation
Madison, James, 77
Maine, Sir Henry, 166, 207n, 233n
Mair, Lucy, 240
Malinowski, Bronislaw, 155, 199n, 208n, 242–43, 268
Manageability of social tasks, 202–5
Managerial direction: as model of social order, 27, 34, 171, 188; distinguished from legislation, 38, 188, 234; and polycentric problems, 116; and contract, 178–79
Mansfield, Lord, 101
Marriage: person / act distinction in law of, 83; mediation in, 148–52; contractual organization of, 149–50, 238; and reform of divorce law, 150–52
Marx, Karl, 185, 193n
Mead, George Herbert, 139
Means and ends, 47–64, 256–60; J. S. Mill on, 49; in architecture, 50–52; Aldous Huxley on, 52–53; Isaiah Berlin on, 53; common assumptions about, 54–58, 200–201; and freedom, 59–60; and equality, 61–64; and law, 252–54
Mediation: as model of social order, 27, 34; and adjudication, 121–22; appropriate contexts for, 125; and contract, 128, 179–80; in collective bargaining, 130–44; dyadic relation in, 130, 133–34; interdependence of parties in, 130, 134–35; element of trade in, 131, 135–38, 155; as drafting of a constitution, 131, 138–40; negotiation by agents in, 131, 140–43; dual role of management in, 131–32, 143–44; source of power in, 134–35; central quality of, 144–45; as antithesis of law, 146–47; oriented toward persons, 147–55; limits of, 148; in marriage counseling, 148–52; in

irrigation water allocation, 152–54; analogues of, in primitive society, 155–57
Menger, Anton, 104
Mill, John Stuart, 38, 49, 59, 202, 269
Miller v. *Miller*, 149n, 238n
Morality: as an element of law, 42–44; procedural, 201. *See also* Legislation: internal morality of
Mosca, Gaetano, 193n, 277

National Labor Relations Act, 300
Natural law method, 169, 296–97, 303
Natural law theory, 294, 295, 296–97; two concerns of traditional, 12, 32; discredited by utilitarians, 13; "core of good sense" in, 24; value of, 276
Nazi law, 160, 162–63
Nietzsche, Friedrich, 57, 285
Nonet, Philippe, 29n, 154n
Norm, social, 148

Oakeshott, Michael, 60
Office of Price Administration, 118
Ortega y Gasset, Jose, 298

Pailler, Mgr. A., 80n
Pareto, Vilfredo, 193n, 277, 302
Parsons, Talcott, 70n, 214
Patterson, Edwin, 12
Pepys, Samuel, 299
Perry, Judge Antonio, 207n
Person / act distinction: in primitive society, 79–80; in religious associations, 80; in criminal law, 82–83, 244–46; in family law, 83, 149–52; in university expulsions, 84; in mediation, 147–55; in enacted law, 244
Piaget, Jean, 201
Polanyi, Michael, 57, 72, 111, 116n, 202
Polycentricity, 111–21
Pothier, Robert J., 296, 297
Pound, Roscoe, 87, 268, 286, 295, 299
Powell, Thomas Reed, 293
Power: formal and real, 193, 196–97; and reciprocity, 195–98
Primitive society, law of, 79–80, 155–57, 182, 216, 219, 221, 222–23, 232, 233, 242–43, 244
Principles of association, 67–85, 90–91, 187n; the legal principle (reciprocity), 67, 71, 72–73, 81, 91; shared commitment (common aims), 67, 71–72, 91; "laws" of interrelation among, 76–78
Promulgation of laws, 159, 164

Property: an adjunct of contract, 27; a product of law, 174; as a legal process, 177–78
Pufendorf, Samuel, 296
Purpose, in science and in legal philosophy, 255–56. *See also* Law, as purposive

Rawle, William, 86
Rawls, John, 28n, 39n
Raz, Joseph, 20n, 31n
Reciprocity: as principle of social order, 67; in contract, 105, 199–200; in mediation, 135–38, 187; in primitive society, 155, 242; and power, 195–98. *See also* Contract
Retrospectivity: of judicial decisions, 109–10; in lawmaking, 159–60, 161–63
Richards, David A. J., 39n
Right, claim of: connection of, to principles, 95; as province of adjudication, 96–98
Robins, Frederick W., 207n
Rodell, Fred, 272
Ross, Alf, 61–63
Rousseau, Jean-Jacques, 38n
Rule of law: and adjudication, 98–103; in international relations, 102; and mediation, 147; in allocation of irrigation water, 152
Rules, legal, and person / act distinction, 146–55
Russell, Bertrand, 255

Salmond, John, 215
Samuelson, Paul, 64n
Schelling, Thomas C., 135, 140n, 143
Schiller, J. C. F. von, 259
Schopenhauer, Arthur, 124
Schulman, Alix, 149n
Searle, John, 28n
Selznick, Philip, 23n, 29n, 31n, 42n
Shils, Edward, 214n
Silber, John R., 81n
Simmel, Georg, 70n, 133, 195n, 220, 235, 239
Social sciences, on the order-creating process, 266–70
Sorel, Georges, 277
Stephen, James Fitzjames, 59
Stravinsky, Igor, 51
Succession, law of, 166–67
Sullivan, J. W. N., 255
Summers, Robert, 75n
Swiss Code of Obligations, 100

Taylor, Fred M., 116n
Taylor, George W., 121

Tocqueville, Alexis de, 77
Tönnies, Ferdinand, 237n
Tucker, Robert, 186n
Tyranny. *See* Despotism

Values: as preferences, 57; as subjective, 285–86. *See also* Means and ends
Vattel, Emeric de, 296
Veblen, Thorstein, 197
Voting. *See* Elections

Walder, Francis, 138n

War Labor Board, 118, 121, 289
War Manpower Commission, 118
War Production Board, 118
Weber, Max, 268, 277
Wicksteed, Philip, 186
Williston, Samuel B., 297
Wilson, John A., 200n
Wittfogel, Karl A., 189–210 passim
Wittgenstein, Ludwig, 161
Wolff, Robert Paul, 29n

Young, Frank W., 77n

Other Duke University Press Books in Paperback

The Roots of Black Poverty
The Southern Plantation Economy after the Civil War
Jay R. Mandle

War and the Christian Conscience
How Shall Modern War Be Conducted Justly?
Paul Ramsey

The Creativity Question
Albert Rothenberg *and* Carl R. Hausman, *editors*

Plantation Societies, Race Relations, and the South
The Regimentation of Populations
Edgar T. Thompson

Black Migration in America
A Social Demographic History
Daniel M. Johnson *and* Rex R. Campbell

Psychology of the Arts
Hans Kreitler *and* Shulamith Kreitler